Learn Unity 4 for
iOS Game Development

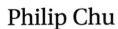

Philip Chu

Learn Unity 4 for iOS Game Development

Copyright © 2013 by Philip Chu

ISBN-13 (pbk): 978-1-4302-4875-0 52032918

ISBN-13 (electronic): 978-1-4302-4876-7   6/13

President and Publisher: Paul Manning
Lead Editor: Michelle Lowman
Technical Reviewer: Marc Schärer
Editorial Board: Steve Anglin, Mark Beckner, Ewan Buckingham, Gary Cornell, Louise Corrigan, Morgan Ertel, Jonathan Gennick, Jonathan Hassell, Robert Hutchinson, Michelle Lowman, James Markham, Matthew Moodie, Jeff Olson, Jeffrey Pepper, Douglas Pundick, Ben Renow-Clarke, Dominic Shakeshaft, Gwenan Spearing, Matt Wade, Tom Welsh
Coordinating Editor: Christine Ricketts
Copy Editor: Mary Bearden
Compositor: SPi Global
Indexer: SPi Global
Artist: SPi Global
Cover Designer: Anna Ishchenko

Distributed to the book trade worldwide by Springer Science+Business Media New York, 233 Spring Street, 6th Floor, New York, NY 10013. Phone 1-800-SPRINGER, fax (201) 348-4505, e-mail orders-ny@springer-sbm.com, or visit www.springeronline.com. Apress Media, LLC is a California LLC and the sole member (owner) is Springer Science + Business Media Finance Inc (SSBM Finance Inc). SSBM Finance Inc is a Delaware corporation.

For information on translations, please e-mail rights@apress.com, or visit www.apress.com.

Apress and friends of ED books may be purchased in bulk for academic, corporate, or promotional use. eBook versions and licenses are also available for most titles. For more information, reference our Special Bulk Sales–eBook Licensing web page at www.apress.com/bulk-sales.

Any source code or other supplementary materials referenced by the author in this text is available to readers at www.apress.com. For detailed information about how to locate your book's source code, go to www.apress.com/source-code/.

Contents at a Glance

Contents

About the Author

Philip Chu is a general-purpose programmer, accidental game developer, and aspiring writer (he wishes he wrote Snow Crash). Since his first encounter with an Apple II in high school, Phil has over two decades of professional software development experience in the semiconductor, defense/government, computer graphics, Internet, mobile and video game industries. He received a Bachelor's degree in Computer Science and Engineering from MIT (Course 6-3, for those in the know) and a Master's degree in Computer Science from Johns Hopkins University.

Phil is currently living the self-employed indie life in sunny Huntington Beach, California, where he performs contract work under his own consulting firm, Technicat, LLC. Projects have included 3D content creation tools (Nendo), video games (Darkwatch, Tech Deck: Bare Knuckle Grind), virtual worlds (Blue Mars, Playstation@Home), and some occasional Java work. But he still misses working on Lisp machines.

For his own projects, Phil develops and self-publishes Mac/PC, web and mobile games with the Unity engine, under the Fugu Games and HyperBowl brands (the latter is licensed from Hyper Entertainment). Check them out at http://fugugames.com/ and http://hyperbowl3d.com/.

Phil blogs and tweets regularly (http://fugutalk.com/ and @fugugames), and maintains game development reference material and software development essays on http://technicat.com/, some of which have been included as reading material in college courses and published in venues such as the MIT Entrepreneurial Review and the Nintendo Developer Support Group site, as well as the Nook and Kindle. Phil has snippets of open source code on http://github.com/technicat, including the Unity projects for this book.

About the Technical Reviewer

Marc Schärer is an interactive media software engineer delivering interactive learning, training, and entertainment experiences to mobile, desktop, and web platforms for customers from all over through his company Gayasoft (http://www.gayasoft.net) located in Switzerland.

He uses Unity, which he has been using since the technologies 1.x days in 2007, and enhances its capabilities through extensions where suitable.

Marc has a strong background in 3D graphics, network technology, software engineering, and interactive media, which he started building in his teenage years and later solidified through education in computer science and computational science and engineering at the Swiss Federal Institute of Technology in Zürich.

He applied this knowledge to usage in Popper (http://www.popper.org), an interactive three-dimensional behavioral research platform by a Harward   powered by Unity, Mathlab, and the ExitGames Photon platforms developed by Gayasoft.

With the rise of serious games, Marc is currently focusing his and his company's efforts to research options and technologies for the next generation of interactive and immersive experiences through Augmented Reality and Virtual Reality technologies (Metaio, OpenCV, Oculus Rift) and new forms of input (Razer Hydra, Leap Motion).

Acknowledgments

Before we get started, I'd like to give special mention to the people who helped me get started back in my Apple II days: my parents, who bought the Apple II that I ended up programming (and also a printer after they saw me typing out code listings on a typewriter—that junior high typing class really paid off!); my fellow high school Apple II programmers, Dave Lyons (now actually at Apple) and Cam Clarke (who made it to Silicon Valley but left us all too early); and Mr. Leaman, the programming teacher who let us hide out in the computer lab during pep rallies. That was time well spent.

Introduction

How I Met Unity

Technically, I first started programming on a TRS-80 in my junior high school library, but really I just typed in the same BASIC code listing from a magazine every day until the librarian mentioned I could save the program on a cassette. I'm embarrassed to recall my first reaction when I heard the library had a computer: "What's it good for?"

A year later, I saw the light when I got my hands on an Apple II. After cracking open the user manual and learning how to draw graphics in BASIC, I was hooked. Soon I was writing Reversi games (one in BASIC, one in 6502 assembly) and even a 3D wireframe display program.

In the intervening years I wandered the Windows wasteland and worked in small and large groups developing computer graphics and games. But fast forward to six years ago, when I happily got back into the Apple fold (now with Unix!) and attended my first Apple World Wide Developer Conference. Joachim Ante, one of the cofounders and the CTO of Unity Technologies, gave me an impromptu demo of Unity 1.5, and it was exactly what I'd been looking for—an inexpensive 3D game engine that ran on a Mac and was able to target multiple platforms, including Windows, Mac, and web browsers.

So I bought a Unity 1.5 Indie license as soon as I returned home (this was when Unity Indie wasn't free), later upgraded to Unity Pro, and was pleasantly surprised a couple of years later that Unity would support iOS. I love it when a plan comes together!

In the meantime, my former employers at Hyper Entertainment granted me a license to port HyperBowl, a 3D arcade bowling game I worked on over ten years ago, to Unity and various platforms supported by Unity, so now I had a meaty project to work with, besides the smaller apps I'd been experimenting with.

It took me six months to get the first version of the HyperBowl remake running as a Unity webplayer, with standalone Mac and PC executables, and on the iPhone (and by the way, also Android, Linux, and Flash). And really, I only spent three months using Unity if you subtract the time I spent figuring out how to extract the art and audio assets from the original game.

With each new version of Unity, HyperBowl and my other games got faster and better-looking, utilized more iOS features and ran on more iOS devices (and, eventually, Android devices). I added capabilities using third-party plugins, a new pause menu, and even an entire new HyperBowl lane (level) with packages from the Unity Asset Store, which is conveniently integrated within the Unity Editor.

This has all taken place with a development team of one (not counting all the work put into the original licensed assets), and I didn't have to learn a single line of Objective-C or create my own art. In a sense, I feel like I've returned to my programming roots, working on my own projects for fun, and as a bonus, profit! Hopefully, I can distill my experience with Unity over the past six years (both mistakes and successes) into this book.

About This Book

With any game development book there's the problem of trying to be all things to all people; there are plenty of areas in game development, Unity, and iOS that could easily take up whole books in themselves. This book is an introduction to developing games for iOS with Unity, so my goal is to get everyone acquainted with Unity and moving into Unity iOS development smoothly, following the same progression I've made over the years (but in less time!)

On the way, we'll go through step-by-step project examples to learn the Unity Editor and how to incorporate graphics, audio, physics, and scripting to make games, and then we'll move on to developing specifically for iOS. We'll take advantage of free art and audio from the Unity Asset Store, so we won't be creating 3D models or sound samples from scratch and can stay within the comfy confines of Unity (except when we have to dabble in Xcode when making iOS builds). We will, however, do plenty of scripting with Unity's version of JavaScript. Our focus will be on using the built-in Unity script functions, but I'll point you to Unity plugins and packages that provide further capability.

You can find the source code on Apress.com at http://www.apress.com/9781430248750 or on http://learnunity4.com/.

Explore Further

No one knows everything. That's why a key to successful development is knowing how to find the tools, assets, information, and help you need. So at the end of each chapter, I'll suggest some reading and resources for you to explore further.

I'll start here, with a recommendation of other worthwhile Unity books. Even on the same topic, it's useful to read different books for their different takes on the subject. For example, Will Goldstone wrote one of the first Unity books, *Unity Game Development Essentials,* Sue Blackman's *Beginning Unity 3D Development* is a hefty tome from an artist's viewpoint that presents an adventure game, and Jeff Murray covers Unity iOS in *Game Development for iOS with Unity 3D*, using a kart racing game as an example.

Since I waxed nostalgic on Apple computers, I should follow up with some Apple historical reading. *Revolution in the Valley* is a fun collection of Mac development anecdotes by Andy Hertzfeld. *iWoz* by Steve Wozniak is an interesting peek at early Apple history and at the Woz himself, and

Apple Design: The Work of the Apple Industrial Design Group by Paul Kunkel portrays the lineup of classic Macs (and by classic, I mean everything before 1997).

Although this book makes heavy use of example game projects, there won't be much discussion on game design. But there's certainly a lot of interesting reading on the subject. My favorite game design book is Richard Rouse's *Game Design*: *Theory and Practice*, mostly a collection of interviews with famous game designers. And there's a bounty of game design articles and blogs on the web site Gamasutra (`http://gamasutra.com/`).

Getting Started

Unity is a cross-platform 3D game development system developed by a company called Unity Technologies (originally named Over the Edge). What does it mean to call Unity cross-platform, exactly? Well, it's cross-platform in the sense that the Unity Editor, the game creation and editing tool that is the centerpiece of Unity, runs on OS X and Windows. More impressively, Unity is cross-platform in the sense that from the Unity Editor we can build games for OS X, Windows, web browsers (using either Flash, Google Native client, or Unity's browser plug-in), iOS, Android, and game consoles. And the list keeps growing (shortly before this book's publication, Unity Technologies announced support for the BlackBerry 10)!

As for 3D, Unity is a 3D game development system in the sense that Unity's built-in graphics, sound, and physics engines all operate in 3D space, which is perfect for creating 3D games, but many successful 2D games have also been developed in Unity.

This book describes the latest version of Unity as of this writing, which is Unity 4.1.2, but Unity is a fast-moving target, with new features and user interface changes appearing even in minor releases (which are appearing more frequently, since Unity Technologies has introduced a faster incremental update schedule starting with Unity 4). This caveat applies to everything else, of course, including products, licenses, and prices from Unity, Apple, and third-party vendors.

Prerequisites

Before the fun part, learning how to use the Unity Editor and build games, you need to download Unity, install it, and activate a license. Although you'll spend the first several chapters working with step-by-step examples in the Unity Editor and not get into iOS development until later (by the way, iOS originally stood for iPhone Operating System, but now includes the iPod Touch and iPad), it's not a bad idea to get started on the iOS development prerequisites, too.

Prepare Your Mac

For iOS development, you'll need a Mac running the Lion or Mountain Lion version of OS X (that is, version 10.7 and up). Unity 4 can still run on older versions of OS X, like Snow Leopard, but Lion and Mountain Lion are currently required to run the latest version of Xcode, the software tool required by Apple for iOS development. Typically, the latest or fairly recent version of Xcode is required to target the latest version of iOS.

Register as an iOS Developer

It's worth visiting the Apple developer site to register as an iOS developer as soon as possible, since the approval process can take a while, particularly if you're registering a company. First, you'll need to register on the site as an Apple developer (free) and then log in and register as an iOS developer ($99 per year membership). This is required to deploy your apps on test devices and to submit those apps to the App Store.

Download Xcode

Although you won't need Xcode until we reach the iOS portion of this book, you can download Xcode now from the Mac App Store (just search for "xcode") or from the Apple developer site at http://developer.apple.com/. When you start building Unity iOS apps, I'll go over the Xcode installation in more detail.

Download Unity

To obtain Unity, visit the Unity web site at http://unity3d.com/ and go to the Download page. There you will find a download link for the latest version of Unity (at the moment, Unity 4.1.2) and also a link to the release notes (which are included with the installation). There is also a link to a list of older versions in case you need to roll back to a previous version of Unity for some reason.

> **Tip**   While you're on the Unity web site, take a look around. Check out the demos, the FAQ, the feature comparisons among the various licenses, and the support links to the documentation, user forum, and other community support sites. You'll certainly have to come back later, so you might as well figure out where everything is now!

There is only one Unity application, with additional features and platform support activated by licenses. For example, the product name Unity iOS Pro specifies Unity with an added Unity Pro license and also a Unity iOS Pro license. I'll elaborate on the various licenses a little bit later in this chapter when I introduce the License Management window in Unity.

Unity version numbers are in the form major.minor.patch. So Unity 4.1.2 is Unity 4.0 with an incremental upgrade to Unity 4.1, with a couple of bug fix updates. Major upgrades, such as Unity 3 to Unity 4, require a license upgrade purchase and may require changes to the project.

> **Tip**   In general, once a Unity project has been upgraded, it may become incompatible with older versions of Unity. So it's a good idea to make a copy of your project before upgrading it, just in case you need to revert back to the previous version of Unity.

To start the Unity installation process, click the download link (as of this writing, it's a button labeled Download Unity 4.1.2). The file is around 1GB in size, so the download will take a while, but we're on our way!

Install Unity

The Unity download file is a disk image (DMG file), which at this time is a file named unity-4.1.2.dmg. Once the file is downloaded, double-click it to see the disk image contents (Figure 1-1).

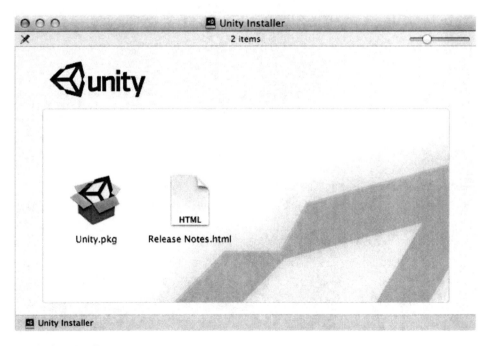

Figure 1-1. The Unity installer files

The installer disk image only contains two files: the release notes and the standard OSX installer package for Unity in the form of a file named Unity.pkg.

Run the Installer

Double-click the Unity.pkg file to start to begin the Unity installation (Figure 1-2).

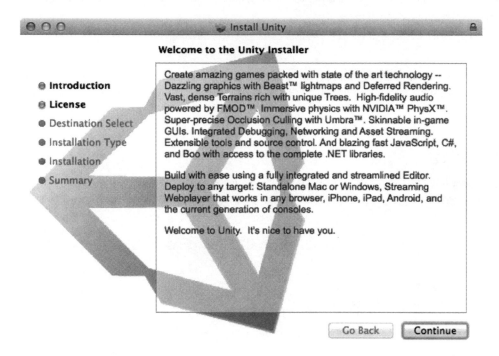

Figure 1-2. The Unity installer

The installer will proceed through a typical installation sequence (the steps are listed on the left side of the installer window), and at the end, a Unity folder will be placed in your Applications folder.

> **Tip**   If you happen to be upgrading from an older version of Unity, this process will just replace that old version. If you want to keep the previous copy around, rename the old folder first. For example, if you're upgrading from Unity 3.5 to Unity 4, first rename your Unity folder to "Unity35" before performing the new installation. Then you can run both versions of Unity.

The Unity installation folder contains the Unity application and several associated files and folders (Figure 1-3).

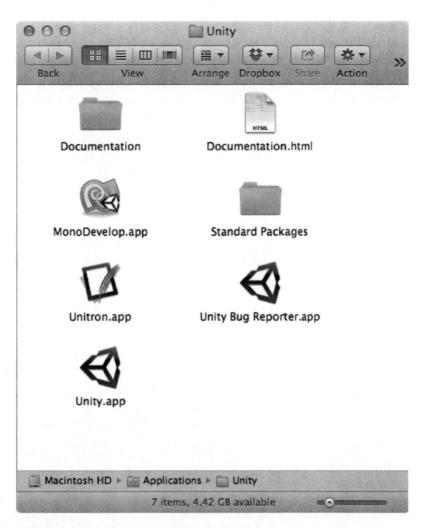

Figure 1-3. Contents of the Unity installed folder

The most important file in the Unity installation folder, and the only one you really need, is the Unity app, which provides the environment used to construct your games. This app is sometimes more specifically termed the Unity Editor, as distinct from the Unity runtime engine, or Unity Player, that is incorporated into final builds. But usually when I just say "Unity," the context is clear (I also refer to Unity Technologies as Unity).

The Documentation folder contains the same User Manual, Component Reference, and Script Reference viewable on the Unity web site (under the Learn tab). Each of these files can be brought up within a web browser from the Unity Help menu, and you can always double-click Documentation.html directly to see the front page of the documentation.

The Standard Packages folder contains several files with the .unityPackage extension. These Unity package files each hold collections of Unity assets and can be imported into Unity (and from Unity, you can export assets into a package file). For example, the Standard Package file named Scripts. unityPackage contains several generally useful scripts.

The MonoDevelop app is the default script editor for Unity and is a custom version of the open source MonoDevelop editor used for the Mono Project, known as Mono for short. Mono is an open source version of Microsoft's .NET framework and forms the basis of the Unity scripting system.

The Unitron app is an earlier and simpler script editor that is also derived from another program, a text editor called Smultron developed by Peter Borg. Although customized for Unity and still included in the Unity installation, Unitron is no longer officially supported.

Finally, there's the Unity Bug Reporter app, which is normally run from the Report a Bug item in the Unity help menu. However, you can always launch the Unity Bug Reporter directly from the Unity installation folder. That's pretty helpful if you run into a bug where Unity doesn't even start up!

Activate a License

Go ahead and double-click the Unity app to run it. If this is the first time Unity has been installed on your machine, you'll be presented with a license activation window. Of the three options presented, two are applicable to Unity iOS development: entering the serial number for a Unity license purchased in the Store section of the Unity web site (Figure 1-4) and registering for a free one-month trial of Unity Pro with Unity iOS Pro and Unity Android Pro (Figure 1-5).

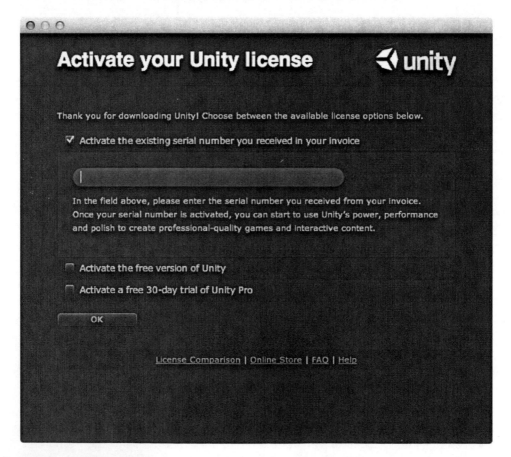

Figure 1-4. Activating a paid Unity license

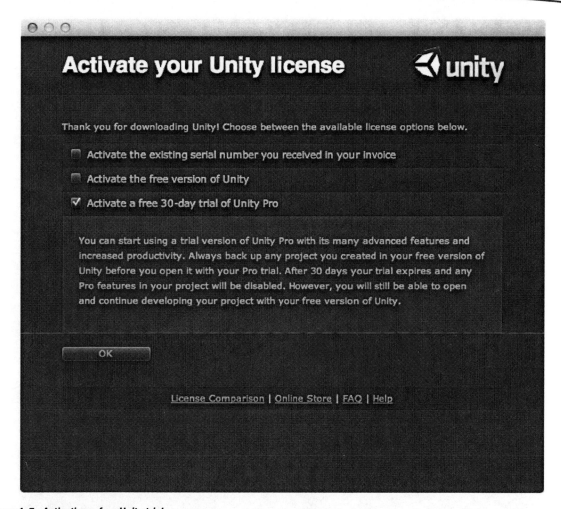

Figure 1-5. Activating a free Unity trial

The free version of Unity, which is Unity without the Pro features and is officially called just Unity (although sometimes it's referred to as Unity Basic, and I still call it Unity Indie, since it's only supposed to be used by entities making less than $100,000 a year), doesn't include Unity iOS. You can still start with free Unity for the portion of this book leading up to the iOS chapters and then add Unity iOS for $400, but keep in mind the Unity Pro and Unity iOS Pro features won't be available.

To clarify, your license determines which core version of Unity is enabled and which add-ons, if any, are enabled. The core product and the add-ons are available in non-Pro and Pro versions, and Unity Pro must be licensed for any Pro version of the add-ons to be licensed. So, developing with the non-Pro version of Unity iOS will cost you $400 in Unity licenses, but developing with Unity iOS Pro will cost $1,500 for Unity Pro and another $1,500 for Unity iOS Pro, for a grand total of $3,000. Unity Technologies sometimes offers discounts, especially when they're introducing a new major version of Unity, and prices can change, of course (after all, Unity Indie used to cost $400 and now it's free). In any case, the availability of the free trial Pro license means you don't have to worry about that immediately.

Welcome to Unity!

After you get the licensing taken care of, the Unity Editor window will appear with a friendly "Welcome To Unity" window appearing on top (Figure 1-6). The welcome window suggests some resources you should look at to get started. You can click each item to bring up that resource.

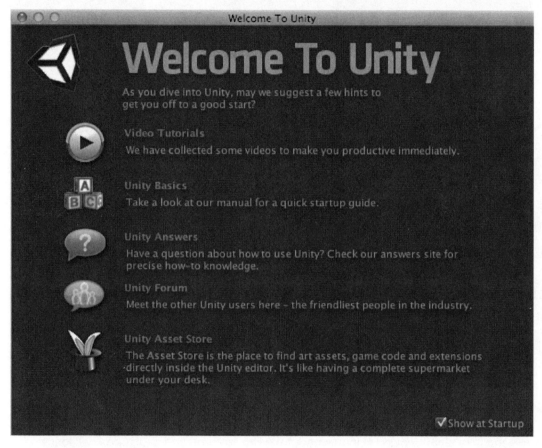

Figure 1-6. The Unity Welcome screen

The Welcome window will appear every time you start up Unity until you uncheck the "Show at Startup" check box in the lower right corner of the window. It's a good idea to look at the suggested resources before doing that, although you can always bring up the Welcome window again using the Unity Help menu (Figure 1-7).

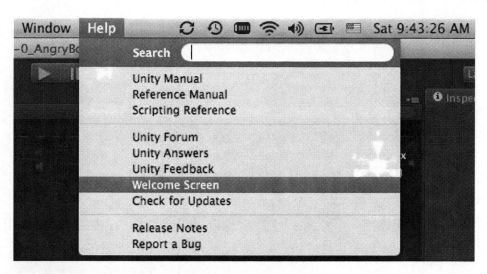

Figure 1-7. Bringing up the Welcome screen from the Unity Help menu

Manage Unity

Before getting into actual game development with Unity, this is a good time to look at some of the administrative features in the Unity Editor.

Change Skins (Pro)

The Unity Editor appears in one of two skins, Dark or Light. If you're using Unity Pro, you'll initially see the Dark skin (Figure 1-8), and if you're using the non-Pro version of Unity, you'll only see the Light skin (Figure 1-9).

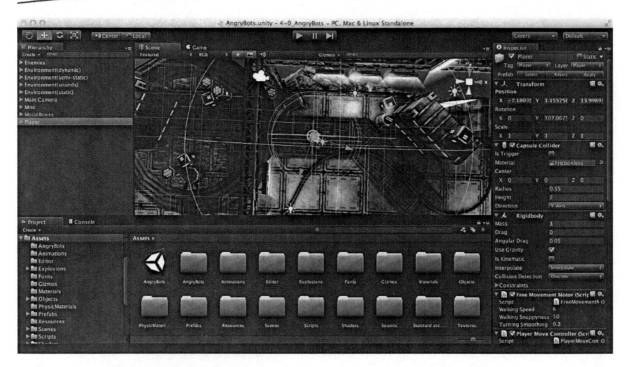

Figure 1-8. *The Unity Editor with the Pro (Dark) skin*

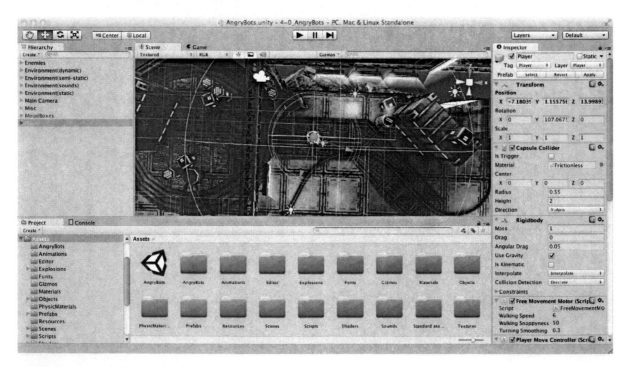

Figure 1-9. *The Unity Editor using the Indie (Light) skin*

For the rest of this book, I use the Dark skin for screenshots, but aside from the hue, there is no difference in the user interface. If you're using Unity Pro and prefer the Light skin, you can change skins in the Unity Preferences window. First select Preferences in the Unity menu (Figure 1-10).

Figure 1-10. The Preferences menu item in the Unity Editor

Now with the Preferences window up, you can change the skin from Dark to Light or Light to Dark (Figure 1-11). This is a Unity Pro-only feature. If you're using Unity Indie, you're stuck with the Light skin.

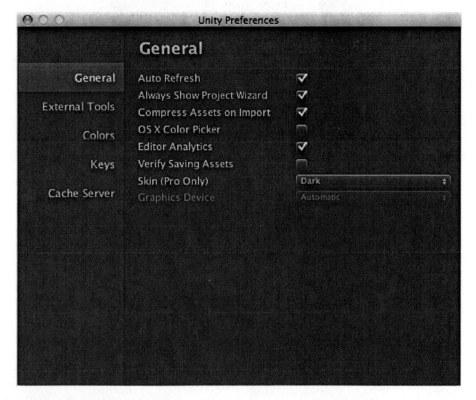

Figure 1-11. General Preferences in the Unity Editor

While you're in the Preferences window, I recommend making sure "Always Show Project Wizard" is checked. That will ensure Unity brings up the project selection dialog when it starts up, instead of automatically opening the most recently opened project, which can be time-consuming and is not always what you want. In particular, you don't want to accidentally upgrade a project to a new version of Unity before you're ready.

Update the License

Eventually, you may need to update your license, either because you're using the free trial and it has expired, to upgrade your license to Pro versions, to add another build platform, or because you need to switch your license to a different machine. At that point, you can bring up the Unity menu on the menu bar and select Manage License (Figure 1-12).

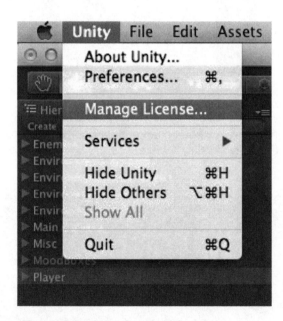

Figure 1-12. Bringing up the License Management window from the Unity menu

The resulting License Management window gives you the option of entering a new serial number or returning the license for this machine so you can use it for another (Figure 1-13).

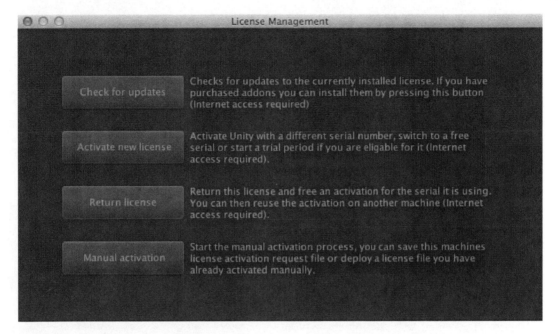

Figure 1-13. The License Management window

A single Unity license can be used on two machines. In its early years, when the Unity Editor only ran on OS X, a Unity license was only good for one machine, but the number was increased to two after Windows support for the Unity Editor was added.

Report Problems

If you use Unity for a significant period of time, you'll certainly encounter bugs, real or imagined. That's not a knock on Unity. The 3D game engines are very complicated, at least internally, and the pace of their development is remarkable (I started with Unity 1.6 when it only ran on OS X and only deployed builds for Windows and OS X). Bugs don't fix themselves, especially when they're not reported. That's where the Unity Bug Reporter comes in. As I mentioned when going over the Unity installation files, the Bug Reporter is available in the Unity folder but normally is launched from the Help menu in the Unity Editor (Figure 1-14).

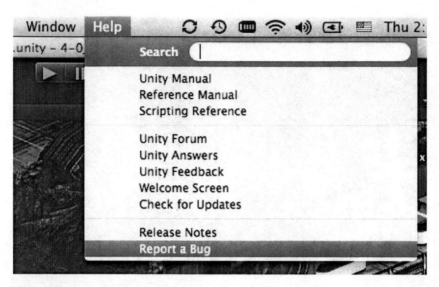

Figure 1-14. The Report a Bug option in the Help menu

> **Tip**   The Bug Reporter, as you can see in the list of files in the Unity installation, is a separate application from the Unity Editor. So if you encounter a bug that prevents the Unity Editor from starting up properly, you can always launch the Bug Reporter directly by double-clicking that file in the Finder.

The resulting Bug Reporter window (Figure 1-15), prompts you to select where the bug occurs (in the Unity Editor or in the Unity Player, i.e., a deployed build), the frequency of the bug's occurrence, and an e-mail address to which Unity Technologies will send responses about this bug.

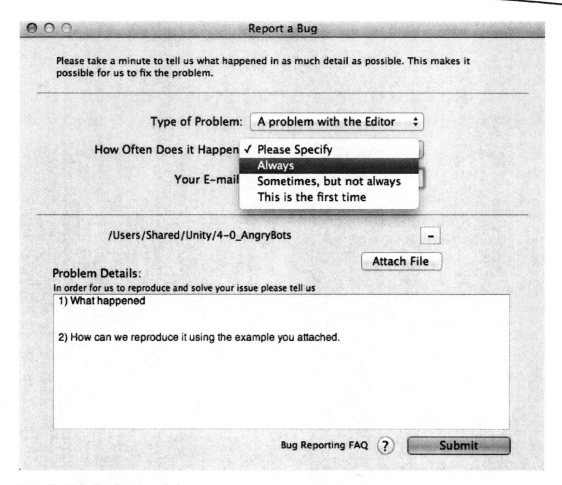

Figure 1-15. The Unity Bug Reporter window

Below that, in the middle of the window, is the list of attachments. Unity automatically starts off this list with the current project, and you might include supplemental files like screenshots or log files. You can remove the current project from this list, but normally you should include the project so that Unity support can reproduce the problem.

By the same token, you should fill in the problem description with a detailed enough explanation that Unity support would know how to replicate the undesired behavior and understand why it's undesired. Basically, you want to avoid responses in the mode of "We can't reproduce the problem" and "This is not a bug. It's by design."

Shortly after submitting a bug report, you should receive an e-mail confirmation from Unity Technologies with a case number and a link to a copy of the report in the Unity bug database, which you can check to see the status of the bug.

Check for Updates

If you're lucky, your bug report will result in a fix. And if you're really lucky, that fix will show up in the next Unity update. You can always check if there's a new update by selecting the Check for Updates command from the Window menu on the menu bar. The resulting window will display whether or not an update is available (Figure 1-16).

Figure 1-16. The Unity Editor Update Check

Notice the version number displayed in Figure 1-16 is Unity 4.1.2f1. The suffix represents the most granular releases, including emergency hot fixes. Out of some caution, Unity Technologies usually doesn't make newly released updates immediately available to the Editor Update Check, so if you're waiting anxiously for a bug-fix update, you can always check the Unity web site, too.

Explore Further

My favorite technical books, like Peter Van Der Linden's *Just Java* (a very detailed but easygoing introduction to Java for nonprogrammers), provide a nice break at the end of each chapter by reciting an interesting anecdote, a bit of trivia, or some relevant history. Alas, I won't be doing that in this book. However, I do find simple chapter summaries and recaps dull (I always skip them as a reader), and I feel one of the major challenges facing new Unity developers is that they need to get in the habit of finding Unity information on their own, and they need to know where to find that information, which isn't always easy!

Therefore, at the end of each chapter, and including this one, I'll direct you to documentation and other resources related to the topics you just learned, so you'll know where to find the definitive and comprehensive information sources and can take things further when you've finished this book. I'll focus on the official Unity manuals and the Unity web site but also mention some third-party resources. So now that you have Unity installed, before putting it to use in this book, take a break and browse the web sites and reference documentation that you will surely be utilizing heavily from now on. It's always a good idea to figure out where to find what you need, before you need it!

iOS Development Requirements

At the beginning of this chapter, I mentioned it's a good idea to get the ball rolling on downloading Xcode and registering for Apple's iOS Developer Program.

Requirements for iOS development, including required hardware and details about the iOS Developer Program, are listed on Apple's developer support page (http://developer.apple.com/support).

Information about Xcode requirements and downloading Xcode can be found at http://developer.apple.com/xcode.

The Unity Web Site

Along with the growth of Unity features and platforms, the Unity web site (http://unity3d.com/) has grown, too. It's all worth browsing, but in particular, for general information about Unity, check out the FAQ section on the Unity web site (http://unity3d.com/unity/faq).

The license activation process and License Management window are documented on http://unity3d.com/unity/activation. This chapter mentioned the distinct Pro and non-Pro versions of Unity and Unity iOS, but the license comparison table at http://unity3d.com/unity/licenses provides a more comprehensive table of features and their availability for the various licenses. Many instructional videos are available on the Unity Video archive (http://video.unity3d.com/) and Unity has recently introduced a Learn tab on their web site for easy access to documentation and tutorials.

Unity Manuals and References

The top section of the Unity Help menu (Figure 1-17) lists the official Unity documentation consisting of three documents: the Unity Manual, the Reference Manual, and the Scripting Reference. Although the Unity Manual doesn't have much information on the installation and licensing procedure discussed in this chapter, the manual otherwise provides good general instruction and conceptual explanations on using Unity. The Reference Manual and Scripting Reference will become increasingly important as you create and script scenes throughout this book.

Figure 1-17. The Help menu

The Unity Help menu items bring up the locally installed copies of those manuals, but they are also available under the Learn tab of the Unity web site.

The Unity Community

The first three items in the middle of the Unity Help menu are links to the official Unity community sites. The forum (http://forum.unity3d.com) is where users can bring up just about anything related to Unity (the forum does have moderators, though).

The Unity Answers site (http://answers.unity3d.com/) follows the format of Stack Exchange and provides some quality control over questions and answers. The Unity Feedback site (http://feedback.unity3d.com) allows users to post feature requests and vote on feature requests, whether they're their own or posted by someone else.

> **Tip**   Although the bug type selector offers Feature Request as a Type of Bug, Unity encourages everyone to submit feature requests to their Feedback site.

Welcome to the Unity community!

A Unity Tour

Now that you have Unity installed, it's time to get acquainted with the Unity Editor. The Editor (I'll use the terms Unity, Unity Editor, and Editor interchangeably, as long as the meaning is clear) is where you create, test, and build a game for one or more target platforms. The Editor operates on a single Unity project containing assets included in a game.

This chapter will introduce the Unity Editor using the Angry Bots demo project that is installed with Unity. I won't delve into the inner workings of Angry Bots here, but it's a convenient ready-made project you can use to get acquainted with Unity, even to the point of building Angry Bots as an OS X app to get a feel for the build process. Hopefully, this will get you comfortable with Unity's workflow, user interface, and various file types before learning how to create a new project from scratch in the next chapter.

> **Tip** Filename extensions are hidden by default in OS X, but anyone performing any kind of development should be looking at complete filenames. To ensure extensions are displayed, go to the Advanced tab in the Finder Preferences window and check "Show all filename extensions."

Bring out the Angry Bots

During the installation process of the previous chapter, an example Unity project called Angry Bots was installed in the Users ➤ Shared ➤ Unity folder. If you're a longtime Unity user, you probably have some other projects left there from older versions of Unity. For example, Figure 2-1 shows my Unity shared example folder. Besides the latest version of Angry Bots (the more recent ones have the corresponding Unity version in their file names), I still have the Star Trooper example project that came with Unity 2.

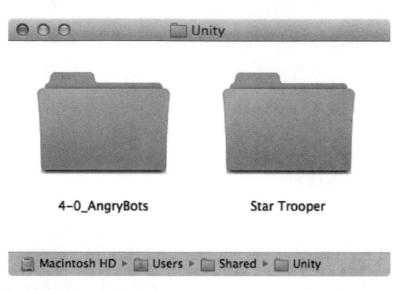

Figure 2-1. *The Unity shared folder of example projects*

Open the Angry Bots Project

Unity will automatically open the Angry Bots demo project when you bring up the Unity Editor for the first time. If for some reason Unity doesn't immediately open Angry Bots, or if you want to return to it later (as we will in Chapters 10 and 11 where we will use Angry Bots to get acquainted with Unity iOS), select the Open Project item in the File menu on the Unity menu bar (Figure 2-2).

Figure 2-2. *The Open Project menu item*

The Project Wizard will appear (the same Project Wizard referred to by the Always Show Project Wizard item in the Preferences window). Select the AngryBots project from the list of recent projects in the Project Wizard (the same one that will show up every time you start Unity if you left the box checked) or click the Open Other button (Figure 2-3).

Figure 2-3. Selecting Angry Bots from the Open Project wizard

Open the Angry Bots Scene

With the Angry Bots project open, the Unity Editor should now display the main scene of the project, named AngryBots. The title bar of the window should list the scene file, AngryBots.unity, followed by the project name and the target platform (Figure 2-4).

Figure 2-4. The Angry Bots project opened with a new scene

The scene name is displayed along the upper border of the Editor window, and the scene contents are reflected in the Hierarchy View, Scene View, and Game View. I'll explain views in a bit and spend a good portion of this chapter going over each view in detail.

A scene is the same as a level in a game (in fact, the Unity script function that loads a scene is called Application.LoadLevel). The purpose of the Unity Editor is to construct scenes, and thus it always has one scene open at a time.

If the Editor doesn't open an existing scene at startup, it will open a newly created scene, the same as if you had selected New Scene from the File menu on the Unity menu bar.

If you're not looking at the AngryBots scene right now, then select the Open Scene command in the File menu (Figure 2-5).

Figure 2-5. The Open Scene menu item

The resulting file chooser will start off in the top level of the project's Assets folder, where you can select the AngryBots scene file (Figure 2-6). All scene files are displayed with a Unity icon and have the .unity filename extension.

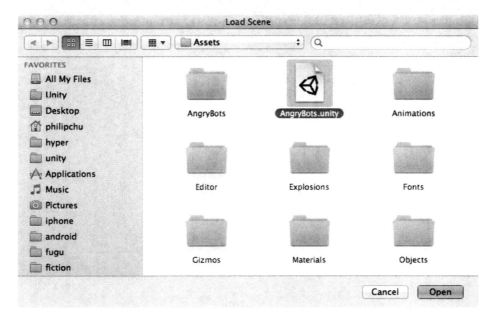

Figure 2-6. Selecting the AngryBots scene in the Load Scene chooser

Play Angry Bots

With the desired scene open, click the Play button at the center top of the Editor to start the game. The Game View will appear and display the running game, which can be played with standard keyboard and mouse controls (Figure 2-7).

Figure 2-7. The Play mode in the Editor

Use the AWSD keys to move forward, back, left, and right, respectively, move the mouse to look around, and press the Esc key to pause. Clicking the Play button again will stop the game and exit Play mode. The two buttons next to the Play button are used to pause and step through the game.

Build Angry Bots

During normal development, you would alternate between editing a scene and playing it.

When you're satisfied how the game plays in the Editor, then you're ready to build the app for the target platform. You won't start building for iOS until Chapter 10, but to get a feel for the build process, go ahead andl build an OS X app version of Angry Bots right now. Select the Build Settings item from the Unity File menu to bring up the Build Settings window (Figure 2-8).

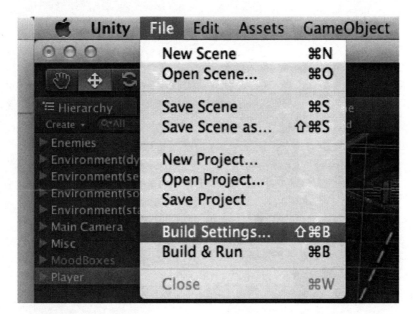

Figure 2-8. Bringing up the Build Settings window

The upper portion of the window lists the scenes to include in the build. Just the scene you have open should be checked. Any unchecked or unlisted scenes won't be included in the build (Figure 2-9).

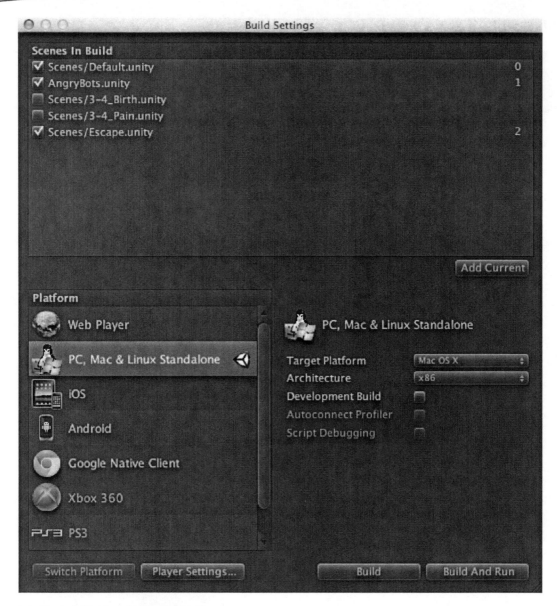

Figure 2-9. The Build Settings for the Mac platform

The default platform selected in the Platform list on the left is PC, Mac & Linux Standalone, matching the platform listed on the Editor title bar. The default specific Target Platform on the right is set as a Windows executable, but since you're operating on a Mac, let's set the Target Platform in the menu on the right to Mac OS X. Then click the Switch Platform button on the lower left. This will initiate a conversion of the project assets to formats suitable for use on a Mac. After the conversion is complete, the title bar of the Editor will update to reflect the new platform.

Now you can click either the Build or Build and Play button in the Build Settings window. Clicking Build will generate an OS X app version of our game. Clicking Build and Play will do the same but also run the game, which just saves the effort of bringing up a Finder window and double-clicking the new app. Unity will prompt you for a file name and location for the app, defaulting to the top level of the project directory, which is fine (Figure 2-10).

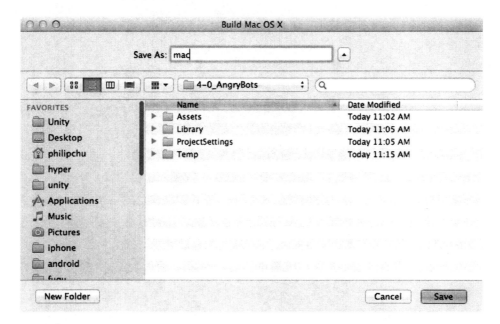

Figure 2-10. Saving an OS X app build

When the build is complete, double-click the generated app to run the game. Or if you selected Build and Run, the game should start automatically. Unity-generated OS X apps start with a resolution-chooser window (Figure 2-11).

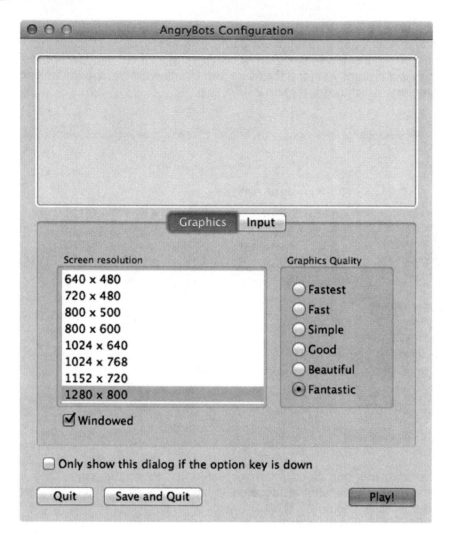

Figure 2-11. Startup dialog for a Unity OS X app

After selecting the desired resolution and clicking Play!, you'll see a game window with the size you just specified. Now you have Angry Bots running in its own Mac window (Figure 2-12).

Figure 2-12. Angry Bots as an OS X app Mac app

The Editor Layout

Now that you've got a feel for the Unity test-and-build workflow with the Angry Bots project, let's take a closer look at the layout of the Unity Editor. The main window is divided into areas (I'm used to calling them panes, but I'll call them areas since that's the term used in Xcode). Each area holds one or more tabbed views. The currently displayed view for an area is selected by clicking the view's tab. Views can be added, moved, removed, and resized, and the Editor supports switching among layouts, so a layout essentially is a specific arrangement of views. For example, the default layout of the main window (Figure 2-13) has an area containing a Scene View (Figure 2-14) and a Game View (Figure 2-15).

> **Note**   The Unity documentation is somewhat inconsistent in naming views. It's obvious from their names that the Game View and Scene View are views. But the Console and Inspector are also views. In this book, I'll include View in all of their names to make clear they are all views and can be manipulated the same way.

Figure 2-13. The default layout of the Unity Editor

Figure 2-14. The Scene View selected in a multitabbed area

Figure 2-15. The Game View selected in a multitabbed area

Preset Layouts

The default layout is just one of several preset layouts. Alternate layouts can be selected from the menu in the top right corner of the main window (Figure 2-16). Go ahead and try them out. Figures 2-17 through 2-20 show the resulting layouts.

Figure 2-16. The Layout menu

Figure 2-17. The 2-by-3 layout

Figure 2-18. The 4-split layout

Figure 2-19. The Tall layout

Figure 2-20. The Wide layout

I'll describe the individual types of views in more detail shortly, but for now note that the 2-by-3 layout (Figure 2-17) is an example of a layout where the Scene View and Game View are in separate areas instead of sharing the same one. The 4-split layout (Figure 2-18) has four instances of the Scene View (reminiscent of tools used for computer-aided design), demonstrating that a layout is not restricted to one of each type of view.

Custom Layouts

The preset layouts provide a variety of workspaces, but fortunately you're not restricted to using them exactly as they are. Unity provides the flexibility to completely rearrange the Editor window as you like.

Resize Areas

For starters, you may notice while trying out the various preset layouts that some of the areas are too narrow, for example, in the left panel of the Wide layout (Figure 2-20). Fortunately, you can click the border of an area and drag it to resize the area.

Move Views

Even cooler, you can move views around. Dragging the tab of a view into another tab region will move the view there. And dragging the tab into a "docking" area will create a new area. For example, start with the Default layout, drag the Inspector tab to the right of the Hierarchy tab. Now the Inspector View shares the same area as the Hierarchy View. And then drag the Console tab into the bottom region of the Hierarchy/Inspector View. That effectively splits the area into two, the bottom half now containing the Console. The result should look like Figure 2-21.

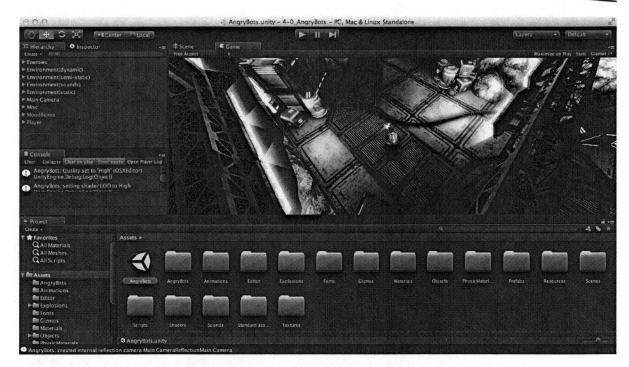

Figure 2-21. A workspace customized with views moved

Detach Views

You can even drag a view outside the Editor window so that it resides in its own "floating" window, which can be treated just like any other area. Drag the Scene tab outside the Editor so it resides in a floating window, and then drag the Game tab into its tab region. The result should look like Figure 2-22. Likewise, dragging a tab into a docking region of the floating window will add another area to the window.

> **Tip**   I like to detach the Game View into a floating window, since I normally don't need to see it while I'm working in the Editor until I click Play, and this allows me to maximize the Game View to fill up to the entire screen.

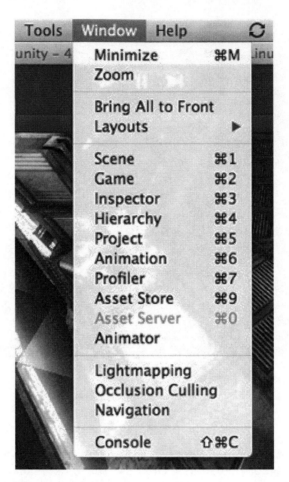

Figure 2-22. The list of views in the Windows menu

Floating windows are often covered up by other windows, so the Windows menu on the menu bar has menu items for making each view visible (Figure 2-22). Notice there is a keyboard shortcut for each, and there is also a Layouts submenu that is identical to the layout menu inside the Editor.

Add and Remove Views

You can also add and remove views in each area using the menu at the top right corner of the area (Figure 2-23). The Close Tab item removes the currently displayed view. The Add Tab item provides a list of new views for you to choose from.

Figure 2-23. *Adding a view to an area*

You may want to have different layouts for different target platforms, or different layouts for development vs. play testing, or even different layouts for different games. For example, I have a custom layout specifically for HyperBowl that preserves the Game View in a suitable portrait aspect ratio. It would be a hassle to manually reconfigure the Editor every time you start up Unity. Fortunately, you can name and save layouts by selecting the Save Layout option in the layout menu, which will prompt you for the new layout name (Figure 2-24).

Figure 2-24. *The Save Layout menu*

After saving, the new layout will be listed in the layout menu and also in the list of layouts available for deletion if you select Delete Layout (Figure 2-25).

Figure 2-25. The Delete Layout menu

If you've messed up or deleted the original layouts, you can select the Restore Factory Settings option in the area menu (Figure 2-26). This will also delete any custom layouts.

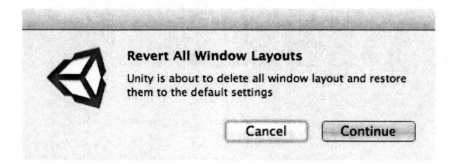

Figure 2-26. The Restore Factory Settings prompt

If you change a layout and haven't saved the changes, you can always discard them by just reselecting that layout in the layout menu.

The Inspector View

The best view to describe in detail first is the Inspector View, since its function is to display information about objects selected in other views. It's really more than an inspector, since it can typically be used to modify the selected item.

The Inspector View is also used to display and adjust the various settings that can be brought up in the Edit menu. For example, you might notice that the Assets folder in the Angry Bots installation has a lot of files with a .meta extension, as shown in Figure 2-27. In fact, there is one of these files for each asset file. Unity tracks the assets in a project using these meta files, which are in text format to facilitate use with version control systems like Perforce and Subversion (or newer distributed version control systems like Git and Mercurial).

Figure 2-27. The meta files in the Angry Bots project

But if you aren't using a version control system (or if you are using the Unity Asset Server, which is a product from Unity Technologies and requires another license), you can turn off version control compatibility in the Editor Settings and get rid of those unsightly files. Bring up the Editor Settings by going to the Edit menu and selecting Editor Settings from the Settings submenu (Figure 2-28).

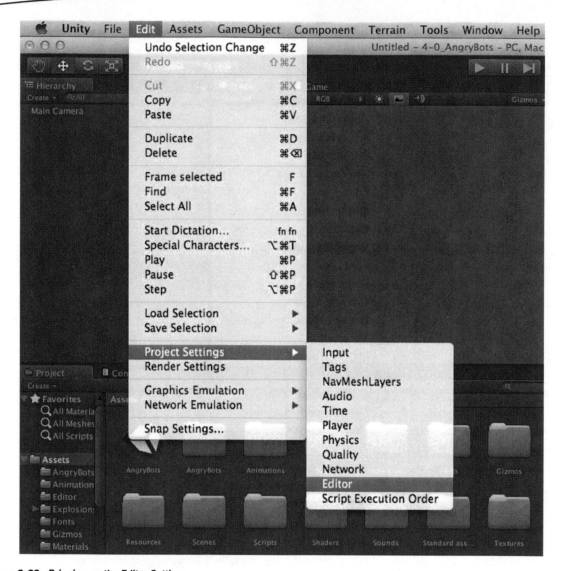

Figure 2-28. Bringing up the Editor Settings

Now the Inspector View displays the Editor Settings. If the project currently has meta files, then the Version Control Mode is set to Meta Files (and if you're using the Asset Server, this option is set to Asset Server). To remove the meta files, set the Version Control Mode to Disabled (Figure 2-29).

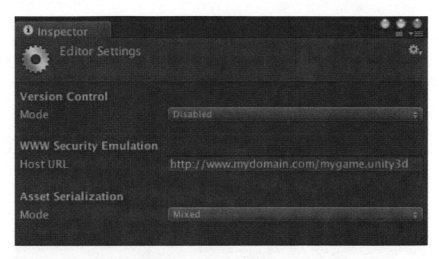

Figure 2-29. Editor Settings in the Inspector View

With the Version Control Mode set to Disabled, Unity will remove the meta files (Figure 2-30). The asset tracking is now handled within binary files inside the Library folder of the project.

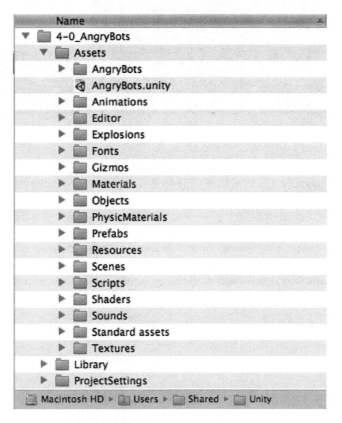

Figure 2-30. The Angry Bots project folder minus the meta files

Note   Unity Pro users who are using meta files for version control support also have the option of setting Asset Serialization Mode to Force Text. In that mode, Unity scene files are saved in a text-only YAML (YAML Ain't Markup Language) format.

Normally, the Inspector View displays the properties of the most recently selected object (when you bring up the Editor Settings, you really selected it). But sometimes you don't want the Inspector View to change while you're selecting other objects. In that case, you can pin the Inspector View to an object by selecting the Lock option in the menu at the top right of the view (Figure 2-31).

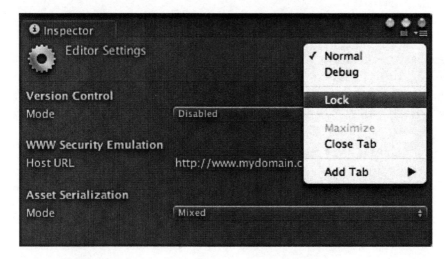

Figure 2-31. Locking the Inspector View

The Project View

While the Inspector View can be thought of as the lowest-level view in the Editor, since it displays the properties of just a single object, the Project View can be considered the highest-level view (Figure 2-32). The Project View displays all of the assets available for your game, ranging from individual models, textures and scripts to the scene files which incorporate those assets. All of the project assets are files residing in the Assets folder of your project (so I actually think of the Project View as the Assets View).

Figure 2-32. Top level of the Project view

Switch Between One-Column and Two-Columns

Before Unity 4, the Project View had only a one-column display. That option is still available in the menu for the Project View (click the little three-line icon at the top right of the view), so you can now switch between one and two columns.

Notice how the Project View of Angry Bots project (Figure 2-32) resembles how the project's Assets folder looks in the Finder (see Figure 2-30). It actually looks more like a Windows file view, where you navigate the folder hierarchy in the panel on the left and view the contents of the selected folder in the right panel.

Scale Icons

The slider on the bottom scales the view in the right panel—a larger scale is nice for textures and smaller is better for items like scripts that don't have interesting icons. This is a good reason to partition assets by asset type (i.e., put all textures in a Textures folders, scripts in a Script folder, and so on). Chances are, a single-scale slider setting won't be good for a mixture of asset types.

Inspect Assets

Selecting an asset on the right will display the properties of that asset in the Inspector View. For example, if you select a sound sample, the Inspector View displays information about the sound format, some of which you can change, like the compression, and it even lets you play the audio in the Editor (Figure 2-33). I'll explain the sound properties in a later chapter, but for now feel free to select various types of assets in the Project View and see what shows up in the Inspector View.

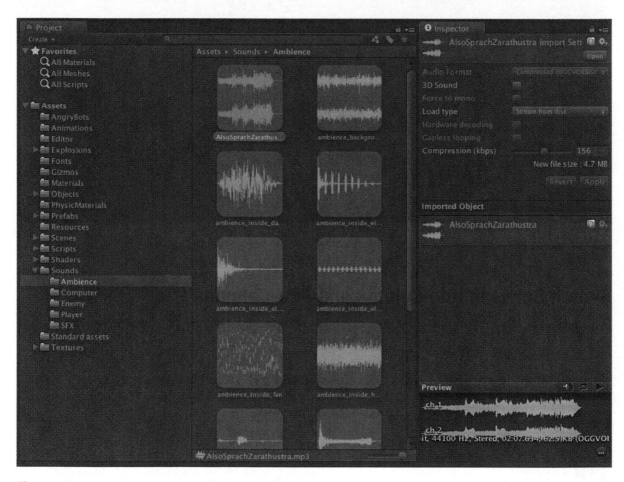

Figure 2-33. Inspecting a selected asset in the Project View

Search for Assets

In a large and complex project, it's difficult to manually search for a particular asset. Fortunately, just as in the Finder, there is a search box that can be used to filter the results showing in the right panel of the Project View. In Figure 2-34, the Project View displays the result of searching for assets with "add" in their names.

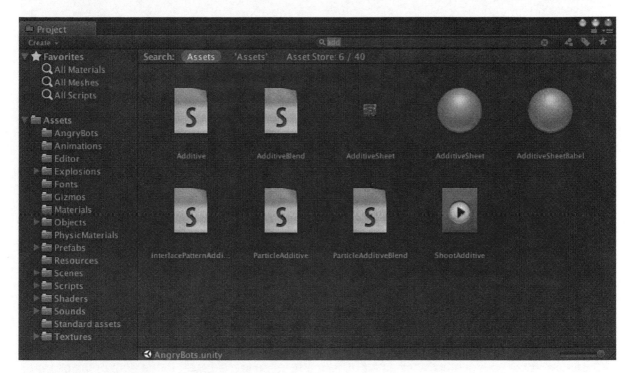

Figure 2-34. Searching for assets with "add" in the name

The right panel displays the search results for everything under Assets (i.e., all of our assets). The search can be narrowed further by selecting one of the subfolders in the left panel. For example, if you know you're looking for a texture, and you've arranged your assets into subfolders by the type of asset, you can select the Textures folder to search (Figure 2-35).

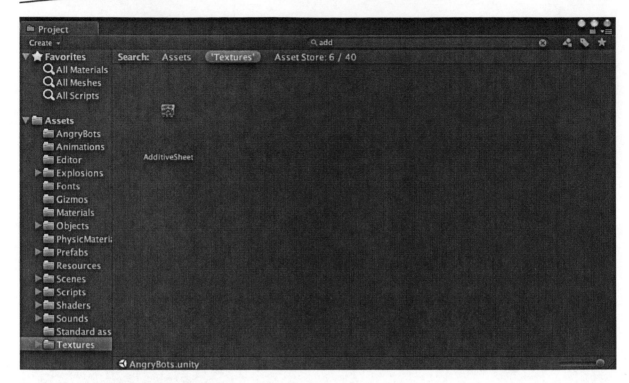

Figure 2-35. Searching assets in a folder

Notice just below the search, there is a tab with the name of the folder that was selected. You can still click the Assets tab to the left to see the search results for all your assets, both locally and on the Unity Asset Store, which we'll make copious use of in this book.

You can also filter your search by asset type, using the menu immediately to the right of the search box. Instead of just searching in the Textures folder, you could have selected Texture as the asset type of interest (Figure 2-36). Notice how that resulted in "t:Texture" being added to the search box. The "t:" prefix indicates the search should be filtered by the following asset type. You could have just typed that in without using the menu.

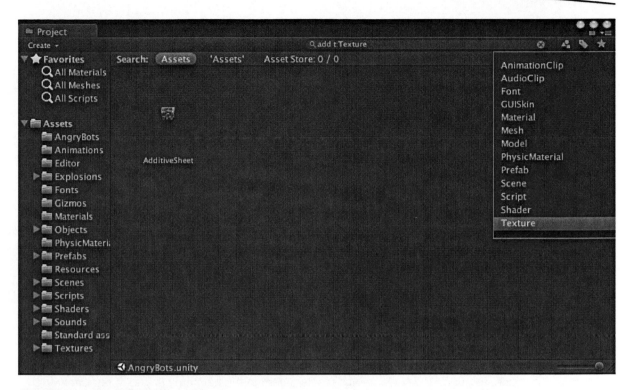

Figure 2-36. A search filtered by asset type

The button to right of the asset type menu is for filtering by label (you can assign a label to each asset in the Inspector View), which is also pretty handy for searching the Asset Store. And the rightmost button, the star, will save the current search in the Favorites section of the left panel.

Operate on Assets

Assets in the Project View can be manipulated very much like their corresponding files in the Finder.

Double-clicking an asset will attempt to open a suitable program to view or edit the asset. This is equivalent to right-clicking the asset and selecting Open. Double-clicking a scene file will open the scene in this Unity Editor window, just as if you had selected Open Scene in the File menu.

You can also rename, duplicate and delete, and drag files in and out of a folder just as you can in the Finder. Some of the operations are available in the Unity Edit menu and in a pop-up menu when you right-click on an asset. You'll get some practice with that in the next few chapters.

Likewise, in the next chapter you will work on adding assets to a project. That involves importing a file or importing a Unity package, using the Assets menu on the menu bar or just dragging files into the Assets folder of the project using the Finder.

The Hierarchy View

Every game engine has a top-level object called a *game object* or *entity* (CryEngine, for example) or something else (Second Life has prims) to represent anything that has a position, potential behavior, and a name to identify it. Unity game objects are instances of the class GameObject.

> **Note**   In general, when we refer to a type of Unity object, we'll use its class name to be precise and make clear how that object would be referenced in a script.

The Hierarchy View is another representation of the current scene. While the Scene View is a 3D representation of the scene that you can work in as you would with a content creation tool, and the Game View shows the scene as it looks when playing the game, the Hierarchy View lists all the GameObjects in the scene in an easily navigable tree structure.

Inspect Game Objects

When you click a GameObject in the Hierarchy View, it becomes the current Editor selection and its Components are displayed in the Editor. Every GameObject has a Transform Component, which specifies its position, rotation, and scale, relative to its parent in the hierarchy (if you're familiar with the math of 3D graphics, the Transform Component encapsulates the transformation matrix of the object).

Some Components provide a function for the GameObject (e.g., a light is a GameObject with a Light Component attached). Other Components reference assets such as meshes, textures, and scripts. Figure 2-37 shows the Components of the Player GameObject (in the Hierarchy View, the entire Player tree of GameObjects is displayed in blue because it's linked to a prefab, a special type of asset that is used to clone a GameObject or group of GameObjects).

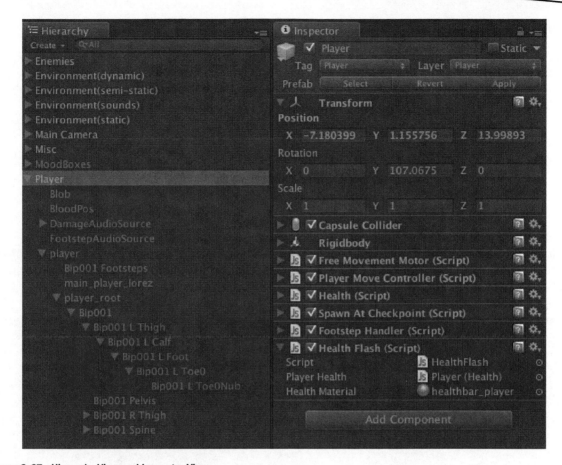

Figure 2-37.   Hierarchy View and Inspector View

Parent and Child GameObjects

Notice that many of the GameObjects are arranged in a hierarchy, hence the name of this view (in computer graphics, this is commonly known as a *scene graph*). Parenting makes sense for game objects that are conceptually grouped together. For example, when you want to move a car, you want the wheels to automatically move along with the car. So the wheels should be specified as children of the car, offset from the center of the car. When the wheels turn, they turn relative to the movement of the car. Parenting also allows us to activate or deactivate whole groups of game objects at one time.

The Scene View

Whereas the Hierarchy View allows you to create, inspect, and modify the GameObjects in the current scene, it doesn't provide a way to visualize the scene. That's where the Scene View comes in. The Scene View is similar to the interfaces of 3D modeling applications. It lets you examine and modify the scene from any 3D vantage point and gives you an idea how the final product will look.

Navigate the Scene

If you're not familiar with working in 3D space, it's a straightforward extension from working in 2D. Instead of just working in a space with x and y axes and (x,y) coordinates, in 3D space you have an additional z axis and (x,y,z) coordinates. The x and z axes define the ground plane and y is pointing up (you can think of y as height).

> **Note**   Some 3D applications and game engines use the z axis for height and the x and y axes for the ground plane, so when importing assets you might have to adjust (rotate) them.

The viewpoint in 3D space is usually called the *camera*. Clicking the x, y, and z arrows of the multicolored Scene Gizmo in the upper right corner is a quick way of flipping the Scene View camera so that it faces along the respective axis. For example, clicking the y arrow gives you a top-down view of the scene (Figure 2-38), and the text under the Scene Gizmo says "Top."

Figure 2-38. A top-down view in the Scene View

The camera here is not the same as the Camera GameObject in the scene that is used during the game, so you don't have to worry about messing up the game while you're looking around in the Scene View.

Clicking the box in the center of the Scene Gizmo toggles the camera projection between perspective, which renders objects smaller as they recede in the distance, and orthographic, which renders everything at their original size whether they are close or far. Perspective is more realistic and what you normally see in 3D games, but orthographic is often more convenient when designing (hence its ubiquity in computer-aided design applications). The little graphic preceding the text under the Scene Gizmo indicates the current projection.

You can zoom in and out using the mouse scroll wheel or by selecting the Hand tool in the upper right toolbar of the Editor window and click-dragging the mouse while holding the Control key down. When the Hand tool is selected, you can also move the camera by click-dragging the view, and you can rotate (orbit) the camera by dragging the mouse while holding the Option (or Alt) key down, so you're not restricted to just the axis camera angles, like in Figure 2-39.

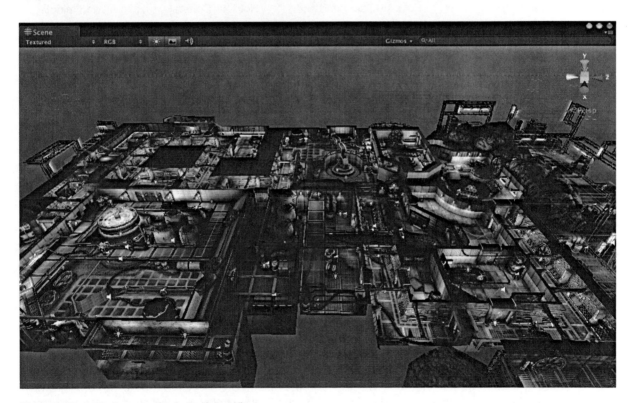

Figure 2-39. A tilted perspective in the Scene View

Notice that when you're looking from an arbitrary angle, the text under the Scene Gizmo says Persp or Iso, depending on whether you're using perspective or orthographic projection (Iso is short for isometric, which is the tilted orthographic view common in games like Starcraft and Farmville).

The other buttons on the toolbar activate modes for moving, rotating, and scaling GameObjects. There's no reason to change the Angry Bots scene, so those modes will be explained in more detail when you start creating new projects.

> **Tip**   If you accidentally make a change to the scene, you can select Undo from the Edit menu. If you made a lot of changes you don't want to keep, you can just decline to save this scene when you switch to another scene or exit Unity. In the meantime, note that you can still move the camera while in those modes, using alternate keyboard and mouse combinations. Table 2-1 lists all the possible options.

Table 2-1. *Available Scene View Camera Controls*

Action	Hand tool	1-button mouse or trackpad	2-button mouse	3-button mouse
Move	Click-drag	Hold Alt-Command and click-drag	Hold Alt-Control and click-drag	Hold Alt and middle click-drag
Orbit	Hold Alt and click-drag	Hold Alt and click-drag	Hold Alt and click-drag	Hold Alt and click-drag
Zoom	Hold Control and click-drag	Hold Control and click-drag or two-finger swipe	Hold Alt and right-click-drag	Hold Alt and right-click drag or scroll wheel

There are a couple of other handy keyboard-based scene navigation features. Pressing the Arrow keys will move the camera forward, back, left, and right along the x–z plane (the ground plane). And holding the right mouse button down allows navigation of the scene as in a first-person game. The AWSD keys move left, forward, right, and back, respectively, and moving the mouse controls where the camera (viewpoint) looks.

When you want to look at a particular GameObject in the Scene View, sometimes the quickest way to do that is to select the GameObject in the Hierarchy View, then use the Frame Selected menu item in the Edit menu (note the handy shortcut key F). In Figure 2-40, I clicked on the x axis of the Scene Gizmo to get a horizontal view, then selected the Player GameObject in the Hierarchy View, and pressed the F key (shortcut for Frame Selected in the Edit menu) to zoom in on and center the player character in the Scene View.

You can also select a GameObject directly in the Scene View, but you have to exit the Hand tool first. Just as selecting a GameObject in the Hierarchy View will result in that selection displaying in the Scene View and Inspector View, selecting a GameObject in the Scene View will likewise display that selection in the Inspector View and display it as the selected GameObject back in the Hierarchy view. In Figure 2-40, after I invoke Frame Selected on the Player, I clicked the Move tool (the button directly right of the Hand tool button in the top right corner of the Editor window) and then clicked a GameObject near the Player in the Scene View. The Hierarchy View automatically updates to show that GameObject is selected, and the GameObject is also displayed in the Inspector View.

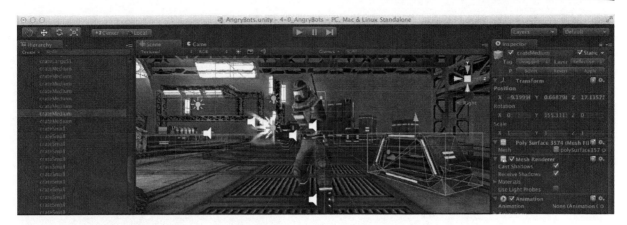

Figure 2-40. Selecting a GameObject in the Scene View

Scene View Options

The buttons lining the top of the Scene View provide display options to assist in your game development. Each button configures a view mode.

The leftmost button sets the Draw mode. Normally, this mode is set to Textured, but if you want to see all the polygons, you can set it to Wireframe (Figure 2-41).

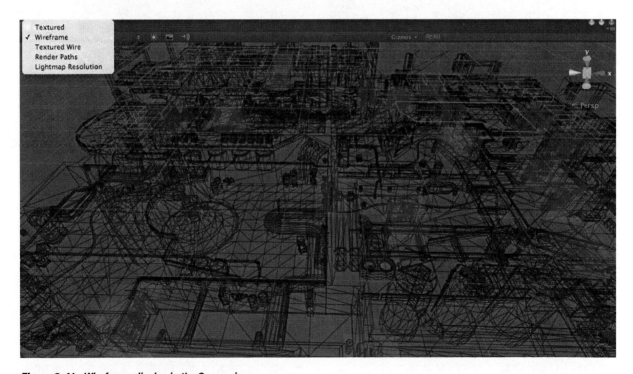

Figure 2-41. Wireframe display in the Scene view

The next button sets the Render Paths, which controls whether the scene is colored normally or for diagnostics.

The three buttons to the right of the Render Paths mode button are simple toggle buttons. They each pop up some mouse-over documentation (otherwise known as *tooltips*) when you let the mouse hover over them.

The first of those controls the Scene Lighting mode. This toggles between using a default lighting scheme in the Scene View or the actual lights you've placed in the game.

The middle button toggles the Game Overlay mode, whether the sky, lens flare, and fog effects are visible.

And finally, there is the Audition Mode, which toggles sound on and off.

Scene View Gizmos

The Gizmos button on the right activates displays of diagnostic graphics associated with the Components. The Scene View in Figure 2-42 shows several gizmos (not to be confused with the Scene Gizmo that controls the Scene View camera). By clicking the Gizmos button and checking the list of available gizmos, you can see those icons represent a Camera, a couple of AudioSources, and a few Lights.

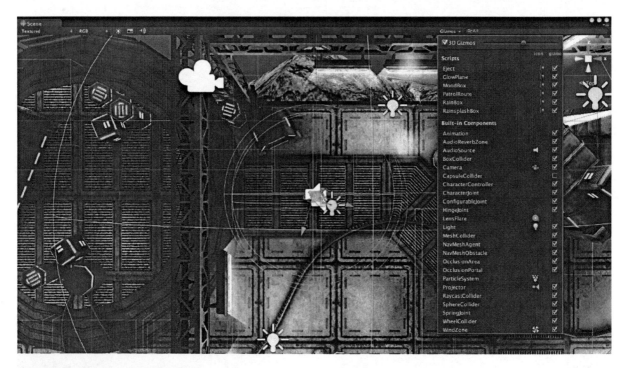

Figure 2-42. Gizmos in the Scene View

You can select and deselect the various checkboxes in the Gizmos window to focus on the objects you're interested in. The checkboxes at the top left toggles between a 3D display of the gizmos or just 2D icons. The adjacent slider controls the scale of the gizmos (so a quick way to hide all gizmos is to drag the scale slider all the way to the left).

The Game View

Now let's go back to the Game View, which you encountered when playing Angry Bots in the Editor. Like the Hierarchy View and Scene View, the Game View depicts the current scene, but not for editing purposes. Instead, the Game View is intended for playing and debugging the game.

The Game View appears automatically when you click the Play button at the top of the Unity Editor window. If there isn't an existing Game View when you click Play, a new one is created. If the Game view is visible while the Editor is not in Play mode, it shows the game in its initial state (i.e., from the vantage of the initial Camera position).

The Game View shows how the game will look and function when you actually deploy it, but there may be discrepancies from how it will look and behave on the final build target. One possible difference is the size and aspect ratio of the Game View. This can be changed using the menu at the top left of the view. Figure 2-43 shows what happens when you switch from the Free Aspect ratio, which adjusts to the dimensions of the view, to a 5:4 aspect ratio, which results in the scaling down the game display so that it fits within the area and maintains the chosen aspect ratio.

Figure 2-43. The Game View

Maximize on Play

Clicking the Maximize on Play button will result in the Game View expanding to fill the entire Editor window when it is in the Play mode (Figure 2-44). If the view is detached from the Editor window, the button has no effect.

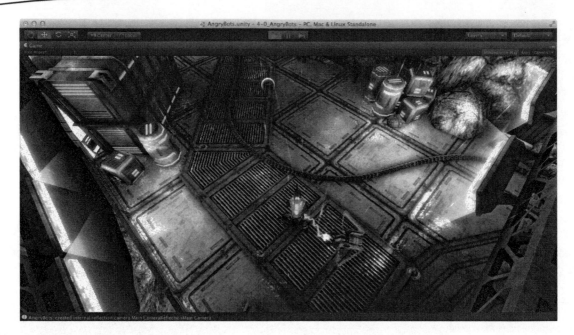

Figure 2-44. Game View with Maximize on Play

Stats

The Stats button displays statistics about the scene (Figure 2-45) that update as the game runs.

Figure 2-45. Game View with Stats

Game View Gizmos

The Gizmos button activates displays of diagnostic graphics associated with the Components. The Game View in Figure 2-46 shows two icons that are gizmos for lights. The light gizmo located at the player's position also reveals the light radius (i.e., the area affected by the light). The list to the right of the Gizmos button allows you to select which gizmos you want displayed.

Figure 2-46. The Game View with Gizmos

Both the Game View and Scene View are both depictions of the current scene. A Unity project consists of one or more scenes, and the Unity Editor has one scene open at a time. Think of the project as a game and the scenes as levels (in fact, some Unity script functions that operate on scenes use "level" in their names). Unity GameObjects are made interesting by attaching Components, each of which provides some specific information or behavior. That's where the Inspector View comes in. If you select a game object in the Hierarchy View or Scene View, the Inspector View will display its attached components.

The Console View

The remaining view in all the preset layouts, the Console View, is easy to ignore but it's pretty useful (Figure 2-47).

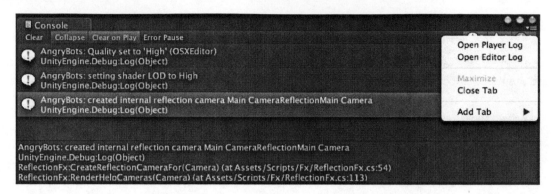

Figure 2-47. The Console View

Informational, warning, and error messages appear in the Console View. Errors are in red, warnings in yellow, and informational messages in white. Selecting a message from the list displays it with more detail in the lower area. Also, the single-line area at the bottom of the Unity Editor displays the most recent Console message, so you can always see that a message has been logged even if the Console view is not visible.

> **Tip** Warning messages are easy to ignore, but you ignore them at your peril. They are there for a reason and usually indicate something has to be resolved. And if you let warnings accumulate, it's difficult to notice when a really important warning shows up.

The Console can get cluttered pretty quickly. You can manage that clutter with the leftmost three buttons on top of the Console View. The Clear toggle button removes all the messages. The Collapse toggle button combines similar messages. The Clear on Play toggle will remove all messages each time the Editor enters Play mode.

The Error Pause button will cause the Editor to halt on an error message, specifically when a script calls a Log.LogError.

While operating in the Editor, log messages end up in the Editor log, while messages generated from a Unity-built executable are directed to the Player log. Selecting Open Player Log or Open Editor Log from the view menu (click the little icon at the top right of the Console View) will bring up those logs, either in a text file or in the Console app (Figure 2-48).

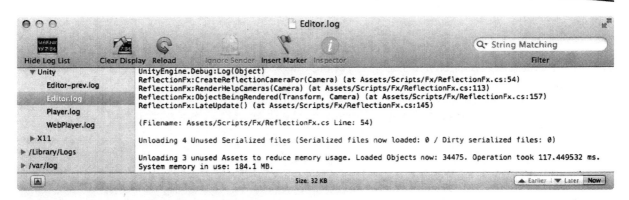

Figure 2-48. *The Unity logs in the Mac Console app*

Explore Further

We've come to the end of this Unity tour and our play time with Angry Bots demo. Beginning with the next chapter, you'll be creating Unity projects from scratch to learn the game engine features. But this won't be the last you'll see of Angry Bots, as we'll return to that project in Chapters 10 and 11, repeating this process to introduce Unity iOS development. Until then, starting with the next chapter, you'll be creating Unity projects from scratch and exploring general and mostly cross-platform Unity game engine features. And from this point on, there are plenty of official Unity resources that expand on the topics I will be covering.

Unity Manual

As you can see, there's a lot of Unity user interface, and we've hardly covered it all. This is a good time to get serious about reading the Unity Manual, either from within the Unity Editor (the Welcome screen or the Help menu) or on the Unity web site (http://unity3d.com/) under the Learn tab in the "Documentation" section. The web version is pretty handy when you want to look something up or just read about Unity without having a Unity Editor running nearby.

Most of what was covered in this chapter matches topics in the "Unity Basics" section of the Unity Manual, particular the sections on "Learning the Interface," "Customizing Your Workspace," "Publishing Builds," and "Unity Hotkeys" (although I think a better reference is just to check the keyboard shortcuts listed in the menus).

I did jump ahead into the "Advanced" section of the Unity Manual and touch on Unity's support for version control. That's covered more in depth with the Unity Manual's page on "Using External Version Control with Unity."

Tutorials

Besides the "Documentation" section, the Learn tab on the Unity web site also includes a "Tutorials" section that features an extensive set of Beginning Editor videos. As the name implies, these videos provide an introduction to the Unity Editor, and in fact the set of videos cover much of what was discussed in this chapter, including descriptions of the most important views (the Game View, Scene View, Hiearchy View, Inspector View and Project View) and even the process of publishing a build.

Version Control

Although I only discussed version control briefly, in the context of explaining how to remove meta files, that topic is worth a little more discussion, since a VCS is so important to software development (which you'll realize the first time you lose your project or can't remember what change you made that broke your game!). If you already have a favorite VCS, you may want to use it with Unity, and if you haven't been using one, then you may want to consider it if only to keep old versions of your project around in case you need to roll back, with the ability to check differences between versions.

Among version control systems, Perforce is a popular commercial tool used in game studios, and Subversion (svn) has a long history as an open source option. These days, distributed version control systems like Git and Mercurial are trending. I use Mercurial on Bitbucket (http://bitbucket.org/) for my internal projects and post public projects on GitHub, including the projects for this book (http://learnunity4.com/).

To say Unity VCS support is product agnostic is really another way of saying Unity doesn't have any particular version control system integrated into the Unity Editor (although Perforce and Subversion integration is in-progress at the time of this writing). The meta files, and YAML scene files for Unity Pro users, simply provide better compatibility with text-oriented version control systems that are commonly used for source code. You still have to run the VCS operations yourself outside of Unity. You can find out more about YAML, by the way, on http://yaml.org/

In the meantime, I find it convenient to use the Mac GitHub app provided on the GitHub web site and similarly Sourcetree for Bitbucket, also available on that web site.

And as I mentioned while explaining the options for Version Control Mode in the Editor Preferences, Unity also offers a VCS designed specifically for Unity called the Unity Asset Server. It requires the purchase of a Unity Team License.

Chapter 3

Making a Scene

Playing Angry Bots was fun, but this book is about making games in Unity, not playing games in Unity! Finally, it's time to get started in game development. It's a long journey starting from nothing and ending up with a playable game, and this is the beginning. In this chapter, you'll start with an empty scene in the Unity Editor and populate it with the basic building blocks of a 3D environment: models, textures, lights, a sky, and a camera.

One of the challenges facing a game developer, especially one on a limited budget, is how to obtain these building blocks. The Unity Editor provides some primitive models, and any image can be used as a texture (in the tradition of the Internet, I'll provide you a picture of my cat as a sample texture). And, as mentioned in Chapter 1, the Unity installation includes a set of Standard Assets that can be imported into your project at any time. All of that can only take you so far, though.

Fortunately, the folks at Unity Technologies recognized this need and created the Asset Store, an online marketplace of Unity-ready assets with its storefront integrated directly into the Unity Editor. It turns out that a lot of these assets are free, so we'll take advantage of that fact and incorporate some of these free assets into the Unity project created in this chapter.

Each chapter in this book (with the exception of Chapters 10 and 11 where the Angry Bots project stages a brief comeback) builds upon the project from the previous chapter. So by the end of this book, the simple static scene created in this chapter will have evolved into an optimized bowling game with sound and physics, running on iOS with leaderboards, achievements and ads. The project created in this chapter, along with the projects for each consecutive chapter, is available on http://learnunity4.com/ but minus any assets from the Asset Store or Standard Packages.

So without further ado, let's get started!

Create a New Project

If you still have the Unity Editor running from the previous chapter, create a new Unity project using the New Project item in the File menu (Figure 3-1).

Figure 3-1. The New Project menu item

The resulting Project Wizard (Figure 3-2) is the same as the one we used when selecting Open Project in the previous chapter, but now it has the Create New Project tab selected. If you're starting up a fresh Unity session and are presented with the Project Wizard, you can just click this tab to create a new project instead of opening an existing one.

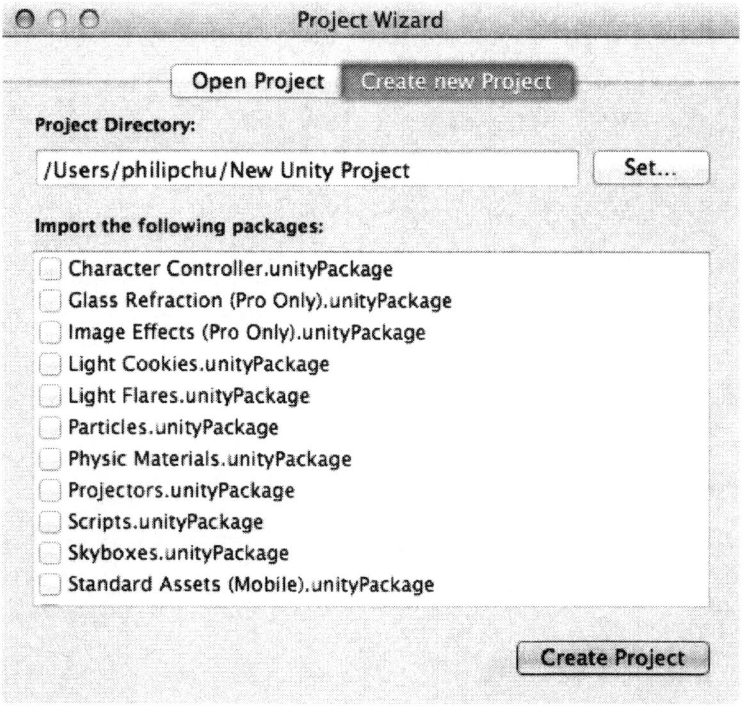

Figure 3-2. Creating a new project with the Project Wizard

The Project Wizard prompts for the file name and location of the new project, defaulting to your home folder and the name New Unity Project (if the folder already exists, a number is appended, e.g., New Unity Project 1, or if that also exists then New Unity Project 2, and so forth). The Set button brings up a file chooser so you can browse for a directory location instead of typing it in.

You can name the project as you please or just use the default for now. The Unity project itself doesn't care about its name, so you can rename the project folder in the Finder later (just make sure you exit Unity or switch to another project first, to avoid wreaking havoc with your current session).

> **Tip** If you have a project that you want to keep around for a while, it's a good idea to give it a meaningful name. More than once, I've discovered an old New Unity Project folder on my Mac and wondered if it was something important.

The Project Wizard presents a list of Unity packages that we can immediately import into our new project. These are the Standard Assets that were installed with Unity in the previous chapter. You don't need to select any right now, as you can always import what you need later.

The Unity Editor will now appear, showing a new and empty project (Figure 3-3). The Project View displays no assets (you can confirm in the Finder that the Assets folder in your project contains no files), and the current scene is an untitled and unsaved scene consisting only of a GameObject named Main Camera.

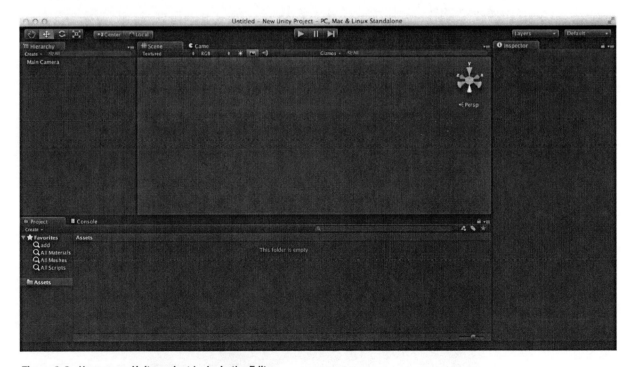

Figure 3-3. How a new Unity project looks in the Editor

The first thing you should do is save and name this scene. The Save Scene option is found in the File menu (Figure 3-4) and has the same Command+S shortcut that is conventional with application save operations (you could think of scenes edited and managed by Unity as analogous to documents edited and managed by a word processing application).

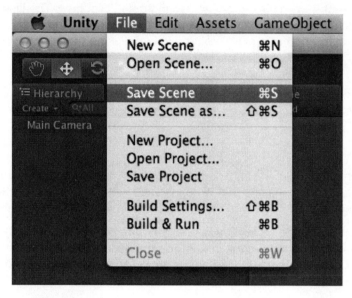

Figure 3-4. The Save Scene menu item

The resulting chooser will provide the project's Assets folder as the default location, which is fine; the scene is an asset and part of the project, so the scene file has to go in the Assets folder. A default name is not provided, so you need to provide one. Let's call it cube, since this scene will just showcase a cube. The new scene will show up in the Project View, with a Unity icon (Figure 3-5).

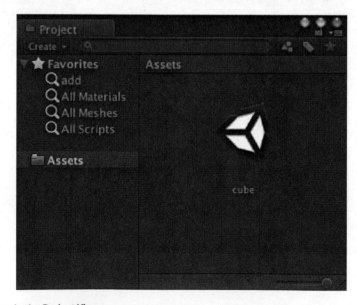

Figure 3-5. The new scene in the Project View

When you exit Unity or switch scenes or projects, Unity will prompt you to save the scene if there are unsaved changes (sometimes those changes are innocuous user interface changes, so don't be alarmed). But it's a good practice to save frequently, in case there's a crash.

The File menu also has a Save Scene As command that is similar to the Save As command of other applications. It lets you save the scene under a new name at any time, effectively making a copy of the scene.

> **Tip**   Instead of using the Save Scene As command, it's often simpler to select the scene file in the Project View and either rename (press Return) or duplicate (Command+D) the scene in the Project View.

You might be wondering about the difference between Save Scene and Save Project in the File menu. Save Project saves any changes to the project but not the current scene, while Save Scene also saves any changes in the current scene, i.e., changes to the GameObjects in the scene or changes to per-scene settings (Render Settings). Save Scene is what you'll want to use most of the time. Save Project is appropriate when you've made some changes to project settings or assets that you want to save but have scene changes you're not ready to save or maybe even have a new scene open that you don't want to save at all.

The Main Camera

The Hierarchy View of the new scene lists just one GameObject, named Main Camera. Every new scene starts with that Camera GameObject, which acts as our eyes in the scene when we play the game. The Main Camera is special in that it's easily accessible by scripts (it's referenced by the variable Camera.main).

Multiple Cameras

The fact that the camera's name is Main Camera might lead you to believe that multiple Cameras can exist in a scene, and you would be correct. It might seem strange to have multiple simultaneous viewpoints, but multiple Cameras make it possible to have a split-screen display or a window within the screen. Those usages aren't actually supported in Unity for iOS (see the section "Viewport" below), but multiple Cameras are still useful for situations like rendering the game world with the Main Camera and rendering a user interface with another, effectively overlaying one set of GameObjects over another.

Anatomy of a Camera

Let's select the Main Camera so we can see in the Inspector View what a Camera is made of (Figure 3-6).

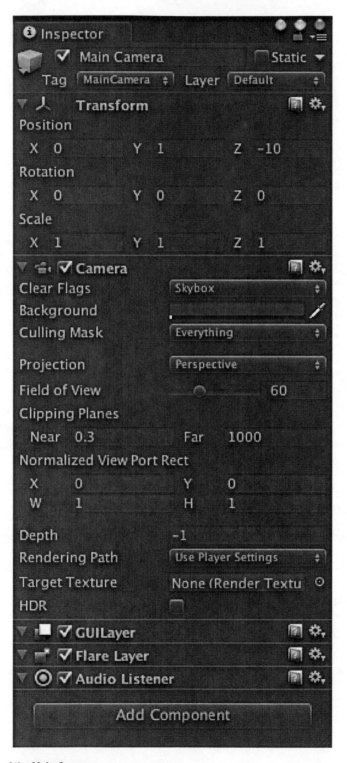

Figure 3-6. Inspector View of the Main Camera

Starting from the top, you can see the name Main Camera. The check box to the left specifies whether this GameObject is active or inactive. If you uncheck the check box, the Camera is deactivated, indicated by a grayed-out appearance in the Hierarchy View, and you won't see anything in the Game View. You can check the check box labeled Static on the right if you know this GameObject will never move. Marking GameObjects as static can facilitate optimization, although that rarely applies to Cameras.

Below the name, you can see this GameObject has MainCamera as its tag, which is really what designates this GameObject as a Main Camera. The name is just for display purposes, so you could edit the name here in the Inspector View without any repercussions.

The Layer menu for this GameObject is on the right. While names are used for description and tags for identification, layers are used to group GameObjects. You can think of these layers sort of like Photoshop layers. This Layer menu should not be confused with the Layers menu at the top right of the Editor window (they are unfortunately close to each other in the Default layout). The Layers menu at the top right controls which GameObjects are visible in the Scene View (it really should be located in the Scene View).

The Transform Component

Like every other GameObject, the Main Camera has a Transform Component that specifies the position, rotation, and scale of the GameObject. Scale is meaningless for Cameras, but the position and rotation allow you to place and point the Camera.

Click the little question mark icon on the top right of the Component. That will bring up the Reference Manual documentation for the Transform Component in a web browser window.

> **Tip**   Every time you encounter a new Component, the first thing you should do is check the documentation.

The Reference Manual page for each Component describes the properties of the Component and explains the usage of the Component. Each Reference Manual page also features a link to the corresponding Script Reference page for the Component, detailing how to access the Component from within a script.

The Camera Component

The Camera Component is what makes this GameObject a Camera. To be perfectly precise, Main Camera is a GameObject that has a Component which specifically is a subclass of Component called Camera. But it's convenient to say Main Camera is a Camera (since that is its function), and say Camera Component to make clear that we're talking about the Component.

Again, clicking on the question mark icon of this Component will bring up the corresponding Reference Manual page, listing the Camera Component properties. But I'll go through them briefly here, in top-down order as they're displayed in the Inspector View.

Clear Flags

The Clear Flags property specifies how the Camera initializes the color and depth buffers at the beginning of each rendering pass. The color buffer contains the pixels the Camera renders, and the depth buffer holds the distance from the Camera of each pixel (this is how it determines if a newly drawn pixel should replace the previous pixel at that location).

Solid Color indicates the color buffer will be cleared to the specified color, essentially using it as a background color, and the depth buffer will be cleared.

Skybox also clears the depth buffer and renders the specified Skybox textures in the background (defaulting to Solid Color if no Skybox is supplied).

Depth Only leaves the color buffer alone and only clears the depth buffer. This is useful when adding a Camera that renders after the Main Camera and over its results, e.g., to render a user interface or HUD (heads-up display) over the rendering of the game world. In that case, you don't want the second Camera to clear the screen before rendering.

Culling Mask

This is where the usefulness of Layers becomes apparent. The Culling Mask specifies which Layers are rendered by the Camera. In other words, a GameObject will only be visible to the Camera if its Layer is included in the Camera's Culling Mask.

The default, Everything, corresponds to all Layers, but, for example, if you had an HUD Camera, you might define an HUD Layer for all your HUD GameObjects and set the Culling Mask for the HUD Camera to only render the HUD Layer. And then you would set the Culling Mask of the Main Camera to include everything except the HUD Layer.

Projection

By default, the Camera is set to use a perspective projection, which as I mentioned in describing the Scene View in the previous chapter, means objects are smaller as they recede from the Camera (the effect is called *foreshortening*). In this mode, the Camera has a viewing volume resembling a four-sided pyramid (not counting the base of the pyramid) emanating from the Camera position in the view direction. This viewing volume is called a *frustum* and is defined by a Field of View (FOV), near and far plane.

The Field of View is analogous to the FOV of a real-world camera. The FOV is the vertical viewing angle, in degrees. The horizontal viewing angle is implicitly defined by the combination of the FOV and the aspect ratio of the Camera. The near and far planes specify how far the screen is in front of the Camera and how far away the base of the frustum is. Nothing outside the frustum is visible to the Camera.

To get a better idea of how the frustum looks, take a look at the Scene View. Figure 3-7 shows how the frustum of the Main Camera looks when you press the y-axis arrow on the Scene Gizmo, changing the vantage to a top-down view. Press the F key (shortcut for the Frame Selected command in the Edit menu) to center the Main Camera in the Scene View, then zoom out until you can see the entire frustum. You should also uncheck the 3D Gizmos check box in the Gizmos menu so that the Camera icon doesn't shrink to nothingness when you zoom out.

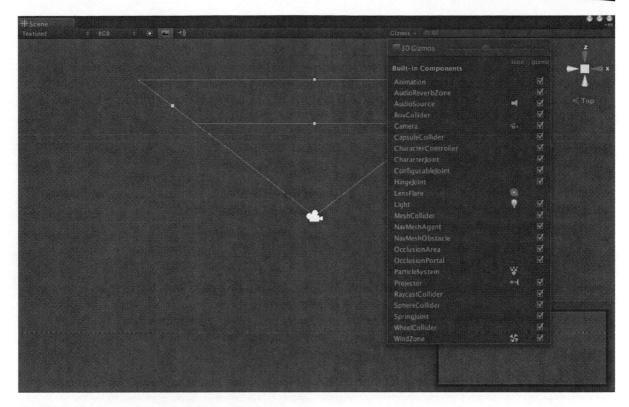

Figure 3-7. The Camera frustum in the Scene View

The Scene View also displays a Camera Preview in the lower right corner. This is what the Camera would render right now, which is also what the Game View would display right now (you can take a look at the Game View right now to confirm). There's nothing visible in this scene yet, but this will be a handy feature later.

Note that the frustum outline and the Camera Preview only display when the Camera is selected and the Camera Component in the Inspector View is open (every Component in the Inspector View can be opened or closed by clicking the little triangle in the upper left). This is generally true of any Component that has an extra graphic display in the Scene View. Opening and closing the Component in the Inspector View will toggle that display.

The alternative to perspective is orthographic, which has no foreshortening and thus is appropriate for 2D games, isometric games user interfaces, and HUDs. The only Camera property specific to orthographic mode is the orthographic projection size, which is the half-height of the orthographic view in world units.

Viewport

The Viewport of (0,0,1,1) indicates the Camera covers the whole screen. The numbers are normalized screen coordinates, meaning the coordinates across the width and height of the screen range from 0 to 1. For a split screen or a window within the screen, you would have multiple Cameras, each with different viewports, (0,0,1,.5) covers half of the screen. However, Unity iOS doesn't support viewports that don't cover the full screen.

Depth

Depth is another property useful when there are multiple Cameras in the scene. During each rendering update, the Cameras will perform their rendering passes in the order of their depth values, lowest to highest. So if you had a second Camera for viewing an HUD, for example, you might specify that the Main Camera has a depth of 0 and the HUD Camera a depth of 1 to ensure the game world renders first and the game HUD renders on top of that.

Rendering Path

The Rendering Path determines how the scene is rendered. Each Camera can have its own Rendering Path or default to the one specified in the Player Settings. Vertex Lit is the simplest but fastest path, Forward Rendering supports more advanced graphics, and Deferred is the fanciest but slowest and not available in Unity iOS.

Target Texture (Pro)

The render-to-texture feature is only available in Unity Pro and Unity iOS Pro. If a texture is assigned to this property, the Camera renders to that texture instead of the screen. The texture can then be placed in the scene, for example, as a television display or the rear-view mirror in a car.

HDR

This property enables High Dynamic Range (HDR), which handles pixels with RGB components outside the normal 0-to-1 range and facilitates rendering of extremely high-contrast scenes. HDR is not available in Unity iOS.

FlareLayer Component

When a Camera GameObject is created from the GameObject menu, both a Camera Component and a FlareLayer Component are automatically attached. The FlareLayer Component allows the Camera to render Light Flares (described later in this chapter).

The FlayerLayer Component is a little unusual in that it's not exposed to scripting, so it does have a Reference Manual page, but no Script Reference page. However, a FlareLayer Component can still be accessed from a GameObject using its class name, i.e., by calling GetComponent("FlareLayer").

GUILayer Component

A GUILayer Component is also automatically attached to a Camera GameObject. This component allows the Camera to render GUIText and GUITextures, which are 2D elements often used for user interfaces.

> **Note**   GUILayer, GUIText and GUITexture (and GUIElement, which is the parent class of GUIText and GUITexture) have nothing to do with UnityGUI, which is a newer built-in GUI system.

You may have noticed that the Inspector View displays GUILayer as one word and Flare Layer as two words. The Editor attempts to present class names in a more English-like fashion by introducing spaces in the names where an upper-case letter follows a lower-case one. That works fine for

FlareLayer but not GUILayer. In any case, this book will stick to the original class name, since that is what will be referenced in scripts.

AudioListener Component

The AudioListener Component is only automatically attached to the Main Camera, since there can only be one active AudioListener at a time. Whereas the Camera Component is analogous to your eyes, responsible for rendering everything visible to it on your computer screen, the AudioListener Component is like your ears, responsible for routing all the audible AudioSources in the scene to the computer speakers.

Add a Cube to the Scene

You'll already have noticed the Camera Preview and Game View display nothing, and the same happens in the Game View when you click the Play button. Of course, that's because you don't have anything in the scene besides the Camera. Let's rectify that with the time-honored tradition of creating a cube.

Make the Cube

Under the Create Other submenu of the GameObject menu, Unity provides a number of GameObjects bundled with Components. Among these is a Camera GameObject, if we wanted to add another one. There is also a Cube GameObject along with a number of other primitive shapes (Figure 3-8).

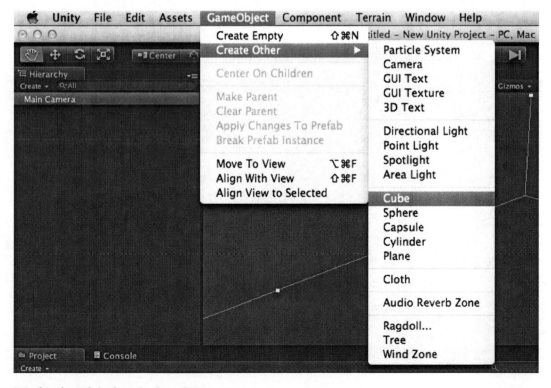

Figure 3-8. Creating a Cube from the GameObject menu

Select the Cube item from the GameObject menu. That will create a Cube GameObject and add it to the current scene. The Cube will appear in the Hierarchy View (Figure 3-9) as the second GameObject of the scene.

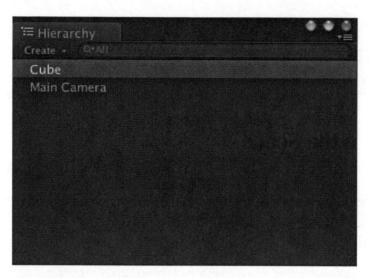

Figure 3-9. *A new cube GameObject in the Hierarchy View*

Frame the Cube

Although the Cube is in the scene, it may not be immediately visible in the Scene View. To ensure the Cube can be seen in the Scene View, select the Cube in the Hierarchy View and press the F key (shortcut for the Frame Selected command in the Edit menu), which will center the Cube in the Scene View (Figure 3-10).

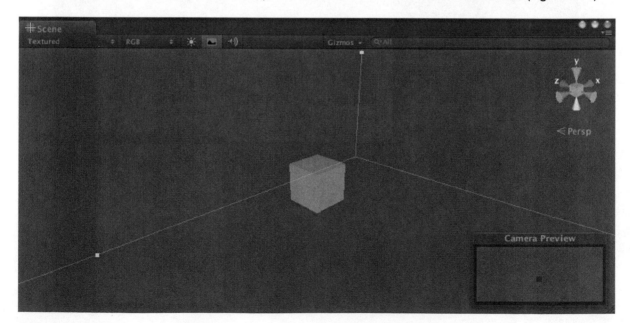

Figure 3-10. *The Cube in the Scene View*

Move the Cube

Remember, the Frame Selected command moves the Scene View camera, not the GameObject you're looking at. The Cube may have been created at an arbitrary position, so set its position to the world origin, (0,0,0) in the Inspector View, by typing those coordinates into the x,y,z Position fields of the cube's Transform (Figure 3-11). Don't worry if you make a mistake.You can always Undo and Redo changes like this with the Undo and Redo commands in the Edit menu. In this case, you can Undo the Position change and then Redo it.

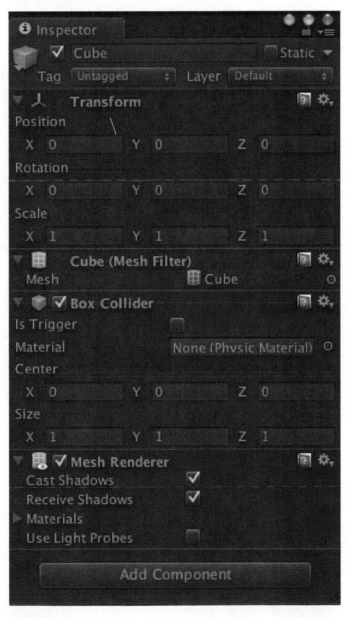

Figure 3-11. The Inspector View of a cube

Anatomy of a Cube

While you have the Cube displayed in the Inspector View, take a look at what it's made of. Or, in other words, see what Components of the Cube make it a Cube.

Transform Component

Of course, as with every GameObject, there's a Transform Component, which provides the position, rotation, and scale of the Cube.

MeshFilter Component

The MeshFilter Component references the 3D model, known in Unity as a Mesh, which consists of triangles and per-vertex information such as texture coordinates. When not referencing a built-in Mesh like the Cube, this property is assigned a Mesh from the project assets.

MeshRenderer Component

Hand-in-hand with the MeshFilter is the MeshRenderer Component, which determines how the mesh is rendered and is largely dictated by the Material (or list of Materials, if the Mesh is split into submeshes). You can think of a Material like the fabric on a sofa—the Mesh provides the shape and the Material wraps around the Mesh to provide the surface appearance.

The MeshRenderer also controls whether the Mesh receives shadows or casts shadows (I'll introduce shadows later in this chapter).

BoxCollider Component

The MeshFilter and MeshRenderer Components together only make the Cube visible. The BoxCollider Component provides a physical surface that is used for collisions in the Unity physics system. Since there's nothing that can collide with the Cube in this scene, you don't need this Component. There's no harm in leaving it there, but you could also disable the Component by unchecking its check box. Or you could remove the Component entirely from the GameObject by right-clicking it and selecting Remove Component from the resulting menu (Figure 3-12).

Figure 3-12. *Removing a Component*

Align With View

Since you moved the Cube, you can press the F key again to center it in the Scene View. But that doesn't affect the Main Camera, as you can see from the Camera Preview in the Scene View and if you check the Game View.

Fortunately, there's a convenient way to sync the Main Camera with the Scene View camera. Select the Main Camera, and then under the GameObject menu, invoke Align With View (Figure 3-13). Now the Main Camera has the same position and rotation as the Scene camera, and you can see in the Camera Preview that the Scene View and Game View are identical.

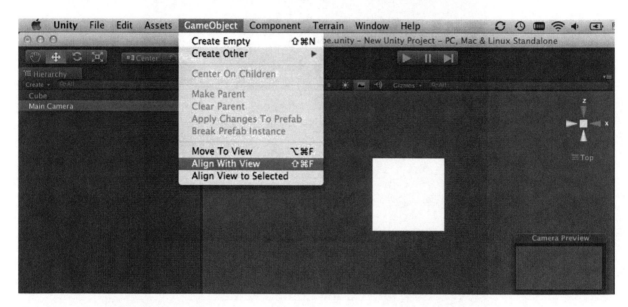

Figure 3-13. The Align With View command

Camera Control

Now if you click the Play button, you can see the Cube, but there's not much going on. The Cube just sits there, and there is no interactivity. The first thing I like to do with a scene that has just one object like this is add a Camera orbit script so I can inspect the object from all angles. Conveniently, Unity comes with several Camera control scripts in the Standard Assets, including a MouseOrbit script.

Import the Script

To import that script, go to the Assets menu and select the Import Package submenu. This is the same list of Standard Assets packages presented when we created a new project (Figure 3-14).

Figure 3-14. Importing scripts from Standard Assets

From this list, selecting Scripts will present a window displaying all the scripts in the Scripts package (Figure 3-15). The scripts ending in the .js extension are written in JavaScript and the ones ending in the .cs extension are written in C#. You can import just the MouseOrbit script or all of the scripts. It's easy enough to delete unwanted assets later.

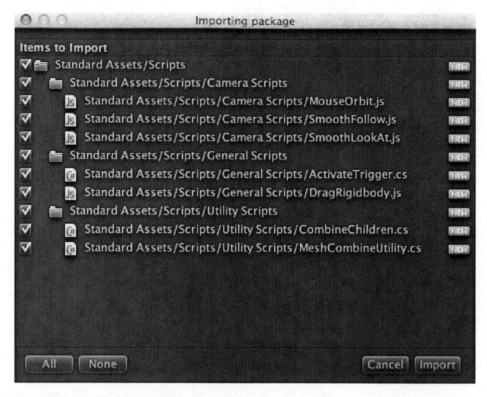

Figure 3-15. The available Standard Assets scripts

Now the scripts and their containing folders are displayed in the Project View (Figure 3-16). The Project View doesn't list the .js extension of the file names, but you can see from the icons that they are JavaScripts, and selecting a script will display the full name on the line at the bottom of the Project View.

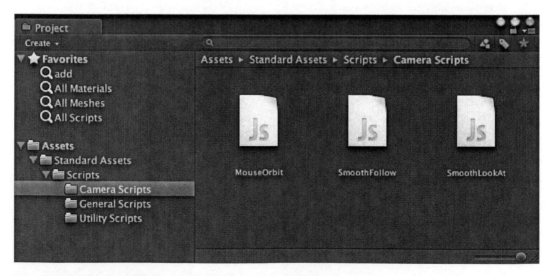

Figure 3-16. Standard Assets scripts in the Project View

If you select the MouseOrbit script in the Project View, the code in that script shows up in the Inspector View (Figure 3-17).

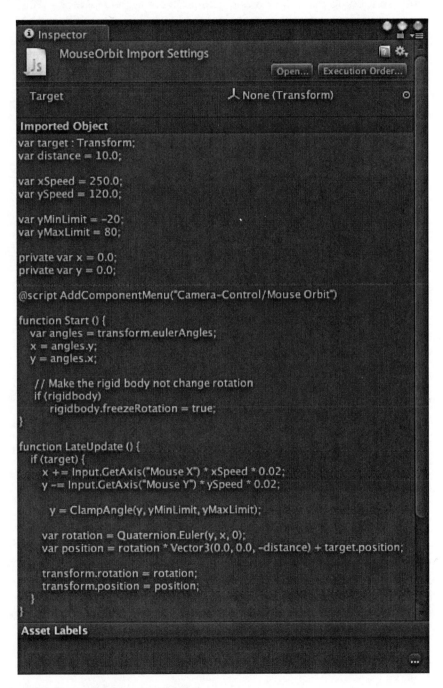

Figure 3-17. The Inspector View of the MouseOrbit script

Attach the Script

Drag the MouseOrbit script onto the Main Camera GameObject in the Hierarchy View. That attaches the script onto the GameObject, so now if you select the Main Camera, the MouseOrbit script will show up as one of its Components (Figure 3-18).

Figure 3-18. *The* MouseOrbit *script attached to the Main Camera*

The first property of the MouseOrbit Component is a reference to the MouseOrbit script (notice how Unity pretty-prints the Component type as Mouse Orbit, but don't be fooled, it's MouseOrbit!). You could actually change the script referenced by that property by dragging another one from the Project View into that field or by clicking the little circle on its right, which would pop up a list of available scripts to choose from (which right now are all the Standard Assets scripts you just imported).

The script itself determines the properties that follow. Notice that each of those properties in the MouseOrbit Component corresponds to a public variable declared at the top of the MouseOrbit script (each line beginning with var is a public variable, while those starting with private var are private).

> **Tip**   Selecting the Debug option in the Inspector View menu (top right corner) will display private variables as properties, too, which can be useful for debugging. Try it now and you'll see the private variables x and y show up. The Debug option also adds diagnostic properties of built-in Components.

The first property defined by the script is Target, which is the GameObject the Camera will orbit around. It defaults to nothing (or in the code, null), so if you click Play, there is nothing for the Camera to orbit around. To rectify that, drag the Cube from the Hierarchy View into the Target field (Figure 3-19).

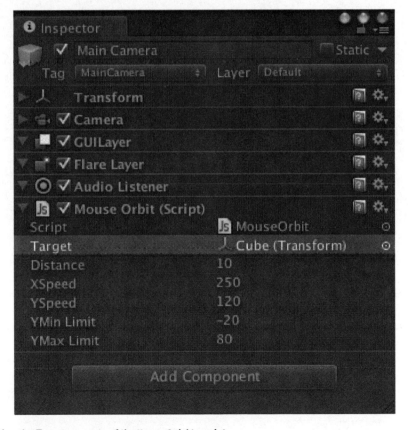

Figure 3-19. Assigning the Target property of the MouseOrbit script

Now when you click the Play button, the Camera orbits the Cube as you move the mouse. While in Play mode, you can adjust the other properties until you find values you like. The Distance property is the distance maintained between the Camera and the Target. Changing it to 3 brings the Camera close enough to the Cube so it fills up the Game View (Figure 3-20). The XSpeed and YSpeed properties control how much the Camera orbits in relation to the mouse movement, and the YMin Limit and YMax Limit properties set the angle limits of the Camera's up and down rotation.

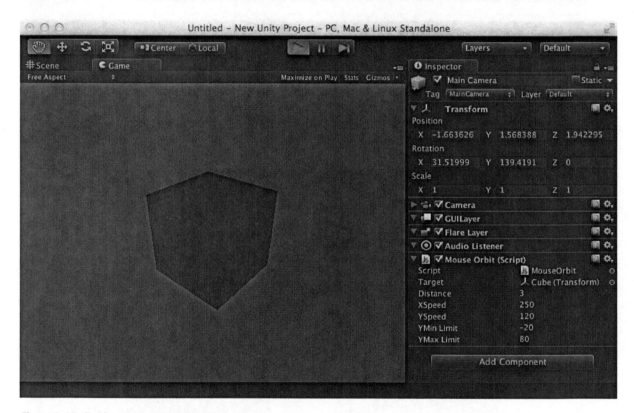

Figure 3-20. Testing the MouseOrbit script

When you exit Play mode, the properties revert to the values they had before you entered Play mode. At that point it's necessary to enter the desired values again. If you end up with property values that you don't like, you can always start over by clicking the icon on the top right of the Component and selecting Reset to revert back to the default property values.

Add a Light

You've probably been thinking the Cube looks awfully dark. Well, let's add a Light! Under the Create Other submenu of the GameObject menu, several types of Lights are listed (Figure 3-21). Let's choose Point Light.

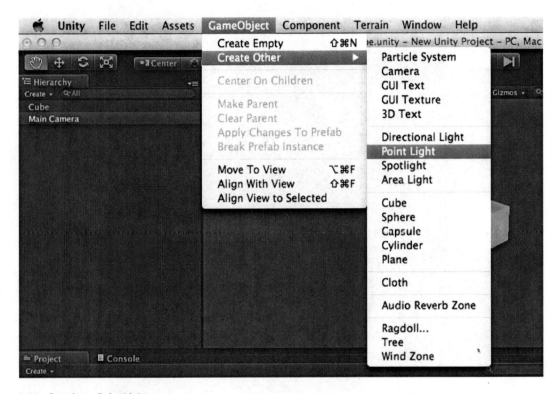

Figure 3-21. Creating a Point Light

The Point Light now appears in the Hierarchy View and the Scene View (Figure 3-22), and you can see that its distinguishing component is a Light Component, with its Type set to Point. A Point Light only lights objects within its radius. So you should adjust its position or radius so that the cube will be lit. Here you can set its position to 5,5,5 (remember, the cube is at 0,0,0) and set the radius to 10.

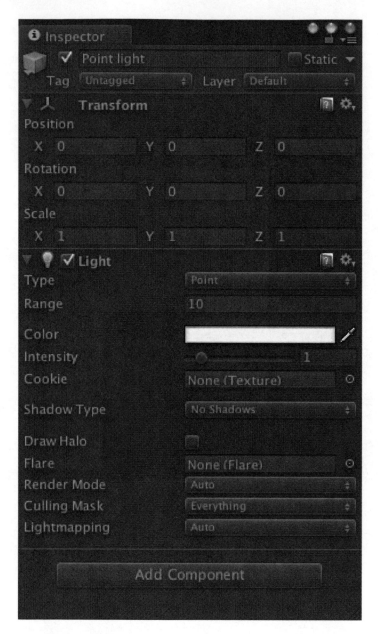

Figure 3-22. The Inspector View of a Point Light

Anatomy of a Light

In the same way that a GameObject becomes a Camera when it has a Camera Component attached, a GameObject behaves as a Light when it has a Light Component attached. Like the Camera Component, the Light Component has several properties, which we'll go over here in top-down order as shown in the Inspector View.

Type

The Type of a Light specifies whether it is a Point Light, Directional Light, Spot Light, or Area Light. Since this GameObject was created as a Point Light, it's Type was automatically set to Point. In contrast to a Directional Light, which acts as a light source infinitely far away (it's sometimes called an *infinite light*), a Point Light has a position (and is thus often known as a positional light) and radiates in every direction. A Spot Light also has a position, but radiates in a certain direction, like a cone. An Area Light is only used in generating light maps (lighting that is precalculated and "baked" into textures).

Range

The Range property for Point Lights specifies the radius of the Light. Only objects within the radius are affected by the Light.

Color

The Color property is the color emitted by the Light. Clicking the little color rectangle brings up a color chooser to assign this property.

Intensity

The Light Intensity ranges from 0 to 1, where 0 is unlit and 1 is maximum brightness.

Shadow Type

The Shadow Type property of a Light specifies whether it the Light projects shadows, and if so, whether they are Hard Shadows or Soft Shadows. Shadows are only available in Unity Pro and Unity iOS Pro and even then only for.Directional and Point Lights (in Unity iOS Pro, only Directional Lights).

Cookie

Directional and Spot Lights can project a cookie texture onto a surface, typicall to simulate a shadow.

Culling Mask

The Culling Mask property specifies the layers that the Light will affect. Very much like how the Culling Mask of the Camera Component dictates what objects are visible to the Camera, the Culling Mask of the Light dictates what objects are lit by a Light.

Flare

The Flare property, when assigned a Flare asset, produces a lens flare effect emanating from thsi Light.

Draw Halo

The Draw Halo property produces a halo effect around the position of the Light. When this property is enabled, an additional property for the halo color is made available.

Render Mode

The Render Mode of a Light specifies whether the Light is Important, Not Important, or Auto, which means its importance is determined automatically, based on the Light's brightness and the current Quality Settings. A Light's importance determines whether it is applied as a pixel light or not. Pixel lights are required for effects like shadows and cookies.

Lightmapping

The Lightmapping property determines whether this Light is used for dynamic lighting, generating lightmaps, or both. You won't be using lightmaps for these examples (they take a long time to generate), so RealtimeOnly or Auto will be fine for these Lights.

Adjust the Light

As with Cameras, when you have the Point Light selected and its Light Component open in the Inspector, more information about the Light is depicted in the Scene View. For a Point Light, the radius is displayed, so you can see what objects are affected by the Light (Figure 3-23). In order for the Cube to be affected by the Point Light, it must be within the Light's radius. But remember, a Point Light radiates outward from its position, so you can't have the Point Light at the same position as the Cube, because then the Light would be radiating from within the Cube and wouldn't illuminate the Cube's outer surface.

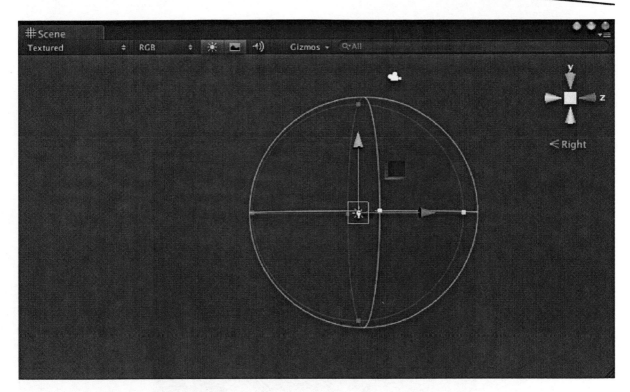

Figure 3-23. The Scene View of a Point Light

You can adjust the Light properties solely in the Inspector View, but try using the Scene View. Click the Move button in the button bar on the top left of the Editor (it's the button with arrows directly right of the Hand tool). Now with the Point Light selected, the Scene View displays arrows centered at the Light that correspond to the x, y, and z axes of the Light. Click-dragging on any of those arrows will move the Light along the corresponding axis.

The circles around the Light delineate the range of the Light. You can adjust the range by click-dragging the little yellow rectangles just inside the circles. Anything within the range is lit by the Light, and anything outside the range won't be affected by the Light.

Warning   An object in exactly the same position as a Point Light won't be affected by that Light.

Go ahead and move the Light and adjust its radius as necessary to make sure the Cube is lit. Now when you click the Play button, the Cube is lit, and the lighting varies as you orbit the Camera around the Cube.

Make a Halo

Right now the Point Light itself is invisible when you're in Play mode. The Light's presence is only evident through the GameObjects that it illuminates. However, you can see where the Light is coming from if you enable its halo. Enable the Draw Halo property in the Inspector View, and while you're at it, click the Color property to change the Light's color (Figure 3-24).

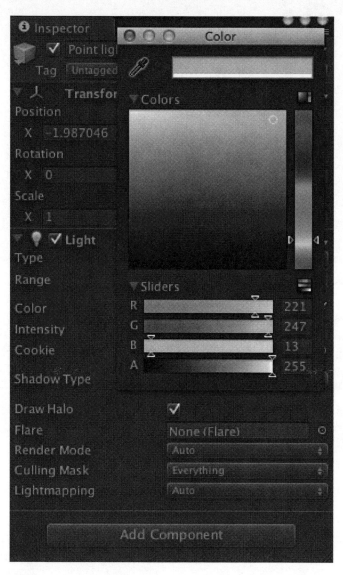

Figure 3-24. Selecting a halo color

This affects not only the color of the Light that is reflected off objects, but it's also the color used to draw the halo. You can see the halo in the Scene View (Figure 3-25) and when you click Play (Figure 3-26).

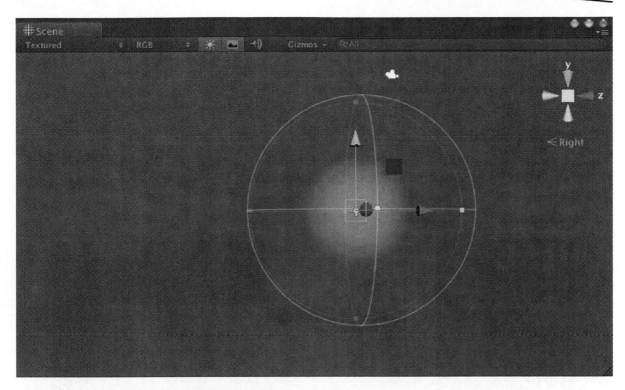

Figure 3-25. The Scene View of a Point Light with a halo

Figure 3-26. The Game View of a Point Light with a halo

Add a Skybox

The Cube is looking more interesting, but the background is still blank, so let's liven it up a bit by adding a sky. Specifically, you can add a *skybox*, which is a sky depicted by six textures comprising the six faces of the inside of a cube that surrounds it.

Import the Skybox

You can import Skyboxes from the Standard Assets just like you did for the Camera scripts. Under the Import Package submenu of the Assets menu, select Skyboxes (Figure 3-27).

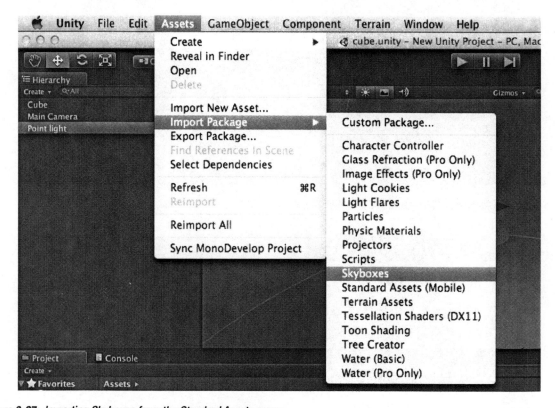

Figure 3-27. Importing Skyboxes from the Standard Assets menu

The resulting Import window (Figure 3-28) lists a whole bunch of Skyboxes. The .mat extension of the filenames indicates that Skyboxes are actually a kind of *material*, which is an object that describes how a surface is rendered. Skyboxes are sort of special-case Materials since they're not applied to Meshes, just used for rendering the sky.

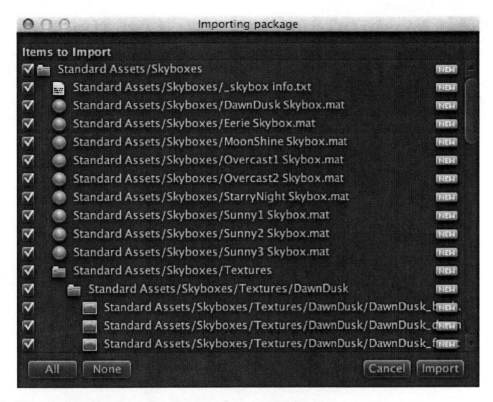

Figure 3-28. Skyboxes in Standard Assets

Go ahead and click the Import button. The Skyboxes and their supporting textures will appear in the Project View (Figure 3-29).

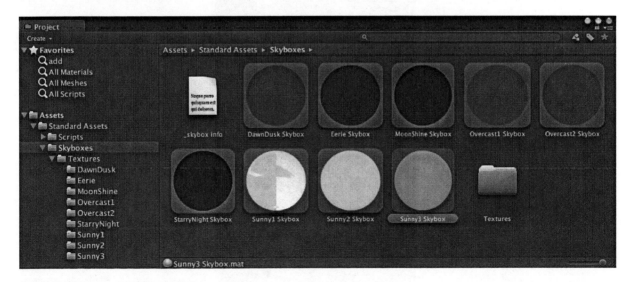

Figure 3-29. The Project View of Skyboxes

Anatomy of a Skybox

To get a better idea of the a Skybox's composition, select the Sunny3 Skybox and examine it in the Inspector View (Figure 3-30). Since it's a Material, the Skybox has a shader, which is a program instructing the graphics hardware how a polygon should be rendered, along with some parameters for the shader. Usually (but not always), the parameters for a shader include one or more textures. In the Inspector View, you can see the Skybox uses a RenderFX/Skybox shader, six textures for the Skybox sides, and a color that tints those textures.

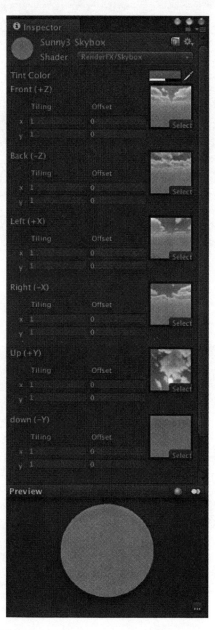

Figure 3-30. The Inspector View of a Skybox

Apply the Skybox

To apply the Skybox to the scene, first make sure you have the Clear Flags property of the Main Camera set to Skybox. Then bring up the Edit menu and select Render Settings (Figure 3-31).

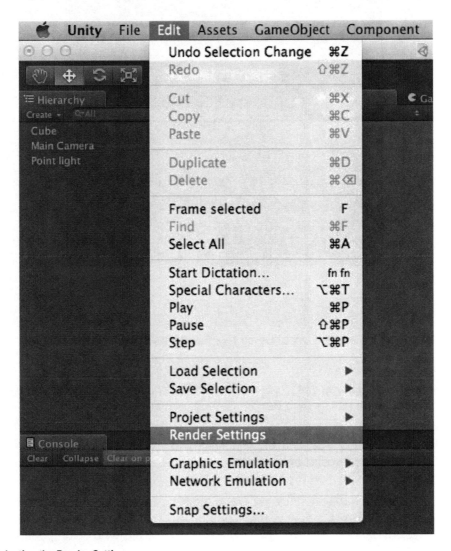

Figure 3-31. Selecting the Render Settings

The Render Settings are rendering properties that apply to the whole scene, including Fog, Ambient Light, and the Skybox (Figure 3-32).

Figure 3-32. The Render Settings

> **Tip**   *If you use fog, it's a good idea to make the fog color match the tint color of the Skybox.*

Note that the Render Settings you see apply only to the currently open scene. If you have multiple scenes in your project, each has its own Render Settings (otherwise you're stuck with the same Skybox in each scene).

Drag the Sunny3 Skybox into the Skybox Material field, and you should see those blue skies and fluffy white clouds in the background of the Scene View and Game View (if you get tired of blue skies, try changing the Tint Color on the Skybox).

Another way to incorporate a Skybox into a scene is to add a Skybox Component to the Main Camera and assign the Skybox Material to that Component. That Skybox would override any Skybox assigned in the Render Settings. The only reason to use a Skybox Component is if you have multiple Cameras that have different Skyboxes.

Add a Flare

There's an obvious analogy between Unity Cameras and, well, real cameras. That analogy can be stretched with the addition of Flares, which simulate lens flares, which are actually technical imperfections in camera lenses but used as effects by filmmakers (you may have seen quite a few, for example, in *Firefly* and J. J. Abrams's *Star Trek*).

Import Flares

As with Skyboxes, Unity provides some built-in Flares in Standard Assets. Go to the Assets menu under Import Package submenu and choose Light Flares (Figure 3-33).

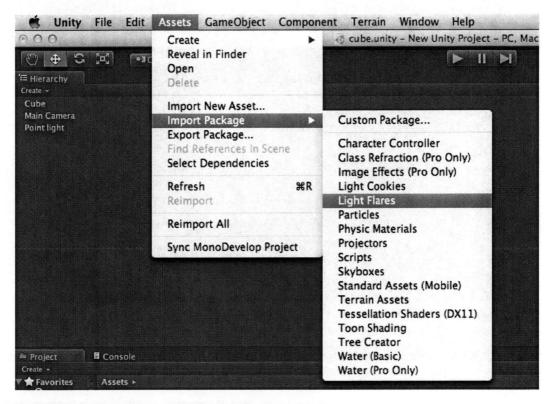

Figure 3-33. The Assets menu item for importing Flares

The package import window (Figure 3-34) reveals each Flare file has a .flare extension and contains a flare Material and a texture (notice that Unity conveniently supports .psd files for textures).

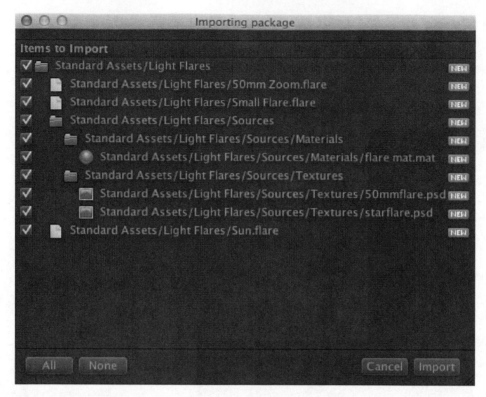

Figure 3-34. Flares in Standard Assets

Once the package is imported, the Flares show up in the Project View, represented by icons that resemble lens flares (Figure 3-35).

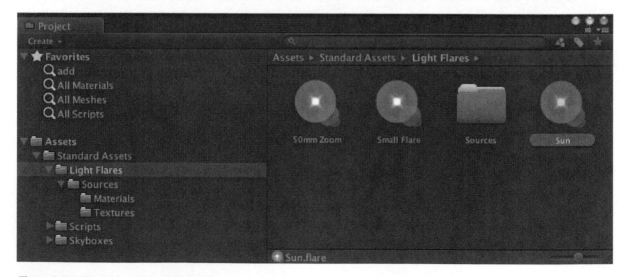

Figure 3-35. The Project View of Flares from Standard Assets

Apply the Flare

Let's use the 50-mm Zoom Flare (that happens to be one of my favorites as it stretches farther along the Flare direction than the others). Drag that Flare into the Point Light's Flare field (Figure 3-36).

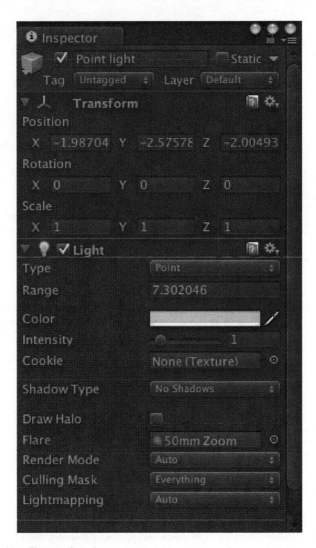

Figure 3-36. The Point Light with a Flare assigned

Now you can see the Flare in the Scene View emanating from the same position as the Point Light, and it looks even better when you click Play and orbit the Camera around the Cube (Figure 3-37). It's a very cool effect!

Figure 3-37. The Game View with a Flare

A more flexible way to incorporate a Flare into the scene is to create a GameObject with a LensFlare Component and assign a Flare to that Component. This method allows placement and alignment of a Flare independent of any Light and provides additional brightness and color adjustment of the Flare.

Textures

Our scene is beginning to look pretty good, now that we have a Skybox and a Light with a halo and Flare, but the Cube still looks drab. It's really the only thing left that doesn't have a texture, but that is easily fixed!

Import a Texture

Just about any image file (.jpeg, .png, .tiff, .psd) on your Mac can be imported as a texture by invoking the Import Asset command in the Assets menu (Figure 3-38) and selecting the image file in the resulting chooser.

Figure 3-38. Importing a new asset

For this example, I've chosen a cat picture from my Photos directory, where it was stored by iPhoto. Feel free to use this file by downloading it from `http://learnunity4.com/` (it's in this chapter's project, under the Textures folder). But if you have any image on your Mac in one of the supported file formats, that will be fine. After importing the image file, the resulting texture will appear in the Project View (Figure 3-39).

Figure 3-39. The Project View of a newly imported texture

Select the texture and examine its Import Settings in the Inspector View (Figure 3-40). The default Texture Type, Texture, is the preset type that is generally suitable for textures applied to models. If there are unapplied Import Settings, the Apply button is enabled and should be clicked (or Unity will prompt you to when it tries to use the texture).

Figure 3-40. *The Inspector View of an imported texture*

Notice how the Preview panel at the bottom summarizes the imported size and format of the Texture. The original image file has not been changed in any way, so importing the file effectively creates a duplicate of the original that is appropriate for our target platform. You never have to worry about messing up the original asset. In fact, you can always start over by right-clicking it in the Project View and selecting Reimport.

Note   We've been using the term *texture* generically and without capitalization. There actually is a Texture class, that is the parent class of all types of textures, but the actual class name of the texture asset created by importing an image file is Texture2D (the other subclasses of Texture include Texture3D, MovieTexture and RenderTexture).

To apply the texture to the Cube, drag the texture onto the Cube in the Hierarchy View. This automatically creates a Material using the texture and applies that Material to the Cube, replacing the previous Material that was there. (Figure 3-41).

Figure 3-41. A texture applied to the Cube

In the Project View, you can now see the newly created Material is placed in a Materials folder located by the texture. Now if you click Play again, the Cube looks cool! (Figure 3-42).

Figure 3-42. The Game View of the textured Cube

Shop the Asset Store

Unity doesn't have a built-in texture library in Standard Assets (although there are many textures used in the various packages). However, the Unity Asset Store, a marketplace of Unity-ready assets, has several free texture packs. Conveniently, the Asset Store is integrated into the Unity Editor. Under the Window menu (Figure 3-43), select the Asset Store item.

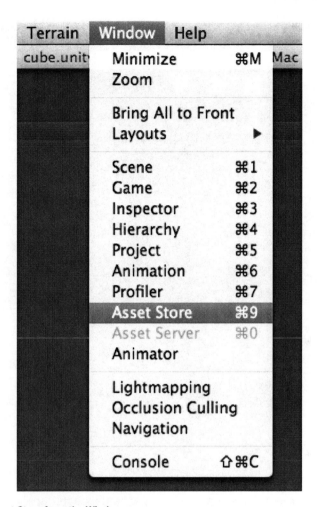

Figure 3-43. Selecting the Asset Store from the Window menu

This will bring up the Asset Store window and display the Asset Store front page (Figure 3-44), which lists the latest releases (both paid and free), categories, and featured items.

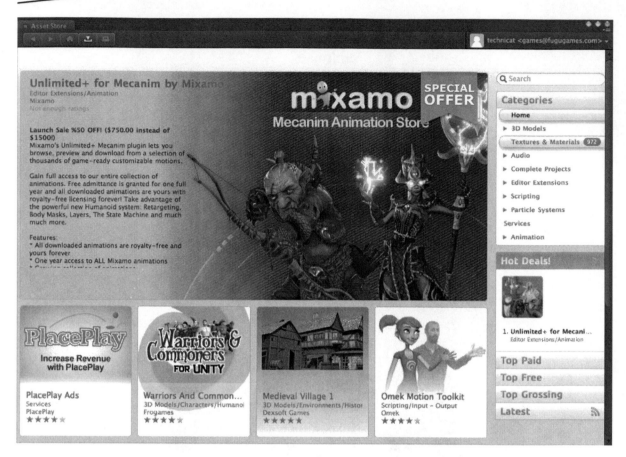

Figure 3-44. The Unity Asset Store

Let's look for some free textures. Click the Textures & Materials category in the upper-right section of the page, and then select Price in the Sort By section on the left (Figure 3-45).

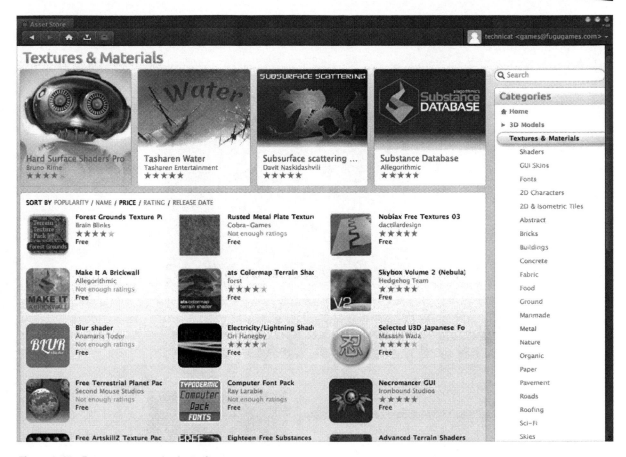

Figure 3-45. *Free textures on the Asset Store*

There are plenty of good candidates here, but if you scroll down, you should be able find to my favorite free texture library, the Free ArtskillZ Texture Pack. Click it to see the full product page (Figure 3-46). It includes the product description, screenshots, list of the individual files, and reviews.

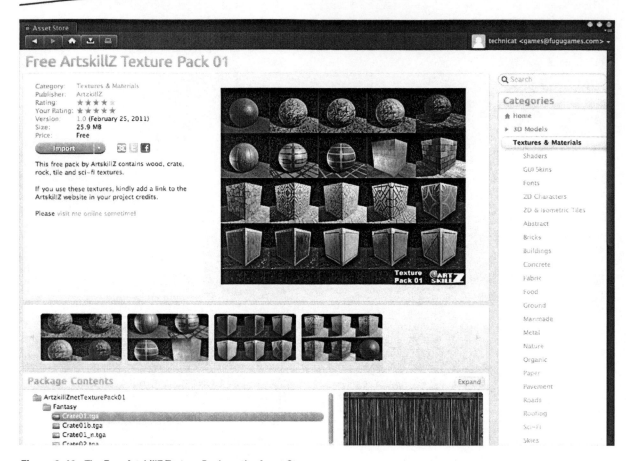

Figure 3-46. The Free ArtskillZ Texture Pack on the Asset Store

Import the Texture

Click the Import button, and you'll see the same type of Import window that you saw when importing the built-in Unity assets. Go ahead and import everything.

Now you'll find all those textures in your Project View, separated into three folders categorizing them by genre (Figure 3-47).

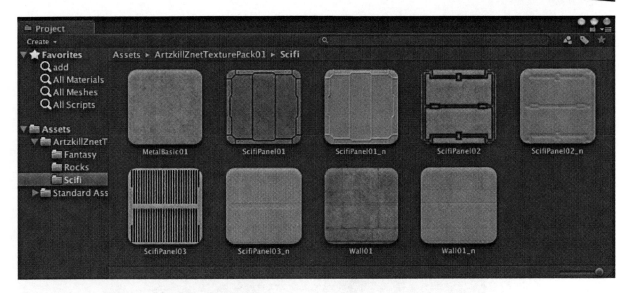

Figure 3-47. *The Project View of the ArtskillZ Textures*

The textures displayed with blue icons are normal maps and are listed as such in their Texture Type fields. A normal map gives the illusion of a nonflat surface (sometimes the term *bump map* is used, although it's not technically exactly the same).

Apply the Texture

For starters, we'll try the ScifiPanel01 Texture. Drag it to the Cube and Unity automatically creates a new Material named after the texture and applies that Material to the Cube. But we want to use the normal map that accompanies that texture, so use the Shader selector of the Material in the Inspector View to change the shader to Bumped Specular. This shader accepts a second texture labelled Normalmap and also has a slider to control the Shininess property (it should be noted that the slider moves left to approach 1 and right to approach 0). Drag the normal map texture, ScifiPanel01_n, into the Normalmap field (Figure 3-48).

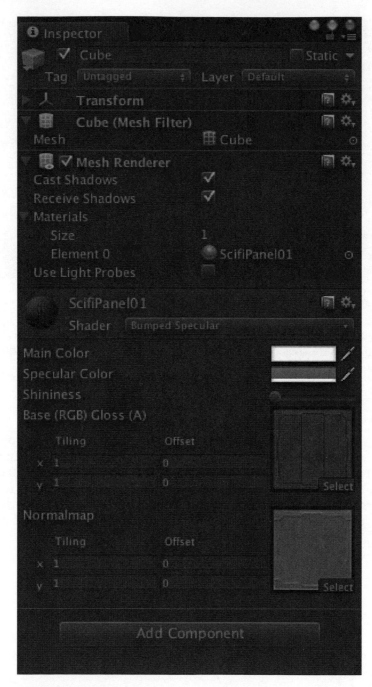

Figure 3-48. *Scifi Texture applied to the Cube*

Click Play, and you'll now see the textured Cube (Figure 3-49).

Figure 3-49. The Game View of the Cube with a specular bump map texture

You could have also searched for free textures using the search field in the Project View. We'll use that option in ensuing chapters as we make use of more Asset Store packages.

Explore Further

This chapter may have seemed like it covered a lot of material (no pun intended) just to create a simple static scene, but a lot of basic Unity concepts were explored along the way, particularly the relationship between Components and GameObjects. As a result, now you have a scene with a bump-mapped and textured Cube, illuminated by a Point Light that's sporting a Flare, and surrounded by a Skybox. The scene was populated with assets imported from local files, the Unity Standard Assets, and the Unity Asset Store. And the scene isn't completely static, due to the MouseOrbit script attached to the Main Camera. Scripting will play a dominant role in this book, starting with the next chapter as we move beyond a static scene.

Before moving on to that, take a break and go over the official Unity documentation on the features used so far, if only to get familiar with where to find this documentation for future reference.

Unity Manual

The Unity Basics section of the Unity Manual was mostly relevant to the previous chapter, describing the user interface, but that section does have a "Creating Scenes" page. More relevant is the "Building a Scene" section, which describes the relationship among GameObjects, Components, and scripts, how to use the Inspector View to edit Component properties, and how to navigate the

Scene View and move GameObjects, all of which was covered in this chapter. Lights and Cameras are also explained. One feature listed in this section that won't be used in this book is the Terrain Engine (it is available in Unity iOS but slow). Terrain is a significant and impressive Unity feature, though, so it's worth a read.

The "Asset Import and Creation" section describes the asset types used in this chapter: Meshes, Materials, textures and scripts. The process of importing assets and the Asset Store are also explained.

We haven't arrived at a point where we have gameplay, but the "Creating Gameplay" section has a page on "Transforms," which as we saw is fundamental to understand even just for placing static GameObjects.

Reference Manual

Getting more in depth than the Unity Manual, the Reference Manual describes each Component in detail, explaining its properties and documenting the use of the Component. The Reference Manual also documents the asset types and gives an explanation of GameObject.

As a rule, you should read the Reference Manual documentation for every Component and asset type you use. Remember, there is a Help icon on each Component in the Inspector View that will bring up the appropriate Reference Manual page when you click it. Like the Unity Manual, the Reference Manual is available not just from the Unity Help menu but als on the Unity web site under the Learn tab (which can be reached directly at `http://docs.unity3d.com/`).

The "Settings Manager" section of the Reference Manual includes a page on the Render Settings, which is where the Skybox in this chapter was assigned.

The "Transform Components" section lists just one Component, naturally, the Transform Component, which is attached to very GameObject.

The "Mesh Components" section is more interesting, as it describes both the MeshFilter and MeshRenderer Components necessary for any GameObject with Mesh, such as the Cube created in this chapter.

The "Rendering Components" section is more bountiful, yet, featuring the Camera Component and its associated GUILayer Component and FlareLayer. The Light Component is also documented here.

Although assets aren't really Components, the Reference Manual has a section titled "Asset Components," which lists the various asset classes. In this chapter, Flare, Material, Mesh and Texture2D were incorporated into the scene (remember that Skybox is really a Material).

The most fun reading is in the section titled "Built-In Shader Guide," which describes in detail (and with pictures) all of the built-in shaders, ranging from the simple and fast to very fancy. The Cube in this chapter started out with the default Diffuse shader and was replaced with a deluxe Specular Bump Map shader. As mentioned in this chapter, a shader is really a program, so if you can't find a built-in shader that suits your needs, you can write your own by following the examples and instructions in the "Shader Reference" section.

Asset Store

This chapter begins our book-long practice of using free assets from the Unity Asset Store. I recommend browsing the Asset Store regularly to check the latest releases. Besides the free textures, models, and scripts, there are plenty of reasonably priced packages that can save you a lot of time and work. The Asset Store can also be viewed with a regular web browser at `http://assetstore.unity3d.com/` (but without the ability to purchase or download any assets).

Computer Graphics

Computer graphics is a huge and intricate area of study. This chapter worked with 3D models, textures, bump maps, light flares, skyboxes, and we're just getting started. So it's well worth reading up on basic (and advanced) computer graphics, such as the popular and comprehensive text *Real-Time Rendering*, by Tomas Akenine-Möller, Eric Haines, and Naty Hoffman. Mark Haigh-Hutchinson's *Real-Time Cameras* is an entire book devoted to the subject of virtual Cameras and their control schemes.

I won't be covering the process of creating assets that can be imported into Unity, but Luke Ahearn has two books that may be generally helpful: *3D Game Textures: Create Professional Game Art Using Photoshop* and *3D Game Environments: Create Professional 3D Game Worlds.* And you can tell from the title of Wes McDermott's *Creating 3D Game Art for the iPhone with Unity* that it's an appropriate complementary text for this book.

Chapter 4

Making It Move: Scripting the Cube

Now that you know how to construct a static 3D scene by placing GameObjects, it's time to make the scene dynamic, and more interesting, by adding movement to GameObjects while the game is played. After all, a 3D graphics scene is nice, but an animated 3D graphics scene is even better!

But applying animation data isn't the only way to move a GameObject. Making a GameObject physical will cause it to move in response to collisions and forces, including gravity. And a script can also move a GameObject by changing the position and/or rotation values in its Transform Component. In fact, any method for moving a GameObject, whether it's animation, physics, or a script, ultimately changes the Transform Component, which always represents the position, rotation and scale of the GameObject.

This chapter will focus on moving GameObjects by scripting, demonstrating how to rotate the formerly static Cube created in the previous chapter and even introducing tween-style animations implemented with the open-source iTween library. In the process, I'll present basic concepts and tools (editing and debugging) of the Unity scripting system.

The scripts you'll be writing are available on http://learnunity4.com/ in the project for this chapter, but I recommend creating them from scratch. You have the best chance of understanding how code works (and doesn't work) when you type it in yourself

Organize the Assets

It's easier to view and browse assets in the Project View when they're partitioned by type. So before you start adding scripts, this is a good time to get organized and create some folders for the scripts and textures in the project.

Launch the Unity Editor, if you don't already have it open from the previous chapter, and make sure you have the project from the previous chapter loaded and the cube scene open. Then click the Create button in the top left of the Project View (Figure 4-1) to bring up a menu of new assets that you can add to the project (alternatively, you can right-click in the Project View and select the Create submenu). Select the Folder item in the menu, and a folder titled New Folder will appear in the Project View. Rename the folder to Textures and drag any textures into it that you imported in the previous chapter (like my cat photo). Although you haven't created any scripts, yet, go ahead and create a Scripts folder, too.

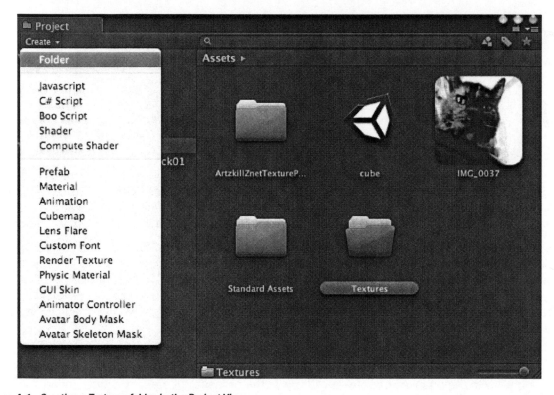

Figure 4-1. Creating a Textures folder in the Project View

Create the Script

Select the newly-added Scripts folder and then, also from the Create menu of the Project View, select JavaScript (Figure 4-2). A script called New Behaviour (U.S. readers, you'll just have to get used to the British spelling) will appear in the Scripts folder. If you accidentally created the new script file outside the Scripts folder, just drag the script into the folder.

> **Note**   Although the Create menu in the Project View lists "Javascript," with just the first letter capitalized, I'll pretend it says "JavaScript," which is the official capitalization and used in the Unity documentation (who knows, a Unity update may fix the menu spelling at any time). Also, this book will use the phrase "a JavaScript" to refer to a script, instead of the more correct but clumsier-to-say "a JavaScript script."

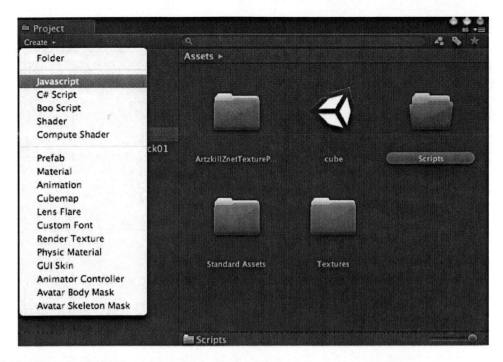

Figure 4-2. Creating a JavaScript

Since this new file is a JavaScript, it has a .js extension. The Project View does not display filename extensions, but the language of the script is evident from its icon (Figure 4-3). And if the script is selected, its full name is shown in the line at the bottom of the Project View.

Figure 4-3. The Project View of the new script

Name the Script

New Behaviour is not a very meaningful name for a script, so the first order of business is to give it a new name. An obvious choice is Rotate, since the eventual purpose of the script is to rotate the Cube. But with overly general names, you can run into a conflict (Unity will report an error) if there are two scripts with the same name, even if they reside in different folders. This is because each script defines a new class (a subclass of MonoBehaviour, to be specific), and you can't have two classes with the same name.

One approach is to name each script with a standard prefix (much like how Objective-C classes start with NS, harkening back to the NextStep origins of OS X). This is a common technique adopted by third-party Unity user interface packages. If everyone names their button class Button, they can't coexist!

> **Note**   C# scripts have the option of partitioning classes among namespaces to avoid name clashes. This book uses JavaScript nearly all the way through, but examples of C# scripts and namespaces are provided in Chapter 17.

Sometimes, I use the game name as a script name prefix, if the script is specific to the game (in HyperBowl, I have a lot of scripts that start with Hyper). However, I usually prefix my script names with Fugu, corresponding to my game brand, Fugu Games. This book will stick with that convention, so go ahead and name the new script FuguRotate (Figure 4-3). Of course, in general, you're free to choose your own script name convention.

Anatomy of a Script

If you select the FuguRotate script in the Project View, the Inspector View displays the source code, or at least as much as will fit in the Inspector View display (Figure 4-4).

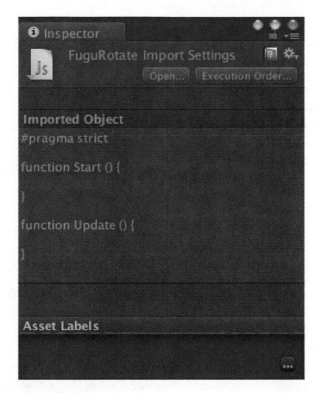

Figure 4-4. The Inspector View of the new script

As the Inspector View shows, when Unity creates a new script, it includes three items (Listing 4-1).

Listing 4-1. The Contents of a New Script

```
#pragma strict

function Start () {
}

function Update () {
}
```

The top line of the script, #pragma strict, instructs the script compiler that all variables have type declarations, or at least have types that are easily inferred by the compiler. This is not a requirement for Unity desktop builds, but it is required for Unity iOS, so you might as well make a habit of it.

> **Note**   All of the complete script listings in this book start with `#pragma strict`. Any code that doesn't include that line is only an excerpt from a script.

The two functions in the script are callbacks, which are called by the Unity game engine at well-defined moments in the game. The `Start` function is called when this script is first enabled. A Component is not completely `enabled` unless the GameObject it's attached to is also active. So if a GameObject is initially active in a scene and it has an enabled script attached, then the `Start` function of that script is called when the scene starts playing. Otherwise, the `Start` function is not called until the script is enabled (by setting the `enabled` variable of the script Component) and the GameObject is made active (by calling the `SetActive` function of the GameObject).

In contrast to the `Start` function, which is only called at most once in the lifetime of a script Component, the `Update` function is called every frame (i.e., once before each time Unity renders the current scene). Like the `Start` function, `Update` is only called when the script is (completely) enabled, and the first call to `Update` happens after the one and only call to `Start`. Thus, the `Start` function is useful for performing any initialization needed by the `Update` function.

Attach the Script

Like other assets in the Project View, a script has no effect until you add it to the scene, specifically as a Component of a GameObject. Ultimately, you want the `FuguRotate` script to rotate the Cube, so drag it from the Project View onto the Cube GameObject in the Hierarchy View. The Inspector View now shows the script is attached to the Cube as a Component (Figure 4-5).

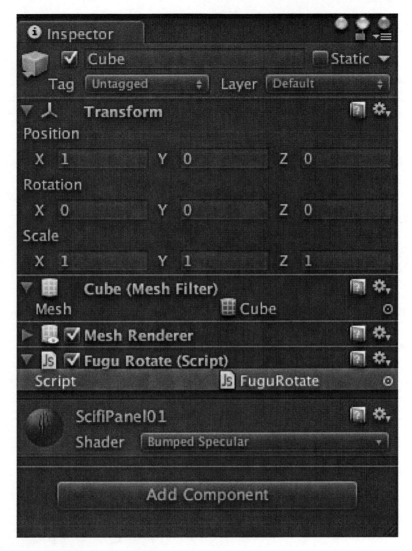

Figure 4-5. The FuguRotate script attached to the Cube

Unity often offers two, and sometimes three, ways to perform the same operation. For example, you could also have attached the FuguRotate script to the Cube by clicking the Add Component button in the Inspector View of the Cube and then selecting the FuguRotate script from the resulting menu. Or you could have dragged the FuguRotate script into the area below the Add Component button (but that's difficult if there isn't much space displayed below the button).

Edit the Script

Now it's time to fill out the script. Select the FuguRotate script in the Project View, and then in the Inspector View click the Open button to bring up the script editor. Double-clicking the script in the Project View, or selecting Open from the right-click menu on the script will work, too. The default script editor for Unity is a customized version of MonoDevelop, a code editor and debugger tailored for Mono, the open source framework underlying Unity's scripting system (Figure 4-6).

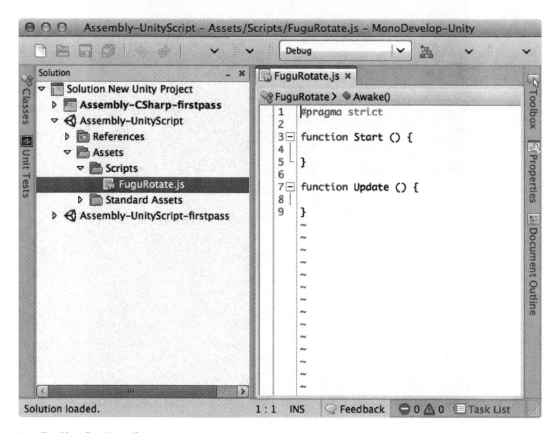

Figure 4-6. The MonoDevelop editor

If you prefer to use another script editor, you can change the default by bringing up the Unity Preferences window, selecting the External Tools tab, and then browsing for the application of your choice (Figure 4-7). Unitron, no longer officially supported but still included in the Unity installation, is an option, but scripts are text files, so any text editor can be used as a script editor. For example, as an old school programmer, I like to use Aquamacs, an OS X version of Emacs.

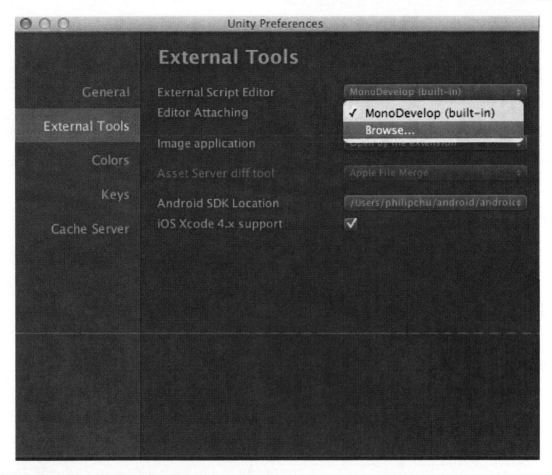

Figure 4-7. Choosing a different script editor

The FuguRotate script as it stands won't do anything noticeable, since the callback functions are empty, having no code between their brackets. Let's start off with some tracing code in the Start and Update functions to demonstrate when those callbacks are invoked (Listing 4-2).

Listing 4-2. FuguRotate.js with Calls to Debug.Log

```
function Start () {
        Debug.Log("Start called on GameObject "+gameObject.name);
}
function Update () {
        Debug.Log("Update called at time "+Time.time);
}
```

One cool feature of Unity's MonoDevelop is its code autocompletion. For example, Figure 4-8 shows that as you type Time.t, MonoDevelop pops up a list of functions and variables that are members of the Time class and looks for one that starts with "t."

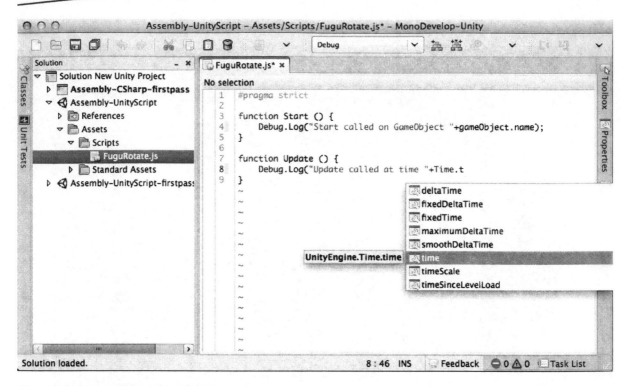

Figure 4-8. Autocompletion in MonoDevelop

Understand the Script

Now that the FuguRotate script is doing something, let's try to understand what that is. Both Start and Update call the function Debug.Log to print messages to the Console View. Log is a static function defined in the Debug class, meaning you can call that function by specifying its class name before the function name, instead of an object (functions defined in classes are also called *methods*).

> **Note** Static functions and variables are also called *class* functions and variables, since they are associated with a class instead of instances of that class.

The variable gameObject references the GameObject this component (the script) is attached to (in this case, the Cube), and every GameObject also has a name variable that references the name of this GameObject (in this case, "Cube"). The + operator can be used to concatenate two strings (it's not just for addition, anymore), so the Start function will print "Start called on GameObject" followed by the name of the GameObject.

Similarly, the Update function calls Debug.Log, concatenating "Update called at time" with the value of the static variable Time.time, which holds the time elapsed (in seconds) since the game started (in the case of running from the Unity Editor, when you click the Play button). Time.time is of type float (a floating point number, which can represent non-integer values), but the + operator will convert the number to a String before appending it.

Read the Scripting Reference

Besides autocompletion, another handy feature of MonoDevelop is the ability to bring up the Scripting Reference documentation for any Unity class, function, or variable. Clicking on Debug at the beginning of a Debug.Log call in the script and pressing Command+' will bring up the Scripting Reference documentation for the Debug class in a browser window. Clicking on Log will bring up the specific documentation for the Debug.Log function.

> **Tip**   Every time you see a Unity class, function, or variable you're not familiar with, the first thing you should do is read the Script Reference documentation on it.

The Scripting Reference is available in the Unity Help menu (Figure 4-9).

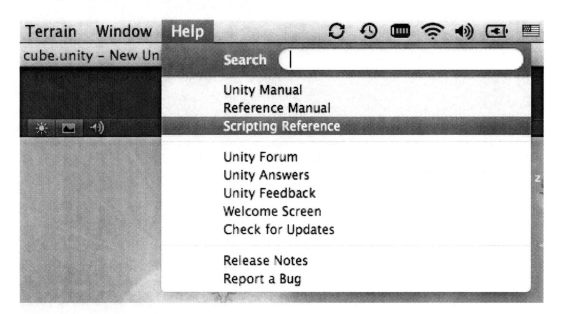

Figure 4-9. Bringing up the Scripting Reference from the Help menu

The Scripting Reference contains documentation for all Unity classes plus their functions and variables (Figure 4-10). I find the fastest way to look up an arbitrary Unity class, function, or variable in the Scripting Reference is to type it in the search box. Command+' in MonoDevelop effectively performs that search when it doesn't know exactly what definition you're looking for. For example, perform Command+' on Start in the FuguRotate script and a list of search results for Start will appear.

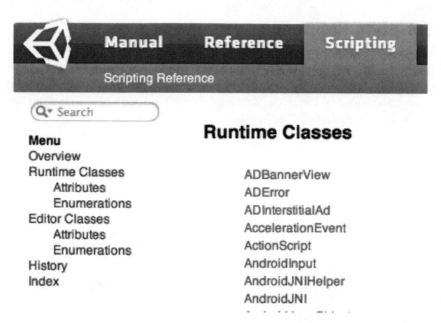

Figure 4-10. The Scripting Reference

However, clicking Runtime Classes on the left of the Scripting Reference will give you the entire list of classes, indented so the class hierarchy (i.e., which classes are subclasses of others) is apparent (Figure 4-11). Some classes, such as Debug and Time, are static classes, meaning they contain only static functions and variables (there are no Unity functions that don't reside in a class) and there's no reason to subclass them.

```
Object
        AssetBundle
        AudioClip
        Avatar
        Component
                Behaviour
                        Animation
                        Animator
                        AudioChorusFilter
                        AudioDistortionFilter
                        AudioEchoFilter
                        AudioHighPassFilter
                        AudioListener
                        AudioLowPassFilter
                        AudioReverbFilter
                        AudioReverbZone
                        AudioSource
                        Camera
                        ConstantForce
                        GUIElement
                                GUIText
                                GUITexture
                        GUILayer
                        LensFlare
                        Light
                        MonoBehaviour
```

Figure 4-11. The class hierarchy of runtime classes

Most classes, however, act as types of objects. The Cube in the scene is an instance of the class GameObject. And GameObject is a subclass of Object, meaning it inherits all of the documented variables and functions of Object. Conceptually, and in object-oriented parlance, the Cube *is a* GameObject and thus also *is an* Object. Contrast this with the relationship between GameObject and Component. The Cube *is a* GameObject and it *has a* MeshFilter (which *has a* Mesh).

From the Runtime Classes list, you can see that just about everything that can be in a scene is a subclass of Object, including GameObject and Component. Many Component subclasses, including Light and Camera, are also subclasses of Behaviour, which is a Component that can be enabled or disabled (as evidenced by their checkboxes in the Inspector View). Some are not, though, like Transform, which is a direct subclass (no intervening classes) of Component and cannot be disabled (no checkbox in the Inspector View).

Each script is actually a subclass of MonoBehaviour, which is a subclass of Behaviour (so you can enable and disable scripts). Thus, the FuguRotate script defines a subclass of MonoBehaviour called FuguRotate. This class declaration is implicit in JavaScript, although you could make it explicit, as shown in Listing 4-3.

Listing 4-3. A Version of FuguRotate.js with an Explicit Class Declaration

```
#pragma strict

class FuguRotate extends MonoBehaviour {

function Start () {
            var object:GameObject = null;
            Debug.Log("Start called on GameObject "+object.name);
    }

    function Update () {
            Debug.Log("Update called at time "+Time.time);
    }

}
```

Run the Script

Proper programming is a lot like the scientific method you learned in school. You should have a general theory on how things work, hypothesize about what your code should be doing, and then you're ready to run an experiment to validate that hypothesis. In other words, it's time to run your code and see if it does what you expect. When you click Play, the messages emitted by Debug.Log will show up in the Console View (Figure 4-12).

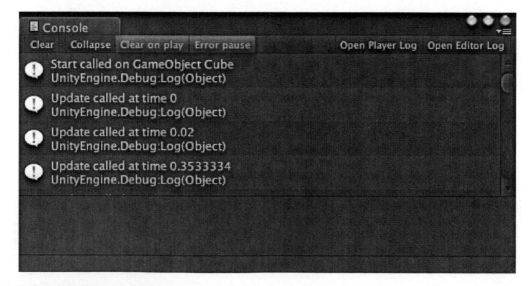

Figure 4-12. Tracing the Start and Update callbacks

If the code doesn't behave as you expect, it is time to revise your theory on what it's doing. This may be a small consolation, but debugging your code is a learning experience!

Debug the Script

Of course, your code will not be perfect as soon as you type it in. On the contrary, usually it will require several iterations of debugging. There are basically two types of errors: compilation errors that appear even before you try to run the game, and runtime errors that occur while the game is playing.

Compilation Errors

Every time a script is saved, it's automatically compiled (converted from the source code to the code format that actually runs). Errors in the script that prevent successful compilation will appear in red at the bottom of the Unity Editor and in the Console View.

Double-clicking the error message at the bottom of the Editor will bring up the corresponding message in the Console View, and double-clicking the message in the Console View will bring up the script editor with the cursor located at the offending line of code. Even without that convenience, the error message will list the file name and line number of the offending code, so it can be found manually.

For example, if you had typed `Time.tim` instead of `Time.time` in the `Update` function, an error message would have appeared as soon as you tried to save the script (Figure 4-13.) Conveniently, Unity will often do a decent job of suggesting what you may have intended to type (although generally computers aren't good at "do what I mean, not what I say").

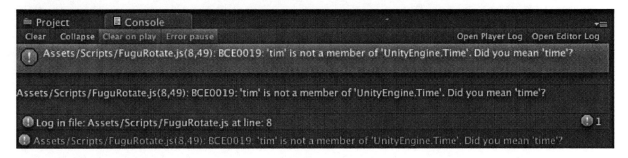

Figure 4-13. A script compilation error

Runtime Errors

Like compilation errors, runtime errors also show up in the Console View. To demonstrate, replace the reference to `gameObject` in your `Start` function with a reference to a local variable named `object` (Listing 4-4). A local variable is declared within a function declaration, and therefore is only accessible within the scope of the function. In this case, `object` is initialized as `null`, meaning it's not referring to any actual GameObject, and is never assigned any GameObject. When you click Play, an error results when the script tries to reference the name of the GameObject (Figure 4-14).

Listing 4-4. Start Function in FuguRotate.js with a Null Reference Error

```
function Start () {
        var object:GameObject = null;
        Debug.Log("Start called on GameObject "+object.name);
}
```

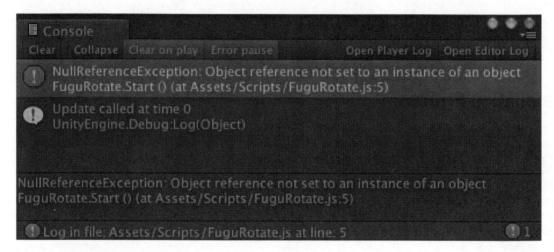

Figure 4-14. A script runtime error

Debug with MonoDevelop

I still perform most of my debugging by calling Debug.Log (old school, again) and examining error messages in the Console View. But modern programmers are accustomed to more sophisticated debugging tools. It turns out that MonoDevelop also provides a full-featured debugger that's been customized to work with Unity. To enable debugging with MonoDevelop, select the Sync MonoDevelop Project command from the Assets menu (Figure 4-15).

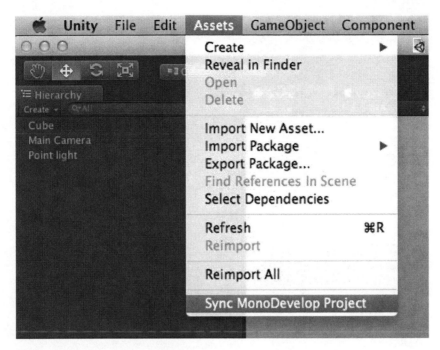

Figure 4-15. Sync MonoDevelop Project to start debugging

The Sync MonoDevelop Project command updates the MonoDevelop project files corresponding to this Unity project and then opens the MonoDevelop project solution file. If MonoDevelop doesn't automatically open that solution file, you can open it from MonoDevelop File menu or double-click the solution file in the Finder (the highlighted file in Figure 4-16).

Figure 4-16. MonoDevelop project files

With the MonoDevelop solution loaded, enable debugging by selecting Attach to Process from the MonoDevelop Run menu (Figure 4-17).

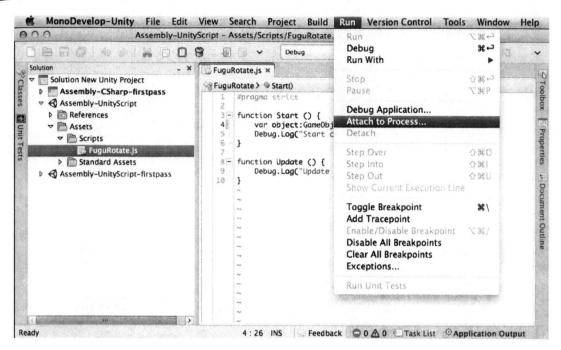

Figure 4-17. The MonoDevelop Attach to Process command

Then choose Unity Editor in the resulting process list (Figure 4-18).

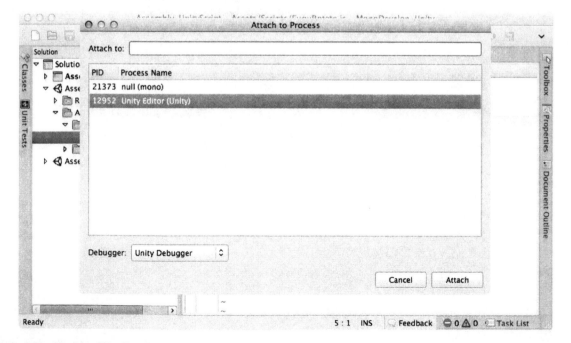

Figure 4-18. Attaching MonoDevelop to the Unity Editor

Click Play, again, and this time MonoDevelop will show not only the line of code where the error occurred, but also the specific type of error (NullReferenceException) and associated information like the stack trace, which is useful in determining what chain of function calls resulted in the error (Figure 4-19).

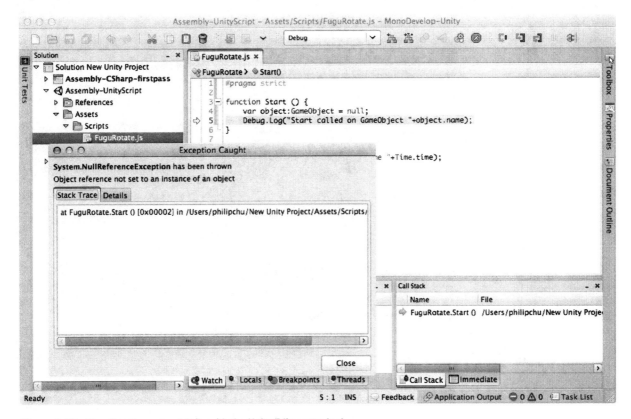

Figure 4-19. *MonoDevelop error details with the Unity Editor attached*

While in debugging mode, the Unity Editor is unresponsive, so when you're finished with a debugging run, select Detach from the Run menu in MonoDevelop to detach the Unity Editor process (Figure 4-20). The Detach command is also available as a button on the MonoDevelop toolbar.

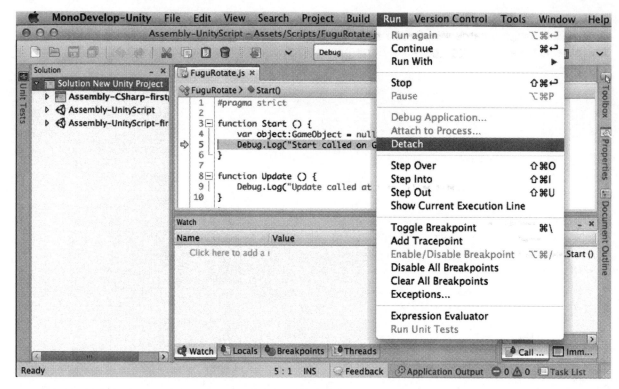

Figure 4-20. Detaching the Unity Editor process from MonoDevelop

Let's fix the null reference problem by changing the initial value of the variable object from null to the script's GameObject (Listing 4-5).

Listing 4-5. Start Function in FuguRotate.js with Null Reference Fix

```
function Start () {
        var object:GameObject = this.gameObject;
        Debug.Log("Start called on GameObject "+object.name);
}
```

The reference to this.gameObject is equivalent to just gameObject. The variable this always refers to the current object, which is this script Component (in some other programming languages, self is used in the same way). Sometimes I like to explicitly prefix variables like gameObject with this. to make it clear that I'm referring to an instance variable, which is a variable defined in the class that is not local to a function and not static, so each instance of the class has its own copy.

Now the script shouldn't break in the Start function (you can click Play in the Unity Editor to confirm). But you can still make execution stop on any line in MonoDevelop by adding a breakpoint. Click to the left of the line in the Update function, and a breakpoint indicator will appear by the line (Figure 4-21).

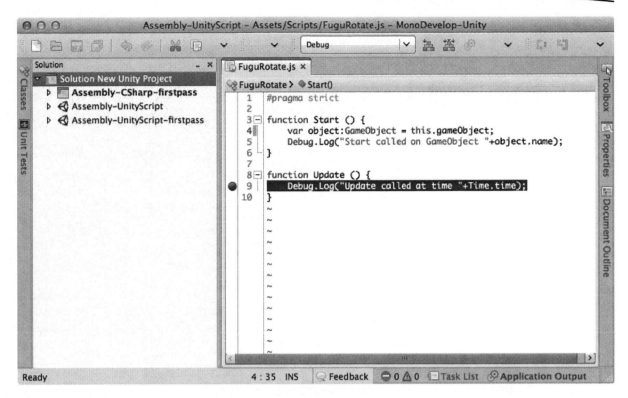

Figure 4-21. Adding a breakpoint in MonoDevelop

Now when you invoke Attach to Process, connect to the Unity Editor, and click Play in the Unity Editor, execution will stop in your Update function just as if there were an error there (Figure 4-22). When execution is halted in MonoDevelop while in debugging mode, you can examine the stack trace and inspect the runtime environment in other ways. For example, Figure 4-22 shows the result of typing gameObject in the Watch panel and then halting at a breakpoint in the FuguRotate Update callback. The current value of gameObject is the Cube GameObject, which can now have its member variables examined.

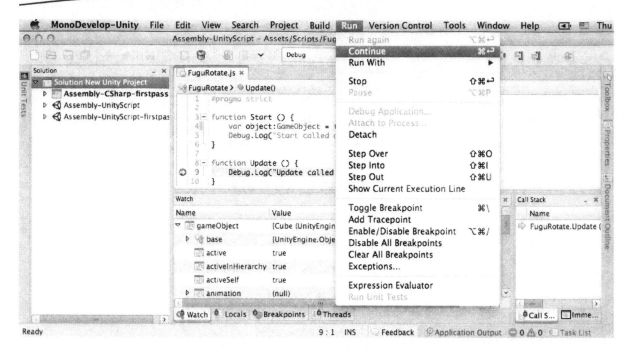

Figure 4-22. Execution halted at a breakpoint

Once you're finished examining the runtime state at the breakpoint, you have an option in the Run menu to Continue until the next breakpoint or error. The Run menu also has commands to Step Over (continue until the next line of code in this function), Step Into (continue until the first line of code any function called by this line of code), or Step Out (continue until you've exited this function), so you can step through your script one line at a time. All of these commands have keyboard shortcuts shown in the Run menu and are also available as buttons on the toolbar.

Make It Rotate

Now that you're familiar with scripts and how to attach, edit, and debug them, we're ready to make this script do what we ultimately want—rotate the Cube.

Rotate the Transform

Moving a GameObject at runtime requires changing its Transform Component. Rotating the GameObject specifically requires changing the rotation value in its Transform Component. Replacing the contents of the FuguRotate script with the code in Listing 4-6 will do the trick.

Listing 4-6. FuguRotate.js Script with Rotation Code in Update

```
#pragma strict
var speed:float = 10.0; // controls how fast we rotate
function Start () {
        var object:GameObject = this.gameObject;
        Debug.Log("Start called on GameObject "+object.name);
}

// rotate around the object's y axis
function Update () {
        //Debug.Log("Update called at time "+Time.time);
        transform.Rotate(Vector3.up*speed*Time.deltaTime);
}
```

Let's go though the new code. First, any line starting with // is a comment and not executed as code. This is a convenient way to deactivate a line of code without deleting it from the file. Comments can also be added within /* and */, which is useful for multiline comments.

> **Note** Some will say code should be written well enough to be self-explanatory, but as a basic rule of thumb, if the intent of the code is not obvious, add a comment. I've wasted plenty of time trying to remember why I wrote some code the way I did.

The speed variable controls how fast the object rotates, and since it's declared as a public instance variable, it's available as an adjustable property in the Inspector View.

You could have just typed var speed=10.0 instead of var speed:float=10.0, since the compiler can infer that speed must be of type float, since it's initialized with a floating point number (this is known as *type inference*). But it's better to be as clear as you can, not just for the Unity compiler, but also for any human reading the code, including yourself!

The variable speed is used in the Update function, which calls the Rotate function defined in the Transform class. Rotate takes a Vector3 as an argument and interprets its x,y,z values as Euler angles (rotation, in degrees, around the GameObject's x,y,z axes). A vector represents a direction and magnitude, but it's common in game engines to use the vector data structure to represent Euler angles.

> **Note** The movie *Despicable Me* has as good a definition of vector as any: "I go by Vector. It's a mathematical term, represented by an arrow with both direction and magnitude. Vector! That's me, because I commit crimes with both direction and magnitude. Oh yeah!"

Vector3.up is a conveniently defined Vector3 with values (0,1,0), so the Update function is rotating around the y axis by speed * Time.deltaTime degrees. Time.deltaTime is the elapsed time since the last frame, in seconds, so, effectively, you're rotating by speed degrees per second. In Update callbacks, you almost always want to multiply any continuous change by Time.deltaTime so that your game behavior does not fluctuate with differences in frame rate. If the multiplication by Time.deltaTime was omitted, the FuguRotate script would rotate objects twice as slow on any machine that's running two times slower.

As intended, the variable speed shows up in the Inspector View and you can edit it (Figure 4-23).

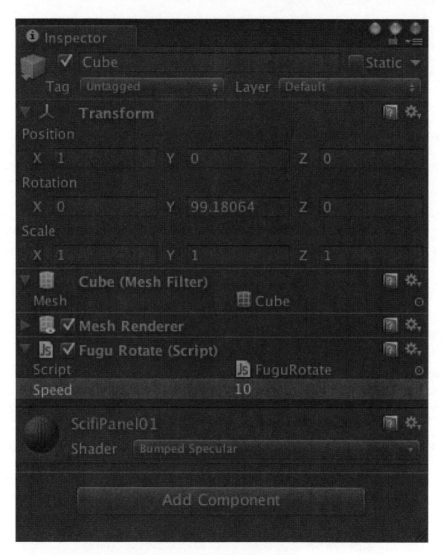

Figure 4-23. *The Inspector View of the FuguRotate script with adjustable speed*

If you click Play, the Cube now spins at a moderate rate, and continuous change in the Transform Component's y rotation value will be displayed in the Inspector View. You can edit the Speed value of the FuguRotate script in the Inspector View to slow it down or speed it up.

Other Ways to Rotate

`Transform.Rotate` is a good example of why you should read the Scripting Reference for every function you encounter. It turns out `Transform.Rotate` is an *overloaded* function, meaning it has variations with different parameters.

> **Note**   The term *parameter* is used when describing the function declaration and *argument* refers to the same value when its passed at runtime, but it's a subtle distinction. Parameter and argument can usually be used interchangeably without confusion.

The documentation for `Transform.Rotate` lists several combinations of arguments that it can take. Instead of accepting a `Vector3` to rotate around and an angle (in degrees), `Transform.Rotate` can take the x, y, and z axis rotations separately. Listing 4-7 shows an alternative version of our `Update` function that just passes in the x, y, and z rotations.

Listing 4-7. Version of Transform.Rotate That Takes Rotation in x, y, and z Angles

```
function Update () {
        transform.Rotate(0,speed*Time.deltaTime,0);
}
```

Or the x, y, and z rotations can be packaged into a `Vector3`, as shown in Listing 4-8.

Listing 4-8. Version of Transform.Rotate That Takes Rotation in a Vector3

```
function Update () {
        transform.Rotate(Vector3(0,speed*Time.deltaTime,0));
}
```

Although a vector has a precise mathematical definition, Unity follows a common practice among 3D application programming interfaces of reusing its vector data structure to represent anything that has x, y, and z values. For example, if you read the Scripting Reference page on `Transform` (and you should), you'll see its position, rotation, and scale are all `Vector3` values.

Rotate in World Space

Each of the `Transform.Rotate` variations also has an optional parameter, which defaults to `Space.Self`. This specifies that the rotation takes place around the transform's (and thus the GameObject's) local axes, which correspond to the axis handles you see in the Scene View when the GameObject is selected. If you specify `Space.World`, as shown in Listing 4-9, the rotation takes place around the world axes (the x, y, z axes centered at 0,0,0).

Listing 4-9. Rotating Around the World Axes

```
function Update () {
        transform.Rotate(Vector3.up,speed*Time.deltaTime,Space.World);
}
```

Tween Rotation

Changing a GameObject's transform steadily over time is straightforward, but the coding can be more involved and substantial for more complicated motions, such as moving a GameObject from one position to another smoothly over a certain period of time. This is the type of thing that Flash programmers use the ActionScript Tween class for. Although Unity doesn't have a built-in Tween class, Unity users coming from a Flash background will be happy to learn there are multiple third-party solutions.

The tween package I use for HyperBowl is called iTween. I have around 200 iTween animations in that game. A sample usage: After a strike is bowled, the 3D STRIKE text is scripted with iTween so that the letters slide onto the screen one letter a time, bob a bit, then fly off the screen while rotating.

Conveniently, iTween is on the Asset Store. In Chapter 3, we searched for packages in the Asset Store window, but this time, let's use the search function in the Project View. Type "itween" in the search box, and click the Asset Store link in the breadcrumbs. iTween will show up in the Free Assets results (Figure 4-24).

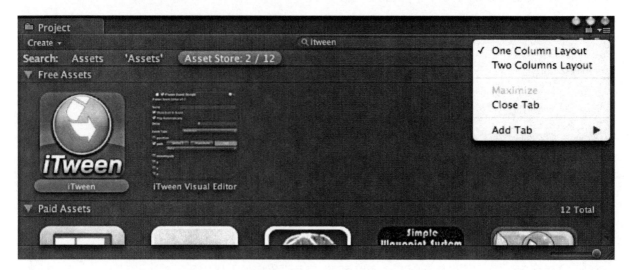

Figure 4-24. Searching for iTween on the Asset Store

> **Tip** Figure 4-24 shows the view menu in the Project View allows switching between One Column Layout and Two Columns Layout. Two Columns Layout is new in Unity 4, but One Columns Layout is still nice to have, particularly when performing a search in the Project View instead of navigating with the left panel.

Select iTween in the Project View and a description of the package will show up in the Inspector View (Figure 4-25), along with options to import the package or preview the full description in the Asset Store window. Go ahead and click the Import package button.

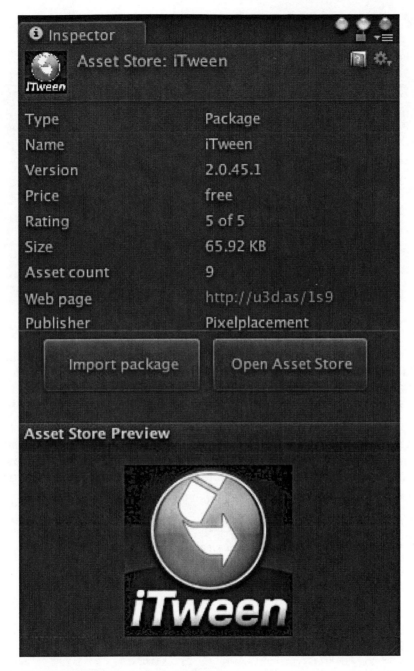

Figure 4-25. The Inspector View of the iTween on the Asset Store

The resulting iTween installation shown in the Project View includes sample and documentation files, but the entire iTween code library is a single script located in the iTween ➤ Plugins folder (Figure 4-26).

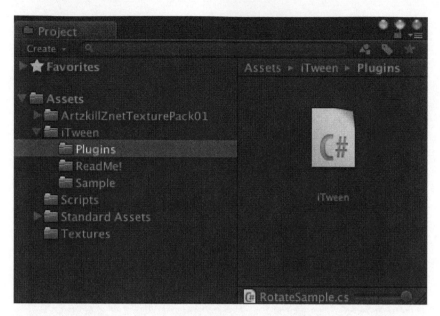

Figure 4-26. Project view of iTween

As you can see in Figure 4-26, iTween is a C# script, with .cs as its filename extension. JavaScript can call functions and refer to variables in C# scripts, but only if the C# scripts are located in a few special folders that are designated to load before all other scripts. One of those folders is Assets ➤ Plugins, so you can just drag the iTween ➤ Plugins folder up a level to just below Assets.

To get a flavor of iTween, add the third line in Listing 4-10 to the Start function in the FuguRotate script. That line starts a rotation tween, and, following the arguments in order from left to right, rotates around the local y axis 1 multiple of 360 degrees over 2 seconds, eases in as the target rotation is achieved, and eases back out as the rotation bounces back in the other direction.

Also, use /* and */ to comment out the Update function so you don't have two pieces of rotation code fighting for control.

Listing 4-10. FuguRotate.js with iTween Called in the Start Function

```
#pragma strict
var speed:float = 10.0; // controls how fast we rotate

function Start () {
        var object:GameObject = this.gameObject;
        Debug.Log("Start called on GameObject "+object.name);
        iTween.RotateBy(gameObject, iTween.Hash("y", 1, "time", 2, "easeType", "easeInOutBack",
"loopType", "pingPong"));
}

// rotate around the object's y axis
/*
```

```
function Update () {
        //Debug.Log("Update called at time "+Time.time);
        transform.Rotate(Vector3.up*speed*Time.deltaTime);
}
*/
```

Children of the Cube

A scene with just one cube is not very interesting, so let's make it slightly more interesting by adding more cubes. You could repeatedly create new cubes in the same manner as the first one. Or you could save some time by duplicating the existing Cube (select the Cube and then invoke the Duplicate command on the Edit menu or use the Command+D keyboard shortcut). But let's take this opportunity to learn about prefabs.

Making Prefabs

A *prefab* is a special type of asset created for cloning a GameObject. The prefab can then be used to create identical copies of that GameObject. In that sense, Unity prefabs are like prefabricated housing, but better. If you make a change to one instance of a prefab, you can have that change automatically propagate to all other instances of the prefab.

First, in keeping with our asset organization, create a new folder in the Project View named Prefabs. Then, with the Prefabs folder selected, click Prefab on the Create menu in the Project View to create an empty prefab in that folder. You can then fill out the prefab by dragging the Cube from the Hierarchy View onto the empty prefab.

Alternatively, instead of starting with an empty prefab, you can just drag the Cube directly into the Prefabs folder, and a prefab will automatically be created and named after the original GameObject (Figure 4-27).

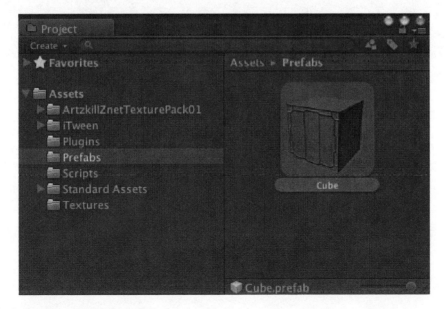

Figure 4-27. The Project View of the Cube prefab

You can now drag the prefab into the Hierarchy View every time you want to create a new cube that looks just like the original Cube GameObject. But instead of having multiple independent cubes in the scene, let's add some cubes as children of the existing cube. Drag the prefab directly onto the Cube in the Hierarchy View twice, and you'll now have two new cubes underneath Cube. In the Inspector View (Figure 4-28), you can see the new cubes are identical to Cube, featuring the same Components and Component properties. Let's name the new cubes child1 and child2 (by the way, this is a good time try out the Lock feature of the Inspector View, so you can inspect two GameObjects at the same time).

Figure 4-28. Editing the child cubes

As children of Cube, the positions of child1 and child2 displayed in the Inspector View are relative to the position of their parent, Cube. Which means if a child cube has position (0,0,0), it is in the exact same position as its parent. So let's set the positions of child1 and child2 to (2,0,0) and (-2,0,0). The two child cubes now are spaced out from their parent Cube like satellite cubes (Figure 4-29).

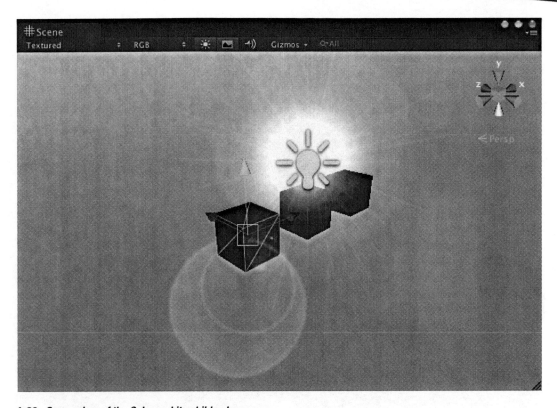

Figure 4-29. Scene view of the Cube and its child cubes

Before you click Play, change the FuguRotate script to the simple transform.Rotate call (Listing 4-11).
Now when you click Play, the main Cube rotates as before, and the child cubes follow around like
the spokes in a wheel. The child cubes also spin around their own axes since they're running their
own copies of the FuguRotate script (all three cubes would rotate around the same world origin if you
had supplied Space.World in the Transform.Rotate call).

Listing 4-11. FuguRotate.js Reverted to Rotation in Update

```
#pragma strict
var speed:float = 10.0; // controls how fast we rotate

function Start () {
        var object:GameObject = this.gameObject;
        Debug.Log("Start called on GameObject "+object.name);
        //iTween.RotateBy(gameObject, iTween.Hash("y", 1, "time", 2, "easeType", "easeInOutBack",
        "loopType", "pingPong"));
}

// rotate around the object's y axis
function Update () {
        //Debug.Log("Update called at time "+Time.time);
        transform.Rotate(Vector3.up*speed*Time.deltaTime);
}
```

Change the FuguRotate Speed property for child2 from 10 to 50, click Play, and you will see that cube spins faster than the others. You can easily make the same change in child1, but imagine if you had 50 cubes to change. That would be tedious! This is where the power of prefabs comes in. Select child2 and then invoke Apply Changes To Prefab in the GameObject menu (Figure 4-30).

Figure 4-30. Applying changes to a prefab

Now child1 is identical to child2 again (except for the name and position, which Unity reasonably assumes you don't want the same in every instance of the prefab). When you click Play, the child cubes are now spinning at the same faster speed.

Breaking Prefabs

But the main Cube is also spinning faster due to the updated rotation speed. If that isn't what you intended, you can change the Cube's Speed back to 10, and then to ensure that you don't propagate changes in the child cubes to the main Cube, you can select the main Cube and invoke Break Prefab Instance in the GameObject menu (Figure 4-31).

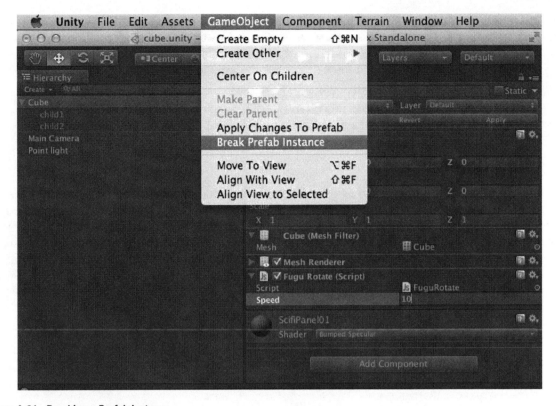

Figure 4-31. Breaking a Prefab Instance

Now the Cube no longer has a relation to the prefab, and any change to the child cubes will not be propagated to the Cube.

Explore Further

The scene has evolved from pretty and static to pretty and dynamic, merely with the addition of simple scripted movement. We'll jazz up the scene some more in the next chapter with animation and sound, but the major milestone you've reached at this point really is learning how to create, edit and debug scripts. From now until the end of the book, you'll be adding scripts, so get used to it!

Unity Manual

The "Building Scenes" section of the Unity Manual has two pages relevant to the work in this chapter—a description of "Prefabs" and an explanation of the "Component-Script Relationship."

The one new type of asset introduced in this chapter (besides prefabs) is the script. The page in the "Asset Import and Creation" section on "Using Scripts" introduces the basic concepts covered in our rotation script—creating a script, attaching it to a GameObject, printing to the Console View (using the print function instead of Debug.Log as you did), declaring a variable, and even applying a rotation in the Update function.

It's worth mentioning the page on "Transforms" again, since our rotation script is in the business of modifying Transforms. That page also describes the parent–child GameObject relationship, which technically is among Transforms, but since there's a one-to-one relationship between GameObjects and Transforms, it's less confusing to think of the linkage among GameObjects, as displayed in the Hierarchy view.

We dipped into one Advanced topic in this chapter—"Debugging." This section describes the Console View, the MonoDevelop debugger, and where to find Log files on your file system.

Scripting Reference

I've mentioned two of the three main pieces of official Unity documentation so far—the Unity Manual and the Reference Manual. The third piece is the Scripting Reference. This chapter presented our first foray into scripting, so everything in the "Scripting Overview" section of the Scripting Reference is worth reading at this point. The list of "Runtime Classes" illuminates the inheritance relationship among the Unity classes. After that, I recommend making frequent use of the search box on that page anytime you see anything in a script you don't recognize (or even if you do recognize it, if you haven't read its documentation).

Asset Store

We downloaded iTween from the Asset Store, but iTween users should also visit Bob Berkebile's official iTween web site with comprehensive documentation and demo projects on `http://itween.pixelplacement.com/`.

Although iTween is popular and one of the first tween packages for Unity, at this point several tween implementations are available (just search for "tween" in the Asset Store), including Holoville's HOTween, documented and also available on `http://holoville.com/hotween/`, and Prime31 Studio's GOKit, source code available on GitHub, `http://github.com/prime31/GoKit`.

Scripting

Although we're only working with JavaScript in this book, there's enough JavaScript and C# out in the Unity world that you should get comfortable with both. The book *Head First C#* by Andrew Stellman and Jennifer Greene is a great visual step-by-step introduction to C#.

And since C# was created by Microsoft as part of its .NET framework, the official C# documentation and other resources can be found by searching for C# on the Microsoft Developer Network (MSDN) at `http://msdn.microsoft.com/`.

While you're on MSDN, search also for .NET documentation, as the Unity scripting engine is implemented with Mono, which is an open source version of .NET. The official Mono web site is `http://mono-project.org/`

You probably don't need to worry about Boo, the other Unity scripting language (I have yet to see a Boo script in the wild), but if you're curious, the official Boo web site is `http://boo.codehaus.org/`.

Put two programmers together in a room, and if there's anything they'll fight about, it's coding conventions. My rule of thumb is to go along with the convention of the official language and framework that I'm coding in. It's a dull topic with fun names.

For example, Unity uses a combination of camel case and Pascal case in its capitalization rules (or camelCase and PascalCase, if we apply the conventions to themselves). You can look up "camel case" on Wikipedia.

Bracket placement is also a common source of contention. The convention I use here (and by Unity, at least when creating the template for new scripts) is called Egyptian style, according to Jeff Atwood (of StackExchange fame) on his popular blog Coding Horror (http://www.codinghorror.com/blog/2012/07/new-programming-jargon.html). The article also terms the practice of applying a standard prefix to class names "Smurf naming."

Chapter 5

Let's Dance! Animation and Sound

Of the three ways to move GameObjects in Unity, scripted control of the Transform Component was covered in the previous chapter, and physics will play a significant role in the bowling game example initiated in the next chapter. Scripted movement is ubiquitous. For example, even in the upcoming bowling game, which relies heavily on physics to control and simulate the bowling ball and its collision with the floor and bowling pins, the Camera following behavior is implemented by a script that modifies its Transform Component (much like the MouseOrbit script used in the cube scene). Not only that, every moving GameObject is reset between rolls and frames by restoring the values in its Transform Component.

Before proceeding on to that bowling game, you'll spend a little more time in this chapter building on the cube scene constructed so far, enhancing it with a dancing character animation to get a feel for Unity's animation support. And it wouldn't be a dance demo without music, so the scene will incorporate looping sound. It will still be a non-physical and only mildly interactive scene, but hopefully it will provide a pretty and entertaining way to introduce Unity's animation and audio support before delving into a lot of physics (a big topic, spanning two chapters) and even more scripting (a bigger topic, spanning the rest of this book).

Quality animations, particularly character animations, are not easy to create if you're not a professional. The same goes for music. Fortunately, there are plenty of music and character animation packs on the Unity Asset Store, many of them free, including the Skeletons Pack and General Music Set used in this chapter. Those assets are not included in the corresponding project on http://learnunity4.com/, but that project can be used as a starting point if you're just jumping in at this point and don't have the cube scene constructed from the previous chapter.

Import the Skeletons Pack

As demonstrated in the previous chapter, you can search the Asset Store from within the Project View. Type "skeleton" in the search field, and the skeleton asset from the Skeletons Pack will show up in the Free Assets results (Figure 5-1).

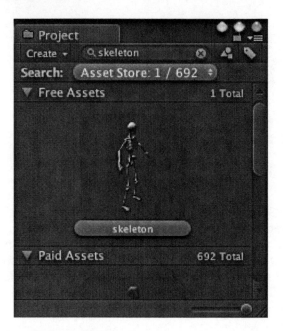

Figure 5-1. The Project View search results for the Skeletons Pack

> **Tip**   Search terms in the Project View are matched against individual assets already imported in the project and available for import from the Asset Store, but the Asset Store portion of the search can be disabled in the Unity Preferences.

Select the skeleton asset and confirm in the Inspector View that the package is indeed the Skeleton Pack (Figure 5-2). You can click the Import package button to import the Skeleton Pack immediately, or you can click the Open Asset Store button to see the full description in the Asset Store window first and import the package from there.

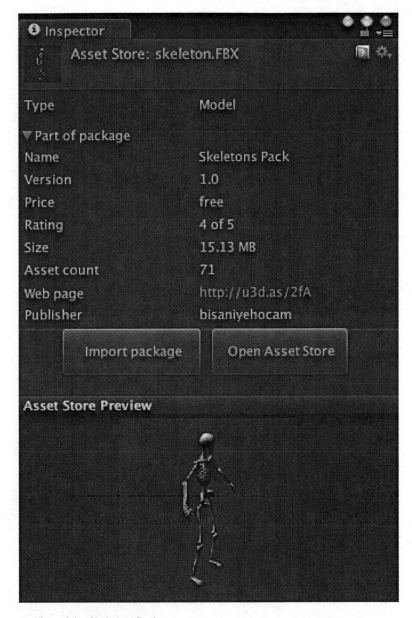

Figure 5-2. The Inspector View of the Skeletons Pack

However you choose to import the Skeletons Pack, the installation will add a SkeletonData folder in the Project View along with several prefabs in the Prefabs folder (Figure 5-3).

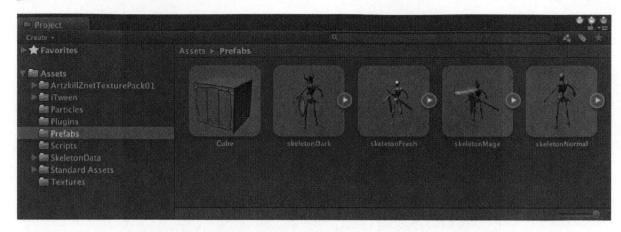

Figure 5-3. The Project View of the Skeletons Pack prefabs

Add a Skeleton

The four prefabs installed by the Skeletons Pack all have the same skeleton but sport different gear, such as a sword and shield. However, it turns out the prefabs with armed skeletons look like they're chopping their own limbs off when dancing, so let's just stick with the skeletonNormal prefab, which has just the bare bones (ha!) skeleton. Add an instance of the skeletonNormal prefab to the scene by dragging that prefab into the Hierarchy View (Figure 5-4).

Figure 5-4. The cube scene with the skeleton active and the Cubes deactivated

The skeletonNormal GameObject has an Animation Component that references the animation data of the skeleton. skeletonNormal also has two child GameObjects. One, named Bip01, is actually a hierarchy of GameObjects that represents the bones of the skeleton. As the skeleton moves, so does the arm, and any hand movement is relative to the arm, and so on. The skeleton hierarchy is reminiscent of the "Dem Bones" song—"The thigh bone's connected to the hip bone . . ."

The other child GameObject, skeleton, is a GameObject with a SkinnedMeshRenderer Component. SkinnedMeshRenderer, like MeshRendererer, is a subclass of Renderer. However, the SkinnedMeshRenderer Component renders the Mesh that wraps around the skeleton and follows its joints as they move. The Mesh essentially forms the skin around a skeleton, so the process of mapping such a Mesh to a skeleton is often called *skinning*.

The skeletonNormal GameObject also contains a couple of particle effects, implemented with ParticleEmitter Components. Particle effects consist of many tiny animated primitives and are great for creating flames, explosions, smoke, or any kind of sparkly effects.

> **Note**   The particle effects included in the Skeletons Pack work with Unity's Legacy particle system, not the newer Shuriken particle system introduced in Unity 3.5. The Legacy system uses the ParticleEmitter Component, while Shuriken uses the ParticleSystem Component.

Hide the Cubes

This scene is all about the dancing skeleton, so you can dispense with the Cubes that featured in the previous two chapters. Instead of deleting the Cubes from the scene (by selecting them and invoking Delete from the Edit menu or using the Command+Delete shortcut), they can be made invisible, out of sight and out of mind, by deactivating them. Select the parent Cube in the Hierarchy View, uncheck the top-left check box in the Inspector View, and the entire tree of Cubes in the Hierarchy View is now grayed out to indicate they are inactive (Figure 5-4).

All the child Cubes are effectively inactive because the parent's active status overrides the children's. In other words, a GameObject is *really* active only if it's marked as active and its parent is marked as active and its parent's parent is marked as active, and so on. Any inactive GameObject has its Components effectively disabled. Its Renderer Component no longer renders, its Collider Component no longer collides, and any attached scripts do not have their callbacks called, with the exception of OnEnable and OnDisable.

Orbit the Skeleton

Although the Cubes are deactivated, the MouseOrbit script on the Main Camera still has the main Cube as its target. The Main Camera should now orbit the skeleton, so select the Main Camera in the Inspector View and then drag the skeletonNormal GameObject from the Hierarchy View into the Target field of the MouseOrbit script (Figure 5-5).

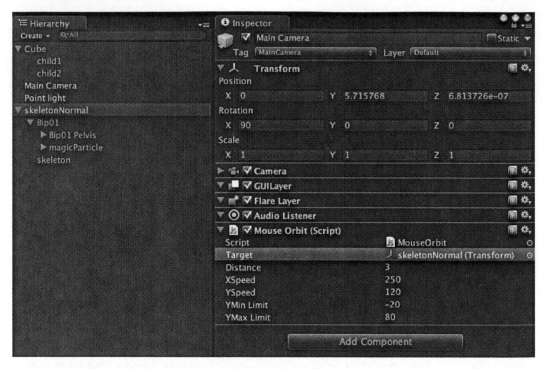

Figure 5-5. The MouseOrbit script on the Main Camera with a skeleton target

Now when you click Play, the Main Camera orbits the skeleton as you move the mouse (Figure 5-6). As a bonus, since the skeleton prefab includes a particle effect, the skeleton appears to be standing amid a sparkly haze.

Figure 5-6. The Game View of an idle skeleton

Make the Skeleton Dance

Right now the skeleton just shuffles around a little instead of dancing. If you select the skeletonNormal GameObject and examine it in the Inspector View, you can see the GameObject has an Animation Component with a field that references an "idle" AnimationClip (Figure 5-7).

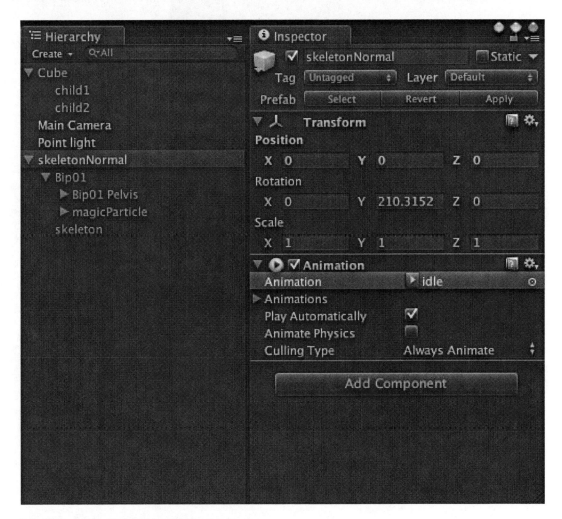

Figure 5-7. Changing the skeleton's position and animation

Notice also that the Play Automatically checkbox is checked, which is why the animation runs as soon as you click Play. This option would be unchecked if the animation is intended to be initiated by a script at some time during the game.

To replace the idle AnimationClip with a dancing AnimationClip, click the circle to the right of "idle" to bring up the AnimationClip selection list (Figure 5-8). Select the AnimationClip named "dance."

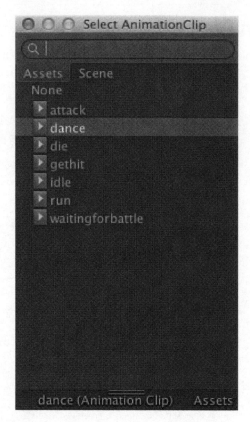

Figure 5-8. *An AnimationClip selection list*

Now when you click Play, the skeleton dances! (Figure 5-9).

Figure 5-9. The dancing skeleton

Make the Skeleton Dance Forever

If you let the skeleton dance for a while, it eventually stops when the AnimationClip ends. But the AnimationClip can be set to loop. In the Inspector View of the skeletonNormal GameObject, click the reference to the dance AnimationClip in the Animation Component. The Project View will show the selected the AnimationClip and associated skeleton Mesh along with the skeleton's other AnimationClips (Figure 5-10).

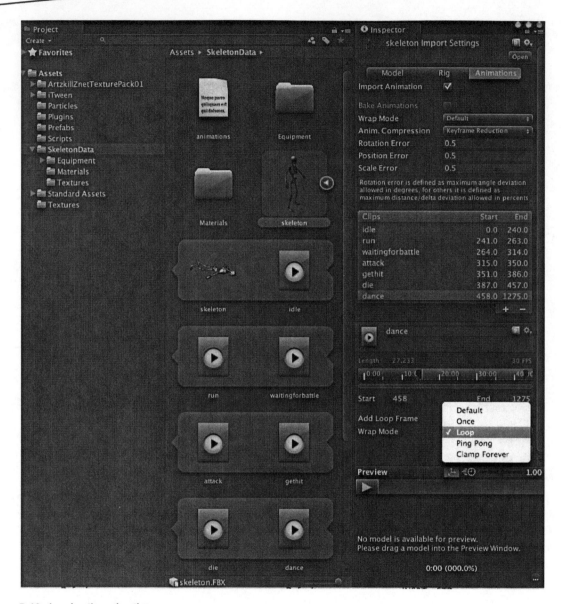

Figure 5-10. Looping the animation

The Inspector View displays a single stretch of animation data that's split into the various AnimationClips. Select the dance clip in that list, and below, the Wrap Mode will display as Default. Change the Wrap Mode to Loop and click the Apply button (just below the Wrap Mode field).

Now when you click Play again, the skeleton will dance, and dance, and dance.

Note This skeleton uses Unity's Legacy animation system. You can verify this by clicking the Rig button shown in Figure 5-10 and see that the Legacy check box is checked. Unity 4 introduced a new animation system called Mecanim, which, among other features, allows you to apply an animation to different skeletons (or avatars, as they are called in Mecanim).

Watch the Hips

Now that the skeleton is dancing properly, let's improve the Main Camera view of the character. Notice how you seem to be looking at the character's feet? That's because the origin (or pivot point, as 3D modelers may know it) of the character is typically at the feet instead of the center of the model. This convention makes it easier to position the character so that its feet are correctly placed on the floor or ground.

One way to have the Main Camera orbit around the midsection of the skeleton is to create a new GameObject for the MouseOrbit target and make it a child of the skeletonNormal GameObject. But skeletonNormal already has child GameObjects representing the bones of the skeleton. In fact, the hip bone, or rather the GameObject named Bip01 Pelvis, is perfect for the MouseOrbit target. Drag the Bip01 Pelvis GameObject into the MouseOrbit Target field and shorten the distance to 2 so that the skeleton fills up more of the screen when you play (Figure 5-11). Then when you click Play, in the Game View you'll be looking at and orbiting the skeleton's hips (Figure 5-12).

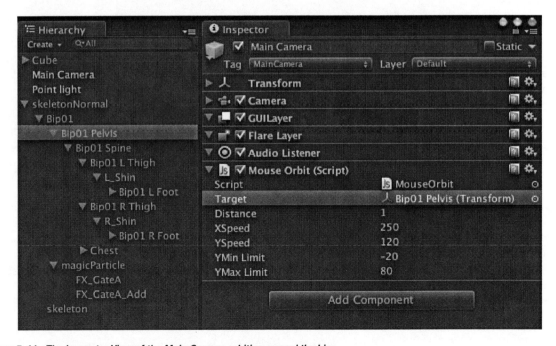

Figure 5-11. The Inspector View of the Main Camera orbiting around the hips

Figure 5-12. The Game View with the Main Camera looking at the hips

By the way, you may have noticed that when you drag a GameObject into the Target field of the MouseOrbit script, the Inspector View appends (Transform) to the displayed GameObject name. If you examine the MouseOrbit script, you can see that the target variable is indeed declared to be of type Transform. Unity's drag-and-drop system conveniently allows you to drag a GameObject from the Hierarchy View into a field of type Transform and automatically assigns the Transform Component of the GameObject to the variable.

Other Components of a GameObject can be used as public variable types, too. But I like to keep the GameObject-Component relationship clear in my own scripts, so I stick to declaring variables as GameObjects in these situations and access the Components through the GameObjects.

Add a Dance Floor

The skeleton looks kind of strange dancing in the sky, so let's give it a floor to dance on. You could make another Cube and scale it, but there's a more suitable primitive GameObject that you can use—a Plane. Like the Cube, you can make a Plane from the Create submenu of the GameObject menu on the menu bar. But this time, try the Create button on the top left of the Hierarchy View (Figure 5-13).

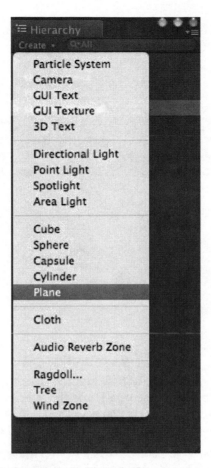

Figure 5-13. Creating a Plane using the Create menu in the Hierarchy View

Note that all the items in the Create menu are available in the GameObject menu on the menu bar, but not all the items that can be created from the GameObject menu are available in the Hierarchy View Create menu.

Now a Plane is listed in the Hierarchy View and displayed in the Scene View (Figure 5-14). A Plane is like a flat Cube—it has a top and bottom but no sides and no height. If we change its x and z scale in its Transform Component, the Plane will stretch out, but changing the y scale (height) makes no difference.

Figure 5-14. The Scene View of the new Plane

Remember, the skeleton position was set to (0,0,0), and the skeleton's origin is at the bottom, coinciding with the skeleton's feet. Select the new Plane that's now shown in the Hierarchy View, and then, in the Inspector View, set the Plane's position also to (0,0,0), so that the floor is placed at the skeleton's feet. Specifically, the y positions (height) of the feet and floor that have to match up.

That's a pretty bland-looking floor, which could benefit from a Material with a texture. The Free Artskillz Texture Pack is already imported and used for the Cube, so you might just as well use it here for the floor. With the cubes, you just dragged a texture onto the Cube in the Hierarchy View and then modified the resulting Material in the Inspector View.

This time around, go straight to the Inspector View of the Plane (Figure 5-15) and change its shader to Bumped Specular. Then drag a main texture and its associated bump (normal map) texture from the Free Artskillz Texture Pack (in the figure, I've chosen the Floor03 and Floor03_n textures from the Fantasy folder of the pack).

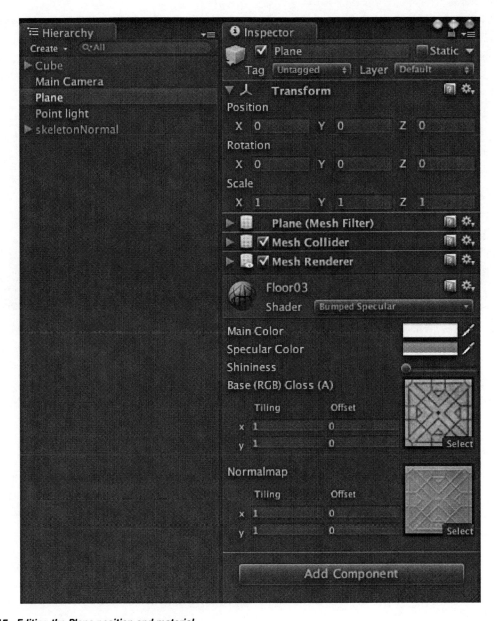

Figure 5-15. *Editing the Plane position and material*

Now when you click Play, the skeleton is dancing on a floor! (Figure 5-16).

Figure 5-16.   The skeleton dancing on a textured Plane

Add a Shadow (Pro)

One of the Light Component properties discussed in Chapter 3 is Shadow Type. Now that the scene has a floor that shadows can be cast on, let's try out this feature.

> **Note**   Dynamic shadows (shadows that move according to the shadow caster's movement) is a Unity Pro and Unity iOS Pro feature, so if you're not running Unity Pro right now, you can still follow along with this exercise, but you won't see the intended shadow.

Select the Point Light (either in the Hierarchy View or Scene View), and in the Inspector View (Figure 5-17), change the Shadow Type from None to Soft Shadows. This provides shadows with a nice soft fuzzy border (the *penumbra* of the shadow), which looks better than the sharp borders of Hard Shadows.

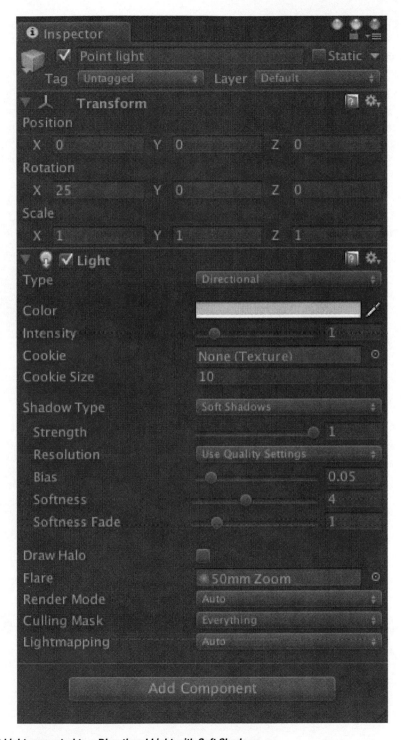

Figure 5-17. A Point Light converted to a Directional Light with Soft Shadows

Now you should change the Type from Point Light to Directional Light. Point Lights can cast shadows, but only Hard Shadows, and only when rendering in Deferred Mode, which isn't available in Unity iOS. Actually, Soft Shadows aren't available in Unity iOS at all, but they look so good, let's try them out here.

Whereas a Point Light radiates light in all directions from a position, a Directional Light is treated as if it were infinitely far away, and thus its position doesn't matter but its rotation does. So in the Transform Component, you can enter 0,0,0 for the position (which doesn't really matter for a Directional Light, but it looks cleaner than having an arbitrary position), and 25,0,0 for the rotation, indicating the Light is rotated 25 degrees around the x axis. In other words, the Light is looking down 25 degrees from horizontal.

Instead of entering a rotation, you could manually rotate the Light in the Scene View (Figure 5-18) by selecting the Light, clicking the Rotate tool in the button bar on the top left of the Unity Editor (third button from the left), and then dragging the circle representing x-axis rotation on the Light.

Figure 5-18. Rotating a Directional Light in the Scene View

There's no reason to use the Move tool (second button from the left on the button bar), since the position of a Directional Light doesn't matter, but it can help visualize what the Light is illuminating if you move it up and away so that it's obviously pointing at the skeleton.

> **Tip**   You can aim a Directional or Spot Light (or anything that can be aimed) in the same way you aimed the Main Camera at the Cube in Chapter 3. In this case, you would select the skeleton, press the F key to Frame Selected, click the leftmost button on the top left toolbar to enter the Hand tool mode in the Scene View, and then in the Scene View alt+click+drag until the Scene View camera is pointing the way you want the Light to point. Then select the Point Light and invoke Align to View from the GameObject menu.

If you click Play at this point, you should see a shadow, but one with room for improvement, even with the Strength set to 1. Unity uses a technique called *shadow maps* for generating shadows, where the shadow quality is dependent on the resolution of the shadow maps. The default setting for the shadow map resolution in the Light Component is Use Quality Settings, which you can override in the Inspector View. But let's go to the Quality Settings, instead, by selecting Project Settings ➤ Quality from the Edit menu (Figure 5-19).

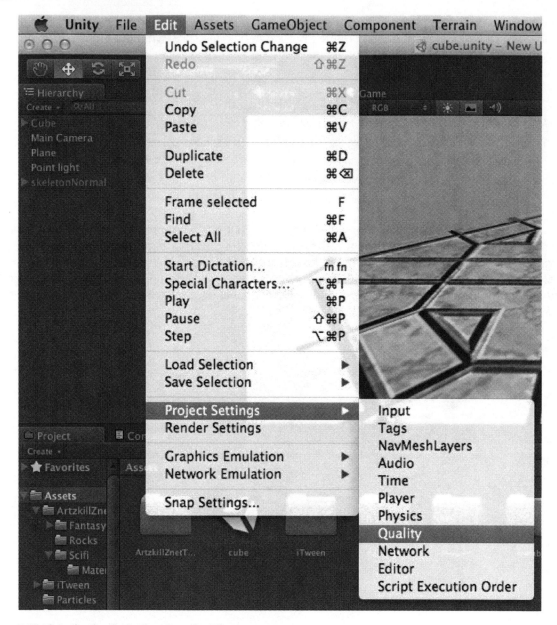

Figure 5-19. Selecting Quality Settings from the Edit menu

The Quality Settings manager appears in the Inspector View (Figure 5-20), displaying a list of Quality Settings and the selected Quality Setting for each build platform. The default Quality Setting desktop platforms is Good. Select that line in the platform-settings table so the individual settings for Good is displayed. The Shadow settings, in particular, control the shadow quality. So change the Shadow Resolution to Very High Resolution and also lower the Shadow Distance to 10, since shorter shadow distances lead to better shadow resolution (but too short, and the shadow won't render).

Figure 5-20. The adjusted Quality Settings for Shadows

Now when you click Play, you have a dancing shadow that should look pretty good! (Figure 5-21).

Figure 5-21. *The Game View of the skeleton with a shadow*

Add Music

No dance demo would be complete without music. Fortunately, there's plenty of free music available in the Asset Store. One music package I've used frequently is Gianmarco Leone's General Music Set. If you enter "general music" in the Project View search field, all of the AudioClips in that package show up in the results (Figure 5-22). Click any one of them, and then import the package from the Inspector View.

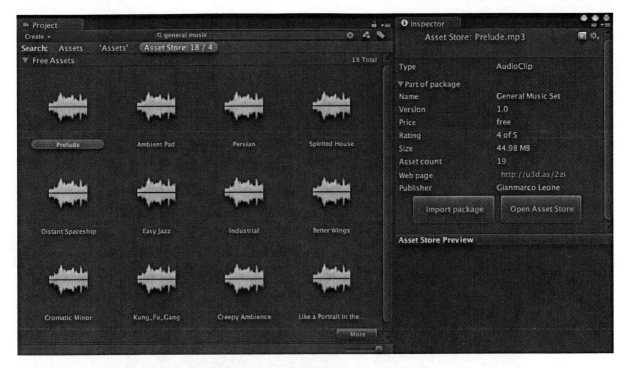

Figure 5-22. *Searching for the General Music Set in the Asset Store*

After the AudioClips install in the Project View (Figure 5-23), select the AudioClip named Caribbean Isle. I think it's got a nice beat, and you can dance to it. But you can decide for yourself by previewing the audio. In the Inspector View (Figure 5-24), click the Play button at the bottom, above the stereo waveform display, to listen to the AudioClip. While you're there, since this AudioClip will be used essentially as background music, not a sound effect with a position, uncheck the 3D Sound checkbox and click the Apply button to reimport the sound.

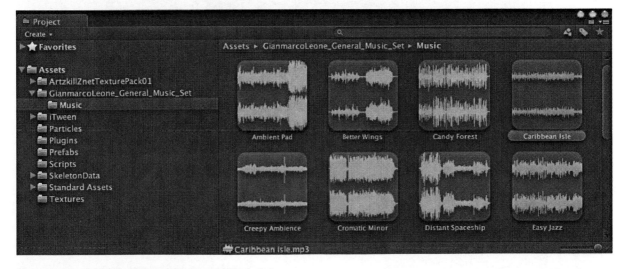

Figure 5-23. *The Project View of the General Music Set*

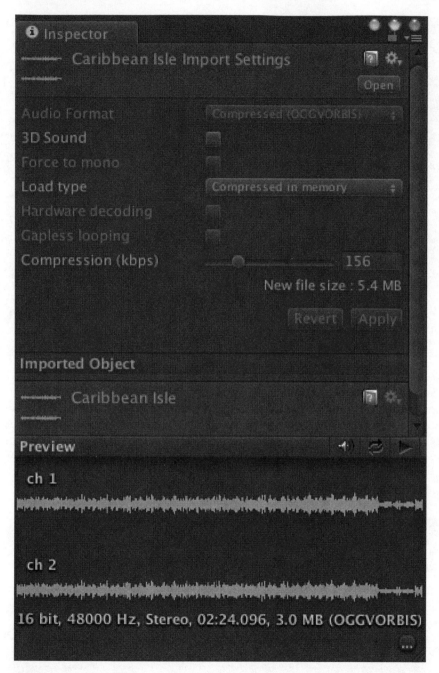

Figure 5-24. The Inspector View of an AudioClip

Now you're ready to add the AudioClip to the scene. Simply drag the AudioClip from the Project View into the Hierarchy View, and a same-named GameObject will automatically be created (Figure 5-25).

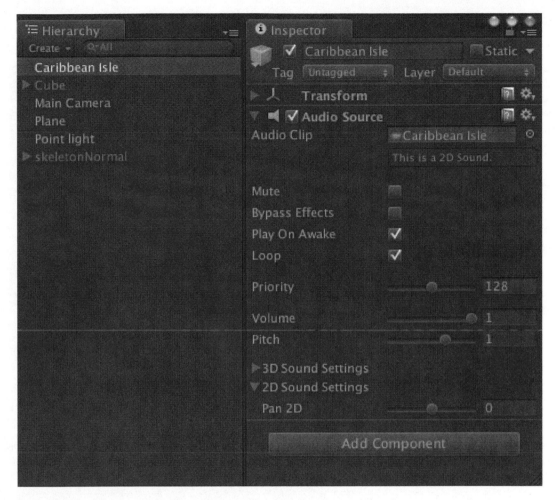

Figure 5-25. Audio in the scene

Select the Caribbean Isle GameObject and you will see in the Inspector View that the it has an AudioSource Component. Among its properties is a reference to the Caribbean Isle AudioClip (described as a 2D sound since you unchecked its 3D sound checkbox), and a Play On Awake checkbox. That specifies the sound will start playing as soon as the scene starts playing. You should check the Loop checkbox too, so the song will keep playing over and over, just like the dancing animation.

Now when you click Play, you have a real music dance party!

Explore Further

Thus ends our dalliance with dancing skeletons. For the rest of this book, you'll be concentrating on developing a bowling game with mostly physics-based motion. But you should already feel a sense of accomplishment, having spent the past three chapters evolving a simple static cube scene into a musical dancing skeleton scene, complete with fancy graphics features like particle effects and dynamic shadows. But fancy features tend to be expensive features in terms of performance, so use them judiciously!

Unity Manual

The "Asset Import and Creation" section covers the two new types of assets introduced in this chapter: audio and animation. The page titled "Audio Files" lists the audio formats recognized by Unity and describes the AudioClip asset that results from importing an audio file.In earlier chapters, we just dipped out toes into the "Creating Gameplay" section of the Unity Manual, but now we've deeper end, adding content described in the pages "Particles," "Legacy Animation System," and "Sound." Also, the "Mecanim Animation System" is the future of Unity animation, so it's worthwhile to read up on that.

Dynamic shadows is a big topic. The "Advanced" section of the Unity Manual has an extensive treatment on "Shadows in Unity", which covers "Directional Shadows," "Troubleshooting Shadows," and "Shadow Size Computation."

Reference Manual

The "Animation Components" section of the Reference Manual has pages on the "Animation" Component and "Animation Clip" asset used by the Legacy animation system. This section also includes several pages on Components used in the new Mecanim animation system.

The "Audio" section lists the audio Components need to add music to the dancing scene constructed in this chapter: "AudioListener" (normally automatically attached to the Main Camera) and "AudioSource" (attached to the sound source). In addition, the section lists "Audio Filter Components (PRO Only)" that can add effects like echo, for example.

The "Effects" section has a page on the new Shuriken particle system and multiple pages on the Legacy particle system.

The Reference Manual also documents the various Settings Managers, including the one for "Quality Settings," which you used to adjust your shadow quality, but it also affects other visual quality elements, such as lighting and particles.

Asset Store

The Asset Store not only offers a lot of music in the Audio category, much of it free, but also provides scripts for playing music. If you want to play more than one song in your dance scene, you could write a script that plays a fixed or random sequence of songs, using the Unity functions defined in the AudioSource class (to play and stop music) and AudioListener class (to control the volume). But it's easier to just download, for example, the Free Jukebox script from the Asset Store (or Jukebox Pro if you're willing to part with a few dollars).

Computer Graphics

I mentioned the book *Real-Time Rendering* at the end of Chapter 3, and it merits a recommendation again for the computer graphics topics you encountered in this chapter: animation, particle effects, and dynamic shadows. There are many books just on character animation, including those on the content-creation side for professional animators, such as George Maestri's *Digital Character Animation*.

Chapter 6

Let's Roll! Physics and Controls

At last, we're ready to begin the main Unity project for this book, a bowling game in the style of HyperBowl, an arcade/attraction game I worked on over ten years ago and ported to Unity just a few years ago. HyperBowl has a unique be-the-ball gameplay where the player constantly rolls the ball around a 3D environment to reach the pins. The bowling game constructed in this book will be much simpler but feature the same style of control.

Even a simple bowling game like this one is a significant project. It will incorporate physics, input handling, camera control, collision sounds, game rules, a score display, and a start/pause menu. And that's even before performing any adaptation for iOS. This chapter just focuses on getting a ball to roll around and will require some physics setup but only a single script for the ball control.

The script is available in the project for this chapter on `http://learnunity4.com/` But it's a fairly simple script and developed incrementally throughout this chapter, so it's best to follow along, implementing it from scratch.

Make a New Scene

The dance scene in the previous chapter was really a modification of the original cube scene we started with in Chapter 3, so we didn't have create the entire scene from scratch again. The skybox, light and floor would be useful in the bowling game, so by the same token we could continue modifying the cube scene and deactivate or remove the skeleton and music before adding content for the bowling game. But there's no rule saying we can have only one scene in a project, so let's leave the cube/dance scene intact and just make a copy of it to use as the beginnings of the bowling scene.

From the previous chapter, you should have the Unity Editor still open to the dance (cube) scene. The quickest way to start working with a copy of this scene is to select Save Scene As in the File menu (Figure 6-1).

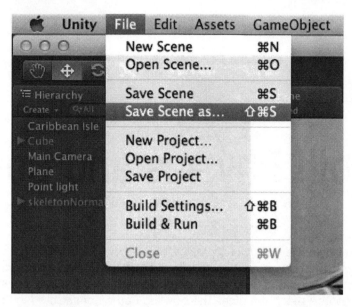

Figure 6-1. *Saving the scene as a new scene*

This will be a bowling scene, so let's name it "bowl" (Figure 6-2).

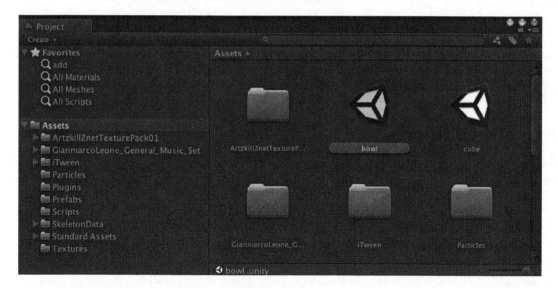

Figure 6-2. *The bowl scene saved at the top level of Assets*

> **Note**   To be consistent with the asset organization system, scenes would go into a Scenes folder, but if
> I have just one or a few scenes, I often just leave them saved at the top level of the Asset folder.

Instead of using Save Scene As, you could have duplicated the scene by selecting it in the Project View and invoking Duplicate from the Edit menu (or the keyboard shortcut Command+D), then renamed the new scene and then switched to it by double-clicking the scene file.

Delete GameObjects

Now you can clean out anything from the scene that's not needed for bowling without fear of mangling the dance scene. So instead of deactivating the skeleton, just delete it by selecting the skeleton GameObject in the Hierarchy View and using the Delete command from the Edit menu (or the Command+Delete keyboard shortcut). Also delete the Cube hierarchy and Caribbean Isle GameObject (Figure 6-3), as cubes and music won't be necessary for bowling, either.

Figure 6-3. Deleting unneeded GameObjects from the bowling scene

Adjust the Light

Once again, a little housekeeping is in order before starting work on a new the scene. Let's start with the color of the Light. Beginning with white lights until all the assets are in the scene allows you to see everything in its full original colors. So let's change the Light color to white by clicking in its Color field and selecting white in the color chooser (Figure 6-4).

Figure 6-4. Set the Light color to white

Also, since the Point Light was actually changed to a Directional Light in the previous chapter to support soft shadows (for Unity Pro users), the name "Point Light" is misleading. This is a good time to change its name to just "Light," which will keep your options open if you want to change its type again, later.

Retile the Floor

The shiny patterned floor from the dance scene doesn't look much like a bowling lane, so let's change its appearance. This is an opportunity to try out Unity's support for procedural materials, which is based on Allegorithmic's Substance technology. Procedural materials use textures generated from algorithms instead of image files. This allows a lot of variation in the materials by tweaking the texture-generation parameters and also potentially offers space savings, since the procedural materials don't require loading image files as textures.

Let's try out a procedural material for the floor. Search for "substance" in the Asset Store window (the Project View searches among individual assets, so in this case it won't bring up any Asset Store results). A number of free Substance packages from Allegorithmic will appear in the Asset Store window (Figure 6-5).

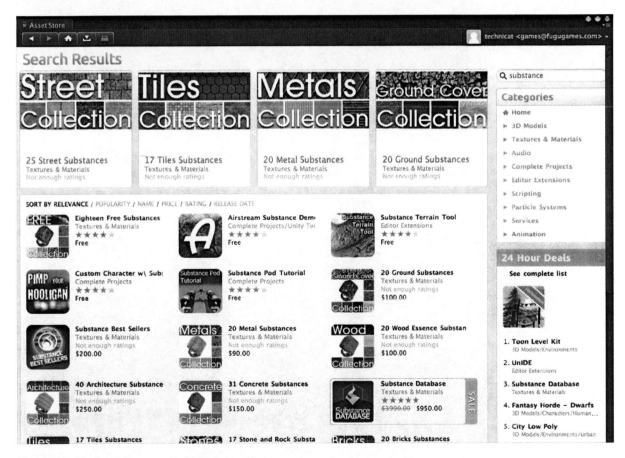

Figure 6-5. The Asset Store results for "substance"

The package we want is Eighteen Free Substances. Select and import that package, and 18 Substance archives (files with the .sbsar extension) will show up in the Project View in a Substances_Free folder (Figure 6-6). The Substance file that will provide a wood floor look is Wood_Planks_01, listed at the end.

Figure 6-6. *The Project View of the 18 Free Substances package*

Each Substance archive contains one or more ProceduralMaterial assets (`ProceduralMaterial` is a subclass of `Material`) and their supporting textures and scripts. Clicking the right arrow of the Wood_Planks_01 icon will change it to a left arrow and expand to show the ProceduralMaterial of Wood_Planks_01 followed by its associated textures (Figure 6-7).

Figure 6-7. *An expanded view of the Wood_Planks_01 Substance archive*

The wood planks ProceduralMaterial looks like a decent candidate for a bowling lane floor (at least better than our fantasy and sci-fi textures), so drag the wood planks ProceduralMaterial (not the archive) to the Plane in the Hierarchy View. You can see in the Scene View that the Plane now has wood planks (Figure 6-8).

Figure 6-8. The Plane with the Wood_Planks_01 procedural material

The planks look overly large, but you can adjust how the textures (there's a main texture and a normal map texture) stretch across the Plane by editing the UV scale fields of the textures. Select the Plane in the Hierarchy View, and in the Inspector View set the x and y Tiling values of both textures to 5 instead of 1 (Figure 6-9).

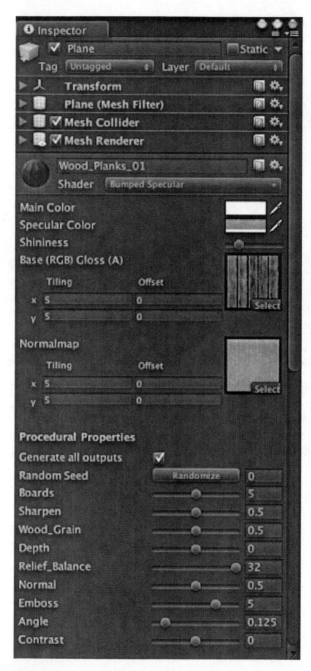

Figure 6-9. *The Inspector View of the Plane with a procedural material*

Now the textures are tiled five times, where before you just had one (Figure 6-10). In the Inspector View, notice that you have a number of procedural properties you can play with to vary the appearance of the generated textures.

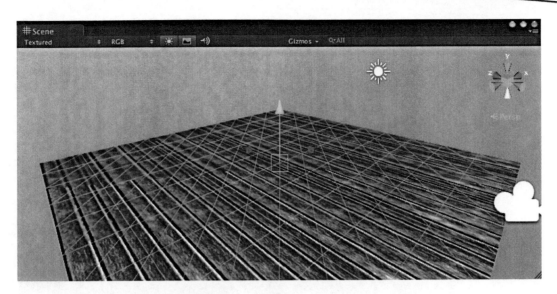

Figure 6-10. The Plane with its Tiling values set to 5

And as with the Light, while you have the Inspector View up, this is a good time to change the name in the top text field and rename the Plane to Floor, to make its function more obvious.

Reset the Camera

The MouseOrbit script attached to the Main Camera isn't suitable for the bowling game, so you can disable that script. Better yet, remove the script entirely from the Main Camera by selecting the Main Camera in the Hierarchy View, and then in the Inspector View, right-click the MouseOrbit component and select Remove Component (Figure 6-11).

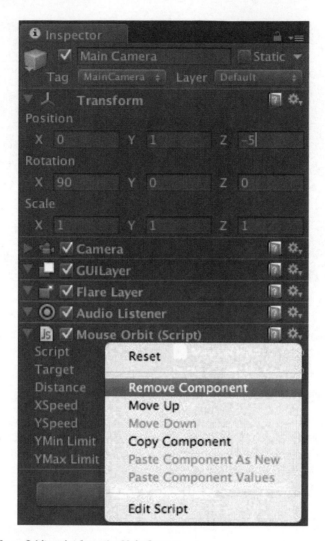

Figure 6-11. *Removing the MouseOrbit script from the Main Camera*

While you're at it, set the Main Camera position to (0,1,-5) and its rotation to (0,0,0). Now you should be looking at a nice floor and sky and not much else (Figure 6-12).

Figure 6-12. *The Game View with a fixed Main Camera*

Make a Ball

Now the scene has a Skybox, Light, Flare, and a Floor, and a Main Camera with a fixed viewpoint. It's time to add the bowling ball.

Make a Sphere

Two primitive GameObjects have been used so far in this book: Plane and Cube. For a ball, there's another primitive that's perfect: Sphere. Like Plane and Cube, Sphere can be selected from the Create submenu of the GameObject menu on the menu bar, but a Sphere can also be instantiated using the Create button on the top left of the Hierarchy View (Figure 6-13).

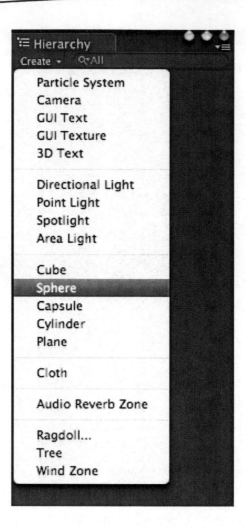

Figure 6-13. Creating a ball

After selecting Sphere from the Create menu, a new GameObject named Sphere should be listed in the Hierarchy View. Select the Sphere GameObject in the Hierarchy View so it can be examined in the Inspector View (Figure 6-14).

Figure 6-14. The Inspector View of the Ball

Like the Cube and Plane primitives, the Sphere GameObject has a MeshFilter Component and a MeshRenderer Component, plus a Collider Component that is of the same shape as the primitive (in this case, a SphereCollider). First, in the spirit of meticulously naming GameObjects, change the name of the Sphere to Ball so it's clear that this GameObject is the bowling ball. Then set the Ball position to (0,1,0), which places the center of the Ball 1 m above the Floor. Since the radius of the ball is 0.5 meters (the SphereCollider Radius shown in Figure 6-14 is a good hint), this gives some clearance between the Ball and Floor. And when you click Play, the Ball will hang in the air above the Floor (Figure 6-15).

Figure 6-15. The Ball in the air

This is as expected, of course. Just like everything else created so far—the floor, cubes, even the dancing character—the Ball will go or stay where it's told.

Make It Fall

For the Ball to fall in response to gravity and respond to other forces, the Ball must be made physical. A GameObject is made physical by addding a Rigidbody Component.

> **Note**   Most game physics is known as *rigid body simulation*, which is pretty much what it sounds like—simulating how hard objects with nonchanging shapes react to forces and collision. A bowling ball is perfect for rigid body simulation. A blob of tapioca pudding, on the other hand, is not.

To add a Rigidbody Component to the Ball, select the Ball in the Hierarchy View, and then in the Component menu on the menu bar, choose the Physics submenu, then Rigidbody (Figure 6-16). You could also click the Add Component button on the bottom of the Inspector View to add a Rigidbody Component.

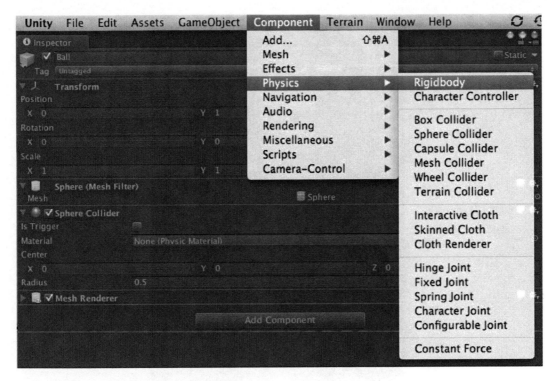

Figure 6-16. Adding a Rigidbody Component to the Ball

The Inspector View now shows a Rigidbody Component attached to the Ball (Figure 6-17).

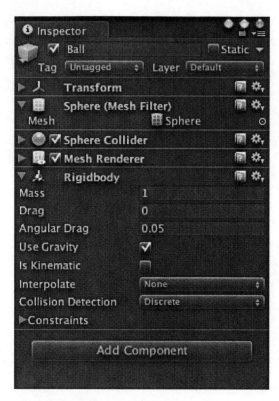

Figure 6-17. The Inspector View of the Ball with a Rigidbody Component

Most of the Rigidbody properties can be used with their default values, but a Mass of 1 kilogram is a bit light for a bowling ball. Let's set it to 5, as 5 kg is in the ballpark for a bowling ball weight.

The minimal values for Drag (air resistance) and Angular Drag (the drag experienced from rotating) are fine. There's no reason to increase drag unless, say you're bowling underwater.

The Use Gravity property specifies that the Ball will respond to gravitational force. If the checkbox is not checked, then the Ball will behave as if it were in a zero-G environment (Bowling in Space!).

The Is Kinematic property is used for GameObjects that move and collide but don't respond to forces (e.g., an elevator platform). Any GameObject with a Collider Component that is going to move should also have a Rigidbody Component attached, and if the movement is not from physics but from scripting or animation, then it should be a Kinematic Rigidbody.

> **Note**   A GameObject that is a Kinematic Rigidbody should not be moved by directly changing its Transform Component, as that results in horrible performance. Instead, it should be moved by calling the `Rigidbody.MovePosition` and `Rigidbody.MoveRotation` functions on the GameObject's Rigidbody Component.

The Interpolation property allows smoothing of the GameObject's movement (at a computational cost).

Likewise, the Collision Detection property provides improved collision detection, in particular for fast-moving GameObjects (again, at a computational cost).

The Constraints property can limit how the GameObject can move in response to forces. For example, a GameObject can be limited to movement along one plane or even just one direction.

With the Rigidbody Component properties appropriately set, click Play again. Now the Ball drops, and even better, it lands on the Floor! (Figure 6-18).

Figure 6-18. The Game View of the Ball landing on the Floor

The default gravitational force, by the way, is standard Earth gravity, approximately 9.8 m/s^2. This can be customized in the PhysicsManager (Figure 6-19), available under the Project Settings submenu of the Edit menu.

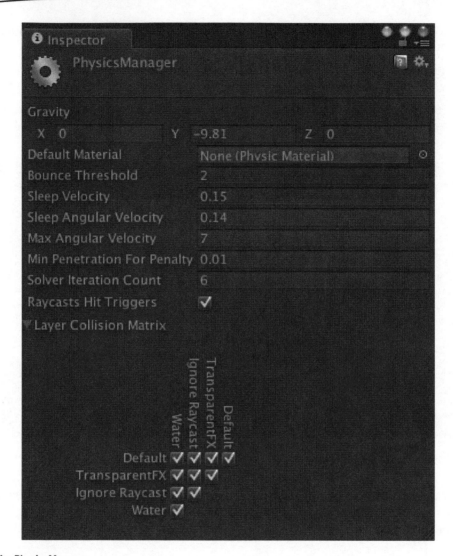

Figure 6-19. The PhysicsManager

The Gravity property of the PhysicsManager is a vector (specifically, a Vector3 if you access the PhysicsManager from a script), with the only nonzero value in the y direction (and negative, so the force is downward). Thus, not only could you change the gravitational force to, say, that of the Moon, you could even change its direction! If you change the y value from -9.81 to 9.81, the ball will fall upward, and if you change the gravitational vector from (0,-9.81,0) to (1,0,0), the Ball will fall sideways at 1 m/s^2. And if you want weightlessness, a gravitational force of (0,0,0) will do the trick.

Customize Collision

A Collider Component provide a GameObject with a collision shape. If you examine the Ball and Floor in the Inspector View, you'll see each has a Collider Component that was automatically attached and has a shape matching its Mesh. The Floor has a MeshCollider Component, which always matches the GameObject's Mesh, and the Ball has a SphereCollider Component, which always has a spherical shape. When you select the Ball or Floor, the Scene View highlights not only the Mesh of the GameObject but also the shape of its Collider Component. You can toggle the display of Collider gizmos using the Gizmos menu in the Scene View.

There is almost a one-to-one correspondence among primitive GameObjects and primitive colliders (by "primitive" I mean it's built in to Unity and also that the shape is simple, which is a good thing for performance). There are exceptions, though. For example, there is a primitive Cylinder GameObject that you can create from the GameObject menu but no available Collider in the shape of a cylinder. Instead, if you create a Cylinder, it automatically uses a CapsuleCollider Component.

The MeshCollider is a special case. Automatically following the shape of the associated Mesh sounds good, but it's only a good idea for static (i.e., nonmoving) GameObjects. Anything that is moving or might move should have a primitive collider or an aggregation of primitive colliders (more about that in the next chapter). A MeshCollider also has to have its Convex property (checkbox) enabled if it's to collide with other Mesh Colliders.

PhysicMaterials

Collider Components dictate at what point two GameObjects will collide, but what actually happens when the collision is detected? Does one GameObject bounce off the other, and if so, by how much? Will the Ball slide or roll along the floor or just stick to it? That's where the Material property of a Collider Component comes in. The property name is a little bit misleading, as the Material of a Collider Component isn't the same Material used with MeshRenderer Components to determine the appearance of a Mesh surface. Instead, a Collider Component uses a PhysicMaterial to determine the collision properties of the the collision surface. The spelling is a little odd, but I think of a PhysicMaterial as a *physics material* or *physical material*.

> **Note** Unlike ProceduralMaterial, the `PhysicMaterial` class is not a subclass of `Material`.

The Material property for Collider Components defaults to the Default Material property in the PhysicsManager (Figure 6-19), which is None. To customize its collision behavior, a Collider Component has to have a PhysicMaterial assigned.

Standard PhysicMaterials

You can create a new PhysicMaterial from scratch from the Project View Create menu, but Unity conveniently provides a package of various PhysicMaterials in its Standard Assets. From the Assets menu on the menu bar, select Import Package and then Physic Materials (Figure 6-20).

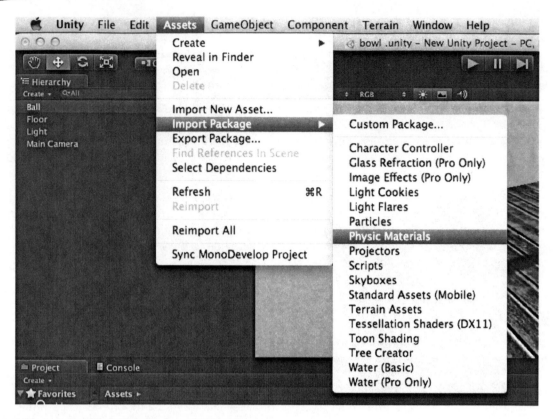

Figure 6-20.   Importing PhysicMaterials from Standard Assets

In the Project View, the new PhysicMaterials will show up in a Standard Assets subfolder named Physic Materials (Figure 6-21).

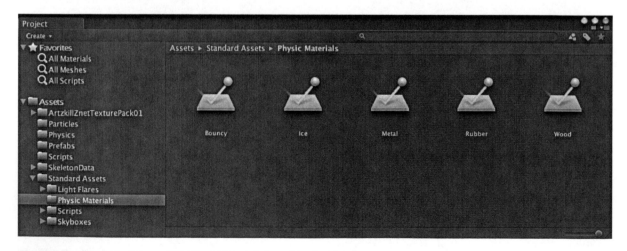

Figure 6-21.   The Project View of the PhysicMaterials from Standard Assets

Anatomy of a PhysicMaterial

Select among the various PhysicMaterials and compare their values in the Inspector View. For example, check out the differences between the Bouncy and Ice PhysicMaterials (Figure 6-22).

Figure 6-22. Comparison of Bouncy and Ice PhysicMaterials

Notice how Ice has particularly low friction values. Dynamic Friction is the friction that occurs while one object is sliding over another. Static Friction is the friction of an object resting on the other. The range for friction is 0-1, where 0 is frictionless and 1 means no sliding at all. Ice also has a Bounciness value of 0, which makes sense, since ice doesn't bounce. And the Bouncy Physic Material has the maximum Bounciness value of 1.

What happens when a collision occurs between GameObjects with two different Physic Materials? Their Friction and Bounciness values are combined according to the Friction Combine and Bounce Combine values, respectively. The Friction Combine value for Bouncy indicates that when it collides or slides along another PhysicMaterial, the applied friction is the average of the friction values from the two materials. And the Bounce Combine value for Bouncy specifies that the maximum bounciness from the two PhysicMaterials will be used (and since Bouncy already has the maximum bounciness value of 1, that will always be the result).

You might be wondering what happens if the two PhysicMaterials have different combine values, as do Bouncy and Ice. Which one will be used? Well, as of this writing, it's not actually documented officially, but the precedence order, from low to high, appears to be Average, Multiply, Minimum, and Maximum. So if Bouncy and Ice collide, it will result in Minimum friction, which is the Ice friction at 0.1, and Maximum bounciness, which is the Bouncy bounciness of 1. Which is what we would expect!

The last three properties shown in the Inspector View of the PhysicMaterials allow for anisotropic friction, meaning different friction values in different directions. If the Friction Direction property is filled in with a nonzero vector, then the secondary static and dynamic friction takes effect in that direction. For the wood-tiled Floor, you might specify a secondary friction direction that runs along the grain of the wood and lower static and dynamic friction values along that direction.

Apply the PhysicMaterial

You can drag any of these standard PhysicMaterials into the Material fields of the Floor and Ball Colliders or click the little circle on the right of the Collider's Material field to select from a pop-up (Figure 6-23). Or you can drag the PhysicMaterial from the Project View onto the GameObject in the Inspector View, and the PhysicMaterial will show up in the right place, i.e., the Material field of the Collider Component.

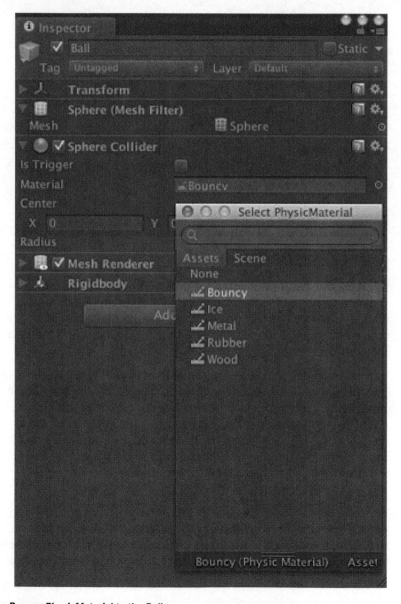

Figure 6-23. Adding a Bouncy PhysicMaterial to the Ball

Go ahead and try out some different PhysicMaterials on the Floor and Ball. Choose the Bouncy PhysicMaterial for the Ball and Metal for the Floor. Then click Play and watch the Ball bound and bounce and bounce, then switch the Ball to Ice, and watch the Ball land with a thud.

Instead of swapping different PhysicMaterials in and out of a Collider Component, you could adjust the PhysicMaterials themselves. For example, you could select the Bouncy PhysicMaterial in the Project View and then in the Inspector View edit the PhysicMaterial properties. But since those PhysicMaterials are in a Standard Assets package, they could get replaced if you ever reimport the package (either accidentally or deliberately if there is an upgrade). Also, if a PhysicMaterial is used by more than one GameObject, changing its properties would affect all of those GameObjects.

The clean and safe solution here is to create a new PhysicMaterial for every GameObject that needs one. Conceptually, you would expect a unique PhysicMaterial anytime you also need a unique Material. Or, to put it another way, a unique surface would have its own Material and PhysicMaterial. For instance, the Ball and the Floor should each have its own PhysicMaterial, while all of the bowling pins (that you'll create in the next chapter) should share the same PhysicMaterial.

Make a New PhysicMaterial

Before creating new PhysicMaterials, for organizational purposes, you should create a folder to contain them. Select the top level Assets folder in the left panel of the Project View, then using the Create menu in the Project View, create a new folder and name it "Physics" (it's shorter and less oddly spelled than "PhysicMaterials").

You can make a brand new PhysicMaterial using the Create menu in the Project View and then fill in all the properties of the new PhysicMaterial in the Inspector View. But you can save yourself some work by copying a PhysicMaterial from Standard Assets, preferably one that is already close to what you want. Given that the Floor has a wood Material, it's convenient to start with the Wood PhysicMaterial in Standard Assets. Make a copy of the Wood PhysicMaterial by selecting it in the Project View and invoking Duplicate from the Edit menu (or Command+D for the keyboard shortcut).

Drag the copy of the Wood PhysicMaterial to your new Physics folder in the Project View and rename it "Floor," since you'll apply it to your Floor GameObject. Then Duplicate the Floor PhysicMaterial and name the new one Ball (Figure 6-24), since you'll apply that one to your Ball GameObject.

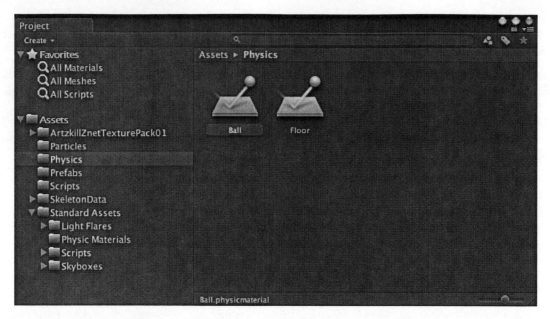

Figure 6-24. *Custom PhysicMaterials*

Now there's a PhysicMaterial for the Floor and one for the Ball. To use these PhysicMaterials on their intended GameObjects, drag the Floor PhysicMaterial onto the Floor GameObject in the Hierarchy View and drag the Ball PhysicMaterial onto the Ball GameObject (you may want to check the two GameObjects in the Inspector View to verify the PhysicMaterials are showing up in the Collider Material fields). Now you're ready to start tweaking the PhysicMaterial properties.

As one would expect, the Wood PhysicMaterial already has values reasonable for a wood floor, so you can leave it alone. But you want to tweak the Ball Physic Material, so select the Ball PhysicMaterial and set its values as shown in Figure 6-25.

Figure 6-25. Adjusted values for the Ball PhysicMaterial

The Ball to shouldn't bounce on the Floor (or off the bowling pins when you add them later), so set the Bounciness value to 0 and Bounce Combine to Minimum, which will ensure that the Ball never bounces at all no matter what it collides with. Then set the Dynamic and Static Friction values to 1 and Friction Combine to Maximum so the Ball always has maximum friction whether it's at rest or rolling. The maximum friction values ensure the Ball rolls instead of slides.

Now when you click Play, the Ball should just drop on the Floor and come to rest without bouncing.

Make It Roll

To get the ball rolling, you'll need to add some controls to the game (for it to be even a game, in fact). The original arcade version of HyperBowl was controlled by a real bowling ball that acted as a large trackball. Spinning that ball would impart a spin on the ball in the game (resulting in comical body movement while trying to bowl up the hills of San Francisco).

Of course, building an air-supported bowling ball peripheral is outside the scope of this book, but the PC version of HyperBowl provided a mouse-based version of this control, in which pushing the mouse would impart a spin on the ball in that direction. This control is fairly straightforward to implement with just a single script.

Create the Script

Select the Scripts folder in the Project View, create a new JavaScript using the Create button on the top left of the Project View, and name the new script FuguForce, since you'll be using it to apply a force to the Ball (I'm tempted to call it FuguRoll for the sushi connotation, but I don't want the name to imply that we're applying a torque, a rotational rather than a linear force). Then drag the FuguForce script onto the Ball in the Hierarchy View, so you'll be ready to test it as soon as you add some code to the script.

Update: Gather Input

Attempting to calculate rotations and translations (changes in position) to simulate rolling the Ball would be complicated, involving collision detection and responses with the floor and pins, taking in account gravity and friction and bouncing...all the calculations that the physics engine already does. It would be a waste not to leave that aspect up to the Unity physics system.

And because the Ball already has a Rigidbody Component, it is already a physical object subject to forces, including gravity, and responding to collisions, including the Floor. So all that's needed to roll the Ball is a push. How much of a push depends on the input, which, in our design, is the movement of the mouse.

> **Note**   The original, non-Unity version of HyperBowl applied a torque (rotational force) to the bowling ball, effectively spinning it. Unity does have a script function to apply torque to a Rigidbody, Rigidbody.AddTorque, but I've found that it works better in Unity to roll the ball by pushing it with a linear force using Rigidbody.AddForce.

The mouse movement, and input in general, can be checked every frame, so the input gathering code and computation of the corresponding push should go in the Update callback of the script, as shown in Listing 6-1. Copy that listing into the FuguForce script.

Listing 6-1. Update Callback in FuguForce.js

```
#pragma strict
var mousepowerx:float = 1.0;
var mousepowery:float = 1.0;

private var forcex:float=0.0;
private var forcey:float=0.0;

function Update() {
        forcex = mousepowerx*Input.GetAxis("Mouse X")/Time.deltaTime;
        forcey = mousepowery*Input.GetAxis("Mouse Y")/Time.deltaTime;
}
```

The script begins with variables mousepowerx and mousepowery used to scale force applied the Ball. mousepowerx affects the force resulting from moving the mouse left or right, and mousepowery affects the force resulting from moving the mouse forward and backware. The variables are public so they can be adjusted in the Inspector View.

The final calculated force is stored in the private variables forcex and forcey, also corresponding to left-right and forward-backward mouse movement, respectively.

> **Tip**   It's a good idea to always specify an initial value for variables in their declarations. That makes the meaning of the code more clear and avoids errors due to wrong assumptions about the initial values (C and C++ programmers especially know to be wary of mystery bugs from uninitialized variables).

The Update callback is where forcex and forcey are calculated from mousepowerx and mousepowery and the mouse movement. Input in Unity is queried using the Input class. For example, the mouse position can be checked by examining the static variable Input.mousePosition, so the mouse movement could be ascertained by saving the mouse position in each Update call and comparing the current position with the saved position from the previous frame.

But the higher-level Input.GetAxis function does that work, already. Input.Getaxis returns a value from -1 to 1 for left-right or forward-backward movement from a mouse, joystick, or keyboard, depending on the argument passed to the function.

In the Update callback, Input.GetAxis("Mouse X") is called to obtain the left-right mouse movement and Input.GetAxis("Mouse Y") is called for the front-back movement that occurred over the previous frame. The results are assigned to the variables forcex and forcey, respectively, after taking into account how much time elapsed during the frame (our old friend Time.deltaTime) and multiplying by scaling factors mousepowerx and mousepowery.

With this code in the FuguForce script, you can see the public mousepower variables show up in the Inspector View of the Ball (Figure 6-26).

Figure 6-26. The Ball with the FuguForce.js script

And when you click Play, you still don't have any control over the Ball, since you haven't added the actual ball-pushing code yet. However, if you select the Debug option in the Inspector View menu, the private forcex and forcey variables will display, and you can see them change as you move the mouse.

FixedUpdate: Use the Force

Functions that affect physics, including Rigidbody.AddForce, should be invoked in the FixedUpdate callback. Unlike the Update callback, which is called once per frame and can take any amount of time, the FixedUpdate callback takes place after every fixed time step has elapsed. For good results, physics simulations need to run at a fixed interval, typically with more frequency than Update. Varying intervals between physics computations can result in varying behavior and long lags between physics updates. In Unity, this time step is set in the TimeManager (Figure 6-27), which is available in the Project Settings submenu of the Edit menu.

Figure 6-27. The TimeManager

The FixedUpdate callback is called at these physics update intervals (I think of FixedUpdate really as PhysicsUpdate and the Fixed Timestep as the Physics Timestep), so this is where any change to the physics simulation should take place, especially any action on a Rigidbody.

Since the force for pushing the Ball is already calculated in the Update callback, the FixedUpdate callback just needs to apply those values in a call to Rigidbody.AddForce on the Ball's Rigidbody Component (Listing 6-2).

Listing 6-2. FixedUpdate Callback in FuguForce.js

```
function FixedUpdate() {
        rigidbody.AddForce(forcex,0,forcey);
}
```

The Rigidbody function AddForce is called on the variable rigidbody, which is a Component variable that always references the Rigidbody Component or this GameObject. The GameObject class also has a rigidbody variable, so a reference to gameObject.rigidbody would be equivalent.

The three values passed to RigidBody.AddForce are the x, y, and z values of the force, which is a vector since it has direction and magnitude. The direction of the force is in world space, and from the viewpoint of the Main Camera in this game, x is left-right and z is forward-backward. So forcex is passed in for the x argument and forcey for the z argument. The controls don't push the Ball up ro down, just forward and sideways, so 0 is passed in as the y argument.

> **Note** Be sure to check the Scripting Reference page on RigidBody.AddForce. It is an overloaded function with a variation that takes the force as a Vector3 instead of three separate numbers. Also, both variations take an optional argument that can specify the value applied to the Rigidbody is a quantity besides force—either acceleration, an impulse, or an instantaneous change in velocity.

Now when you click Play and move your mouse, the Ball rolls in that direction. Try changing the mousepowerx and mousepowery values in the Inspector View to get the roll responsiveness you want.

Is It Rolling?

You might notice that if you move the mouse while the Ball is falling, you can actually push the Ball while it's still in the air, which doesn't seem right. Moving the mouse should only roll the Ball when it's on a surface.

Fortunately, Unity has callback functions, each prefixed by OnCollision, that are called when a GameObject collides with another GameObject and when the contact ceases. Each of the callbacks takes one argument, a Collision object which contains information about the collision, such as a reference to the other GameObject that was involved.

The FuguForce script could check if the colliding GameObject is the Floor by checking if it's name is "Floor" (using the GameObject name variable). But in general it's a better practice and more efficient to find and identify GameObjects by their tags (using the GameObject tag variable). If you select the Floor GameObject and examine it in the Inspector View, you can see in the upper left it has the default tag Untagged. To change the GameObject's tag to Floor, the Floor tag must first be created by selecting Add Tag from the Tag menu of the GameObject (Figure 6-28).

Figure 6-28. Adding a new Tag

This brings up the TagManager in the Inspector View. The TagManager manages tags and layers. Tags are used to identify GameObjects, so you can create practically an unlimited number of them. Layers, on the other hand, are used to label groups of GameObjects, and at most 32 layers can be defined, since they are implemented as bits in a 32-bit number. This makes it convenient to specify combinations of layers, for example, in the Culling Mask properties of Cameras and Lights.

To create a new tag named Floor, just type "Floor" into the first empty tag field in the TagManager (Figure 6-29). Then select the Floor GameObject in the Hierarchy View again, click the Tag menu in the Inspector View again, and the new Floor tag is available for selection.

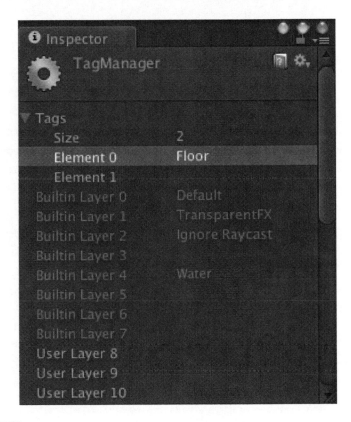

Figure 6-29. The TagManager

Now the FuguForce script can be augmented with collision callbacks to see if the Ball is on the Floor (Listing 6-3).

Listing 6-3. Collision Callbacks in FuguForce.js

```
private var isRolling:boolean=false;
private var floorTag:String = "Floor";

function OnCollisionEnter(collider:Collision) {
        if (collider.gameObject.tag == floorTag) {
                isRolling = true;
        }
}
```

```
function OnCollisionStay(collider:Collision) {
        if (collider.gameObject.tag == floorTag) {
                isRolling = true;
        }
}

function OnCollisionExit(collider:Collision) {
        if (collider.gameObject.tag == floorTag) {
                isRolling = false;
        }
}
```

Two private variables are added. The first variable, isRolling, is true when the Ball is on the Floor. The second variable, floorTag, is the tag assigned to the Floor.

> **Tip** Defining a variable for the tag avoids having to spell out the tag in multiple locations (and avoids hard-to-debug spelling errors), and if the name of the tag is changed later, only the variable needs to be updated. Each of the three collision callbacks checks if the GameObject the Ball collided against is the Floor by checking the tag of the tag of the colliding GameObject. If the GameObject is not the Floor, then the collision callback doesn't do anything.

The OnCollisionEnter callback is called by Unity when the Ball collides with another GameObject, so that function sets isRolling to true. Conversely, OnCollisionExit is called by Unity when contact ceases between the Ball and a GameObject, and in that case isRolling is set to false.

In the meantime, OnCollisionStay is called while the Ball stays in contact with a GameObject, so it also ensures that isRolling stays true.Now the FixedUpdate callback can check if isRolling is true, indicating that the Ball is on the Floor, before applying a push to the Ball (Listing 6-4).

Listing 6-4. Add a Rolling Check in FixedUpdate of FuguForce.js

```
function FixedUpdate() {
        if (isRolling) {
                rigidbody.AddForce(forcex,0,forcey);
        }
}
```

Limit the Speed

Finally, as a bit of polish, the ball control script can check the Ball's speed before pushing the Ball, avoiding cases where the Ball ends up rolling much faster than we intended, due to some freak combination of existing velocity, frame rate, and input values (Listing 6-5).

Listing 6-5. Add a Speed Check in FixedUpdate of FuguForce.js

```
var maxVelocitySquared:float=400.0;

function FixedUpdate() {
        if (isRolling && rigidbody.velocity.sqrMagnitude<maxVelocitySquared) {
                rigidbody.AddForce(forcex,0,forcey);
        }
}
```

This is a pretty simple change, requiring only the addition of a variable maxVelocitySquared to hold our maximum velocity value, actually the square of the maximum velocity value. Then FixedUpdate, in addition to checking if the Ball is on the Floor, also checks if the Ball if the squared magnitude of the Ball's velocity is below maxVelocitySquared. In other words, FixedUpdate is checking the square of the Ball's speed.

The velocity variable of Rigidbody is a Vector3, which in turn has a magnitude variable that gives you the length of the Vector3. But finding the length of a Vector3 involves a square root operation (remember the Pythagorean theorem from high school geometry?), and square roots require more computation. So whenever you need to compare the length of two Vector3's, you should instead compare the square of their lengths.

The Complete Script

Listing 6-6 presents the complete listing for the Ball controller script, FuguForce.js, put together so far, available in the Chapter 6 project on http://learnunity4.com/.

Listing 6-6. Complete Listing of FuguForce.js

```
#pragma strict

var mousepowerx:float = 1.0;
var mousepowery:float = 1.0;

var maxvelocity:float=400.0;

private var forcey:float=0.0;
private var forcex:float=0.0;

private var isRolling:boolean=false;
private var floorTag:String = "Floor";

var maxVelocitySquared:float=400.0;

function Update() {
        forcex = mousepowerx*Input.GetAxis("Mouse X")/Time.deltaTime;
        forcey = mousepowery*Input.GetAxis("Mouse Y")/Time.deltaTime;
}
```

```
function FixedUpdate() {
        if (isRolling && rigidbody.velocity.sqrMagnitude<maxVelocitySquared) {
                rigidbody.AddForce(forcex,0,forcey);
        }
}
function OnCollisionEnter(collider:Collision) {
        if (collider.gameObject.tag == floorTag) {
                isRolling = true;
        }
}

function OnCollisionStay(collider:Collision) {
        if (collider.gameObject.tag == floorTag) {
                isRolling = true;
        }
}

function OnCollisionExit(collider:Collision) {
        if (collider.gameObject.tag == floorTag) {
                isRolling = false;
        }
}
```

Be the Ball

The Ball control works pretty well at this point, but the Main Camera just sits there while the Ball rolls off into the distance. This is a glaring deficiency, as any decent 3D game has some kind of camera movement. In HyperBowl, the Main Camera follows the ball as you roll, but always facing the same direction (toward the pins). It turns out Unity has a Camera follow script in Standard Assets. The Scripts package was already imported from Standard Assets in Chapter 3 to obtain the MouseOrbit script. The follow script is also located in the Camera Scripts folder of the Scripts package and called SmoothFollow (Figure 6-30).

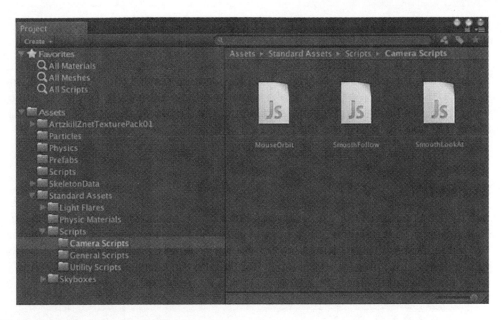

Figure 6-30. *The Camera scripts in Standard Assets*

Drag the SmoothFollow script from the Project View onto the Main Camera in the Hierarchy View. Then select the Main Camera in the Hierarchy View so you can edit the SmoothFollow script properties in the Inspector View (Figure 6-31).

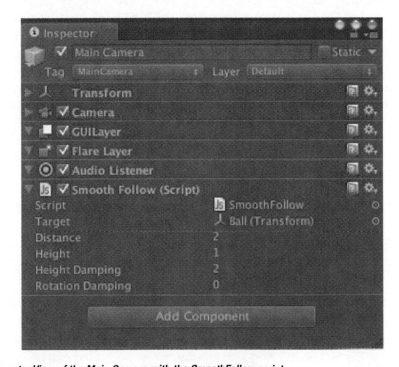

Figure 6-31. *The Inspector View of the Main Camera with the SmoothFollow script*

The Main Camera should follow the Ball, so drag the Ball GameObject from the Hierarchy View into the SmoothFollow script's Target field in the Inspector View.

As for the other SmoothFollow properties, set the Distance to 2, which will leave the Main Camera trailing 2 meter behind the Ball, and Height to 1, so the Camera stays 1 meter above the Ball instead of following right behind it. Height Damping of 2 allows the Main Camera to spring up and down a bit while following the Ball's height, and a Rotation Damping of 0 ensures the Main Camera will always stay behind the Ball and not swing around to the left or right.

Now click Play, and as you roll around, you're rolling and following!

Explore Further

Now we have the beginnings of real gameplay. It's not a complete bowling game, yet, but it has physics (a ball rolling on a floor), interactive control (pushing the ball), and camera movement (following the ball). Each of those features are rich topics in game development, but in particular we'll be digging deeper into physics in the next chapter with the addition bowling pins and collision-based sound effects. Then the game will look a lot more like a bowling game!

Unity Manual

In the "Asset Import and Creation section," the page on "Procedural Materials," which you used on the Floor, describes the Substance archive format a little bit and provides an overview of the tools used to create and analyze procedural materials.

In the "Creating Gameplay" section, the page on "Input" describes the Input class and its GetAxis function used in the FuguForce script implemented in this chapter and lists the joystick and keyboard values passed to that function. The lower portion of that page describes Input functions and variables available for iOS, so you can read that for a preview of this book's chapter on iOS input.

This chapter has been mostly about physics, so the page on "Physics" is the most important to read. It lists all the collider types, including the SphereCollider, BoxCollider, and MeshCollider Components used in this chapter. The page describes the differences between Rigidbodies (the ball) and static colliders (the floor), and how PhysicMaterials and their properties affect collision behavior.

Reference Manual

In the "Asset Components" section, the page on "Procedural Material Assets" explains what you see in the Project View and Inspector View for procedural materials.

The section on "Physics Components" lists all the available colliders in detail, along with the available joints (including hinges and springs), constant force, and cloth components (cloth is not supported in Unity iOS).

A new Settings Manager was introduced in this chapter, the "TagManager," which was used to create a new tag for the Floor.

In the "Scripting Concepts" section, the page titled "What Is a Tag?" expands on how to create a tag and apply it to a GameObject, along with an example of how a tag can be used to find a GameObject at runtime.

The page on "Rigidbody Sleeping" explains how a Rigidbody "goes to sleep" when it rests. This is a nice optimization that reduces unnecessary physics computation.

Scripting Reference

In the Runtime Classes listing, the page for the "MonoBehaviour" class lists the collision callbacks that were introduced in this chapter: "OnCollisionEnter," "OnCollisionStay," and "OnCollisionExit."

We queried the "Collision" class for information on collisions: relative velocity, the GameObject collided against. Other data like actual point of contact are available.

I introduced the "Rigidbody" Component in this chapter, and the Scripting Reference page for this class is worth reading in its entirety. It's variables correspond largely to the properties available in the Inspector View, and besides the "AddForce" function you used to push the Ball, there are many related functions: "AddRelativeForce," AddTorque, AddRelativeTorque, AddExplosionForce, AddForceAtPosition.

"Component" has several variables that act as shortcuts to reference other Components often attached to GameObjects. Of the two scripts created so far in this book, the FuguRotate script references the "transform" variable, and the FuguForce script references the "rigidbody" variable. The Component variables mirror the same set of variables in "GameObject."

The one function in the "Input" class that we used is "Input.GetAxis." If you plan on making any desktop or web games, you'll want to check out the various functions used to query the keyboard, mouse, and joystick. This page also lists the Input functions available for mobile applications.

On the Web

The physics implementation in Unity is based on an older version (2.x) of the PhysX engine, originally developed by NovodeX, acquired by Ageia who bundled it with a hardware physics accelerator, and now a product of nVidia. The latest version (3.x) is available on the nVidia Developer Zone (https://developer.nvidia.com/physx). The PhysX Software Development Kit is worth a look just to get a better idea what physics engine features underlie the Unity physics Components and script functions.

The fairly new Learn section on the Unity web site (http://unity3d.com/) includes an extensive set of physics tutorials covering much of what was discussed in this chapter and what will be discussed in the next chapter.

7

Let's Bowl! Advanced Physics

At this point, we have the glimmerings of a bowling game, or at least a scene in the Unity Editor where the player can roll the ball around on the floor. But the game won't look like a bowling game until it at least has bowling pins. That will be remedied in this chapter and involve more Unity physics, including collisions between Rigidbodies (among the ball and pins) and compound colliders (to accommodate the shape of a bowling pin). On top of that, we'll add collision-based sounds effects so the game will sound like a bowling game, too.

This additional functionality will require the construction of several new scripts, available in the Unity project for this chapter on `http://learnunity4.com/` However, the barrel model used for the bowling pins and the audio for pin collisions and the ball rolling sound are taken (free) from the Asset Store and not included in the online project.

Lengthen the Lane

Before adding bowling pins to the bowl scene, which should be open in the Unity Editor as we left it in the previous chapter, we need some more room to roll. Select the Floor in the Hierarchy View, and in the Inspector View (Figure 7-1) set Scale to 10 for X, Y, and Z.

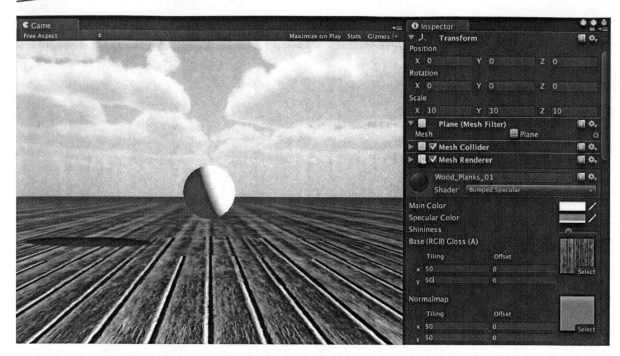

Figure 7-1. The larger Floor GameObject, scaled up by a factor of 10

> **Tip**   For performance reasons, it's best to avoid changing the scale in the Transform Component (for imported models, change the scale in the Import Settings, instead). And if you have to change the scale, change it uniformly along all three axes.

The Floor is now ten times larger (except in height, since a Plane has zero height). But the textures on the Floor are also stretched, resulting in some really wide planks. To compensate, you should also adjust the Tiling for the Floor's Main and Normalmap textures by a factor of 10, which results in a new Tiling factor of 50 in each direction and the wooden planks looking as they originally did.

Make Some Pins

Now that there's room to roll, it's time to add the pins. In lieu of a bowling pin model, you can make a simplistic version of a bowling pin with the Capsule primitive.

Select Capsule from the Create menu of the Hierarchy View (Figure 7-2). Capsule, like the other primitive models, is also available in the GameObject menu on the menu bar.

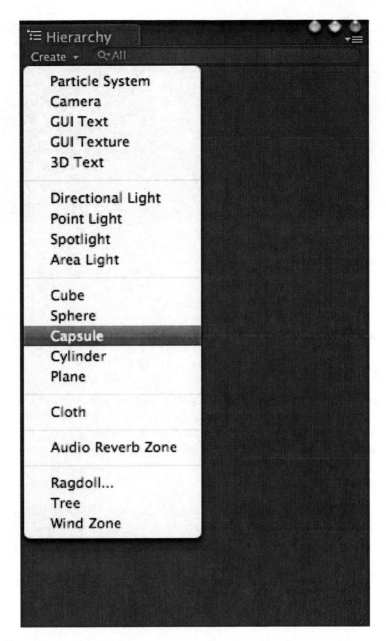

Figure 7-2. Creating a Capsule

Name the resulting GameObject Pin. To create ten pins, you could duplicate the Pin nine times, but in the same way the Cube was cloned in the cube scene, it's better to make a prefab first. This way, any changes you make to a single pin can be applied to all ten of the pins.

So go ahead and drag the Pin into the Prefabs folder in the Project View to create the prefab (Figure 7-3).

Figure 7-3. The Pin prefab in the Project View

But dragging nine copies of the prefab into the scene and manually placing them would be laborious and error-prone. A task fitting that description is a good candidate for implementing in a script! So plan on spawning all of the pins in the game using a script and the Pin prefab. In that case, the Pin GameObject in the scene is redundant, so delete it (by selecting the GameObject in the Hierarchy View and invoking Delete from the Edit menu or the keyboard shortcut Command+Delete).

Make a Game Controller

Besides spawning the pins, the bowling game will surely require more scripting to implement the rules of the game and the playing sequence. In fact, any game that's not really simple can benefit from having a single game controller script that implements the the overall flow of the game. So let's plan on implementing the pin creation as the first action in the bowling game controller.

Create the Script

In the Project View, create a new JavaScript, place it in the Scripts folder, and name it `FuguBowl` (we'll follow a convention of naming the game controller script after the game itself). Then add the code in Listing 7-1, which consists of a few variables, a `CreatePins` function, and an Awake callback that calls the `CreatePins` function.

Listing 7-1. Pin Instantiation Code in FuguBowl.js

```
#pragma strict

var pin:GameObject; // pin prefab to instantiate
var pinPos:Vector3 = Vector3(0,1,20); // position to place rack of pins

var pinDistance = 1.5; // initial distance between pins
var pinRows = 4; // number of pin rows

private var pins:Array;

function Awake () {
        CreatePins();
}
```

```
function CreatePins() {
        pins = new Array();
        var offset = Vector3.zero;
        for (var row=0; row<pinRows; ++row) {
                offset.z+=pinDistance;
                offset.x=-pinDistance*row/2;
                for (var n=0; n<=row; ++n) {
                        pins.push(Instantiate(pin, pinPos+offset, Quaternion.identity));
                        offset.x+=pinDistance;
                }

        }
}
```

The CreatePins function first creates an Array, which is similar to the built-in array denoted by brackets, but with adjustable size, so it can grow as you add elements and shrink as you remove them. The function then loops through the number of rows specified and in each row instantiates an increasing number of pins: row one has one pin, row two has two pins, and so on. Thus when you have four rows, you end up with a triangle of ten pins as desired!

Instantiate Pins

The Instantiate function takes an Object, position, and rotation as arguments to create an identical Object at the specified position and rotation (in world space, not local space). Instantiate copies the entire Object hierarchy, so if the Object is a GameObject with child GameObjects, then the entire hierarchy is copied. If the Object is a Component, then the GameObject of that Component and all of that GameObject's children are copied.

If the original GameObject is already in the scene, then calling Instantiate is similar to selecting the original GameObject and invoking Duplicate on it from the Edit menu (or Command+D). If the original object is a prefab, as is the case here, then calling Instantiate is similar to dragging the prefab into the scene to create a new GameObject.

The position is a Vector3 and the rotation is passed in as a Quaternion instead of an Euler angle. A quaternion is not a very intuitive representation of rotations (quaternions are complex numbers with three imaginary components), but they have some advantages over Euler angles (e.g., more natural interpolation) and thus are used internally by Unity. In this case, passing in the static variable Quaternion.identity specifies that no rotation takes place (same as a rotation of 0,0,0 in Euler angles).

> **Caution**   Quaternions also have x,y,z values (and one more, w) so be careful about confusing them with Euler angles. In particular, note that the rotation and localRotation variables in the Transform Component are Quaternion values. The Euler angles are stored in the variables eulerAngles and localEulerAngles.

Instantiate is a static function of the Object class. The call to Instantiate in the script is equivalent to calling this.Instantiate, where this is the script Component. And Component is a subclass of Object, so the compiler knows you're calling Object.Instantiate. Instantiate is also an overloaded function, with a variation that takes just one argument: the Object to clone. The newly instantiated Object will appear at the same position and with the same rotation as the original Object.

Namespaces

Normally I'd prefer to explicitly call Object.Instantiate to make it clear that Instantiate is a static function in the Object class and doesn't have to be called on an actual instance of Object (in which case it would be termed an *instance function*). However, spelling out Object.Instantiate in the script results in the Console View error message: *'Instantiate' is not a member of 'Object'* (Figure 7-4).

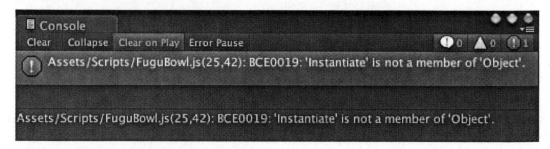

Figure 7-4. A compiler error referencing the (wrong) Object class

The problem here is that there is another Object class defined in Mono. That class acts as the superclass of other Mono classes, just like the Unity Object class is the superclass of most Unity classes (at least the ones that can exist in a scene). The compiler thinks you're referring to the Mono Object class instead of the Unity class. This is the issue we've been trying to avoid by naming classes with a (hopefully) unique prefix. Useful class names like Object and Button are likely to be used by many different developers.

But how can the Unity and Mono versions of Object coexist? The answer is namespaces. Every class defined by Unity is in the UnityEngine namespace, whereas the Mono version of Object is defined in the System namespace. The fully qualified name of every class is the class name preceded by the namespace name, so the Unity Object class is really UnityEngine.Object and the Mono Object is System.Object.

References to Unity classes rarely include the UnityEngine prefix, because JavaScript implicitly imports that namespace (equivalent to adding "import UnityEngine" at the top of the script). This means the compiler will look in the UnityEngine namespace when it's trying to figure out where a class is defined. Unfortunately, JavaScript also implicitly imports the System namespace and Object resolves to System.Object first. So a call to Object.Instantiate generates the the same error as a call to System.Object.Instantiate, since there is no Instantiate function defined for the System.Object class. But a call to UnityEngine.Object.Instantiate works just fine. So just know that any time any call to just plain Instantiate is really a call to UnityEngine.Object.Instantiate!

By the way, there is no such confusion with the Object class in C# scripts, as they do not automatically import the System namespace. And although JavaScript doesn't yet allow declarations of new namespaces, C# does have that support beginning with Unity 4.

Awake

The Awake function is a script callback very similar to Start. Like Start, Awake is called just once, when the GameObject is first made active. Unlike Start, Awake is called regardless of whether the script is enabled. And Awake is always called before Start.

> **Note**   Originally, Awake was called as soon as the GameObject was loaded into a scene or created, regardless of whether the GameObject was active. This behavior didn't work well with prefabs, hence the current behavior where Awake resembles an earlier `Start` callback. You could use either Awake or `Start` in this case, but I like to use Awake for initialization and `Start` for actively commencing the script's behavior.

Create the GameObject

For the game controller script to run, it has to be attached to a GameObject in the scene. Although `FuguBowl.js` could be attached to an existing GameObject, like the Main Camera, it's cleaner to create a new GameObject. The GameObject can be named in a way that clearly indicates the game controller script is attached, and you don't have to worry about the GameObject getting deactivated while it's being used for other purposes.

Going with that strategy, create a new GameObject in the Hierarchy View, name it FuguBowl, same as the script it will hold, and drag the `FuguBowl` script onto the FuguBowl GameObject (Figure 7-5).

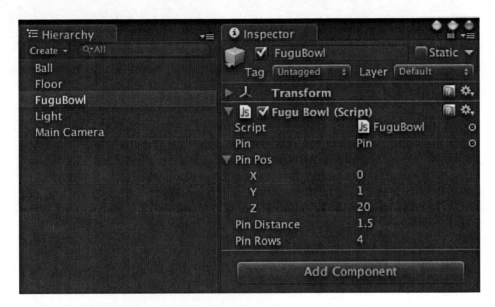

Figure 7-5. The game controller GameObject with FuguBowl.js attached

Most of the properties of the FuguBowl script can be left at their default values, but you do need to drag the Pin prefab from the Project View into the Pin field of the FuguBowl script. Now click Play, and all ten bowling pins appear (Figure 7-6).

Figure 7-6. The bowling with pins

But as you bowl into the pins, the Ball just bounces off them since the pins have Collider Components but are static GameObjects. Like the Ball, each pin has to have a Rigidbody Component in order to react to forces. A Rigidbody Component can be added to the Pin prefab from the Component menu, but this time, let's try it another way. Select the Pin prefab in the Project View and then in the Inspector View click the Add Component button. In the resulting pop-up, under Physics select Rigidbody (or you can find that selection by typing "rigidbody" in the search field of the pop-up). Whichever way you choose, there should now be a Rigidbody Component on the Pin prefab (Figure 7-7).

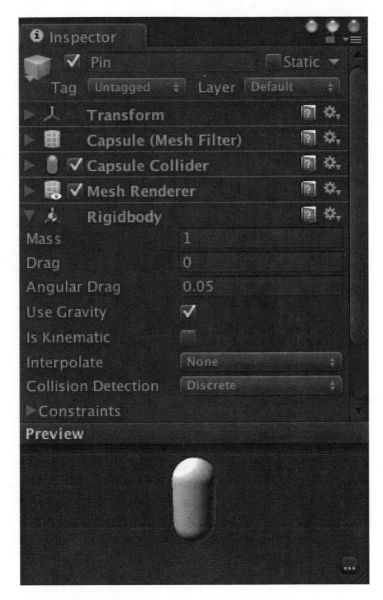

Figure 7-7. The bowling pin prefab with a Rigidbody

Like the Floor and Ball Collider Components, the Pin prefab should have its own PhysicMaterial. A quick way to create a suitable PhysicMaterial is to copy the one used for the Ball, so select the Ball PhysicMaterial in your Physics folder in the Project View, duplicate it using the Edit menu or Command+D, and name the new PhysicMaterial Pin (Figure 7-8).

Figure 7-8. A PhysicMaterial for the Pin prefab

Since the bowling pins should roll just as well as the Ball, leave the Dynamic and Static Friction values at 1 (to avoid slippage while rolling), and leave the Fiction Combine value at Maximum. Unlike the Ball, however, the bowling pins should be fairly bouncy, so set the Bounciness to 0.5 and the Bounce Combine value to Average (taking in account the bounciness of whatever it's bouncing against).

Finally, it's time to assign the Pin PhysicMaterial to the Pin prefab. Select the Pin prefab in the Project View, and then in the Inspector View, click the circle to the right of the PhysicMaterial field of the Collider Component and select the Pin PhysicMaterial from the pop-up chooser (Figure 7-9).

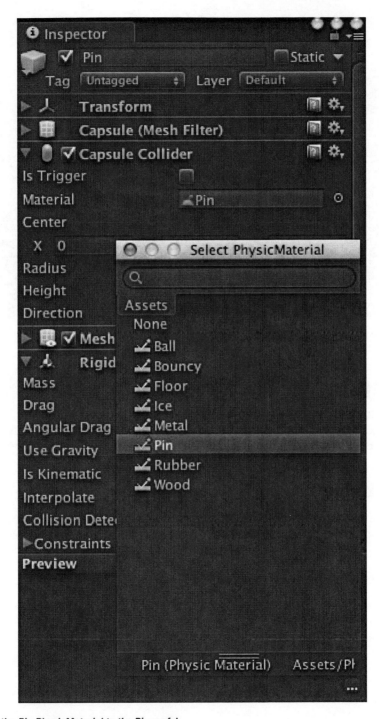

Figure 7-9. Assigning the Pin PhysicMaterial to the Pin prefab

Now when you click Play and roll the Ball into the pins, they get knocked around, as shown in Figure 7-10, bouncing and rolling!

Figure 7-10. Collision with pins that each have a Rigidbody

Keep Playing

It's rather tiresome to have to stop the game and click Play again every time you want to test a roll. And when the Ball rolls off the Floor, you're stuck watching the Ball fall indefinitely. So let's have the Ball, Main Camera, and pins reset if the Ball rolls off the edge of the Floor.

Make It Resettable

First, you need a script that will restore a GameObject to its initial position and rotation (can't forget rotation—if a pin is knocked down you want to reset it to its initial standing orientation). Create a new JavaScript, call it `FuguReset`, with the contents of Listing 7-2.

Listing 7-2. Restoring a GameObject position in FuguReset.js

```
#pragma strict

private var startPos:Vector3;
private var startRot:Vector3;
```

```
function Awake() {
        // save the initial position and rotation of this GameObject
        startPos = transform.localPosition;
        startRot = transform.localEulerAngles;
}

function ResetPosition() {
        // set back to initial position
        transform.localPosition = startPos;
        transform.localEulerAngles = startRot;
        // make sure we stop all physics movement
        if (rigidbody != null) {
                rigidbody.velocity = Vector3.zero;
                rigidbody.angularVelocity = Vector3.zero;
        }
}
```

The Awake function saves the GameObject's position and rotation in a couple of variables and the function ResetPosition restores the GameObject to those settings. ResetPosition also checks if the GameObject has a Rigidbody. If so, then the function stops it from moving or rotating.

The FuguReset script should be attached to every GameObject that will need to reset its position and (and possibly rotation) when you restart the game. That list includes the Ball, the pins, and the Main Camera. Start by dragging the FuguReset script onto the Main Camera and Ball GameObjects in the Hierarchy View. Then select the Pin prefab in the Project View, and in the Inspector View click the Add Component button to add the FuguReset script (Figure 7-11).

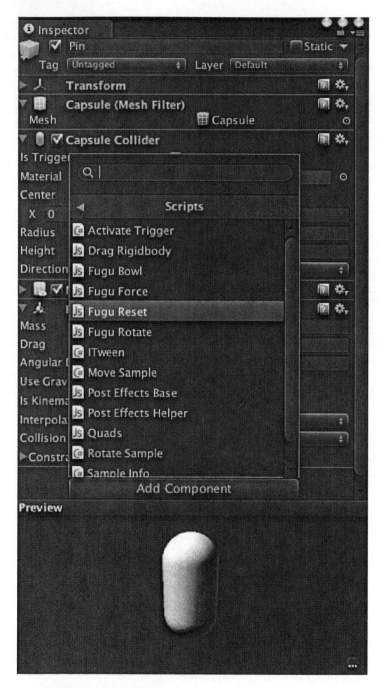

Figure 7-11. Attaching the FuguReset script to the Pin prefab

The Ball, pins, and Main Camera now record their original positions and rotations when the game starts and you have a ResetPosition function ready to call that will restore them to those original positions and rotations.

Send a Message

Normally, calling a function in a script attached to one GameObject from a script attached to another GameObject is a little bit tricky. It involves calling GetComponent on a GameObject to retrieve the script and then referencing that script to call the function.

But in simple cases (e.g., when you don't care about the return value of the function), Unity allows you to call functions by sending messages to GameObjects using either the SendMessage or BroadcastMessage function in the GameObject class. A GameObject receiving a message, which consists of the name of the function to call, will pass that message on to any attached script that might have that function.

Let's add some functions to our game controller script that will send ResetPosition messages (Listing 7-3).

Listing 7-3. Functions to Send ResetPosition Messages in FuguBowl.js

```
var ball:GameObject; // the bowling ball

function ResetBall() {
        ball.SendMessage("ResetPosition");
}

function ResetPins() {
        for (var pin:GameObject in pins) {
                pin.BroadcastMessage("ResetPosition");
        }
}

function ResetCamera() {
        Camera.main.SendMessage("ResetPosition");
}

function ResetEverything() {
        ResetBall();
        ResetPins();
        ResetCamera();
}
```

The additional code begins with a public variable that will refer to the Ball. The script already has a pins Array that references all of the bowling pins, and the Main Camera can always be referenced through the static variable Camera.main, so now the script can access every GameObject that it needs to reset. The functions ResetCamera and ResetBall call SendMessage to send the ResetPosition message to their respective target GameObjects. Every ResetPosition function defined in scripts attached to those GameObjects will be called. Specifically, since the Main Camera and the Ball have the FuguReset script attached, the ResetPosition function in that script will respond to the message.

The ResetPins function is a little bit different in that it calls BroadcastMessage to send the ResetPosition message. BroadcastMessage behaves the same as SendMessage except that the message is also propagated to any child GameObjects of the original recipient GameObject. This will be useful later in this chapter when we swap in some pins that have their Rigidbodies attached to child GameObjects.

ResetPins does generate a warning in the Console about an *Implicit downcast from 'Object' to 'UnityEngine.GameObject'* (Figure 7-12).

Figure 7-12. The Console View of an Implicit Downcast warning

The warning appears because Array is defined to contain elements of type Object, but each element is treated as a GameObject. That's plausible, since GameObject is a subclass of Object, but as far as the compiler knows, not necessarily true. You can remove the warning by adding #pragma downcast to the script, which basically tells the compiler, "trust me."

Check for Gutter Ball

When the Ball rolls off the edge of the Floor, it's essentially a gutter ball, since there's no hope of reaching the pins at this point. So a reset of the game is definitely in order when this happens. The gutter ball can be implemented by checking in every frame whether the y position of the Ball has dropped below a certain level. That can be implemented by adding the public variable sunkHeight and Update callback in Listing 7-4 to the FuguBowl script.

Listing 7-4. Update Callback in FuguBowl.js to Test for Gutter Ball

```
var sunkHeight:float = -10.0; // global y position which we call a gutterball

function Update() {
        if (ball.transform.position.y<sunkHeight) {
                ResetEverything();
        }
}
```

The variable sunkHeight specifies what y position the Ball has to fall below to reset everything. The default value at some of sunkHeight is some distance below zero so the players has some time to see the Ball fall before it resets.The Update callback checks every frame whether or not the Ball's y position is below sunkHeight. If it is, ResetEverything is called, which sends out all the ResetPosition messages to the Ball, Main Camera, and pins. Before you click Play to test this, you need to assign the ball public variable in the script by dragging the Ball GameObject from the Hierarchy View into the Ball field of the FuguBowl script (Figure 7-13).

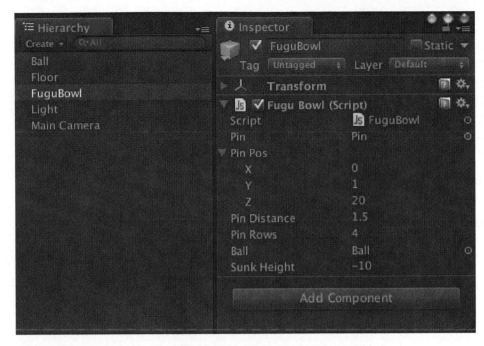

Figure 7-13. Game controller properties in FuguBowl.js to support resetting the ball

Now when the Ball rolls off the Floor, the Ball, Main Camera and pins should pop right back into their beginning positions. Continuous gameplay!

The Complete Listing

The complete game controller script is given in Listing 7-5.

Listing 7-5. The Complete Listing for FuguBowl.js

```
#pragma strict
#pragma downcast

var pin:GameObject;                     // pin prefab to instantiate
var pinPos:Vector3 = Vector3(0,1,20);   // position to place rack of pins
var pinDistance = 1.5;                  // initial distance between pins
var pinRows = 4;                        // number of pin rows

var ball:GameObject;                    // the bowling ball
var sunkHeight:float = -10.0;

private var pins:Array;

function Awake () {
        CreatePins();
}
```

```
function CreatePins() {
        pins = new Array();
        var offset = Vector3.zero;
        for (var row=0; row<pinRows; ++row) {
                offset.z+=pinDistance;
                offset.x=-pinDistance*row/2;
                for (var n=0; n<=row; ++n) {
                        pins.push(Instantiate(pin, pinPos+offset, Quaternion.identity));
                        offset.x+=pinDistance;
                }

        }
}

function Update() {
        if (ball.transform.position.y<sunkHeight) {
                ResetEverything();
        }
}

function ResetBall() {
        ball.SendMessage("ResetPosition");
}

function ResetPins() {
        for (var pin:GameObject in pins) {
                pin.BroadcastMessage("ResetPosition");
        }
}

function ResetCamera() {
        Camera.main.SendMessage("ResetPosition");
}

function ResetEverything() {
        ResetBall();
        ResetPins();
        ResetCamera();
}
```

Bowling for Barrels

Capsules make for very simplistic bowling pins, both in appearance and collision shape. A real bowling pin model would be much better, but, unfortunately, searching for bowling pins on the Asset Store turns up nothing (although that could change at any time if a vendor decides to fill the void). However, there are a lot of other models on the Asset Store, that, if we're flexible, could act as bowling pin substitutes. It turns out there are several packages of barrel models, so we'll go with barrels as pins for our backup plan.

Pick a Barrel

A search for barrel on the Asset Store reveals several free packages of barrel models (Figure 7-14).

Figure 7-14. Free barrels on the Asset Store

Any of the free packages will work fine, but the Barrel package from Universal Image, that one displaying three barrels in its Asset Store icon, already has a prefab set up, so let's download that package. From the Asset Store description, and from the Project View after you import the package, you can see the Barrel package is nicely organized, with a folder named Barrel that contains the Barrel prefab and the Barrel model (Figure 7-15).

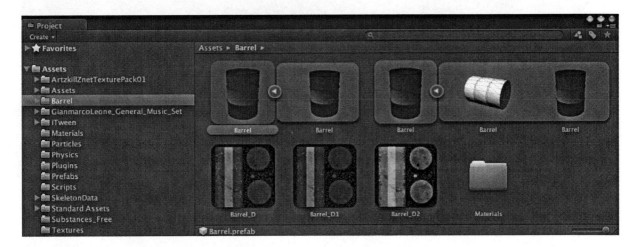

Figure 7-15. The Project View of the Barrel package

The two assets look similar in the Project View, but clicking on the prefab shows the full filename Barrel.prefab at the bottom of the Project View, while clicking on the Barrel model displays Barrel. FBX, indicating it's an imported FBX file (3D format used by Autodesk).

Make a Prefab

We need a Barrel prefab to replace the simple Pin prefab, but we should avoid modifying the original Barrel prefab (another import of the Barrel package would clobber our changes). To make our own copy of the Barrel prefab, select the prefab, press Command+D (or Duplicate from the Edit menu), and drag the copy of the prefab into the Prefabs folder. Then rename it to BarrelPin, since it's a Barrel and we're using it as a bowling pin (Figure 7-16).

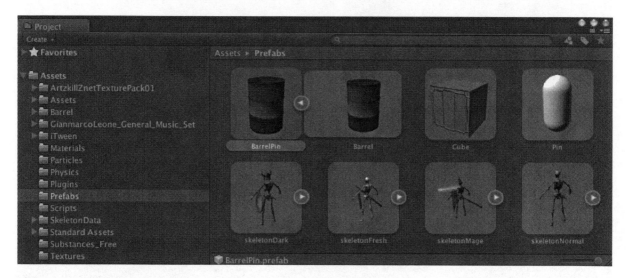

Figure 7-16. Copy of the Barrel prefab

Select the child GameObject of the BarrelPin prefab so that it is displayed in the Inspector View. A MeshFilter Component and MeshRenderer Component are present, but to use this prefab as a bowling pin, it needs a Collider Component and Rigidbody Component so the pins (barrels) are subject to gravity and can collide with each other, the Ball, and the Floor. The prefab also needs a FuguReset script attached to handle the ResetPosition messages sent by the game controller.

For now, let's take care of the Rigidbody Component and FuguReset script and defer adding the Collider Component, as matching the barrel shape will be somewhat involved. With the prefab selected, you choose Rigidbody from the Component menu on the menu bar, or you can click the Add Component button at the bottom of the Inspector View and choose Rigidbody from the resulting menu (Figure 7-17).

Figure 7-17. Adding a Rigidbody and FuguReset script to the Barrel prefab

In the newly attached Rigidbody Component, set the Mass to 2 (kg). That's pretty light for a metal barrel, but the game won't be fun if the Ball can't knock down the barrels-as-pins without too much trouble. In games, fun trumps reality!

The FuguReset script can added to the prefab by dragging the script into the Inspector View or also by using the AddComponent button.

Use the Prefab

To replace the simple capsule-shaped Pin with the BarrelPin prefab, select the FuguBowl GameObject in the Hierarchy View so that it's Components display in the Inspector View, and then drag the BarrelPin prefab into the Pin field of the FuguBowl script, replacing Pin prefab we started with (Figure 7-18). Now when you click Play, ten barrels will appear instead of ten capsules. But they will immediately fall through the Floor, because the pins don't have Collider Components, yet!

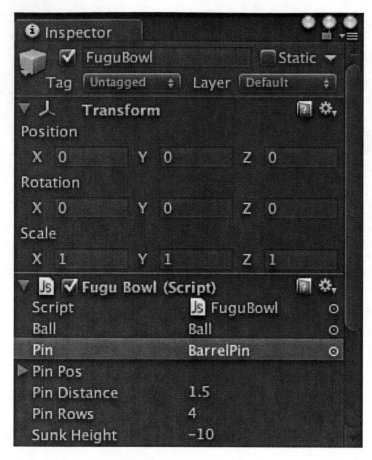

Figure 7-18. Using the BarrelPin prefab as the bowling pin

Add a Collider

We can't avoid it any longer. It's time to take care of the BarrelPin collision. So that we can visualize the BarrelPin and it's collision shape in the Scene View, temporarily place the BarrelPin prefab in the scene by dragging the prefab into the Hierarchy View. Once there, open the BarrelPin GameObject and select the child Barrel GameObject so that it is displayed in the Inspector View, and press the F key to invoke the Frame Selected, which will center the Barrel in the Scene View. Also, change the viewing options (top left pull-down menu in the Scene View) from Textured to Wireframe, so the Mesh and Collider Component's shape can be seen more easily.

Unfortunately, the Component menu doesn't list any primitive colliders that are barrel-shaped (a CylinderCollider would be perfect, but it doesn't exist), and although a MeshCollider would conform to the shape of the barrel, MeshColliders are not appropriate for physical GameObjects because of performance issues. The closest matching shape in the Components menu is the CapsuleCollider. So let's start with a Capsule Collider on our Barrel GameObject and see how well it fits.

Although Unity tries to size a Collider Component to fit the GameObject's Mesh when the Collider Component is added, in this case the fit isn't very good, largely because, as you can see from the rotation in the Transform Component, this GameObject is rotated 90 degrees around its x axis. Without that rotation, the barrel is lying on its side, but the rotation also affects the orientation of the Collier Component. To adjust for the rotation, switch the axis of the Capsule Collider to the z axis. After that, setting the radius to 2 and height to 6 will produce a much closer match between CapsuleCollider and the Barrel (Figure 7-19).

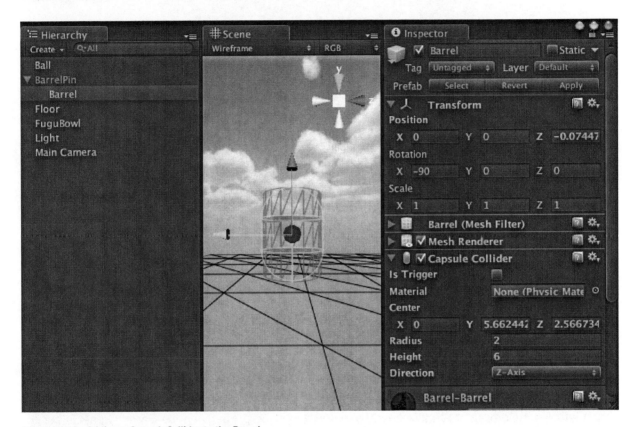

Figure 7-19. Adding a CapsuleCollider to the Barrel

The Capsule matches the Barrel shape pretty well around the side but not on the top and bottom, which should have flat surfaces instead of just the endpoints the capsule. For flat surfaces, BoxColliders are the obvious choice. So this is a situation where you want to combine multiple Collider Components into a *compound collider*.

Add a Compound Collider

Unity allows more than one Collider Component on a GameObject, but they have to be different types of Colliders. For example, two BoxCollider Components cannot be attached to the same GameObject. However, an arbitrary set of primitive Collider Components can be combined into a compound collider by attaching each of the Collider Components to its own GameObject and making all of those GameObjects children of the Rigidbody's GameObject.

This is the approach we'll take in combining a CapsuleCollider Component and a BoxCollider Component for the Barrel. To hold those two Collider Components, create two child GameObjects of the Barrel in the Hierarchy View and name them box and capsule for their respective shapes (Figure 7-20).

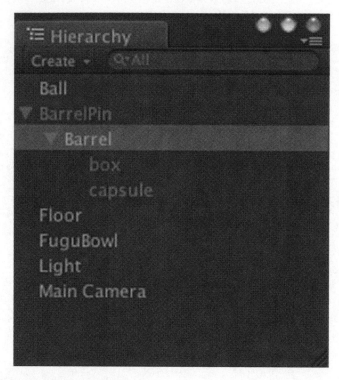

Figure 7-20. Child GameObjects for a compound collider

Rather than create a new CapsuleCollider Component from scratch, let's take advantage of the CapsuleCollider Component that's already oriented and sized properly on the Barrel GameObject by copying that Component. Select the Barrel GameObject, and in the Inspector View, right-click on the CapsuleCollider Component and select Copy Component (Figure 7-21).

Figure 7-21. Copying a Component

Then select the capsule GameObject again, right-click its Transform Component in the Inspector View, and in the pop-up menu select Paste Component As New (Figure 7-22). The capsule GameObject now has a CapsuleCollider Component just like the one created for the Barrel GameObject, so we don't need the original one, anymore. Select the Barrel GameObject, right-click on the CapsuleCollider Component that you just copied, and select Remove Component in the pop-up menu to remove the CapsuleCollider Component. There should be just one CapsuleCollider Component in the Barrel hierarchy, now.

Figure 7-22. Pasting a Component

Let's turn our attention to the BoxCollider Component. You could add it directly to the box GameObject using the Component menu, but if you add the BoxCollider Component to the Barrel GameObject, instead, then Unity will do the work for you in sizing the BoxCollider to the Mesh. So let's repeat the process you went through with the CapsuleCollider Component, only this time with a BoxCollider. With the Barrel GameObject selected, add a BoxCollider Component using the Component menu or the AddComponent button. In the Scene View, you can see the BoxCollider encompasses the Barrel (Figure 7-23).

Figure 7-23. A BoxCollider automatically sized around the Barrel

It's fine that the BoxCollider extends from the top to bottom of the Mesh, since it's desirable to have two flat collision surfaces on both ends. But it's not so desirable to have the BoxCollider extending outside the curved portion of the Barrel. Decrease the width of the BoxCollider by lowering its x and y values of its Size in the Inspector View (remember, the Barrel is rotated) to 2.5. From the top-down vantage of the Scene View (click the y axis of the Scene Gizmo), you can see the BoxCollider now fits inside the barrel (Figure 7-24).

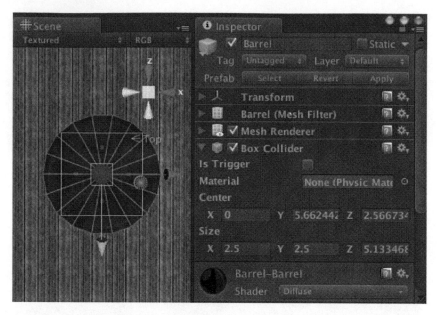

Figure 7-24. Top-down view of a BoxCollider fitting within the Barrel

Now that you have the BoxCollider sized the way you want it, repeat the process for the CapsuleCollider—right-click the BoxCollider in the Inspector View, select Copy Component, select the box GameObject, right-click its Transform Component in the Inspector view, select Paste Component As New. And don't forget to go back to the BoxCollider Component on the Barrel, right-click it to Remove Component. With the Barrel selected, you should see both Collider Components displayed in the Scene View, providing a better approximation of the Barrel shape than either of the Collider Components individually (Figure 7-25).

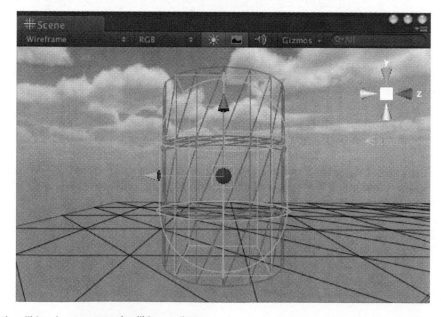

Figure 7-25. Both colliders in a compound collider on display

Update the Prefab

Finally, now that the Barrel is ready to go, select Apply Changes To Prefab in the GameObject menu (Figure 7-26).

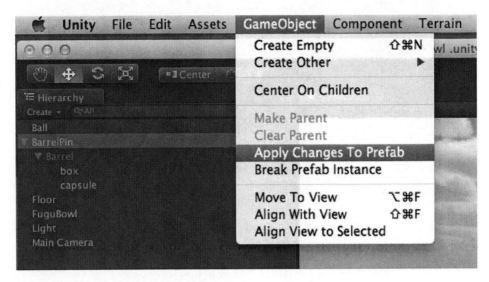

Figure 7-26. Applying changes to the BarrelPin prefab

Tip   It's a good idea to perform a Save Project or Save Scene (which implicitly performs a Save Project), to make sure prefab changes are really saved. Project changes are saved when Unity exits normally, but if it exits abnormally, all bets are off.

With the prefab updated, the Barrel GameObject is no longer needed in the scene and can be removed (Command+Delete or choose Delete from the Edit menu). Now when you click Play, the barrels no longer fall through the Floor, and, as shown in Figure 7-27, they tumble when you roll into them!

Figure 7-27. Bowling into Barrels

A Complex Collider (HyperBowl)

The compound collider created for the BarrelPin prefab is still fairly simple, consisting of just two primitive Collider Components. Compound colliders can be much more complex, depending on the shape they're approximating. As an example of a more realistic bowling pin, take a look at HyperBowl (Figure 7-28).

Figure 7-28. A compound collider for HyperBowl bowling pin

The compound collider for a bowling pin in HyperBowl consists of six primitive colliders: a BoxCollider to provide a flat surface at the bottom, a CapsuleCollider for the neck of the pin, and four SphereColliders of various size to fill out the body and top of the pin.

Add Sounds

Our bowling game is starting to look good, but it's awfully quiet! You could add background music or ambient sound like the looping music to in the dance scene. But a bowling game really should have collision-based sounds, such as a rolling sound for the Ball and collision sounds for each pin.

Get Sounds

First, we need to find some sound files. Once again, let's visit the Asset Store, navigating to the Sound category and then the Sound Effects (FX) subcategory (Figure 7-29).

Figure 7-29. Asset Store search results for free Sound FX

The Free SFX Package from Bleep Blop Audio lists a good variety of audio clips, so let's download that package. The files show up in a Project View folder named Assets inside your Assets folder (submitting packages to the Asset Store is a little tricky so that file organization was probably unintentional).

Add a Rolling Sound

Feel free to play the various sounds by selecting them and clicking the Play button in the Inspector View. But for now we'll use the Sci-Fi Ambiences sound for the Ball rolling sound. It's not a great ball-rolling sound, but it's the only AudioClip in this package that's suitable for looping (Figure 7-30).

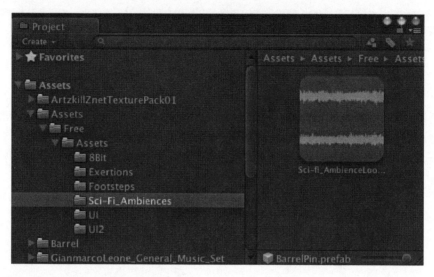

Figure 7-30. The AudioClip used for the Ball rolling sound

Drag the AudioClip to the Ball GameObject in the Hierarchy View and select the Ball. The Inspector View should display a new AudioSource Component that was automatically created to reference the AudioClip (Figure 7-31).

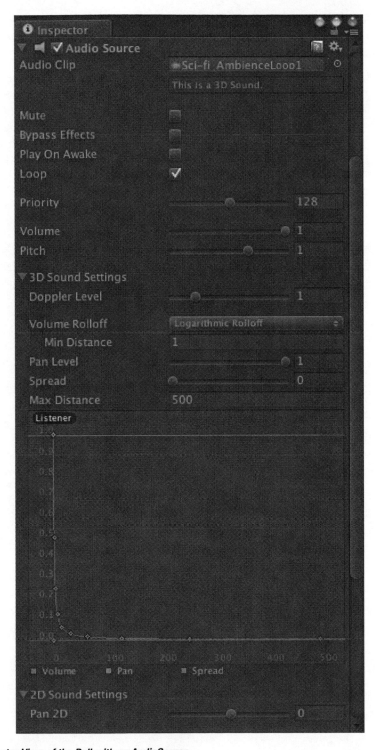

Figure 7-31. The Inspector View of the Ball with an AudioSource

The rolling sound will be controlled by a script and not played automatically, so make sure the Play on Awake checkbox is unchecked. But when the rolling sound is played, it should continue playing until told to stop, so the Loop checkbox should be checked.

The AudioClip is a 3D sound, as indicated in the AudioSource Component below the AudioClip name. That means the sound will attenuate with the distance between the AudioSource Component and AudioListener Component (which is attached to the Main Camera). The attenuation is specified by the graph shown at the bottom of the AudioSource Component. You can adjust the attenuation by selecting among the Volume Rolloff options and also specifying the Min Distance, which specifies at what distance the attenuation begins. If the AudioListener is less than the Min Distance from the AudioSource, then the sound is not attenuated at all. Or you can directly manipulate the attenuation curve by dragging the handle along the curve.

> **Tip**   If you're having trouble hearing an AudioSource, try starting with a high Min Distance to be certain you're hearing it at full volume and then adjust the Min Distance and attenuation curve to your liking. The script to play the rolling sound will be attached to the Ball. Create a new JavaScript, place it in the Scripts folder, and name it `FuguBallSound`. Then add the contents of Listing 7-6 to the script.

Listing 7-6. FuguBallSound.js Script for Ball Rolling Sound

```
#pragma strict

var minSpeed:float = 1.0;
private var sqrMinSpeed:float = 0;

function Awake() {
        sqrMinSpeed = minSpeed*minSpeed;
}

function OnCollisionStay(collider:Collision) {
        if (collider.gameObject.tag == "Floor") {
                if (rigidbody.velocity.sqrMagnitude>sqrMinSpeed) {
                        if (!audio.isPlaying) {
                                audio.Play();
                        }
                } else {
                        if (audio.isPlaying) {
                                audio.Stop();
                        }
                }
        }
}
```

```
function OnCollisionExit(collider:Collision) {
        if (collider.gameObject.tag == "Floor") {
                if (audio.isPlaying) {
                        audio.Stop();
                }
        }
}
```

There is some similarity with the FuguForce script, since both scripts keep track of when the Ball is rolling using collision callbacks and checking the tag of the colliding GameObject to see if it's the Floor. FuguBallSound uses just two of the OnCollision callbacks: OnCollisionStay and OnCollisionExit. OnCollisionEnter isn't implemented, as it would be redundant with OnCollisionStay (the FuguForce script didn't really need OnCollisionEnter, either). Both of the script's collision callbacks reference the audio variable of this Component, which is equivalent to the audio variable of this Component's GameObject and references the attached AudioSource.

When the Ball is on the Floor, OnCollisionStay checks if the Ball is moving faster than a minimum speed, which is specified in a public variable minSpeed so that it can be adjusted in the Inspector View. The script actually compares the square of the Ball speed against the square of minSpeed to avoid the computational expense of square root calculations. If the Ball is on the Floor and moving fast enough, and if the Ball's AudioSource is not already playing its AudioClip, then the script starts playing the AudioClip. If the Ball's speed drops far enough, the rolling sound will stop.

The job of OnCollisionExit is easier, as it just needs to check if audio is playing, and if it is, then stop playing the audio. In other words, if the Ball loses contact with the Floor because it bounced or rolled off, then the rolling sound stops.

Drag the script onto the Ball in the Hierarchy View (Figure 7-32), and click Play to try it out. As the Ball rolls around, the rolling sound should become audible, and the sound should cease when the Ball comes to rest.

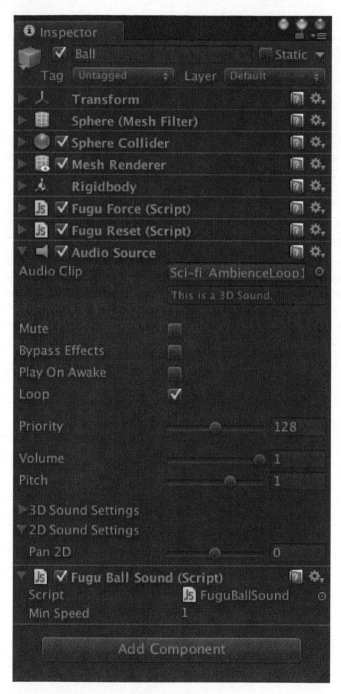

Figure 7-32. The FuguBallSound script attached to the Ball GameObject

Add a Pin Collision Sound

Now you're ready for the pin sound. In place of a real bowling pin sound, we'll make do with the Coin_Pick_Up_03 sound from the Free SFX Pack (Figure 7-33).

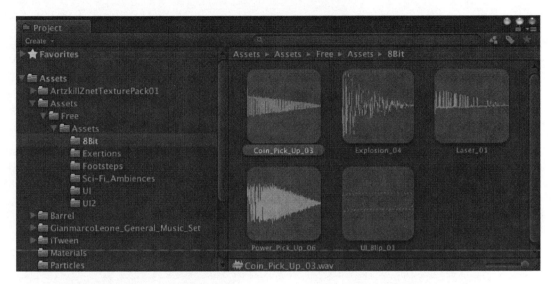

Figure 7-33. The AudioClip used for Pin collision sounds

Select the Pin prefab in the Project View and add an AudioSource Component using the Add Component button at the bottom of the Inspector view. Then click to the right of the AudioClip field of the AudioSource Component to select the Coin_Pick_Up_03 AudioClip. And once again, uncheck the Play on Awake checkbox or you'll hear that sound play whenever the game starts.

Similar to how the Ball rolling sound is played by a script attached to the Ball, the Pin collision sounds will be played by a script attached to each Pin. Create a new JavaScript, place it in the Scripts folder, and name it FuguPinSound. Add the code in Listing 7-7 to the script.

Listing 7-7. Generating Pin Collision Sounds in FuguPinSound.js

```
#pragma strict

var minSpeed = 0.01; // actually the square of the minSpeed

function OnCollisionEnter(collider:Collision) {
        if (collider.relativeVelocity.sqrMagnitude > minSpeed) {
                if (collider.gameObject.tag != "Pin") {
                        audio.Play(); // hit anything besides another pin, play the sound
                } else {
                        // otherwise pin with lower ID gets to play
                        if (gameObject.GetInstanceID() < collider.gameObject.GetInstanceID()) {
                                audio.Play();
                        }
                }
        }
}
```

This script is different from `FuguBallSound` in that it uses the `OnCollisionEnter` callback and not the `OnCollisionStay` or `OnCollisionExit` callbacks. Again, there is a `minSpeed` variable that is compared with the squared magnitude of a velocity. But this time the velocity is the `relativeVelocity` variable of the Collision, since both the Pin and whatever it's colliding with (the Ball or another Pin) may both be moving.

Here it is assumed that each Pin has a tag named Pin, so you can test if the Pin is colliding with another Pin. If the Pin is not colliding with another Pin, then it must be getting hit by the Ball or is falling on the Floor, in which case the script plays the collision sound. If the Pin is getting hit by another Pin, then a decision has to be made which Pin gets to play the collision sound. Otherwise, they'll both play the sound at the same time. A simple trick is used to arbitrate. Each `Object` in Unity has a unique ID number that can be retrieved by the `Object` function `GetInstanceID`. The rule used in the script is that the Pin with the lower ID number wins and gets to play the collision sound.

To attach the `FuguPinSound` script to the Pin prefab, select the prefab in the Project View and use the Add Component button in the Inspector View to select the script. And while you have the Pin prefab in the Inspector View, set its tag to Pin, as the `FuguPinSound` script expects. In the same manner that the Floor tag was create ad assigned to the Floor GameObject, select Add Tag in the Tag menu, add a tag named Pin in the TagManager (make sure you're creating a new tag, not a new layer), and select the Pin prefab again so that you can use the Tag menu to choose the new Pin tag. This, by the way, is an example of how a tag can be used to identify a group of elements rather than uniquely naming one, like we did with the Floor.

The Barrel GameObject in our BarrelPin prefab should now look like Figure 7-34 in the Inspector View.

Figure 7-34. AudioSource and FuguPinSound script attached to the BarrelPin prefab

Now when you click Play and bowl into the barrels, pleasant coin sounds chime in as the barrels bounce around!

Explore Further

The bowling game is starting to look like a bowling game at this point (whereas at the end of the previous chapter, we had at best what could be called a rolling game). But although he player can roll the ball around and knock down bowling pins, we still don't have the rules of the game. Stay tuned for that in the next chapter, which will get much heavier into scripting. In fact, this chapter is sort of a turning point, trending to more and more scripting and less introduction of new Components. So from now on, so you should be spending most of your time in the Scripting Reference of the Unity documentation.

Scripting Reference

The "Instantiate" function in the "Object" class was introduced to create the bowling pins at runtime. This is the function used to spawn GameObjects, typically from prefabs. In other games, you might use Instantiate to spawn anything from pickup items to NPC's. The function is described in the "Scripting Overview" but its page in "Runtime Classes" has more detailed information.

One new callback, "Awake", was introduced as an alternative to the "Start" callback. The "MonoBehaviour" collision callbacks "OnCollisionEnter", "OnCollisionStay", and "OnCollisionExit" were introduced in the previous chapter but used again for rolling and collision sounds. The "Collision" class for information on collisions: relative velocity, the GameObject that was collided against. Other data such as the actual point of contact are also available.

The page for the "Rigidbody" class is worth reading in its entirety. Its variables correspond largely to the properties available in the Inspector view, and besides the "AddForce" function you used to push the Ball, there are many related functions: "AddRelativeForce", "Add Torque", "AddRelativeTorque", "AddExplosionForce", "AddForceAtPosition".

The "Transform" class was used again, this time checking "Transform.position" to determine if the Ball had rolled off the Floor. Since Quaternions were mentioned, take a look at the "rotation" and "localRotation" variables in "Transform" and compare to the "eulerAngles" and "localEulerAngles" variables.From the "GameObject" class, the "SendMessage" and "BroadcastMessage" functions were used to invoke the "ResetPosition" functions in other GameObjects. There's also a "SendMessageUpward" function that works like "BroadcastMessage", except the message is sent up the GameObject's hierarchy instead of down. The message functions are also defined in the "Component" class.

"AudioSource" functions were used to play and stop AudioClips. Other functions are useful if you want to refine your sound code. For example, the HyperBowl rolling sound code changes the volume of the sound (using the "AudioSource.volume" variable) according to the ball's velocity, which not only provides a nicer rolling sound but also a softer cutoff of the sound when stopping.

Assets

We saw the Asset Store has a bountiful selection of free barrel models and sound libraries. And there's much more if you don't restrict yourself to free assets.

Although the Asset Store doesn't yet have bowling pin models, it's not hard to find some on 3D model marketplaces such as `http://Turbosquid.com/`. Free audio, including bowling sounds, are available on the Creative Common licensed `http://freesound.org/`.

Let's Play! Scripting the Game

Our bowling game that has been taking shape over the past few chapters is starting to actually look like a bowling game! It has a bowling ball, bowling pins (or rather, the barrels added in the previous chapter), game controls, and game physics. But it's still more a toy than a game, since it lacks game rules and scoring. That will be remedied in this chapter with a healthy dose of scripting. Most of that will take place in the game controller script, `FuguBowl.js`, which will be filled out with the complete logic for a bowling game laid out as states in a finite state machine (FSM). Just the scoring rules are complicated enough, so those will be encapsulated in a script named `FuguBowlPlayer.js`.

The good news is that, for once, there are no added assets in this chapter besides the `FuguBowlPlayer` script. The bad news is that there's a lot of new code to type in, particularly in the game controller script. Although it may be tempting to just copy the online version of the `FuguBowl` script from the project for this chapter at `http://learnunity4.com/`, it'll be easier to get the hang of implementing game logic for future projects if you put it together from scratch, piece by piece (or in the case of an FSM, state by state). Same goes for the new `FuguBowlPlayer` script.

The Game Rules

First, let's quickly go over the rules of bowling. A game consists of ten frames. In each frame, you have up to two balls to knock down all ten pins. If you knock down all ten with the first ball, it's called a strike, and you advance to the next frame. If you knock down all ten pins with two balls, then it's called a spare. In the tenth frame, if you get a spare or strike, then you're awarded a bonus third (and final) ball.

The final game score is the sum of the scores from each frame. The score for a frame is the number of pins knocked down in that frame, except when it's a spare or strike. If it's a spare, it's the number of pins knocked down (ten), plus the number of pins knocked down with the next ball. If it's a strike, it's also ten, but added to the number of pins knocked down from the next two balls. So a "perfect" game, 12 consecutive strikes, results in a score of 300 (I leave that calculation as an exercise for the reader).

Scoring the Game

The FuguBowl script already defines a class that represents our game, but it makes sense to encapsulate the score code in a player class, since conceptually there is a player (and potentially more than one, although not in this particular game) and the score is associated with the player.

Moreover, the scoring rules for bowling are not simple. Placing the code for bowling score calculation in a separate script not only keeps the game controller script smaller and more readable, but it also allows reuse of the score code for other bowling games.

To begin, create a new JavaScript, name it FuguBowlPlayer, and place it in the Scripts folder (Figure 8-1).

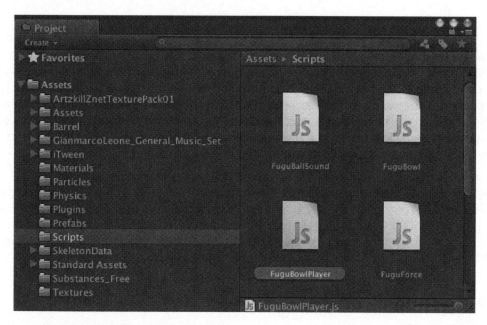

Figure 8-1. Creating the FuguBowlPlayer script

The Frame Score

In the FuguBowlPlayer script, before implementing the FuguBowlPlayer class, let's start with a supporting class called FuguBowlScore that represents the score for a single bowling frame (Listing 8-1). It's small enough and not a MonoBehaviour in its own right (no Start or Update callbacks, for example), so it's fine to just add it to the FuguBowlPlayer script.

Listing 8-1. The FuguBowlScore Class in FuguBowlPlayer.js

```
class FuguBowlScore {
        var ball1:int; // pins down for ball 1
        var ball2:int; // pins down for ball 2
        var ball3:int; // pins down for ball 3
        var total:int; // total score for this frame (may include future rolls)
```

```
function Clear() {
        ball1 = -1;
        ball2 = -1;
        ball3 = -1;
        total = -1;
}

function IsSpare():boolean {
        // doesn't handle spare on ball3
        return !IsStrike() &&
                (ball1 + ball2 == 10);
}

function IsStrike():boolean {
        return ball1 == 10;
}
}
```

The FuguBowlScore class is very simple and doesn't inherit from any other class (it could well be defined as a struct instead of a class, except JavaScript doesn't support defining new structs). The class includes instance variables that represent the score for the first ball rolled, the second ball, and (only relevant in the tenth frame), the bonus ball. FuguBowlScore also has a variable to hold the total score for the frame, which can depend on the result of future rolls if the current frame is a spare or strike.

Each of the variables needs a way to indicate that its score hasn't been calculated. The scores for ball1, ball2, and ball3 aren't available until that ball has been rolled. The total score isn't available until the bowling for this frame is complete, and even then, if the result has been a spare or strike, the score still cannot be calculated until the next ball or two has been rolled.

Leaving the score values as zero won't work, since zero is a valid score when the player doesn't knock down any pins. But there's no way a negative score can be rolled, so -1 will work fine as an indicator a score has not been calculated, yet. The Clear function in FuguBowlScore initializes this frame by setting all the variables to this number.

Besides the Clear function, the FuguBowlScore class has two other member functions. IsStrike returns true if there has been a strike rolled in this frame. That can be tested easily by seeing if the number of pins knocked down with the first ball is ten. The IsSpare function is only slightly more complex; it returns true if the sum of the pins knocked down by the first and second balls is ten, but only if there isn't a strike in this frame (in other words, if you're not adding ten pins from the first ball and zero pins from the second ball).

Notice the :boolean that is added to the two function declarations. That makes it clear that each of these functions returns a boolean value, although the compiler can infer the return type from the code.

The Player Score

With the FuguBowlScore class defined, now we're ready to add the FuguBowlPlayer class, which will aggregate the frame scores for the total game score (Listing 8-2). As with FuguBowlScore, the FuguBowlPlayer class is declared explicitly, even though it has the same name as the script file, and it doesn't inherit from MonoBehaviour (otherwise the class declaration would include extends MonoBehaviour). Besides not having any Unity callback functions, this means the FuguBowlPlayer class is not a subclass of Component and therefore the script can't be attached to a GameObject. In other words, the FuguBowlPlayer script acts as a code library containing classes used by other scripts.

Listing 8-2. The Beginnings of the FuguBowlPlayer Class in FuguBowlPlayer.js

```
class FuguBowlPlayer {
       var scores:FuguBowlScore[]; // all 10 frames of the game

       // constructor
       function FuguBowlPlayer() {
              scores = new FuguBowlScore[10];
              for (var i:int=0; i<scores.length; ++i) {
                     scores[i] = new FuguBowlScore();
              }
              ClearScore();
       }

       function ClearScore() {
              for (var score:FuguBowlScore in scores) {
                     score.Clear();
              }
       }

       function IsSpare(frame:int):boolean {
              return scores[frame].IsSpare();
       }

       function IsStrike(frame:int):boolean {
              return scores[frame].IsStrike();
       }
}
```

The FuguBowlPlayer class naturally contains information about the player, and, for example, could have a String variable for the player's name. However, for the purposes of this book, we'll confine ourselves to tracking the player's bowling score. Therefore, the class has just one instance variable, scores, which is a built-in array of FuguBowlScore objects. Each FuguBowlScore element in the array represents the score for one frame of the bowling game.

> **Note**   Built-in arrays are accessed with indices just like instances of the Array class (used for the pins variable in FuguBowl.js). Built-in arrays have much faster access than instances of Array and can be edited in the Inspector View when declared as public variables. However, built-in arrays, unlike instances of Array, are not resizable at runtime.

The function FuguBowlPlayer within the class definition has the same name as the class, which means it's a *constructor*, a special function called when an instance of this class is created. An explicitly defined constructor isn't always necessary (FuguBowlScore doesn't have one), and it is even prohibited within a MonoBehaviour. But a constructor is warranted in this case, because each newly created FuguBowlPlayer needs to have its *scores* array also created. So the FuguBowlPlayer constructor creates a built-in array of ten entries, declared to be of type FuguBowlScore, and fills the array with newly created FuguBowlScore instances.

The constructor also calls a function ClearScore, which in turn calls Clear on each of the FuguBowlScore objects, ensuring they all start out indicating no score has been registered. The FuguBowlPlayer class also has IsSpare and IsStrike functions that call the same-named functions on the specified FuguBowlScore object, indexed in the scores array by the argument passed in. Since array indices begin at zero, the ten frames of a game are represented by the indices 0-9.

> **Note**   In a sense, the FuguBowlPlayer class acts as a wrapper around the FuguBowlScore class so that other scripts need only know about the FuguBowlPlayer class. As an exercise in polish, you could provide more abstraction by having IsSpare and IsStrike accept frame indices in the range 1-10 and then subtract 1 before using them as array indices.

Setting the Score

As the game progresses, the score has to be updated after each roll of the ball. Let's plan on adding functions named SetBall1Score, SetBall2Score, and SetBall3Score (for the tenth frame) to the FuguBowlPlayer class. Like the IsSpare and IsStrike functions in that class, the additional functions will take a frame index as an argument.

The score for each roll of the ball potentially updates the total score for a previous frame if it had a strike or spare. So first we'll need functions to perform those updates in the FuguBowlPlayer class, named SetSpareScore (Listing 8-3) and SetStrikeScore (Listing 8-4).

Listing 8-3. The SetSpareScore Function in the FuguBowlPlayer Class

```
function SetSpareScore(frame:int) {
      var framescore:FuguBowlScore = scores[frame];
      framescore.total = framescore.ball1+framescore.ball2+scores[frame+1].ball1;
}
```

Listing 8-4. The SetStrikeScore Function in the FuguBowlPlayer Class

```
function SetStrikeScore(frame:int) {
      var framescore:FuguBowlScore = scores[frame];
      framescore.total = framescore.ball1;
      framescore.total+=scores[frame+1].ball1;
      if (frame < 8 && IsStrike(frame+1)) {
            framescore.total+=scores[frame+2].ball1;
      } else {
            framescore.total+=scores[frame+1].ball2;
      }
}
```

The SetSpare function sets the total score to the sum of the first and second ball scores (which should always be ten), plus the score from the next roll, which is the first ball of the next frame.

The SetStrike function is a little more complicated. It sets the total score to the score from the first ball (which should be ten) plus the scores from the next two rolls, which normally consists of the first and second balls from the next frame. But if the next frame is a strike, then the next two rolls are the first ball from the next frame and the first ball from the frame after that.

The use of SetSpareScore and SetStrikeScore is illustrated in the definition of SetBall1Score (Listing 8-5). The first line sets the ball1 variable of the frame with the number of pins knocked down, which is passed in as the second argument of the function. Then, if the current frame is not the first frame, SetBall1Score checks if a spare had been rolled in the previous frame. If that's the case, then the previous frame is waiting for the results of the this roll to calculate the frame's total score, and SetSpareScore is called on that frame to perform that final calculation.

Listing 8-5. The SetBall1Score Function in the FuguBowlPlayer Class

```
function SetBall1Score(frame:int,pinsDown:int) {
      scores[frame].ball1=pinsDown;
      if (frame>0 && IsSpare(frame-1)) {
            SetSpareScore(frame-1);
      }
      if (frame>1 && IsStrike(frame-1) && IsStrike(frame-2)) {
            SetStrikeScore(frame-2);
      }
}
```

If the current frame is not the first or second frame, then SetBal1Score checks if strikes have been rolled in the previous two frames, in which case the first of those frames is waiting for the result of this roll to update its total score, and SetStrikeScore is called for that frame.

Notice SetBall1Score doesn't set the total score for the current frame. If the current roll is not a strike, then the frame isn't over, yet, and if the current roll is a strike, then two more rolls have to take place before the total for this frame can be updated (via SetStrikeScore, of course!).

The SetBall2Score function (Listing 8-6) is more complicated, since it has more cases to handle. As the second argument passed into the function is the number of pins knocked down so far in the frame, the ball2 variable is set to the number of pins down minus whatever was already knocked down for the first ball, except for the special case where the first ball is a strike.

Listing 8-6. SetBall2Score Function in the FuguBowlPlayer Class

```
function SetBall2Score(frame:int,pinsDown:int) {
      var framescore:FuguBowlScore = scores[frame];
      if (IsStrike(frame)) { // we must be in the final frame
            framescore.ball2=pinsDown;
      } else {
            framescore.ball2=pinsDown-framescore.ball1;
      }
      if (!IsSpare(frame) && !IsStrike(frame)) {
            framescore.total= pinsDown;
      }
```

```
        if (frame>0 && IsStrike(frame-1)) {
                SetStrikeScore(frame-1);
        }
}
```

Normally, if the first ball is a strike, the second ball is skipped and SetBall2Score wouldn't even be called. But if a strike occurs on the first roll of the tenth frame, then the second ball is awarded, and ball2 is set to the total number of pins knocked down, because the pins were reset after the strike in the first roll.

The total score for this frame is set to the sum of the first and second balls, except in the case of a spare or strike, in which case one or two future rolls, respectively, have to take place before the total can be resolved.

Given that this is the second roll of the frame, and a spare only adds the first roll of the next frame to its score, there's no way this roll can contribute to a spare score from the previous frame. However, if the previous frame had a strike, calling SetStrikeScore that frame is warranted what that frame, since it's been waiting for the first and second rolls of this frame to complete its total.

The function SetBall3Score (Listing 8-7) is a special case, as a third roll can only occur in the tenth frame, and even then only if there was a strike with the first or second ball or a spare with the first two balls. When SetBall3Score is called, the function sets the ball3 variable with the number of pins down if ball2 was a strike or completed a spare, the two cases where the pins get reset before the third ball. Otherwise, there must have been a strike in the first frame and a something other than a strike in the second, so ball3 is set to the number of pins down minus the pins knocked down by the second ball.

Listing 8-7. The SetBall3Score Function in the FuguBowlPlayer Class

```
function SetBall3Score(frame:int,pinsDown:int) {
        var framescore:FuguBowlScore = scores[frame];
        if (IsStrike(frame) && framescore.ball2 <10) {
                framescore.ball3 = pinsDown - framescore.ball2;
        } else {
                framescore.ball3 = pinsDown; // spare or two strikes
        }
        framescore.total = framescore.ball1+framescore.ball2+framescore.ball3;}
```

Getting the Score

Although implementation of a user interface will take place in the next chapter, we should make sure the FuguBowlPlayer class supports a score display. A typical bowling scoreboard, in real life or in a computer game, displays the score for each roll in each frame, which matches perfectly with the ball1, ball2, and ball3 variables in the FuguBowlScore class. Furthermore, a bowling scoreboard typically has special markings to indicate a spare or strike in each frame, which the IsSpare and IsStrike functions in the FuguBowlPlayer class can accommodate.

However, while FuguBowlScore has a total variable that represents the total score for the frame, a bowling scoreboard usually shows the *game total* score for that frame, i.e., the total cumulative score up to and including that frame. For example, Figure 8-2 shows how the scoreboard in HyperBowl looks after bowling two frames.

Figure 8-2. The HyperBowl scoreboard

The first frame displays the scores for the first and second roll and the resulting total. The second frame displays the score for its first roll and the mark for a spare on the second roll. The game total score displayed in the second frame is the game total score from the first frame plus the additional frame total score from the second frame.

This example provides a clue on how to implement a function that returns the game total score for a frame. Listing 8-8 shows the code for such a function, GetScore, added to the FuguBowlPlayer class. If the specified frame is the first frame of the game, GetScore returns the frame total score. And if the frame total score is -1, meaning not yet available, then GetScore returns -1 to indicate the game total score is not yet available for that frame.

Listing 8-8. The GetScore Function in the FuguBowlPlayer Class

```
function GetScore(frame:int):int {
    if (frame==0 || scores[frame].total==-1) {
        return scores[frame].total;
    } else {
        var prev:int = GetScore(frame-1);
        if (prev==-1) {
            return -1;
        } else {
            return scores[frame].total+prev;
        }
    }
}
```

But if the frame total is available and the frame is not the first frame, then the frame total is added to the game total from the previous frame, unless that game total is not yet available. If the game total is not available from the previous frame, then, again, -1 is returned.

The game total from the previous frame is acquired by calling GetScore on that frame, which in turn will call GetScore on the frame before it, until the first frame is reached. GetScore is an example of a *recursive function*, which is a function that calls itself. Infinite recursion is avoided because eventually GetScore arrives at its *base case*, the first frame, which will always return.

The Complete Listing

The complete listing for the FuguBowlScore script is too unwieldy to show here (it spans four pages), but all of its contents have been shown in this section. The entire script, FuguBowlScore.js, is available in the project for this chapter on http://learnunity4.com/.

If you want to replace a script with the version from http://learnunity4.com/, perform the replacement in the Finder (i.e., drag or paste the file into the Scripts folder of this project). Normally, the ability to just drag a file from the Finder into the Project View is really convenient, but in this case Unity will rename the new file to avoid clobbering the original.

And don't rename the original script yourself, if your intent is to replace it, since any references in the scene will still refer to that script under the new name. Rather, duplicate the original script (either in the Finder or using Duplicate from the Edit menu in the Unity Editor), if you want to keep a copy.

Creating a FuguBowlPlayer

The FuguBowlPlayer class is now all set and ready to use. Since the script is not attached to a GameObject (and can't be, since FuguBowlPlayer is not a MonoBehaviour), a FuguBowlPlayer has to be instantiated at runtime. The natural place to do this is in the FuguBowl script's Awake callback, which is already instantiating the bowling pins (Listing 8-9).

Listing 8-9. Creating a FuguBowlPlayer in FuguBowl.js

```
static var player:FuguBowlPlayer = null;

function Awake() {
        player = new FuguBowlPlayer();
        CreatePins();
}
```

The augmented Awake callback creates a new FuguBowlPlayer instance and assigns it to the variable player, which is declared a static variable for easy access from outside the FuguBowl script (looking ahead to the scoreboard implementation in the next chapter).

To support multiple players, the variable player might instead be an Array of FuguBowlPlayer (a resizable Array instead of a built-in array, to accommodate different numbers of players), and there might be some encapsulating functions like GetPlayer and GetNumberOfPlayers. But for the purposes of this book, we'll keep things simple and focus on a single-player game.

The Pin Status

The FuguBowl script now has a a reference to a FuguBowlPlayer in addition to the bowling pins and ball. But to call the FuguBowlPlayer score functions, FuguBowl must pass in the number of pins that have been knocked down. Rather than adding code to FuguBowl to figure out whether a pin is down, it's cleaner to write that code in a script attached to each pin. Then FuguBowl can just ask each pin if it's down and doesn't have to know about the inner workings of the pins.

For this new pin script, create a new JavaScript, name it FuguPinStatus, and place it in the Scripts folder (Figure 8-3).

Figure 8-3. Create a FuguPinStatus.js script

Next, add the contents of Listing 8-10 to the script.

Listing 8-10. Listing for FuguPinStatus.js

```
#pragma strict

var knockedAngle:float = 45.0;

private var initialAngles:Vector3;

function Awake () {
        initialAngles = transform.localEulerAngles;
}

function IsKnockedOver() {
        return Mathf.Abs(transform.localEulerAngles.x-initialAngles.x)>knockedAngle ||
        Mathf.Abs(transform.localEulerAngles.y-initialAngles.y)>knockedAngle ||

                Mathf.Abs(transform.localEulerAngles.z-initialAngles.z)>knockedAngle;
}
```

The Awake callback in the script saves the GameObject's initial rotation in the private variable initialAngles for comparison later. The function IsKnockedOver returns true or false depending on whether the pin's rotation around any axis has changed by more than the number of degrees specified in the knockedAngle variable.

In the Project View, select the Barrel GameObject in the BarrelPin prefab and use the Add Component button in the Inspector View to attach the FuguPinStatus script (Figure 8-4).

Figure 8-4. The FuguPinStatus script attached to the Barrel pin prefab

Before querying each pin to see if it's been knocked over, the FuguBowl script needs to find the pins. Querying each GameObject in the variable pins would work if the Array is filled with the capsule-based Pin prefab but when the Array is full of BarrelPin GameObjects, the Barrel GameObjects that act as the real pins are children of those BarrelPin GameObjects.

Fortunately, in Chapter 7 we tagged all the "real" pins, the GameObjects with Rigidbodies and Meshes that actually move, with the tag Pin. This makes it possible to retrieve an array of all the real pins using the static function GameObject.FindGameObjectsWithTag. That should take place at the end of the CreatePins function in the FuguBowl script, after all the pins have been instantiated (Listing 8-11). The tagged pins are assigned to a private variable pinBodies.

Listing 8-11. Declaring and Setting the pinBodies Variable in FuguBowl.js

```
private var pinBodies:GameObject[]; // the real physical pins

function CreatePins() {
        pins = new Array();
        var offset = Vector3.zero;
        for (var row=0; row<pinRows; ++row) {
                offset.z+=pinDistance;
                offset.x=-pinDistance*row/2;
                for (var n=0; n<=row; ++n) {
                        pins.push(Instantiate(pin, pinPos+offset, Quaternion.identity));
                        offset.x+=pinDistance;
                }

        }
        pinBodies = GameObject.FindGameObjectsWithTag("Pin");
}
```

The number of pins that have been knocked down are counted by the function GetPinsDown function (Listing 8-12) that loops through the pinObjects array, incrementing a local variable pinsDown for each pin whose IsKnockedOver function returns true. After the loop is complete, the value of the pinsDown counter is returned.

Listing 8-12. The GetPinsDown Function in FuguBowl.js

```
function GetPinsDown():int {
        var pinsDown:int = 0;
        for (var pin:GameObject in pinBodies) {
                if (pin.GetComponent(FuguPinStatus).IsKnockedOver()) {
                        ++pinsDown;
                }
        }
        return pinsDown;
}
```

Besides counting pins that have been knocked down, we can remove them, like the way real pins get scraped away after getting knocked down in a real bowling alley. The function RemoveDownedPins (Listing 8-13) loops through the pinBodies list and calls SetActive(false) on each one that returns true for IsKnockedDown. Calling SetActive(false) is equivalent to unchecking the checkbox on the top left of a GameObject in the Inspector View. Each pin that is knocked down, while not getting completely removed form the scene, is made invisible and does not collide.

Listing 8-13. The RemovePins Function in FuguBowl.js

```
function RemoveDownedPins() {
      for (var pin:GameObject in pinBodies) {
            if (pin.GetComponent(FuguPinStatus).IsKnockedOver()) {
                  pin.SetActive(false);
            }
      }
}
```

Of course, deactivated pins need to be reactivated at some point. The existing ResetPins function (Listing 8-14) is a good place to do that, since ResetPins is called when restoring the pins to their original positions in preparation for bowling a new frame.

Listing 8-14. ResetPins Function in FuguBowl.js

```
function ResetPins() {
      for (var pin:GameObject in pinBodies) {
            pin.SetActive(true);
            pin.SendMessage("ResetPosition");
      }
}
```

In fact, now the loop through the pins Array can be replaced with a loop through pinBodies. Within the loop, SetActive(true) is called on each pin in case it was deactivated and SendMessage can replace BroadcastMessage because each pin in pinBodies is known to have the FuguReset script attached.

The Game Logic

I highly recommend sketching out a game as an finite state machine (FSM) before attempting to code the game logic. A finite state machine represents a program as, surprise, a finite set of states. An FSM is in one state at any time and transitions from state to state.

> **Note** The term state machine often refers to an FSM, but technically there is a whole range of state machines ranging from the FSM, the simplest and least-powerful class of automata, up to the Turing Machine, which has infinite memory and a potentially infinite number of states.

Once you have your game visualized as an FSM, you can be confident that you can code it. Conversely, if you can't visualize your game flow as an FSM, you probably just have a vague idea that you're not yet ready to implement it!

Design the FSM

To sketch out the FSM, think of all the states that the game will go through. All FSMs have an initial state, which in this case is the beginning of a new game. The player starts out in the first frame with the first ball, starts rolling the ball, and when finished rolling, has a strike, a spare, or a regular score. Then the player moves onto either the second ball or back to the first in a new frame, and the process is repeated. If the player is on the second ball, the flow is the same except for the transition back to the first ball of a new frame or possibly the third ball if this is the tenth frame and a the player rolled a strike or spare. After all ten frames have been completed, the FSM transitions to the GameOver state, which may cycle back to a new game.

Figure 8-5 shows how the state machine just described might look.

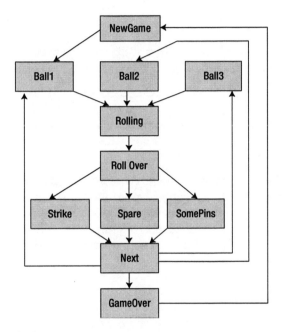

Figure 8-5. A state machine for bowling

It's not important to get it exactly right the first time. Typically, when you sketch out the flow of a program and then start scripting, you'll realize you forgot something or there's a better way, and then you go back and adjust your original design. It's like what one of my professors said about constructing proofs—it's a messy process completing one, but then you go back and clean it up and pretend that's how you planned it in the first place!

Technically, an FSM doesn't have memory, so a really complete state machine for bowling would have a lot of duplicated states for all three balls and even all ten frames. But a state machine with a few hundred states would be hard to understand, which would largely defeat its purpose. We don't have to be purists about this, so let's assume there are variables tracking the current frame that's being played and which ball the player is rolling.

Tracking the Game

The variables defined in the FuguBowl script to track the current frame and current ball are shown in Listing 8-15.

Listing 8-15. The Variables in FuguBowl.js that Track the Current Frame and Ball

```
private var frame:int; // current frame, ranges for 0-9 (representing 1-10)
private var roll:Roll; // the current roll in the current frame

enum Roll {
      Ball1,
      Ball2,
      Ball3
}
```

The variable `frame` tracks the current frame with an `int`, ranging from 0-9 instead of 1-10 because that number will be used as an array index when it's passed to the `FuguBowlPlayer` functions.

The variable `roll` tracks the current roll of the ball and could also have been declared an `int`, choosing a convention where the numbers 0-2 or 1-3 represent the three possible balls in a frame. But it's cleaner to define an `enum` (short for *enumeration*), which essentially allows you to define a new type where the value is one from a list of named values. So roll is declared to be of type `Roll`, which is an enum with values `Ball1`, `Ball2`, or `Ball3`.

By the way, at this point we've encountered several different categories of types: primitive types like `int` and `boolean`, built-in arrays that contain other types, enums like `Roll`, structs like `Vector3`, and classes like `GameObject`, `Component`, and `FuguBowlPlayer`. Of these categories, classes and arrays are *reference types*, meaning different variables can reference the same instance of that type, and modifications to the instance will be visible through every variable referencing that instance.

Starting the State Machine

Okay, now that you've sketched out the state machine, how do you go about coding it? FSMs are useful enough that some game engines, including CryEngine, Unreal, and Second Life, have built-in support for in their scripts. Unfortunately, Unity doesn't, but since this is software, there are a variety of ways to homebrew some FSM support.

One way is to have essentially a big conditional statement inside the `Update` function that performs different actions depending on which state it's in (and we'd probably use an enum to define those different states). However, that method tends to result in unwieldy `Update` functions. In fact, because because the `Update` callback added to the FuguBowl script in Chapter 7 will be obviated by the state machine we're about to add, you should delete that callback from the FuguBowl script right now.

Another way to create an FSM, which I tried for a while, is to represent a state machine with a GameObject that has several scripts attached, where each script represents a state. Whenever the current state is exited, that script would disable itself and enable the next script or state. This method is appealing, since each script or state has its own `Update` function and other callbacks. But I find my state machines easier to understand and work with if the entire FSM is contained in a single script.

So, ultimately I've settled on implementing state machines with *coroutines*, which are functions that can suspend themselves for one or more frames at a time by calling yield (the function is *yielding* control temporarily even though it hasn't finished executing). You can implement each state as a coroutine that returns when the state is exited. While in the state, the coroutine performs whatever action is supposed to take place during that state, but repeatedly yielding so it doesn't block the rest of Unity (including the renderer and physics) from running. And before returning, the coroutine specifies the next state it will transition to.

Some, but not all, callbacks can be used as coroutines. For example, Awake cannot be used as a coroutine, nor Update, but Start can yield and thus can act as an FSM controller (Listing 8-16).

Listing 8-16. Start Callback Running State Machine in FuguBowl.js

```
private var state:String;

function Start() {
        state="StateNewGame";
        while (true) {
                Debug.Log("State "+state);
                yield StartCoroutine(state);
                yield;
        }
}
```

The name of the current state, which is the name of the coroutine implementing that state, is held as a String in a private variable named state. The Start callback loops endlessly, repeatedly calling StartCoroutine with the value of state to invoke the coroutine. Start yields on the call to StartCoroutine so that it waits until the state coroutine has finished executing before starting a coroutine with the next value of state.

There's no guarantee the coroutines called will yield at all, so Start includes an extra yield in the loop for good measure to make sure at least one yield occurs between states and gives the rest of the game engine an opportunity to work.

As a debugging aid, Start calls Debug.Log before executing each state coroutine (Figure 8-6). This is a convenient way to trace the state machine progress when testing the game.

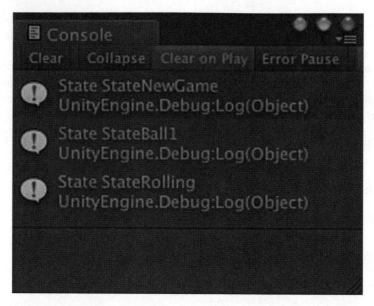

Figure 8-6. The Console View of a state machine debug trace

The States

As a convention, we'll prefix all of the state coroutines with State to indicate those functions are states in a state machine.

StateNewGame

The initial state of the bowling state machine is StateNewGame (Listing 8-17), which starts a new game by clearing the player's score and setting the current frame index to 0, specifying the player is currently bowling the first frame of the game.

Listing 8-17. StateNewGame in FuguBowl.js

```
function StateNewGame() {
     player.ClearScore();
     frame = 0;
     state="StateBall1";
}
```

Before returning (effectively, exiting the state), StateNewGame specifies the next state is StateBall1, which is the state where the player begins rolling the first ball of the frame.

StateBall1

The first action StateBall1 (Listing 8-18) takes is to reset the positions of the pins, Ball, and also the Main Camera. This isn't really necessary the first time the state is entered, i.e., the beginning of the game, but when the player finishes bowling a frame and transitions back to this state, everything needs to be placed in its starting position and rotation (pins that may be knocked over will have their rotations changed).

Listing 8-18.   The State to Start Rolling the First Ball in FuguBowl.js

```
function StateBall1() {
      ResetEverything(); // reset pins, camera and ball
      roll = Roll.Ball1;
      state="StateRolling";
}
```

After performing the reset, this state sets the roll variable to Roll.Ball1, indicating the player is rolling the first ball of the frame. Finally, this state transitions to StateRolling, the state occupied while the ball is rolling toward the pins.

StateBall2

Like StateBall1, StateBall2 (Listing 8-19) starts by resetting the Ball and Main Camera.

Listing 8-19.   The State to Commence Rolling the Second Ball in FuguBowl.js

```
function StateBall2() {
      ResetBall();
      ResetCamera();
      if (GetPinsDown()==10) {
            ResetPins();
      } else {
            RemoveDownedPins();
      }
      roll = Roll.Ball2;
      state="StateRolling";
}
```

If the player has reached this point, normally it means the first ball of the frame didn't result in a strike, and now it's time to try knocking down the remaining pins, after cleaning up the downed pins from the previous roll. But if all the pins are down, it must be that special case in the tenth frame where a strike then results in two more rolls, and the pins are reset.

Before exiting the state, roll is set to Roll.Ball2, and as with StateBall1, the next state is set to StateRolling.

StateBall3

And speaking of the tenth frame, that's the only case where StateBall3 (Listing 8-20) occurs, since that's the only frame in which the player can roll three times.

Listing 8-20. The State to Start Rolling the Third Ball in FuguBowl.js

```
function StateBall3() {
      ResetBall();
      ResetCamera();
      if (GetPinsDown()==10) {
            ResetPins();
      } else {
            RemoveDownedPins();
      }
      roll = Roll.Ball3;
      state="StateRolling";
}
```

StateBall3, just like StateBall2, resets the ball and if you knocked down ten pins from the previous rolls in the frame (either a spare or two strikes), it will reset the pins. Otherwise, the downed pins from the previous roll are cleaned up. Again, the state sets the roll variable, to Roll.Ball3, and transitions to StateRolling.

StateRolling

StateRolling (Listing 8-21) more or less fulfills the Update function created in the previous chapter and discarded earlier in this one. The state yields every frame, doing nothing except waiting until the Ball control should cease.

Listing 8-21. The State for Rolling the Ball in FuguBowl.js

```
function StateRolling() {
      while (true) {
            if (ball.transform.position.z>pinPos.z) {
                  state = "StateRolledPast";
                  return;
            }
            if (ball.transform.position.y<sunkHeight) {
                  state = "StateGutterBall";
                  return;
            }
            yield;
      }
}
```

There are two cases where this roll is definitely done. Either the Ball rolls off the edge of the Floor, which is basically the same situation as a gutter ball in a normal bowling game, or when you've rolled up to the pins (if you don't relinquish control, the game's too easy; you can roll back and forth among the pins like a monster truck!).

Detecting a gutter ball is easy. As in the now-removed Update callback, this state checks if the ball has fallen below the y position specified in the sunkHeight variable. If so, transition to the gutter ball state. The other case is nearly as simple, checking if the ball's z position has passed the first pin's z position. Essentially, the state is checking if the ball has reached the "pin line" stretching left to right across the floor where that pin is placed. If it has, then transition to StateRolledPast.

We actually didn't consider having `StateGutterBall` and `StateRolledPast` when we sketched out our FSM, but it's not a big deal. You can now just insert those states in place of the formerly direct transition between `StateRolling` and `StateRollOver`.

StateRolledPast

After rolling far enough to reach the pins, the `StateRolledPast` state is entered (Listing 8-22). This state "lets go" of the Ball by disabling the Ball and Main Camera controls.

Listing 8-22. The State Entered when Reaching the Pins in FuguBowl.js

```
function StateRolledPast() {
        var follow:Behaviour = Camera.main.GetComponent("SmoothFollow");
        if (follow != null) {
                follow.enabled = false;
        }
        ball.GetComponent(FuguForce).enabled = false;
        yield WaitForSeconds(5);
        state = "StateRollOver";
}
```

To disable the Main Camera `SmoothFollow` script, the state accesses the Main Camera through the static variable `main` in the Camera class and calls `GetComponent` on that GameObject, passing in `SmoothFollow` as the class of the Component to be retrieved. That returns the `SmoothFollow` script that's attached to the Main Camera. The script is then assigned to a local variable named `follow`.

The `follow` variable is declared to be of type `Behaviour`, which is a direct subclass of `Component`. A `Behaviour` can be enabled or disabled by setting its `enabled` variable. `follow` could instead have been declared as a more specific class like `MonoBehaviour` (a subclass of `Behaviour` and the parent class of any script that can be attached to a GameObject) or even `SmoothFollow`, the most specific class of the `SmoothFollow` script, because all of those classes inherit the `enabled` variable from `Behaviour`. But choosing the most general class that's suitable provides the most flexibility. For example, if you declared `follow` to be of type `SmoothFollow` and then later opted to use a different Camera control script, you would have to adjust the type declaration for `follow`.

> **Tip**   For type declarations, use the most general class that implements the functions and variables you need.

Another reason not to declare `follow` to be of type `SmoothFollow` is that the version of this project available on `http://learnunity4.com/` doesn't include any Asset Store or Standard Assets packages, including the `SmoothFollow` script. Referencing the `SmoothFollow` class when it's not available in the project will result in a compiler error.

This is the reason why "SmoothFollow" is passed to `GetComponent` as a String, so that it's not used to find a class until `GetComponent` is called at runtime, at which point `GetComponent` returns null. Attempting to access the `enabled` variable on null will result in an error, so the state first checks if `follow` is null before attempting to disable it. The FuguForce script attached to the Ball is disabled in a similar manner, by calling `GetComponent` on the Ball to retrieve the `FuguForce` script and then settings its enabled variable to false. But, unlike the Main Camera and the SmoothFollow script, because we're certain the Ball has a FuguForce script attached, there's no need to perform a null check test before disabling the script.

Furthermore, GetComponent is an overloaded function with one version taking a String argument and the other taking a class directly. So instead of passing the "FuguForce" to GetComponent, the class FuguForce is passed directly. This way, a compiler error will result if the class name is misspelled (e.g., GetComponent(FuguFource)).

Passing in a misspelled String name of a class (e.g., GetComponent("FuguFource")), won't result in an error at compile time, which may at first sound like a good thing, but it's better to catch problems early. At runtime, that call to GetComponent will return null, which could result in a crash if the code is expecting a non-null result, or just produce aggravating debugging sessions, as you wonder why that script isn't getting disabled as you expect.

> **Tip**   Let the compiler do your error checking whenever possible.

At some point, the SmoothFollow and FuguForce scripts have to be reenabled. The natural place to do that is in the ResetCamera and ResetBall functions (Listing 8-23), as they get called when a roll is over and the Main Camera and Ball, respectively, are reset to start another roll.

Listing 8-23. ResetBall and ResetCamera Functions in FuguBowl.js

```
function ResetBall() {
        ball.GetComponent(FuguForce).enabled = true;
        ball.SendMessage("ResetPosition");
}
function ResetCamera() {
        var follow:Behaviour = Camera.main.GetComponent("SmoothFollow");
        if (follow != null) {
                follow.enabled = true;
        }
        Camera.main.SendMessage("ResetPosition");
}
```

In both the ResetBall and ResetCamera functions, the code to enable the script Component is the same one used to disable the script, except the enabled variable is set to true.

After disabling both the FuguForce and SmoothFollow scripts, StateRolledPast waits five seconds before transitioning to the next state, StateRollOver, allowing time for the Ball to roll into the pins (or past the pins). A while loop that calls yield until the desired amount of time has passed (by checking Time.time) would do the trick, but it's much more convenient to call yield on the function WaitForSeconds, which takes a number of seconds as an argument (in StateRolledPast, the number of seconds is hardcoded to 5, but it could easily be a public variable to allow customization). As a result, the coroutine StateRolledPast will essentially pause (without blocking execution in the rest of Unity) until the given time has elapsed.

StateGutterBall

The gutter ball state is a lot simpler than StateRolledPast. It just transitions directly to StateRollOver (Listing 8-24).

Listing 8-24. The State for a Gutter Ball in FuguBowl.js

```
function StateGutterBall() {
      state = "StateRollOver";
}
```

Although it seems StateRolling could transition directly to StateRollOver instead of passing through StateGutterBall, inclusion of StateGutterBall provides some symmetry with StateRolledPast. And in a polished bowling game, you would most likely implement some kind of feedback that you rolled a gutter ball. For example, in HyperBowl, animated letters spelling out "Gutter" fly across the screen (Figure 8-7), and this animation takes place in StateGutterBall.

Figure 8-7. Animated text for a gutter ball in HyperBowl

Those letters are animated with iTween, by the way. You aren't limited to visual feedback either. In my Fugu Bowl app on the App Store, StateGutterBall plays the sound of kids booing!

StateRollOver

When the roll of the ball is deemed complete (the Ball has guttered by rolling off the Floor or has reached the pin line), the FSM enters StateRollOver (Listing 8-25), which wraps up the current roll by figuring out what was scored.

Listing 8-25. The State for the End of a Roll in FuguBowl.js

```
function StateRollOver() {
        var pinsDown:int = GetPinsDown();
        switch (roll) {
                case Roll.Ball1: player.SetBall1Score(frame,pinsDown); break;
                case Roll.Ball2: player.SetBall2Score(frame,pinsDown); break;
                case Roll.Ball3: player.SetBall3Score(frame,pinsDown); break;
        }
        if (roll == Roll.Ball1 && player.IsStrike(frame)) {
                state = "StateStrike";
                return;
        }
        if (roll == Roll.Ball2 && player.IsSpare(frame)) {
                state = "StateSpare";
                return;
        }
        state = "StateKnockedSomeDown";
}
```

This state first ascertains how many pins are down by calling the GetPinsDown function. That number is passed to the appropriate FuguBowlPlayer scoring function, based on whether this is the first, second or third ball, so the score for this roll is recorded. The next state depends on the result of the roll, whether it was a strike (which can only happen on the first ball), a spare (which can only happen on the second ball), or any other result (StateKnockedSomeDown isn't a great name, considering we might have knocked down zero pins, but I like it better than StateNotSpareOrStrike).

StateSpare, StateStrike, and StateKnockedSomeDown

Like the gutter ball state, the states for bowling a strike, a spare, and anything else have no actions except for transitioning to the next state (Listing 8-26).

Listing 8-26. StateSpare, StateStrike, and StateKnockedSomeDown in FuguBowl.js

```
function StateSpare() {
        state="StateNextBall";
}

function StateStrike() {
        state = "StateNextBall";
}
```

```
function StateKnockedSomeDown() {
        state="StateNextBall";
}
```

All three of these states transition to StateNextBall, so it's tempting to consider these states redundant and remove them entirely. But for a complete bowling game you might initiate some kind of feedback in each of these states, like congratulatory audio and graphics for bowling a strike. I mentioned that Fugu Bowl on the App Store emits a booing sound during a gutter ball. The same app utters a cheer when a strike is bowled, and this happens in StateStrike. And HyperBowl displays animated "SPARE" and "STRIKE" text in StateSpare and StateStrike, respectively.

StateNextBall

StateNextBall is the most complicated state so far (Listing 8-27), because most of the bowling rules kick in here. This is where you must decide whether you're rolling another ball in this frame or advancing to the next frame.

Listing 8-27. The State for Transitioning to the Next Ball in FuguBowl.js

```
function StateNextBall() {
        if (frame == 9) { // last frame
                switch (roll) {
                        case Roll.Ball1: // always has a second roll
                         state = "StateBall2";
                         break;
                        case Roll.Ball2: // bonus roll if we got a spare or strike
                                if (player.IsSpare(frame) || player.IsStrike(frame)) {
                                        state = "StateBall3";
                                } else {
                                        state = "StateGameOver";
                                }
                                break;
                        case Roll.Ball3:
                                state = "StateGameOver";
                                break;
                }
                // all other frames
        } else if (roll == Roll.Ball1 && !player.IsStrike(frame)) {
                        state = "StateBall2";
                } else {
                        ++frame;
                        state = "StateBall1";
                }
        }
}
```

The tenth frame in particular is complex, because you have to check for the end of the game and could potentially have three rolls. So let's first look at the bottom portion of the code, which applies to the first nine frames. If you just finished rolling Ball1 and didn't get a strike, then the next state is StateBall2. Otherwise, you must have rolled Ball2 or got a strike, so either way, the next state is StateBall1, and you increment your frame index. In the tenth frame, you always roll at least twice, so if you just rolled Ball1, you set the next state to StateBall2. If you just rolled Ball2, and the result is a spare or strike, then you set the next state to StateBall3, otherwise you go to the game-over state. And of course if you just rolled Ball3, that's the last possible roll, and you go to the game-over state.

StateGameOver

Finally, you're reached the end-of-game state, StateGameOver (Listing 8-28).

Listing 8-28. The Game Over State in FuguBowl.js

```
function StateGameOver() {
        Debug.Log("Final Score: "+player.GetScore(9));
        state="StateNewGame";
}
```

In lieu of a fancy user interface (the UnityGUI system will be introduced in the next chapter), let's take the opportunity to print out the final score in the Console View using the function Debug.Log. The final score is retrieved by calling the FuguBowlPlayer function GetScore with the array index 9, which indicates you want the total score tallied in the tenth frame.

In a complete bowling game, this is the place to put up a "Game Over" message, submit the score to a leader board, and any other action appropriate at the end of a game (in HyperBowl, the Application.LoadLevel function is called to switch to a scene displaying the score and present a trophy). But for now, let's just transition back to StateNewGame and start a new game.

The Complete Listing

The overhauled FuguBowl script is much larger even than the FuguBowlPlayer script, so the entire listing for FuguBowl.js isn't shown here. The complete script is available on http://learnunity4.com/ and all its contents have been presented in this section, piece by piece (or mostly, state by state).

Explore Further

This chapter was a change of pace, concentrating solely on scripting. Most of that scripting was added to the game controller script, FuguBowl.js, in the form of a state machine, but scoring code was incorporated in a new script, FuguBowlPlayer.js.

If you're tired of writing big chunks of code and long for the little script snippets that we started with, you just have to endure writing one more big script in the next chapter, for the user interface. And, as a counterpart for the scoring code added in this chapter, the next one includes a small additional script to display a scoreboard.

Unity Manual

State machines are useful not only for game control logic but also for anything that can be represented as going through different states (simple examples: a light is on or off, a weapon is locked and loaded, a door is open or closed). State machines are particularly useful for animation (walking, running, throwing) which is why the new Mecanim animation system does have its own FSM capability. This is described in the Unity Manual, under "The Mecanim Animation System" section, in "Animation State Machines."

Scripting Reference

The major scripting technique introduced in this chapter was the use of coroutines, specifically to implement an FSM in the `FuguBowl` script. The "Scripting Overview" section of the Scripting Reference has a page on "Coroutines and Yield," that provides a basic explanation some examples.

The classes related to coroutines include `"Coroutine"` and `"WaitForSeconds"` (both of them inherit from `"YieldInstruction"`). The one function we used is the `"StartCoroutine"` function of `"MonoBehaviour"`. The documentation page for each `MonoBehavior`, callback specifies whether the callback can be used as a coroutine (as we saw, `"Start"` can, but `"Awake"`, `"Update"`, and `"FixedUpdate"` cannot).

The added code in the `FuguBowl` script also had frequent cause to access Components, so the page on "Accessing Components" is relevant. That page lists the "Component" and "GameObject" variables that can be used to access commonly attached Components and also provides examples on how to call the function "GetComponent" (either on a `Component` or a `GameObject`) to access Components, including scripts.

Asset Store

Several more sophisticated FSM frameworks are available on the Asset Store. A search for "fsm" in the Asset Store window brings up several, including a popular visual programming package called Playmaker, developed by Huton Games at `http://hutongames.com/`.

On the Web

Wikipedia (`http://wikipedia.org/`) has an extensive description of bowling and its scoring rules. Just search for "bowling" on the site. And if you search for "state machine" you'll find an article that explains probably more than you'll ever want to know about FSM's!

I mentioned some game engines have FSM's built into their scripting system. It's interesting to compare them and see how FSM's are implemented in those systems. For example, CryEngine has a state-switching mechanism built into its Lua scripts. Visit the CryEngine 3 Free SDK site (`http://freesdk.dev.net/`) and search for "state" to find an article on "Entity States."

I worked on a CryEngine-based virtual world called Blue Mars, which heavily utilized that FSM support. Visit the Blue Mars wiki (`http://create.bluemars.com/`) and search for "entity script" to see the introductory examples (I actually started that wiki entry five years ago!)

And even the most well-known virtual world, Second Life, has FSM support. Search for "state" on the Second Life wiki (`http://wiki.secondlife.com`) to see how states are defined using the Linden Scripting Language (LSL).

Chapter 9

The Game GUI

Over the past several chapters, we've put together a fairly complete bowling game with 3D graphics, physics, sound, player controls, and automatic camera movement. The game has almost every category of feature expected in a 3D game except for one: a graphical user interface (GUI). In particular, the bowling game should have a scoreboard, and games usually have a menu that shows up at the beginning of the game and when the game is paused.

> **Tip** I have had an iOS game rejected by Apple for not having a pause menu, so I do recommend including one, if only for that reason.

In this chapter, we'll implement both a scoreboard and start/pause menu with Unity's built-in GUI system, known as UnityGUI (you can tell how long a Unity feature has been around by the coolness of its name—more recent features have names like Shuriken, Mecanim, and Beast).

The scoreboard and pause menu scripts are available in the project for this chapter on http://learnunity4.com/, but, to iterate a point ad nauseam, entering the code line by line and function by function provides the best learning experience!

The Scoreboard

Let's start off with the scoreboard because it's a simpler case than the menu. The scoreboard only needs to display, with no interaction required. As described in the previous chapter, a typical bowling scoreboard will show the results for each frame (i.e., the first and second ball, and possibly third, in the tenth frame), and also the total score up to that frame. We won't do anything fancy here, just display the scores with text by drawing the scoreboard as a sequence of labels, with each label displaying the score for that frame as text.

Create the Script

Let's get started by creating a GameObject with a scoreboard script attached (this should be a familiar process by now). In the Project View, create a new JavaScript in the Scripts folder and name it FuguBowlScoreboard (Figure 9-1).

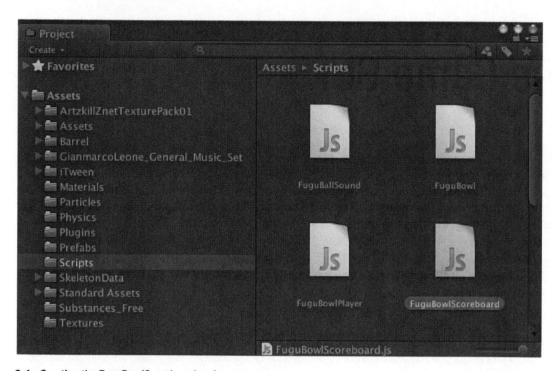

Figure 9-1. Creating the FuguBowlScoreboard script

Next, create a new GameObject in the Hierarchy View, name it Scoreboard, and attach the FuguBowlScoreboard script to it.

Now you're ready to add UnityGUI code to the FuguBowlScoreboard script. If you've developed user interfaces with other GUI systems, you'll probably find UnityGUI a bit unusual. Instead of creating and placing GUI objects that have callbacks responding to events like button clicks, UnityGUI Controls are created inside OnGUI callback functions, which are called every frame (actually a few times a frame). To demonstrate quickly how UnityGUI works, place the contents of Listing 9-1 in the FuguBowlScoreboard script.

Listing 9-1. Testing a Simple UnityGUI Label in FuguBowlScoreboard.js

```
#pragma strict

function OnGUI() {
    GUI.Label(Rect(5,100,200,20),"This is a label");
}
```

All UnityGUI Controls are created with calls to static functions in the GUI class (and also GUILayout, but I'll get to that in the next section). The OnGUI callback of Listing 9-1 calls GUI.Label to draw a label, passing in a Rect (rectangle) that specifies the label is to be drawn at x,y coordinates 5,100 (the coordinate system for UnityGUI has 0,0 at the top left of the screen) and with a width and height of 200 and 20 pixels, respectively. The second argument is the text to display in the label. Click Play and you should see "This is a label" appear on the screen.

Placing user interface code in a single script callback can be cumbersome if the user interface is complex. But for this simple user interface, the OnGUI callback is convenient, and we can expand on it to form a no-frills text-based bowling scoreboard. Let's replace the single-label example in FuguBowlScoreboard with the contents of Listing 9-2.

Listing 9-2. A Bowling Scoreboard

```
#pragma strict

var style:GUIStyle; // customize the appearance

function OnGUI() {
        for (var f:int=0; f<10; f++) {
                var score:String="";
                var roll1:int = FuguBowl.player.scores[f].ball1;
                var roll2:int = FuguBowl.player.scores[f].ball2;
                var roll3:int = FuguBowl.player.scores[f].ball3;
                switch (roll1) {
                        case -1: score += " "; break;
                        case 10: score +="X"; break;
                        default: score += roll1;
                }
                score+="/";
                if (FuguBowl.player.IsSpare(f)) {
                        score +="I";
                } else {
                        switch (roll2) {
                                case -1: score += " "; break;
                                case 10: score +="X"; break;
                                default: score += roll2;
                        }
                }
                if (f==9) {
                        score+="/";
                        if (10==roll2+roll3) {
                                score +="I";
                        } else {
                                switch (roll3) {
                                        case -1: score += " "; break;
                                        case 10: score +="X"; break;
                                        default: score += roll3;
                                }
                        }
                }
```

```
            GUI.Label(Rect(f*30+5,5,50,20),score,style);
            var total:int=FuguBowl.player.GetScore(f);
            if (total != -1) {
                    GUI.Label(Rect(f*30+5,20,50,20)," "+total,style);
            }
        }
    }
}
```

The new OnGUI callback loops through all ten frames, querying the FuguBowlPlayer for the FuguBowlScore representing each frame. At the bottom of the loop, one or two calls to GUI.Label are issued. The first GUI.Label displays the score for each ball of the frame, and the second GUI.Label is drawn below the first, displaying the game total score for that frame if it is available.

Most of the code in the loop is devoted to figuring out what to display for each ball of the frame. For ball1, if it has not been rolled, yet, then the String to display is just a space. If a strike has been rolled, then the letter 'X' is displayed. Otherwise, display the numeric score (1–9).

ball2 is similar to ball1, except it also displays the letter 'I' for a spare. Normally, I would use the slash character '/' for a spare, but that is used here to separate the scores for ball1, ball2, and ball3.

The String for ball3 is constructed only if the frame is the tenth frame (index 9). ball3 is the same as ball2, except it checks for a spare combining ball2 and ball3 instead of ball1 and ball2.

The frame total score is retrieved just by calling the FuguBowlPlayer function GetScore and is displayed as long as long as the score is available, i.e., not –1. The Rect for each GUI.Label is offset from the top left of the screen by an increment based on the frame the GUI.Label is displaying (Figure 9-2).

Figure 9-2. A bowling scoreboard displayed by FuguBowlScoreboard.js

Figure 9-2 shows a game on the second ball of the fourth frame. Three pins have been knocked down on the first ball. Strikes have been rolled on the first two frames and a spare on the third (five pins on the first roll and five on the second).The game total for the first frame is 10 for the strike plus the pins knocked down by the next two balls, which is 10 for the second strike and then 5 for the first ball in the third frame, for a total of 25.

The second frame also has a strike, so it's 10 plus 5 for the first ball of the third frame and 5 for the second ball of that frame, for a total of 20. Add that to the 25 from the first frame, for a game total of 45.

The third frame has a spare, so it's 10 again, but with just the next ball added, which is 3, for a total of 13, and add it to the game total from the previous frame, that's 58. So our scoring code and scoreboard code works!

Style the GUI

The appearance of a GUI Control can be customized with a GUIStyle, which is a collection of properties that affect the display of the Control. Conceptually, it's similar to how Cascading Style Sheets (CSS) are used in formatting web content.

Each GUI function that creates a GUI Control is an overloaded function that comes in two flavors: one that uses the default GUIStyle and one that takes a GUIStyle argument. The initial single-label example just used the default GUIStyle, but the scoreboard uses the version of GUI.Label that takes a GUIStyle argument, which provides a way to customize the scoreboard's appearance.

The GUIStyle passed to the GUI.Label is bound to a public variable named style, which allows customization of the GUIStyle in the Inspector View. For example, since the scoreboard is all text, you can click the Text Color field in the Normal subsection of the style (equivalent to accessing style.onNormal.textColor in the script) to bring up a color chooser and change the color of the scoreboard (Figure 9-3).

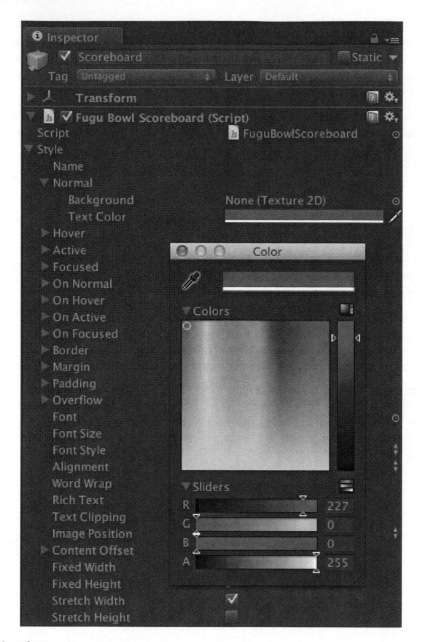

Figure 9-3. GUIStyle options

Among the many other GUIStyle properties, several affect the GUI font, which defaults to Unity's built-in font, Arial. You can change the font by dragging a Font asset from the Project View into the Font field of the GUIStyle (in the script, that would be the variable style.font). Any font in TrueType, OpenType, or dfont format can be imported into Unity.

Other GUIStyle properties control the font size and style (for Font assets imported as dynamic fonts), text alignment, and word wrap.

Rich text format is particularly interesting, as it provides for HTML-like markup in the label text. So really, although the script is simple, your style customization options are plentiful!

The Pause Menu

Compared with the scoreboard, a start/pause menu will take considerably more scripting, so, first, a design is in order. Let's create a main menu and two submenus: one for game options and one to display the game credits. The options menu will have distinct panels for audio, graphics, system, and stats. The logic is not as complicated as for the bowling game controller, but it's another example where you should first sketch out the design as a state diagram (Figure 9-4).

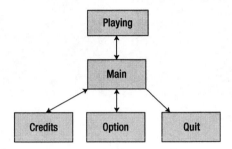

Figure 9-4. A state diagram for a pause menu

The diagram shows that the player can go from the game playing state (or equivalently, the menu-invisible state) to the main pause menu, and from there to a credits screen, an options menu, or quit the game. The options menu in turn can display an audio, graphics, system, or statistics panel, each of which could be listed as states, but for now, let's keep it simple by just thinking of each top-level menu screen as a state.

All states except for Quit (which you can think of as the exit state) can transition back to the state that transitioned to them in the first place, which is why each transition arrow is drawn bidirectionally. This means the player can go from the main menu to the options menu and back to the main menu, and from there can go back to the normal game play mode. But there won't be any shortcuts going from the options menu straight back to gameplay, for example.

Create the Script

Let's start the pause menu implementation by creating a new JavaScript in the Scripts folder of the Project View and name it FuguPause (Figure 9-5).

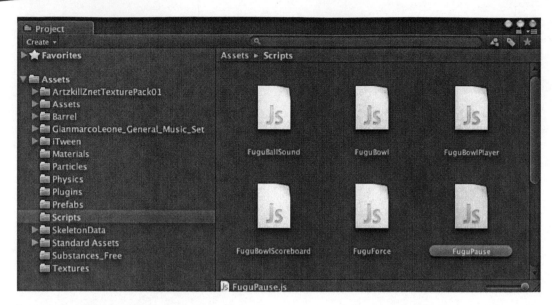

Figure 9-5.   Creating the FuguPause.js script

Now, to add the script to the scene, create a new GameObject in the Hierarchy View, name it
PauseMenu, and attach the `FuguPause` script to the PauseMenu GameObject.

Track the Current Menu Page

The technique used in the `FuguBowl` script of implementing a state machine with coroutines won't
work with UnityGUI, as all of the UnityGUI functions must be called within an `OnGUI` callback. But
the state diagram is still useful as the basis for an implementation. For starters, we can focus on
the states that represent distinct menu screens. Let's call them "pages" to distinguish them from
the more general term "screen." These menu states could be distinguished by strings or integers,
but an enumeration fits the bill when you have several related but distinct values. So let's define an
enum called Page for the menu page states and a variable named `currentPage` to track which page is
currently being displayed (Listing 9-3).

Listing 9-3.   Enumerations for Menu Pages

```
enum Page {
      None,Main,Options,Credits
}

private var currentPage:Page;
```

Following the state diagram, the enum lists a state for no menu (the game is playing), the main menu
page, the options page, and the credits page. Because the variable `currentPage` is of type Page, only
the values `Page.None`, `Page.Main`, `Page.Options`, or `Page.Credits` can be assigned to that variable.

Pause the Game

Making a pause menu involves solving two problems: making a menu and making the game pause. We'll start with making the game pause. The static variable Time.timeScale specifies how fast the simulated game time progresses and defaults to 1. Setting Time.timeScale to 0 effectively pauses the game, suspending physics, animation and anything else dependent on the advance of Time.time. So let's make a PauseGame function that sets Time.timeScale to 0 (Listing 9-4).

Listing 9-4. A Function to Pause the Game in FuguPause.js

```
private var savedTimeScale:float;        // Time.timeScale before we pause

function PauseGame() {
        savedTimeScale = Time.timeScale; // save normal time scale
        Time.timeScale = 0;              // suspend time
        AudioListener.pause = true;      // suspend music
        currentPage = Page.Main;         // start with the main menu page
}
```

PauseGame first saves the current Time.timeScale in a variable savedTimeScale so we can restore Time.timeScale when the game is unpaused (we shouldn't assume Time.timeScale is 1 when the game is paused).

PauseGame also sets AudioListener.pause to true, which suspends any playing sounds (you don't want to do this if you're going to play sounds in the menu).

Finally, the currentPage variable to the is set to Page.Main, indicating the main pause screen should be displayed.

The game is unpaused by reversing all of that (Listing 9-5).

Listing 9-5. Function that Unpauses the game in FuguPause.js

```
function UnPauseGame() {
        Time.timeScale = savedTimeScale;
        AudioListener.pause = false;
        currentPage = Page.None;
}
```

UnPauseGame restores Time.timeScale to the value you saved in the variables savedTimeScale by PauseGame, and sets AudioListener.pause to false to reenable audio.

To see if the game is paused, you can just check if Time.timeScale is 0. Listing 9-6 shows a little convenience function for that. Notice that it's a static function, so any script can call it as FuguPause.IsGamePaused().

Listing 9-6. Checking if the Game is Paused in FuguPause.js

```
static function IsGamePaused() {
        return Time.timeScale==0;
}
```

If the game is to start paused, the Start callback should have a call to PauseGame (Listing 9-7). Adding a public boolean variable startPaused and checking it before calling PauseGame makes the initial pause optional.

Listing 9-7. Pausing the Game in the Start Callback of FuguPause.js

```
var startPaused:boolean = true; // bring up the menu at game start

function Start() {
        if (startPaused) {
                PauseGame();
        }
}
```

Since the default value for startPaused is true, if you click Play, the game will immediately pause, showing the ball suspended in the air. And then you're stuck, since there's no menu. There's also no way to unpause then pause again, so let's have the Escape key (the key labeled ESC on the top left of most keyboards), toggle the pause state. Input handling is usually performed in the Update callback, and this is no exception (Listing 9-8).

Listing 9-8. Handling the Escape Key in the Update Callback of FuguPause.js

```
function Update() {
        if (Input.GetKeyDown("escape"))  {
                switch (currentPage) {
                        case Page.None: PauseGame(); break;   // if not paused, then pause
                        case Page.Main: UnPauseGame(); break; // if paused, then unpause
                        default: currentPage = Page.Main;     // any subpage goes back to main page
                }
        }
}
```

The first line checks if the ESC key has been pressed. If so, then it calls PauseGame, unless the pause menu is already up. The function also treats ESC as a back key, switching from a subpage to the main page or from the main page to an unpaused state.

Check Time.DeltaTime

Setting Time.timeScale to 0 halts the advance of Time.time, so Time.deltaTime is always 0. This works great for Update functions that multiple values by Time.deltaTime, but dividing by Time.deltaTime when time is frozen results in a division-by-zero error. There is such a case in the Update callback of the FuguForce script, so before proceeding with the pause menu, that has to be taken care of (Listing 9-9).

Listing 9-9. Avoiding Divide-by-Zero in FuguForce.js

```
function Update() {
        forcex = 0;
        forcey = 0;
        if (Time.deltaTime > 0) {
                CalcForce();
        }
}
```

```
function CalcForce() {
        var deltaTime:float = Time.deltaTime;
        forcex = mousepowerx*Input.GetAxis("Mouse X")/deltaTime;
        forcey = mousepowery*Input.GetAxis("Mouse Y")/deltaTime;
}
```

Instead of immediately dividing the rolling force values by `Time.deltaTime`, now the `Update` callback checks that `Time.deltaTime` is not 0 before proceeding with the force calculation, now moved into a `CalcForce` function. `Update` always initializes the force values to 0 to ensure that no lingering force is applied to the bowling ball while the game is paused.

Display the Menu

The actual display of the pause menu, as with the scoreboard in the previous section, must take place in an `OnGUI` callback function. Specifically, `OnGUI` needs to check if the game is paused, and if so, then display the current menu page (Listing 9-10).

Listing 9-10. The OnGUI Callback in FuguPause.js

```
function OnGUI () {
        if (IsGamePaused()) {
                switch (currentPage) {
                        case Page.Main: ShowPauseMenu(); break;
                        case Page.Options: ShowOptions(); break;
                        case Page.Credits: ShowCredits(); break;
                }
        }
}

function ShowPauseMenu() { Debug.Log("Main Pause"); }
function ShowOptions() { Debug.Log("Options"); }
function ShowCredits() { Debug.Log("Credits"); }
```

For now, there are placeholders for each of the page display functions, keeping the script in a runnable state (i.e., without compilation errors) as you fill out each of the display functions one at a time. It's a good idea to place `Debug.Log` statements inside these stub functions to verify they're called when expected. For example, if you click Play, you should see "`Main Pause`" appear in the Console View every time you pause the game.

Automatic Layout

For the menu buttons that are stacked vertically and centered in the screen, you can take advantage of the `GUILayout` functions to avoid figuring out each Rect that would otherwise have to be passed for each `GUI.Button`. Between calls to `GUILayout.BeginArea` and `GUILayout.EndArea` you can make calls to create GUI Controls without passing a Rect to each one, using the `GUILayout` versions of the GUI functions. The Controls will be automatically placed and sized within the Rect that was passed to `GUILayout.BeginArea`. Since all of the pause menu pages will be displayed the same way, let's make some convenience functions that wrap around the `GUILayout` functions (Listing 9-11).

Listing 9-11. GUILayout Functions for Positioning Pages in FuguPause.js

```
var menutop:int=25; // y-coordinate for top of the menu

function BeginPage(width:int,height:int) {
        GUILayout.BeginArea(Rect((Screen.width-width)/2,menutop,width,height));
}

function EndPage() {
        if (currentPage != Page.Main && GUILayout.Button("Back")) {
                currentPage = Page.Main;
        }
        GUILayout.EndArea();
}
```

The BeginPage function calls GUILayout.BeginArea, and the area is specified by the width and height passed as arguments, horizontally centered on the screen and with its top edge distance from the top of the screen specified by the public variable menutop.

The EndPage function calls GUILayout.EndArea, but before that, if the current page is not the main page, displays a Back button. If that button is clicked, then the current page is set to the main page.

The Main Page

Now we have all of the pieces to get a menu on the screen. Listing 9-12 shows a fleshed-out ShowPauseMenu function.

Listing 9-12. Function that Displays the Pause Menu in FuguPause.js

```
function ShowPauseMenu() {
      BeginPage(150,300);
      if (GUILayout.Button ("Play")) {
              UnPauseGame();
      }
      if (GUILayout.Button ("Options")) {
              currentPage = Page.Options;
      }
      if (GUILayout.Button ("Credits")) {
              currentPage = Page.Credits;
      }
#if !UNITY_WEBPLAYER && !UNITY_EDITOR
      if (GUILayout.Button ("Quit")) {
              Application.Quit();
      }
#endif
      EndPage();
}
```

All of the GUI code between BeginPage and EndPage effectively takes place between GUILayout. BeginArea and GUILayout.EndArea, so you can use the GUILayout versions of the GUI calls to create elements without passing Rects. For example, instead of calling GUI.Button you could call GUILayout.Button. Aside from the missing Rect parameter, the functions look otherwise identical.

GUILayout.Button is different from GUILayout.Label in that it returns true or false depending on whether the button has been pressed. So each call to GUILayout.Button takes place inside an if test and executes the appropriate statement if the button has indeed been pressed.

When you click Play, you'll now see the main menu, and the Play button in the menu should unpause the screen (Figure 9-6). Application.Quit has no functionality in a Unity web player or in the Editor, so that piece of code is surrounded by a test of the corresponding preprocessor definitions UNITY_ WEBPLAYER and UNITY_EDITOR to see if the build target is a web player or if you're running in the Editor. These definitions are evaluated just before compilation takes place (hence the term "preprocessor"), so if UNITY_WEBPLAYER is false and UNITY_EDITOR is false, the enclosed code is compiled. Otherwise, it's as if the code were never there.

Figure 9-6. The main menu

The Credits and Options buttons won't do anything yet, because the ShowCredits and ShowOptions functions are still empty shells. The Credits page is simpler, so let's start with that one.

The Credits Page

Multiple credit entries can be stored in a String array. A variable credits is defined for that, along with a ShowCredits function to display the credits, in Listing 9-13.

Listing 9-13. Function to Display the Credits Page in FuguPause.js

```
var credits:String[]=[
     "A Fugu Games Production",
     "Copyright (c) 2012 Technicat, LLC. All Rights Reserved.",
     "More information at http://fugugames.com/"] ;

function ShowCredits() {
     BeginPage(300,300);
     for (var credit in credits) {
          GUILayout.Label(credit);
     }
     EndPage();
}
```

Because the variable `credits` is public, you can edit each of the credit entries and add to the array or remove from it in the Inspector View.

The `ShowCredits` function loops through the array of credits and displays each one in a UnityGUI label (Figure 9-7). Notice that there is a simple way to loop through the array using `in` instead of the usual habit of iterating through a sequence of array indices. In this particular case, you don't need an index for anything else, so let's go with the simpler method.

Figure 9-7. The Credits page

Like the main menu, you start with a call to `BeginPage` and end with `EndPage` so you're operating inside a GUILayout area (this time 300 × 300) and can use `GUILayout.Label` instead of `GUI.Label`. `EndPage` ensures that there automatically is a Back button. And remember, the `Update` callback also treats the ESC key as equivalent to clicking the Back button.

The Options Page

The Options page is quite a bit more involved than the Credits page, as it features a toolbar implemented with four tabs: Audio, Graphics, Stats, and System. Listing 9-14 shows the fleshed-out ShowToolbar function, with some supporting variables and functions.

Listing 9-14. The Options Page in FuguPause.js

```
private var toolbarIndex:int=0; // current toolbar selection
private var toolbarStrings: String[]= ["Audio","Graphics","System"]; // tabs

function ShowOptions() {
        BeginPage(300,300);
        toolbarIndex = GUILayout.Toolbar (toolbarIndex, toolbarStrings);
        switch (toolbarInt) {
                case 0: ShowAudio(); break;
                case 1: ShowGraphics(); break;
                case 2: ShowSystem(); break;
        }
        EndPage();
}

function ShowAudio() { Debug.Log("ShowAudio"); }
function ShowGraphics() { Debug.Log("ShowGraphics"); }
function ShowSystem() { Debug.Log("ShowSystem"); }
```

Again, everything in the ShowOptions function is enclosed between calls to the BeginPage and EndPage functions. The first line calls GUILayout.Toolbar to create a toolbar—a row of buttons that acts as a tab or radio button—from a String array, where each String is the label of the button. The function also takes an integer that corresponds to a position in that array of strings. That is the button to make currently active on the toolbar. But if you just had

```
GUILayout.Toolbar (toolbarIndex, toolbarStrings);
```

then toolbarIndex would never change from its initial value (0), and even if you click another button, the next time this is called (in the next invocation of OnGUI), the active button would be set back to that value.

But GUILayoutToolbar returns an integer that represents the currently active button, so you feed that value back into the variable that you passed in, toolbarIndex.

```
toolbarIndex = GUILayout.Toolbar (toolbarIndex, toolbarStrings);
```

Thus, toolbarIndex is 0 initially, but if you click Graphics, it'll change to 1, and if you click Controls it'll change to 2, and so on. Then there is a switch statement that checks toolbarIndex and calls the display function that matches the selected button. As with the main menu, we start with stub functions and implement them on by one. Go ahead and click around, and you should see the corresponding function names show up in the Console View, because that's all you've told it to do!

The Audio Panel

When the Audio tab is selected, it will display a slider for volume control (Figure 9-8).

Figure 9-8. The Audio panel in the pause menu

Adding that slider the ShowAudio function is actually pretty easy, just one line. Well, two lines, since a slider with no label is a bit too mysterious (Listing 9-15).

Listing 9-15. The Audio Panel in FuguPause.js

```
function ShowAudio() {
    GUILayout.Label("Volume");
    AudioListener.volume = GUILayout.HorizontalSlider(AudioListener.volume,0.0,1.0);
}
```

The first line calls GUILayout.Label, which should be familiar by now. The second line calls GUILayout.HorizontalSlider, which takes as arguments the minimum value represented by the slider, the maximum value, and a value that represents the current setting.

The slider reflects the value of AudioListener.volume, which is the master volume of all sounds in Unity. So AudioListener.volume is passed as the current value of the slider, and because AudioListener.volume ranges from 0 to 1, pass those values are passed as the minimum and maximum, respectively. And, in order to register the slider value, the return value of GUILayout.Slider is assigned to back AudioListener.volume. Otherwise, the value of AudioListener.volume will never change and the slider won't budge.

The Graphics Panel

The Graphics panel will display the some of the same graphics quality information shown by the Quality Settings of the Unity Editor (Figure 9-9).

Figure 9-9. Graphics options in the pause menu

The two buttons at the bottom of the panel increase and decrease the Quality Settings level. This panel doesn't require any new UnityGUI controls to implement this panel, but it does access the QualitySettings class (Listing 9-16).

Listing 9-16. Function that Displays the Quality Settings

```
function ShowGraphics() {
      GUILayout.Label(QualitySettings.names[QualitySettings.GetQualityLevel()]);
      GUILayout.Label("Pixel Light Count: "+QualitySettings.pixelLightCount);
      GUILayout.Label("Shadow Cascades: "+QualitySettings.shadowCascades);
      GUILayout.Label("Shadow Distance: "+QualitySettings.shadowDistance);
      GUILayout.Label("Soft Vegetation: "+QualitySettings.softVegetation);
      GUILayout.BeginHorizontal();
      if (GUILayout.Button("Decrease")) {
            QualitySettings.DecreaseLevel();
      }
      if (GUILayout.Button("Increase")) {
            QualitySettings.IncreaseLevel();
      }
      GUILayout.EndHorizontal();
}
```

The ShowGraphics function is fairly straightforward. It retrieves the current Quality Settings level, represented as an integer, by calling QualitySettings.GetQualityLevel, and then uses that integer as an index to the QualitySettings.names array to retrieve the name of that Quality Setting. That name and several Quality Settings properties are displayed in labels, and two buttons are placed at the bottom: one calling QualitySettings.DecreaseLevel and the other calling QualitySettings.IncreaseLevel.

The two buttons allow you to increase and decrease the Quality Settings level, within the range of existing levels, and not only will you see the displayed Quality Settings information change, you might see the graphical quality of the scene change before your eyes, too, since it's still being rendered every frame, even with the game time paused.

The System Panel

The System panel displays information about the hardware platform (Figure 9-10).

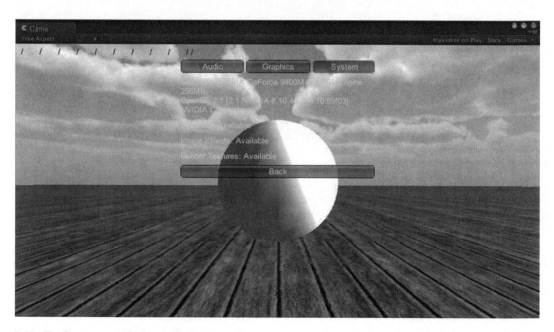

Figure 9-10. The System panel in the pause menu

As in the Graphics page, the information is displayed with labels, but whereas the Graphics page accesses the QualitySettings class, the System panel accesses the SystemInfo class (Listing 9-17).

Listing 9-17. The System Panel in FuguPause.js

```
function ShowSystem() {
        GUILayout.Label("Graphics: "+SystemInfo.graphicsDeviceName+" "+
        SystemInfo.graphicsMemorySize+"MB\n"+
        SystemInfo.graphicsDeviceVersion+"\n"+
        SystemInfo.graphicsDeviceVendor);
        GUILayout.Label("Shadows: "+ Available(SystemInfo.supportsShadows));
        GUILayout.Label("Image Effects: "+Available(SystemInfo.supportsImageEffects));
        GUILayout.Label("Render Textures: "+Available(SystemInfo.supportsRenderTextures));
}
```

The SystemInfo class provides information about the graphics hardware and its capabilities, including some identifying information such as the device name and the name of the vendor, its graphics memory size, and whether the hardware supports some of the more advanced features, such as dynamic shadows, rendering to a texture, or image effects (which requires rendering to a texture).

Customize the GUI Color

You may have noticed the white text in the pause menu is often difficult to read. One solution is to change the static variable GUI.color, which tints the entire GUI with a color value (Listing 9-18).

Listing 9-18. GUI Color Customization in FuguPause.js

```
var hudColor:Color = Color.white;

function OnGUI () {
        if (IsGamePaused()) {
                GUI.color = hudColor;
                switch (currentPage) {
                        case Page.Main: ShowPauseMenu(); break;
                        case Page.Options: ShowOptions(); break;
                        case Page.Credits: ShowCredits(); break;
                }
        }
}
```

We add a public variable hudColor to the FuguPause script so a color can be chosen in the Inspector view. All UnityGUI operations, including setting variables like GUI.Color, must take place within an OnGUI callback, so the assignment to GUI.color is placed inside the OnGUI callback before any of the GUI Controls are created (but after IsGamePaused is called, since there's no reason to set GUI.Color if there's no GUI rendering). Note that you can set GUI.color multiple times within OnGUI to change the color before rendering various parts of the GUI.

Now you can select a color in the Inspector View (Figure 9-11) and see the resulting GUI tint (Figure 9-12).

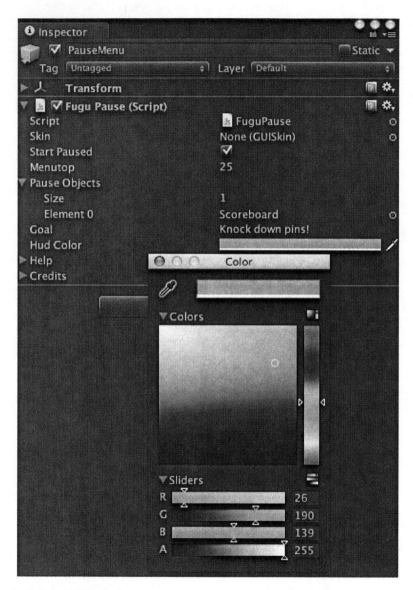

Figure 9-11. Color selection for the pause menu

Figure 9-12. The pause menu with a custom color

Customize the Skin

The default UnityGUI skin is pretty neutral, and it's hard to read the text, as you can see with the pause menu from the previous section. With the scoreboard, you could change the text color by adjusting the style passed to GUI.Label, but if you have a lot of GUI elements, that can be a hassle.

That's where UnityGUI skins come in. A *Skins* is a collections of styles assigned to the various GUI elements. Applying a skin is easy—just declare a public variable of type GUISkin and assign that skin to the variable GUI.skin, within the OnGUI callback, similar to assigning a GUI.Color (Listing 9-19).

Listing 9-19. Adding a GUISkin to the Pause Menu

```
var skin:GUISkin;

function OnGUI () {
      if (IsGamePaused()) {
            if (skin != null) {
                  GUI.skin = skin;
            } else {
                  GUI.color = hudColor;
            }
            switch (currentPage) {
                  case Page.Main: ShowPauseMenu(); break;
                  case Page.Options: ShowOptions(); break;
                  case Page.Credits: ShowCredits(); break;
            }
      }
}
```

You can test this skin support with a really cool-looking free UnityGUI skin from the Asset Store called the Necromancer GUI (Figure 9-13).

Figure 9-13. The Necromancer GUI on the Asset Store

Download and import the Necromancer GUI, then drag its skin file (named Necromancer GUI) into the Skin property that's now in the Inspector View (Figure 9-14).

Figure 9-14. The Necromancer GUI

Then click Play, and you have a much more ornate pause menu. Figure 9-15 shows how the pause menu Graphics panel looks with the Necromancer GUI. Look at all the pretty buttons!

Figure 9-15. The Necromancer GUI skin in action

The Complete Script

The finalized start/pause menu script is significantly longer than the scoreboard script, so the complete listing is omitted here. All the code has been shown in this chapter, and the entire script FuguPause.js is available in the project for this chapter at http://learnunity4.com/.

Explore Further

Finally, the scoreboard display makes our bowling game a fully functional bowling game, and the addition of a start/pause menu provides some of the polish that players expect!

The addition of the game GUI not only completes the bowling game (in a commercial game project, this might be considered a "first playable" milestone) but it also marks the end of our introduction to Unity's basic features typically used in a 3D game.

> **Tip**   Although I left the GUI development to the end of this phase, which is unfortunately common in game development, it's best to include GUI design early in the project. Even just sketching out the menus will help clarify the anticipated game modes and options.

For the most part, although you've been modifying and testing the game solely in the Editor, these are cross-platform features. Right now, you could build this game as a web player or a Mac or Windows executable, and the game would run the same on all platforms, performance differences aside. But the ultimate goal of this book is to get you into iOS development, so, starting with the next chapter, the remainder of this book will be all about Unity iOS.

Unity Manual

The Game Interface Elements link in the "Creating Gameplay" section of the Unity Manual leads to the "GUI Scripting Guide," which is a tutorial-style sequence of pages that goes through the UnityGUI system, from creating a single button to adding various other UnityGUI Controls such as sliders and radio buttons, use of automatic layout vs. fixed layout, creating reusable compound Controls, and customizing the GUI appearance with styles and skins.

The "GUI Scripting Guide" also explains how you can customize the Unity Editor using UnityGUI. It turns out the Editor interface is actually implemented with UnityGUI (which explains why on occasion you may see an OnGUI error message in the Console View that is not related to any of your code)!

Reference Manual

I briefly mentioned how additional fonts besides the built-in Unity font can be imported into a Unity project and then assigned to UnityGUI styles and skins. The Reference Manual has a page in its Asset Components section describing the Font asset and its import options in more detail.

Scripting Reference

Naturally, the Runtime Classes list in the Scripting Reference includes pages describing the UnityGUI functions you've used, starting with the "OnGUI" callback defined in the "MonoBehaviour" class.

Most of the UnityGUI functions used in both the scoreboard and pause menu are the static "GUI" and "GUILayout" functions used to create the various UnityGUI Controls, such as "GUI.Button" and "GUI.Label." It's worth going through the Scripting Reference pages for each of them so you know what GUI Controls are available, along with customization variables like "GUI.color" and "GUI.skin" (and there are others, e.g., to customize the background color). GUIStyle and GUISkin are classes too, and you can change their properties any time in a script.

Besides the UnityGUI classes, a few others are used in the pause menu. The static variable "Time.timeScale" was set to pause and unpause the game, "Application.Quit" called to exit the game, and the "AudioListener," "QualitySettings," and "SystemInfo" classes accessed in the Options page.

Asset Store

The Necromancer GUI looked great in the pause menu, demonstrating how nice UnityGUI can look with a well-crafted GUISkin, but there are many others on the Asset Store. They're all listed, along with the Necromancer GUI, in the "GUI Skins" category under "Textures and Materials." That category is well populated with skins for UnityGUI and also skins for third-party GUI systems, such as the popular EZGUI from Above and Beyond Software (http://anbsoft.com/) and NGUI from Tasharen Entertainment (http://tasharen.com).

Those third-party GUI systems are available under the "Scripting" category, in the well-populated "GUI" subcategory, which is filled with pre-scripted GUIs such as minimaps and menus. In fact, a version of the pause menu implemented in this chapter is on the Asset Store in the "Complete Projects" section (under the name FuguPause).

The Asset Store also has a decent assortment of fonts listed under the "Fonts" category of "Textures and Materials." But since Unity can import TrueType and OpenType fonts, a plethora of free font sites on the web is available to you, along with moderately priced font libraries (I use the MacXWare Font Library).

Chapter 10

Using Unity iOS

Congratulations! You now have a bowling game incorporating the basic features that typically comprise a 3D game: 3D graphics (of course), physics, sound effects, player control (of the bowling ball), camera movement, and a graphical user interface.

The default built target is listed on the title bar of the Editor window as PC, Mac and Linux Standalone. If you were to perform an OS X build of the bowling project right now, the game would run essentially the same as it does in the Editor. Same for Linux, Windows, and even a web player (although a web player build would require you to switch build targets first).

Targeting iOS is another story. You could change the build target for the bowling game to iOS right now and build it without any compiler errors. But the bowling ball control in `FuguForce.js` is designed for mouse input, so that would have to change. Besides reimplementing the input handling, adapting desktop PC games to mobile devices (a process called *porting*) often requires adjustments for the device display and compromises to achieve adequate performance.

Moreover, building an iOS app involves much more in the way of external procedures than the desktop standalone and web player targets. Due to Apple's requirement that all iOS apps be compiled with Xcode, Unity iOS builds an app by first generating an Xcode project, which in turn is compiled by Xcode to create the final app. And to actually run the app on a test device and submit the app to the App Store, a rather complicated sequence of procedures is required, along with registration in Apple's iOS Developer Program.

For now, let's go back to our roots, so to speak, and temporarily return to the Angry Bots demo project that we started with in this book. Conveniently, Angry Bots is ready to run on iOS without modification. If you have an iOS device, go ahead and download Angry Bots from the App Store. A quick way to find the Angry Bots app is to enter "unity technologies" in the App Store search field, and Angry Bots will appear, along with other apps from Unity Technologies (Figure 10-1).

Figure 10-1. Example apps from Unity Technologies on the App Store

Besides Angry Bots, you should also download the Unity Remote app, which acts as a remote control for testing a Unit iOS game in the Editor. While you're at it, you should download and try all the example apps from Unity Technologies. Many of them have not been updated in a while, but they do provide an idea of what kinds of games can be created with Unity.

Once you install Angry Bots from the App Store onto your iOS device and play the game, notice how the game features on-screen virtual joysticks (Figure 10-2) for player movement and weapon fire that up until now, we haven't seen in Angry Bots.

Figure 10-2. The iOS version of Angry Bots with virtual joysticks

Although the iOS version of Angry Bots has different controls, it's built from the same version of Angry Bots installed with Unity. So we'll defer the iOS conversion work on our bowling game and spend these next couple of chapters getting reacquainted with Angry Bots so we can focus on the Unity iOS build and test process. In this chapter, specifically, you'll learn how to test the Unity iOS version of Angry Bots with the Unity Remote and and with the iOS Simulator in Xcode.

Bring Back the Angry Bots

Returning to Angry Bots, select Open Project from the File menu, and Angry Bots should be listed among the recent projects (Figure 10-3).

Figure 10-3. Angry Bots listed among recent projects

If Angry Bots is not listed, then click the Open Other button and look for Angry Bots under the Unity demo folder, Users ➤ Shared ➤ Unity (Figure 10-4).

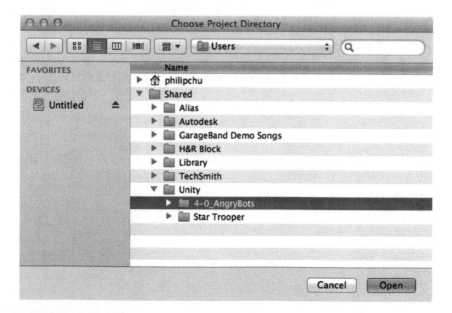

Figure 10-4. Opening the Angry Bots project

Now that we're back in Angry Bots, let's change the build target to iOS. Bring up the Build Settings window using the Build Settings command in the File menu. The available build targets are shown in the Platforms list on the left, with a Unity icon indicating the current build target, which should be PC, Mac & Linux Standalone (Figure 10-5).

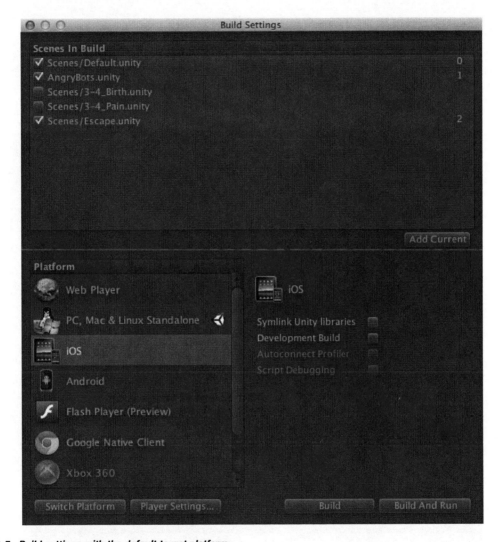

Figure 10-5. Build settings with the default target platform

To build the game for iOS, select iOS in the Platform list and then click the Switch Platform button on the lower left to reimport the project assets in the proper formats for iOS. A progress dialog box will appear while the reimporting process is taking place (Figure 10-6).

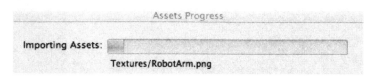

Figure 10-6. *The progress bar for reimporting assets while switching build targets*

Projects with a lot of assets can take a while to reimport, and the Editor will be unresponsive during that period. But once the assets have been converted, the Build Settings will display the Unity icon next to iOS in the Platform list, indicating that iOS is now the build target (Figure 10-7).

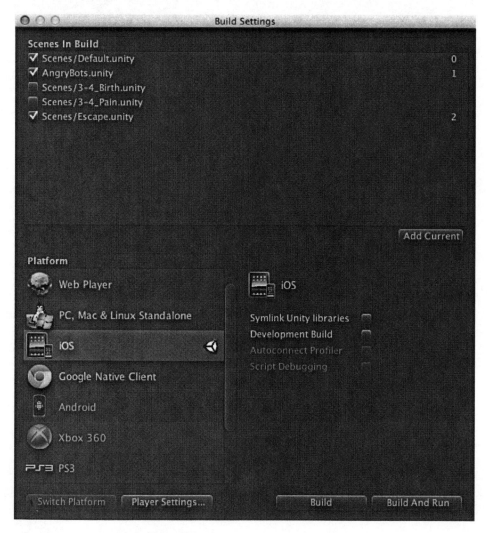

Figure 10-7. *Build Settings with iOS as the build target*

Notice also that the Switch Platform button is now dimmed when you select iOS, indicating that the asset conversion has taken place.

> **Tip**   If you select iOS but neglect to click the Switch Platform button, the project assets will still be converted automatically the first time you perform a build. However, it's best to convert the project assets immediately so you can examine and test the game within the Editor and catch platform-specific issues earlier.

And yet another indication that the build target is now iOS, the title bar of the Editor window, which formerly displayed PC, Mac & Linux Standalone, now sports iPhone, iPod Touch and iPad (Figure 10-8).

Figure 10-8.   The Unity Editor window with iOS as the build target

Now that Angry Bots is configured for iOS, let's open the AngryBots scene, if it's not already open (and it probably isn't, because you switched from the bowling project to the Angry Bots project).

> **Note**   When switching from one project to another, Unity tries to open a scene with the same name as the open scene in the previous project. If no such scene exists, the Editor will open a new scene, just as if you had selected New Scene in the File menu.

The AngryBots scene file is at the top level of the Assets folder (Figure 10-9), so you can double-click that file in the Project View to open the scene, as an alternative to using the Open Scene command in the File menu.

Figure 10-9. The Project View of the AngryBots scene file

And yet another clue that the current build target is iOS, the screen size menu at the top left of the Game View now lists iOS device resolutions (Figure 10-10).

Figure 10-10. iOS screen resolutions in the Game View

Moreover, when you click Play, the same virtual joysticks featured on the version from the App Store are now visible (Figure 10-11).

Figure 10-11. Playing Angry Bots in the Editor with virtual joysticks

Unfortunately, although you can watch the bots in Angry Bots move around, you can't actually play the game, since the mouse and keyboard controls are deactivated, and the code is waiting for touch-screen input to operate the virtual joysticks. But no worries, there is a way to provide touchscreen input while testing in the Editor!

Test with the Unity Remote

Unity has provided a very cool solution for in-Editor testing of Unit iOS projects in the form of the Unity Remote app, which runs on an iOS device and relays touchscreen and accelerometer data from that device over Wi-Fi to the Unity Editor. If you don't have an iOS device, you can skip this section and still get some testing done using the iOS Simulator, described in the next section.

Unity Remote can be found on the App Store in the same way as the Angry Bots app, by entering "unity technologies" in the App Store search box (Figure 10-1). Entering "unity remote" works, too (Figure 10-12).

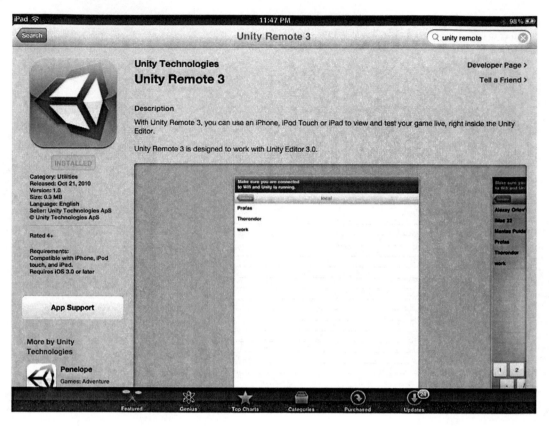

Figure 10-12. The Unity Remote app on the App Store

Once Unity Remote is installed on your iOS device, make sure the device is on the same Wi-Fi network as your Mac that's running Unity. When you launch Unity Remote, the screen should display the name of that Mac (Figure 10-13). Select that computer, and if Unity is not in Play mode, the Unity Remote screen will just wait, displaying a reminder for you to click Play in the Unity Editor.

Figure 10-13. Computer selection in the Unity Remote app

When the Unity Editor is in Play mode, the graphics in the Game View will also appear in Unity Remote, and you can play the game on your device, using its touchscreen! It will look a bit coarse, because Unity is sending copies of the game screen over Wi-Fi to the device. You can improve the performance by minimizing the resolution of the Game View in the Unity Editor (Figure 10-14).

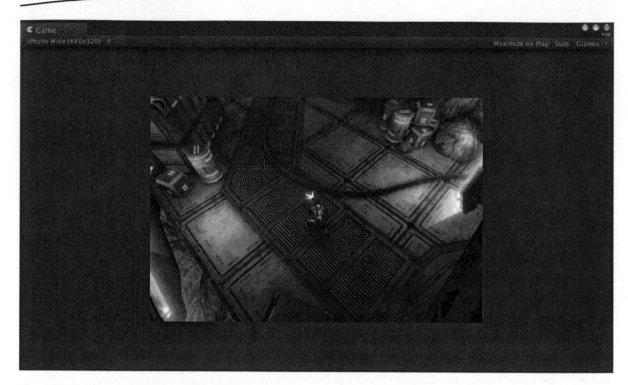

Figure 10-14. Minimized device resolution in the Game View

Regardless of the graphics quality, you are now able to play Angry Bots on an iOS device, although you're really still playing in the Editor and just using the device as a controller. The touchscreen input is sent back to the Unity Editor over Wi-Fi and received by the game running in Play mode, so you still have all the debugging features of the Unity Editor at your disposal during the test run. It's the best of both worlds!

Install Xcode

At some point you have to leave the comforts of the Unity Editor and really start building for iOS. All iOS apps have to be built through Xcode, Apple's official iOS development tool (and also their official OS X development tool), which is why a Unity iOS build first generates an Xcode project, which in turn is built by Xcode to create the app. Xcode is available free from the Apple Developer Site but conveniently also available on the Mac App Store. Search for "xcode" on the Mac App Store and click the Free button to download (Figure 10-15).

Figure 10-15. Xcode on the Mac App Store

After installation, you should see the Xcode application in your Applications folder. Now you're ready to start performing iOS builds from Unity!

Customize the Player Settings

Unity iOS builds invariably require customization of the Player Settings in the Unity Editor (the Unity Player, as opposed the Unity Editor, is the deployed version of the Unity engine). Select Player Settings under the Edit menu, or click the Player Settings button in the Build window, and the Player Settings will show up in the Inspector View (Figure 10-16).

Figure 10-16. Selecting the Player Settings

The Player Settings are partitioned into Cross-Platform Settings at the top and Per-Platform Settings below. The only two Cross-Platform Settings that affect an iOS build are the Product Name and Default Icon, which provide the app name and icon, respectively, that appear on the device.

The Company Name, Default Cursor, and Cursor Hotspot properties are only used in desktop and web player builds, although you might as well provide the appropriate Company Name or your name, just so it's there in the project. If you're wondering why the Cross-Platform Settings aren't entirely cross-platform, keep in mind Unity started out supporting just the web and desktop platforms, iOS support came a few years later (and Android support, even later).

Because we're only interested in the iOS Player Settings now, click the Per-Platform Settings tab that somewhat resembles an iPhone to see the Settings for iOS (Figure 10-17).

Figure 10-17. Player Settings for iOS

The Player Settings are plentiful, so they are organized into several foldouts: Resolution and Presentation, Icon, Splash Image, and the catch-all Other Settings. Chapter 12 is devoted to presentation issues, including the Icon and Splash Image settings, so for now, we'll focus on the Resolution and Presentation and Other Settings.

Resolution and Presentation

Most of the Resolution and Presentation settings have reasonable defaults (Figure 10-18), but I recommend always changing the Default Orientation from Landscape Left to Auto Rotation, since Apple requires iPad apps to autorotate, meaning the display is rotated automatically to stay upright. The other Default Orientation choices are Landscape Right, Portrait, or Portrait Upside Down.

Figure 10-18. Resolution and Presentation in the Player Settings for iOS

If Auto Rotation is selected, then the Allowed Orientations for Auto Rotation are displayed. Because Angry Bots is intended only to run in a landscape mode, select Landscape Left and Landscape Right. As a result, Angry Bots will flip between Landscape Left and Landscape Right as the device is turned around, but never to a portrait mode.

The Use Animated Autorotation option specifies whether the display visibly rotates or just switches instantly. I always opt for the animated rotation because it looks cool. The status bar options specify whether the iOS status bar is visible when the app launches, and if visible, in what style. The 32-bit display buffer dictates the color resolution. If this option is not selected, then 16-bit color is used.

Note   The 32-bit display buffer option is marked with an asterisk. Any setting marked with an asterisk is shared among other mobile platforms, namely Android.

The Show Loading Indicator controls whether the iOS activity indicator, the little spinning graphic at the center of the screen, appears when the app launches. This setting is also covered among presentation options in Chapter 12.

Other Settings

It so happens that many important settings are collected under the generically titled Other Settings (Figure 10-19). The static and dynamic batching options under the Rendering settings are really optimization options, affecting whether and when Meshes are automatically combined for performance reasons. That will be discussed among optimization techniques in Chapter 16.

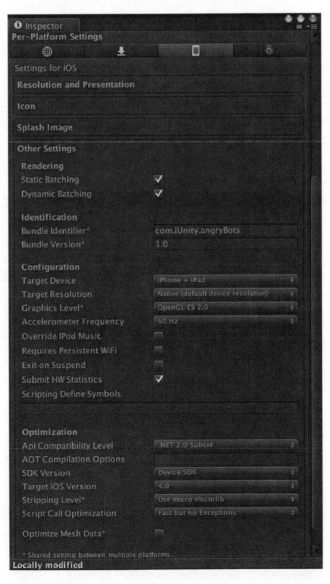

Figure 10-19. Other Settings in the Player Settings for iOS

There are two settings in the Identification section: the Bundle Identifier and the Bundle Version. They are not important for running in the iOS Simulator, but when it comes time for app submission, these settings must match the corresponding information for the app specified in iTunesConnect (covered as part of the app submission process in the next chapter).

The bundle ID is a unique identifier for your app, typically expressed like a URL in reverse. For example, all of my apps have bundle IDs of the form `com.technicat.<appname>`, so I would change `com.unity.angryBots` to `com.technicat.angryBots`.

The bundle version is the same app version number displayed for the app on the App Store. It's usually formatted as two numbers, `<major>.<minor>`, or sometimes three, `<major>.<minor>.<revision>`. This number has to be incremented every time you submit an update for your app on the App Store.

Under Configuration, most of the settings have reasonable defaults, but you do need to decide whether your app will run on iPhones, iPads, or both by selecting the Target Device. Most 3D apps generally run well on a variety of screen aspect ratios, at least better than 2D apps, but iPhones and iPod Touches have narrower screens than iPads. And sometimes, for business reasons, you might want to release an app only for the iPad or only for the iPhone.

For Target Resolution, Native is usually what you want (Figure 10-20). It's equivalent to Best Quality, while Best Performance specifies a lower screen resolution (not available on the iPhone 3GS and its iPod touch counterpart, as they have the lowest-resolution screens). The remaining options are fixed iPhone-only and iPad-only resolutions.

Figure 10-20. The Target Resolution options in the Player Settings for iOS

Scripting Define Symbols allows you to define your own preprocessor definitions, just like the `UNITY_EDITOR` and `UNITY_WEBPLAYER` definitions referenced in the FuguPause script in the previous chapter. For example, if you had some code that calls some functions only available in Unity Pro, then you might wrap the code with `#if UNITY_PRO ... #endif` and then add `UNITY_PRO` to the Scripting Define Symbols in projects that are running with Unity Pro.

Multiple definitions can be added using semicolons as a separator. If you also had a `USE_ADS` preprocessor definition to control whether ads are displayed, you might have `USE_ADS;UNITY_PRO` in the Scripting Define Symbols field.

Some of the Optimization settings have nothing to do with optimization. The application Api Compatibility Level (never mind the weird capitalization of API) specifies the version and extent of the .NET API you need. Usually you won't need to change that.

AOT Compilation Options refers to the ahead-of-time compilation that takes place during a Unity iOS build, as opposed to just-in-time (JIT) compilation. This why `#pragma strict` is required in Unity iOS scripts. It gives the AOT compiler enough information to do its job.

The SDK Version has two options: Device SDK and Simulator SDK. When building for a test device or an app submission, covered in the next chapter, the default value of Device SDK is the correct choice, but in this chapter, Simulator SDK should be selected to run our game in the iOS Simulator.

> **Note**   SDK Version is an odd property name to distinguish between simulator and hardware builds, but it is a holdover from older versions of Unity iOS that required specifying the iOS SDK that was installed with Xcode.

The Target iOS Version specifies the minimum iOS version the app will run on. Leaving it on the default and minimum value, iOS 4.0, maximizes the number of compatible devices and thus potential customers. However, targeting any iOS SDK older than iOS 4.3 will result in a Unity warning of a potential App Store rejection (Figure 10-21).

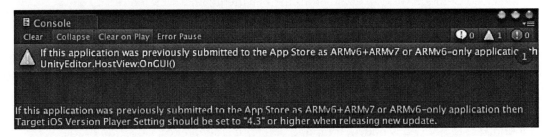

Figure 10-21. Warning when submitting with a Target SDK older than version 4.3

This is only a potential Apple rejection issue if you happen to be upgrading an app already on the App Store that has support for ARMv6 processors, because Unity 4 dropped ARMv6 support and only supports the newer ARMv7 family. As the Unity warning recommends, targeting iOS 4.3 or later is safe, because Apple also dropped ARMv6 support starting with iOS 4.3 (which means they also dropped support for devices older than the iPhone 3GS).

> **Tip**   When I first tried to submit ARMv7-only updates to the App Store (in 2012), the apps were rejected, and eventually, targeting iOS 4.3 or later avoided that problem. Moreover, once an ARMv7-only update was approved on the App Store, I was able to target older versions of iOS again because I was no longer upgrading an ARMv6 app!

Finally, the Stripping Level, Script Call Optimization, and Optimize Mesh Data really are optimization settings, which will be covered among other optmization techniques in Chapter 16. But, briefly, Stripping Level is a Unity iOS Pro option that removes unused code (or if you're unlucky, used code, which is why it's optional), Script Call Optimization can speed up scripts by eliminating exception handling (exceptions, essentially, are errors or "exceptional" conditions that can be caught by calling code), and Optimize Mesh Data removes unused Mesh data (e.g., normals are not necessary when an unlit material is used).

As you can see, there are many options in the Player Settings that affect the appearance and performance of Unity iOS builds. After changing the Player Settings, it's a good idea to save those changes by invoking Save Project or Save Scene (which implicitly performs a Save Project, too) from the File menu. Although many if not most of the Player Settings will be important at some point, the only change you have to make to get Angry Bots running on the iOS Simulator is setting the Device SDK to Simulator SDK.

Test with the iOS Simulator

Now that you have Xcode installed and have the Device SDK set to Simulator SDK, you're ready to build and run Angry Bots on the iOS Simulator. The Build and Run command in the File menu and the Build and Run button in the Build Settings window will perform the Build phase, generating an Xcode project, and then perform the Run phase, invoking a build-and-run within the Xcode project. Normally, that is pretty convenient, but when working with the iOS Simulator, you have more control over the iOS Simulator when performing the Xcode build-and-run manually from Xcode. So let's bring up the Build Settings window again (from the File menu) and click the Build button.

> **Tip**   Before performing a build, check in the Build Settings window that you have the correct set of scenes included.

Unity will bring up a Save As window prompting you for a location and file name of the soon-to-be-built Xcode project (Figure 10-22).

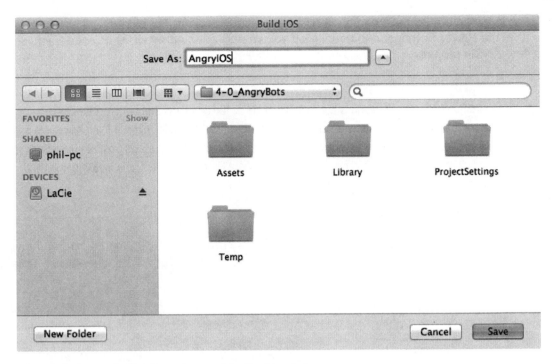

Figure 10-22. Build prompt for location and name of the Xcode project

It usually defaults to the top level of the Unity project folder. Let's call the Xcode project AngryIOS.

Caution   Be careful not to choose a build destination inside the Assets folder, or Unity will try to import an entire Xcode project as project assets.

If this isn't the first time you built this project at this location, Unity will detect that an Xcode project with that name already exists and will ask if you want to replace the project completely or append the project changes (Figure 10-23).

Figure 10-23. Build Append or Replace dialog box

Appending is faster, but sometimes you need a fresh Xcode project. For example, if you change the bundle ID in the Player Settings, and definitely if you've upgraded either Unity or Xcode, you should build a new Xcode project.

> **Tip**   Build and Run from the File menu is not quite the same as the Build and Run button in the Build Settings. The command in the File menu assumes you want to append the build folder, if it already exists and doesn't ask if you want to append or replace it. I prefer to stick with performing builds from the Build Settings window, so I always know what's going on. I've had cases where I copied a project, and invoking Build and Run from the File menu still built to the original location!

In any case, after clicking Build, a progress bar will display during the build (Figure 10-24). As with asset reimporting, this can take a while for a big project, and the Editor will be unresponsive during the build.

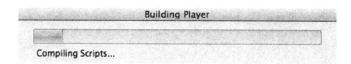

Figure 10-24. The progress indicator during a build

When the build is complete, an Xcode project will folder appear in the location you specified (Figure 10-25).

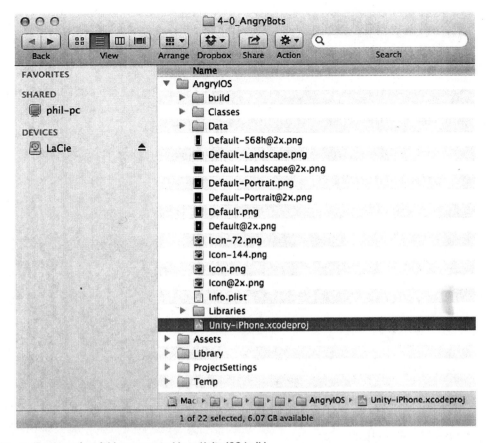

Figure 10-25. An Xcode project folder generated by a Unity iOS build

The Xcode project file is named Unity-iPhone.xcodeproj and is located in the Xcode project folder. Double-click that file to open the project in Xcode (Figure 10-26).

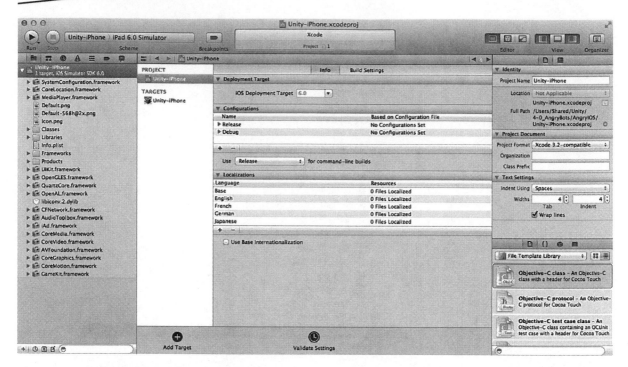

Figure 10-26. Xcode launched with a Unity iOS project

Notice how iPad 6.0 Simulator is displayed at the top left of the Xcode window. That is a menu for selecting the Xcode scheme, which is a collection of build rules in Xcode. The other available scheme is iPhone 6.0 Simulator (Figure 10-27).

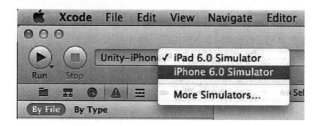

Figure 10-27. Selecting the iPad or iPhone simulator

Performing a Build and Run from Unity would have launched the iOS Simulator automatically without first giving you a chance to choose between the iPad and iPhone simulators. For now, let's stay with the iPad simulator and click the Run button at the top left of the Xcode window. The Run button is really a Build and Run button, as it compiles the project if necessary before attempting to run it. If successful, an iOS Simulator window matching the screen size of an iPad will appear, running Angry Bots (Figure 10-28).

Figure 10-28. Angry Bots running in the iOS Simulator

The iOS Simulator will interpret mouse input as touch-screen events, so you can click and drag on the virtual joysticks to play. In addition, the Hardware menu for the iOS Simulator simulates other device events (Figure 10-29).

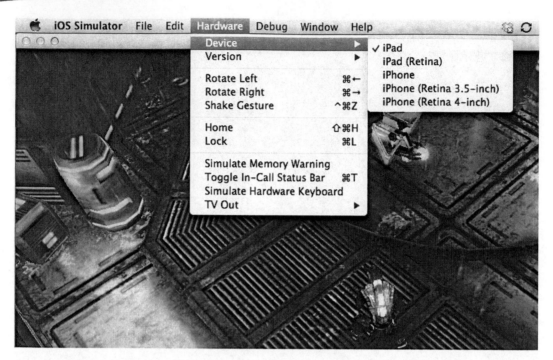

Figure 10-29. iOS Simulator options

For example, the Rotate Left and Rotate Right commands simulate rotating the device orientation (try it out and see the autorotation in action), and invoking Home is the same as pressing the device Home button on a device, which will suspend or exit the app and display the Home screen of the device. The app icon should be there and can be clicked (simulated tap) to restart the app. The Hardware menu also allows you to select different devices and iOS versions to simulate.

Besides testing, the iOS Simulator is useful for taking screenshots, via the Save Screen Shot command in the Tools menu (Figure 10-30). Invoking that command immediately saves the screenshot to the Desktop. The App Store requires screenshots for the devices your app supports, so if you need an iPad screenshot, for example, and you don't have an iPad, the iOS Simulator is a convenient tool for getting that screenshot.

Figure 10-30. The Save Screen Shot command in the iOS Simulator

The iOS Simulator window doesn't have an operable close button, but the Simulator can be exited by the Quit iOS Simulator command in the iOS Simulator menu or its keyboard shortcut Command+Q (Figure 10-31).

Figure 10-31. Exiting the iOS Simulator

The iOS Simulator is fairly complete at simulating iOS features, including iAd and Game Center. So if you don't have an iOS device available for testing, you can still get through the most of the rest of this book just using the iOS Simulator.

Explore Further

You might be experiencing deja vu, because we started with the Angry Bots demo as our first project and now we've returned. The difference of course is now we're building the project for iOS. We've taken baby steps, changing the build target to iOS, testing in the Unity Editor with Unity Remote, and then building with Xcode to run in the iOS Simulator. The next step, building to run on a real iOS device, will take place in the next chapter, and then we'll return to our regular programming, the bowling game. By then, hopefully, you'll be comfortable with the build process and can concentrate on making the game an iOS game!

Unity Manual

Because the discussion has returned to Angry Bots, it's fitting that the first relevant section in the Unity Manual is the "Unity Basics" section, specifically the page on "Publishing Builds."

The Unity Manual also includes several sections specifically about Unity iOS, although you may have to click the iPhone icon at the top of the manual to make that content visible. The section "Getting Started with iOS Development" is somewhat out of date as of this writing, but its page on the "Unity Remote" is still useful to explain how to set up and operate that app.

More recent documentation on Unity iOS is listed in the "Advanced" section of the Unity Manual, including a page on the "Structure of a Unity Xcode Project." It's a good idea to become familiar with the files in the generated Xcode project, but you won't be messing with the Xcode files generated by Unity, except to enable the built-in profiler when you get to Chapter 16.

Reference Manual

Most of the work in getting Angry Bots to build consisted of filling in appropriate values in the Player Settings. This chapter provided a cursory overview of the iOS-specific settings, and only the Default Orientation and Device SDK settings are important for running in the iOS Simulator, but the "Player Settings" page in the Reference Manual details each of the individual cross-platform and iOS-specific Player Settings, along with the settings for other platforms.

iOS Developer Library

Download links and documentation for Xcode are available on the Xcode page at the Apple Developer site (http://developer.apple.com/xcode). One of the great things about using Unity for iOS development is that you can avoid needing to know much about Xcode and Objective-C. But still, learning your way around Xcode and understanding Objective-C code can only help.

In addition to the Xcode documentation you can find under its Help menu, there are links to developer documentation from the Xcode web site http://developer.apple.com/xcode. There are many other articles listed under the Xcode topic, and many are also available in the Xcode Help menu, including the Xcode User Guide and Xcode Basics Help.

The iOS Developer Library Lists Xcode under Topics, and most of the relevant "IDE" section of the Xcode topic can be found in the iOS Simulator User Guide. The guide is extensive, featuring multiple chapters that expand on the introduction in this book to the iOS Simulator, explaining how to launch the simulator from Xcode, how to operate the simulator, and how to invoke simulated device input.

Although, Unity does a lot to shield you from working in Xcode, and in this chapter you literally just had to click the Run button in Xcode to run the iOS Simulator, it's a good idea to read up on the tool in preparation for the next chapter, where you'll learn how to build and run our app for testing and build for submission to the App Store.

Chapter 11

Building for Real: Device Testing and App Submission

Running an iOS version of Angry Bots turned out to be amazingly easy. It was just a matter of switching the build target to iOS, then immediately playing the game in the Editor using the Unity Remote app as the input device, or, to run the game in the iOS Simulator, performing a build with the Target SDK set to Simulator SDK in the Player Settings.

That might seem too easy to be the end of it, and it is. The next step is the painful part, building the Unity project so that it installs and runs on real iOS hardware. The Unity part of this procedure is easy, nearly identical to building a project to run on the iOS Simulator. But to install an app on a test device requires that the app be built with a mobile provisioning profile that is also installed in Xcode and on the test device. Before that, the profile has to be created in Apple's Provisioning Portal using a development certificate associated with the test device and the app's bundle ID. So before that, the test device and bundle ID have to be registered on the Provisioning Portal, and the development certificate has to be generated after creating a certificate request.

And that's just for testing. A similar process is required when building apps for submission to the App Store, but with a separate distribution provisioning profile and corresponding certificate. Furthermore, submitting an app to the App Store also requires adding the app to iTunes Connect, a separate web site for managing apps on the App Store.

If dealing with provisioning profiles sounds like a hassle, you may be tempted to skip this chapter and return later. And in fact, the iOS adaptation of our bowling game in the next couple of chapters can be tested with the Unity Remote (for the input code in Chapter 13) and iOS Simulator (the icon, splash screen, and screen size set in Chapter 12), as we did with Angry Bots in the previous chapter. Plus, access to the Provisioning Portal and iTunes Connect, and the associated nonpublic documentation, requires membership in the iOS Developer Program, so if you haven't acquired that yet, then you'll have to wait anyway.

But you will need an iOS Developer membership to set up Game Center leaderboards and achievements (which I will cover in Chapter 14) and an iAd banner and interstitial ads (which I will cover in Chapter 15), and the performance measurement (which I cover in Chapter 16) won't be very interesting without it being able to run on real hardware. So at the very least, it's best to get the iOS Developer registration process started as soon as possible!

Register as an iOS Developer

As you might expect, the Apple Developer web site (http://developer.apple.com/) is the place to find most of the official Apple developer resources (iTunes Connect is an exception), including all of the Apple developer programs—the Mac Developer Program, the Safari Developer Program, and the one we're interested in, the iOS Developer Program. You can register in the iOS Developer Program as an individual or a company. Registering as an individual is fairly straightforward, as long as you have a credit card and are prepared to pay the $99 yearly fee. Signing up as a company requires the same, but it also requires an actual legal company entity and supporting information about the company, including a DUNS (Data Universal Numbering System) number, which is a unique identifier assigned to a company by Dun & Bradstreet. Both individual and company accounts have to be approved by Apple, but approval for company accounts can take longer than individual accounts (the approval for my company, Technicat, LLC, took three months).

The only additional feature for company accounts is the ability for the account administrator to add team members, so in this book we'll assume we're working with an individual account or, equivalently, as the administrator of a company account.

Once you've been approved as an iOS developer, you'll have login access to the Apple developer site and and also iTunes Connect (http://itunesconnect.apple.com/) using your Apple ID. ITunes Connect is the site where you manage all your apps that are on or being prepared for the App Store.

But before working in iTunes Connect, we'll be logging in to the Apple developer site and working in the Provisioning Portal to create development and distribution provisioning profiles, which are required for test and distribution builds, respectively.

The Provisioning Portal

Assuming you have an iOS Developer Membership (if not, you can skip this chapter and return later), log in to http://developer.apple.com/ and enter the Provisioning Portal.

> **Note**   The Apple developer site has several areas that you can log in to—the Member Center, iOS Dev Center, and Developer Forums—and you can reach the Provisioning Portal from either the Member Center or iOS Dev Center (at this time, the organization is a bit confusing).

Detailed documentation is available on the site once you log in (the Provisioning Portal is one area where Apple doesn't have much in the way of public screen-to-screen documentation), but I'll briefly outline the steps that are involved and the information you need to provide.

Register Test Devices

A development provisioning profile is valid only for a specified set of test devices, so the first thing to do is register in the Provisioning Portal the iOS devices you want to use for testing. You will need to supply the unique device identifier (UDID) for each device. The UDID of a device can be found with iTunes or Xcode. In iTunes, when an iOS device is connected to your Mac, the UDID can be found by clicking the serial number of the device, which switches the serial number display to a UDID display. But that display cannot be copied and pasted, so a better option is to obtain the number from Xcode.

When an iOS device is connected to your Mac, the UDID will show up in the Xcode Organizer window. To bring up the Organizer window in Xcode, launch Xcode if it's not running already, then select Organizer from the Window menu (Figure 11-1).

Figure 11-1. Bringing up the Organizer from the Xcode Window menu

Once the Organizer window is up, all connected iOS devices should be listed in the left panel. Select the device you want to register for testing, and the device information, including the UDID, listed as the Identifier, will be displayed (Figure 11-2).

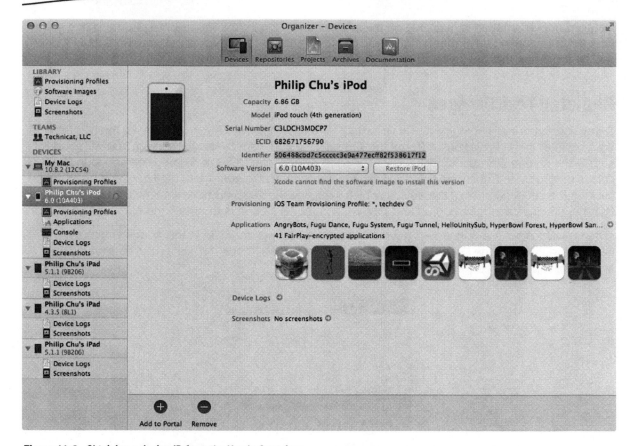

Figure 11-2. Obtaining a device ID from the Xcode Organizer

You can then copy and paste the UDID into the Provisioning Portal to register your test device.

Register App Identifiers

Once you've registered your test devices, you need to register app identifiers, because each provisioning profile is only valid for a single app ID. An app ID corresponds to a bundle ID (the same one specified in the Unity Player Settings for your app) or matches many bundle IDs when it ends with an asterisk (then it's called a *wildcard app ID*). For example, I registered an app ID com.technicat.* that I can use in a single provisioning profile for all my apps, such as com.technicat.fugubowl and com.technicat.hyperbowl.

> **Tip**   Create a wildcard app ID that matches all or most of your bundle IDs, so you don't have to create a new app ID for every bundle ID.

Development Provisioning Profiles

To create a development provisioning profile, you need to generate a development certificate that is associated with the profile. The Provisioning Portal has instructions on how to generate and upload a certificate request, which will in turn result in a new development certificate. Then you can create a development provisioning profile associated with that certificate.

Actually, once you have generated a development certificate, the Provisioning Portal will automatically generate a Team Provisioning Profile for you that uses the asterisk * as an app ID and thus matches any of your bundle IDs, which is a real convenience. But you can also generate any number of other development provisioning profiles with the same certificate and the app ID you specify.

Distribution Provisioning Profiles

Creating a distribution provisioning profile is similar to creating a development provisioning profile. You'll need to create a distribution certificate and then a distribution provisioning profile associated with that certificate.

Tip   You can save a little time by reusing the same certificate request file to create both the development and distribution certificates.

The Xcode Organizer

When your development provisioning profiles are available, you can download them into Xcode. Bring up the Xcode Organizer window (from the Xcode Window menu), select Provisioning Profiles in the sidebar, and click the Refresh button on the lower right of the profiles list. After prompting you for your Apple developer login, the Organizer will retrieve and display all the provisioning profiles you've created in the Provisioning Portal.

Figure 11-3 shows all four of my provisioning profiles. Notice all the app IDs are prefixed with a number. That's generated by the Provisioning Portal and called the *bundle seed ID*. For our purposes here, you can ignore it.

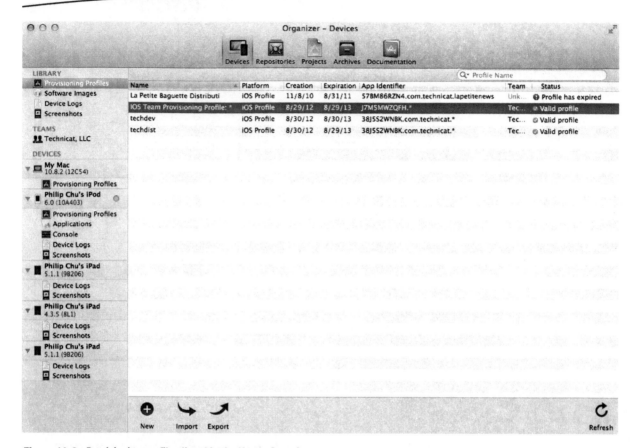

Figure 11-3. Provisioning profiles listed in the Xcode Organizer

The first provisioning profile, named La Petite Baguette Distribution, is a distribution provisioning profile that only matches an app called La Petite Baguette (a restaurant app). Notice that the app ID is fully specified, exactly matching the bundle ID for the La Petite Baguette app. Notice also that the provisioning profile has expired.

The second profile, iOS Team Provisioning Profile, is a development provisioning profile automatically created by the Provisioning Portal. It matches any app's bundle ID.

The third profile, named techdev, is a development provisioning profile I created that will work with any of my apps, as it will match any bundle ID starting with com.technicat.

The fourth profile is my sole distribution provisioning profile. It also matches any app that has a bundle ID starting with com.technicat.

It's not enough for the development provisioning profile to be in Xcode; it also has to be installed on your test devices. With a test device connected to your Mac and listed in the sidebar of the Xcode Organizer, just drag the profile from the Provisioning Profiles list to the device. To verify the profile is installed on the device, launch its Settings app, select the General category, and within that, select Profiles and see if the profile is listed there (Figure 11-4).

Figure 11-4. Provisioning profiles on a test device

Notice the expiration date. Certificates, and thus their associated provisioning profiles, expire after a year, at which point you'll have to replace the expired profile with a new profile created with a new certificate.

You can also create a new provisioning profile within the Xcode Organizer by clicking the + button on the lower left and then, after being prompted for a Provisioning Portal login, filling out the information as shown in Figure 11-5.

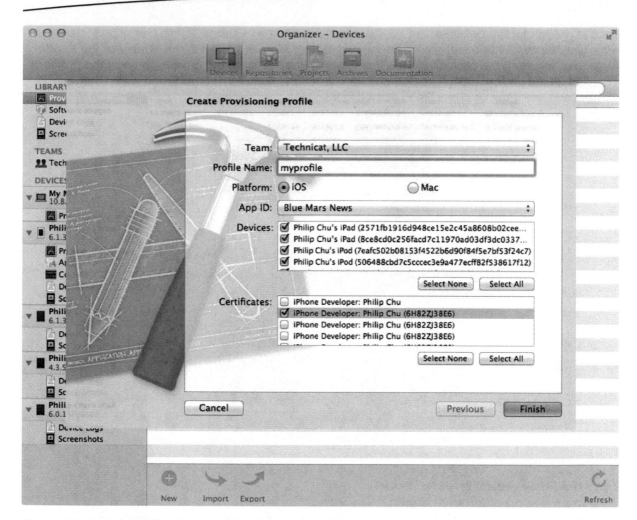

Figure 11-5. Creating a provisioning profile from the Xcode Organizer

This is the same information you would provide in the Provisioning Portal to create a development provisioning profile. Once you have provided enough information (don't forget to enter a name!), the Finish button will be enabled, and after clicking Finish, the new provisioning profile will show up in the list of all your provisioning profiles (Figure 11-6).

Figure 11-6. A newly created provisioning profile in the Xcode Organizer

If you happen to be working in Xcode and need to create a development provisioning profile, this is a convenient option. But I prefer to create my provisioning profiles directly in the Provisioning Portal, because requesting certificates, registering test devices, and creating distribution provisioning profiles have to take place there. And working directly in the Provisioning Portal avoids some flakiness I've encountered from time to time when managing provisioning profiles in the Organizer.

Build and Run

Now you're ready to start testing your device. The process is exactly the same as building and running for the iOS Simulator, except first you will need to go to the Unity Player Settings and set the SDK Version to Device SDK instead of Simulator SDK (Figure 11-7).

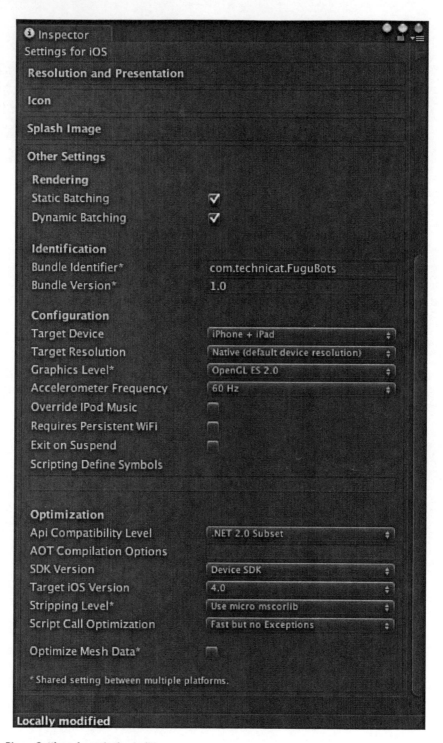

Figure 11-7. The Player Settings for a device build

Before starting a build, because you're building for real hardware, you should make sure the Target iOS Version is compatible with your test device (or vice versa), meaning the Target iOS Version should be at least as old as whatever version of iOS your test device is running. But really, it's a deployment decision, too. Supporting older versions of iOS increases the potential number of customers, but may increase your support burden and prevent use of features available only in later versions of iOS.

It turns out there is data on iOS hardware and versions currently running Unity-based apps, collected by Unity at http://stats.unity3d.com/ Any Unity app you create will contribute to this data, as long as the Submit HW Statistics option is selected in the Player Settings. You can perform a Build and Run, which is equivalent to performing a Build, manually opening the generated Xcode project by double-clicking the project file (Figure 11-8), and then clicking the Run button in Xcode.

Figure 11-8. An Xcode project generated by a Unity iOS build

Either way, instead of building and running in the iOS Simulator, Xcode will build, install, and run on the connected test device.

> **Tip** It's best to disable screen lock completely while using a device for testing. Initiating a run from Xcode will fail if the connected device has the screen locked.

As with the iOS Simulator, any Unity debug text will show up in the Xcode debug area (Figure 11-9) instead of the Console View as in the Unity Editor.

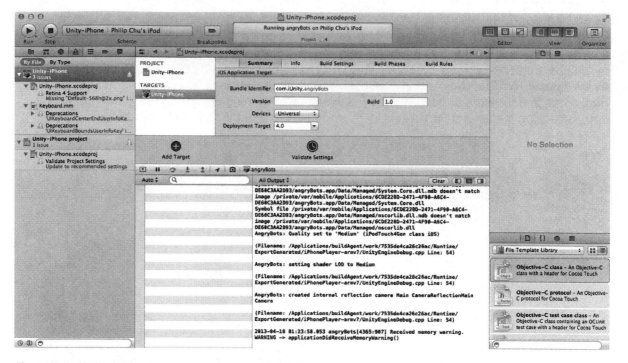

Figure 11-9. Xcode running an app on a test device

> **Note**   The Xcode equivalent of views in the Unity Editor are called *areas*. Unlike views, Xcode areas are spelled in lowercase, e.g., the navigation area, the editor area and the debug area.

You can also make use of the MonoDevelop debugger, although there's more setup involved to debug an iOS app than a game running in the Unity Editor. To enable the app for remote debugging with MonoDevelop, select the Development Build option in the Build Settings window (Figure 11-10). After the Development Build option is enabled, the Script Debugging option becomes available, and you should select that, too.

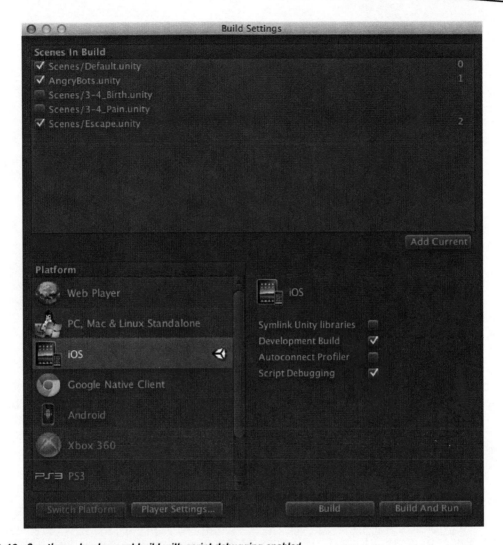

Figure 11-10. Creating a development build with script debugging enabled

Remote debugging has problems interacting with Xcode, including the inability to resume after breakpoints, so first perform a Build and Run to get the app installed on the test device. Click Stop in Xcode to halt the test run, and then manually restart the app on the device (i.e., tap the app's icon just like you would to start the app normally). Finally, in MonoDevelop, perform an Attach to Process, only instead of attaching to the Unity Editor, attach it to the test device (Figure 11-11).

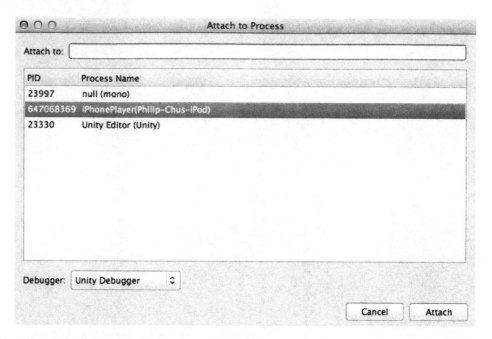

Figure 11-11. Attaching the MonoDevelop debugger to the iOS player

After you're satisfied with the device testing, it's time to submit your app to the App Store. This doesn't require any change within Unity; you only need to rebuild the app within Xcode using a distribution provisioning profile instead of a development provisioning profile. But first, you need to create an App Store entry for the app in iTunes Connect. And before you create the iTunes Connect entry, you should have some graphics ready for the App Store.

Prepare App Store Graphics

You'll need two kinds of graphics for the App Store: an app icon and a set of screenshots for all the devices that you're targeting. iTunes Connect has a tendency to log out after a period of idleness and lose all changes, so you don't want to be messing around with creating an icon and taking screenshots while logged in there.

Create an Icon

iTunes Connect will ask for a 1024 × 1024 version of your app icon, either in .png or .jpeg format, that will accompany the App Store description of your app. If you planned ahead when creating the app icon, you're all set. Otherwise, you'll have to create it now before proceeding to iTunes Connect.

Ideally, you'd have a professional icon designer create the icon, but if you're low on both funds and art skills, you can do what I do in a pinch—grab a large screenshot from the Unity Editor game view and scale it to 1024 × 1024. It's better to scale from large to small. Scaling up a smaller existing icon usually doesn't create good results and is discouraged by Apple, although it probably happens a lot because until fairly recently apps were submitted with a 512 × 512 icon uploaded.

> **Caution**   Apple may reject an app if the App Store icon does not match any of app's icons that are displayed on a device. So if you create an entirely new 1024 × 1024 for the App Store, you should set that as the default icon in the Unity Player Settings.

Take Screenshots

iTunes Connect will also ask you for screenshots in three sizes: matching the iPhone 4 (640 × 960 or 960 × 640), iPhone 5 (640 × 1136 or 1136 × 640), and iPad (768 × 1024 or 1024 × 768 or double that for the new iPad). That's assuming you selected iPhone + iPad as the supported hardware in the Unity Player Settings. If you only selected iPhone, then you don't need to supply the iPad screenshot, and if you only selected iPad, then you only need to supply the iPad screenshot.

There are three fairly convenient ways to take screenshots: using the iOS Simulator, from a device using the Xcode Organizer window, and on the device itself by pressing some buttons.

Taking screenshots with the iOS Simulator is easy. Use the Screenshot command in the Edit menu, and the resulting screenshot is saved on the Desktop. It may be inconvenient to use the iOS Simulator if your game does not play well with the limited iOS Simulator input. But if you don't have an iPhone 4 and 5 series, plus an iPad, this is one way to get screenshots.

Taking Xcode screenshots is almost as simple. With a device attached to your Mac, select the Screenshots panel of the device as it appears in the Xcode Organizer window (all attached devices will display with a green dot).

Then click the New Screenshot button on the lower right when you see a screen you like, as you play your game on the test device. The screenshot will appear in the Screenshots panel (Figure 11-12), and you can drag any screenshot from there (the smaller preview on the left or the big one on the right) to the Desktop for easy access.

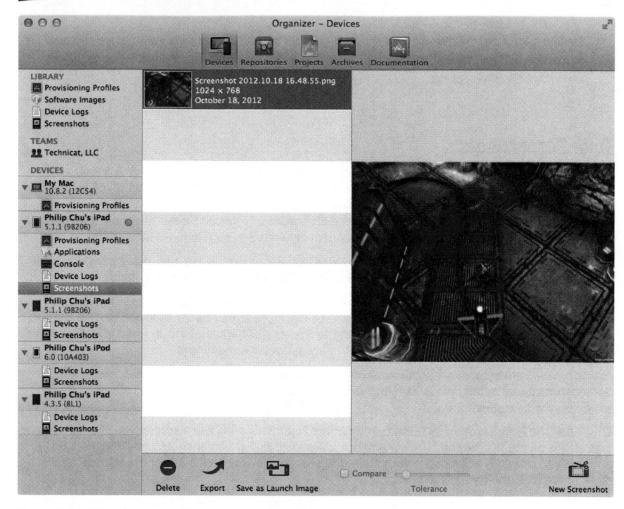

Figure 11-12. Taking device screenshots in the Xcode Organizer

Otherwise, if you need to access them in the Finder, the screenshots are in the Library ➤ ApplicationSupport ➤ Developer ➤ Shared ➤ Screenshots folder.

Tip   OS X normally hides the Library folder. You can unhide it by opening the Terminal application and entering `chflags nohidden ~/Library`.

My favorite way to take a screenshot is directly on the device by pressing the Home and Power buttons simultaneously. The resulting screenshot is saved to Photos on the device, which can later be synced to iPhoto on the Mac and accessible in the Finder from there. This method allows me to take screenshots at my leisure, and anywhere I want, like on the sofa, instead of being tethered to a Mac. And it's easier to quickly take a screenshot at a propitious moment than trying to grab a mouse and quickly click the New Screenshot button in the Xcode Organizer.

Add an App on iTunes Connect

Now that you've got your icon and screenshots ready, you can start adding your app information to iTunes Connect. Log in to `http://itunesconnect.apple.com/` and you'll see the main menu, as shown in Figure 11-13.

 Sales and Trends
Preview or download your daily and weekly sales information here.

 Contracts, Tax, and Banking
Manage your contracts, tax, and banking information.

 Payments and Financial Reports
View and download your monthly financial reports and payments.

 Manage Users
Create and manage both iTunes Connect and In App Purchase Test User accounts.

 Manage Your Applications
Add, view, and manage your applications in the iTunes Store.

 iAd Network
View ad performance and manage the ads that appear in your apps.

 Catalog Reports
Request catalog reports for your App Store content.

 Developer Forums
Find solutions and share tips with Apple developers from around the world.

 Contact Us
Having a problem uploading your application? Can't find a Finance Report? Use our Contact Us system to find an answer to your question or to generate a question to an iTunes Rep.

Access the Developer Guide.   **FAQs** Review our answers to common inquiries.

Figure 11-13. The main menu in iTunes Connect

Click Manage Your Applications to get started. Now you'll see a list of apps that you've already added and an Add New App button. Figure 11-14 shows this page in my iTunes Connect account, displaying some of my apps, each with a version number and a dot that is color coded according to the app's status.

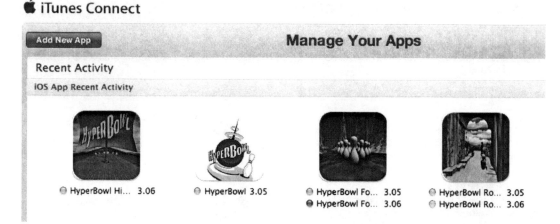

Figure 11-14. Add or manage apps in iTunes Connect

A green dot means the app is live on the App Store, and red means it has been rejected. Yellow has all kinds of meanings, but often means the app has not been uploaded yet. An app that is already live and has an update submitted or in progress will list the status of both. If this is your first app, of course, no apps will be listed.

Select App Type

When you click Add New App, the next page (Figure 11-15) asks you to select an app type, either an iOS App for the App Store or a Mac OS X app for the Mac App Store.

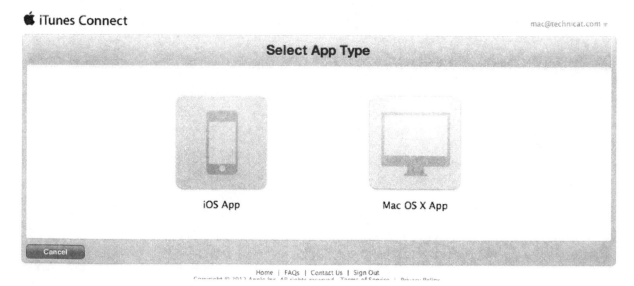

Figure 11-15. Selecting the new app type in iTunes Connect

Clicking iOS App will bring up a series of web pages, each with a form to fill out, and advance to the next page or form by clicking the Continue button.

App Information

After selecting iOS as the app type, you'll be presented with a page for entering the app name and bundle ID. These should match the Product Name and bundle ID specified in the Player Settings of the Unity Editor. The list of bundle IDs is taken from the list of app IDs you added to the Provisioning Portal. If you added a wildcard app ID, you can select that and then the suffix of the specific bundle ID for the app you're adding.

For example, in Figure 11-16, I have the info for our modified Angry Bots project, renamed Fugu Bots. The wildcard ID com.technicat.* and suffix FuguBot matches the bundle ID com.technicat.FuguBot I have in the Unity Player Settings.

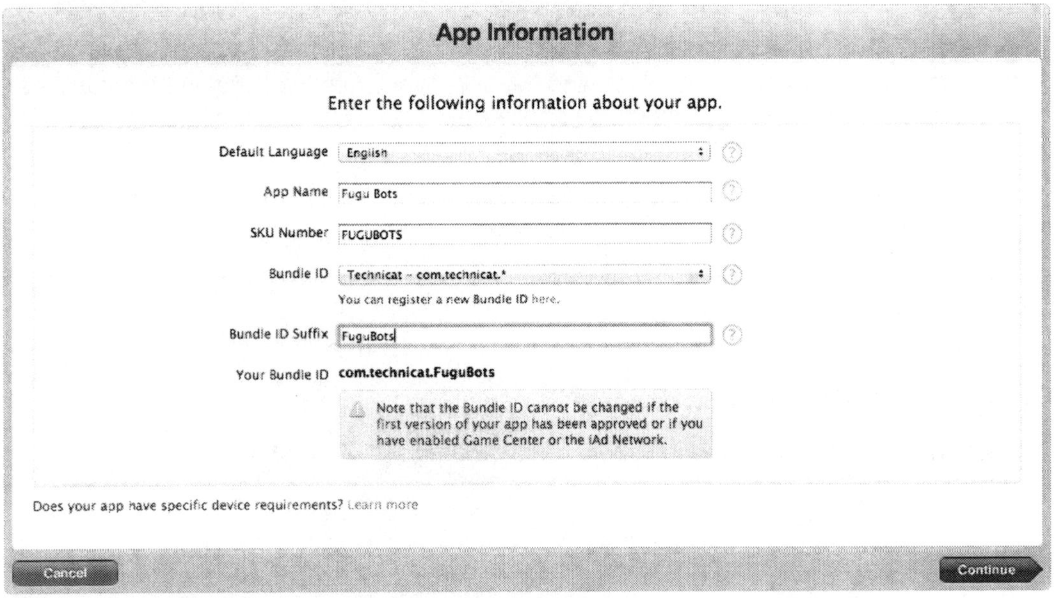

Figure 11-16. Specifying the app name and bundle ID on iTunes Connect

The default language indicates the primary language you'll be using for all the assets and descriptions you're submitting with this app.

The SKU Number can be anything you want, but it has to be unique among your apps and should be readily identifiable with your app if you see it in reports.

Availability and Price

Upon continuing from the App Information page, iTunes Connect will ask you to specify the price of the app and when you would like the app to become available on the App Store (Figure 11-17).

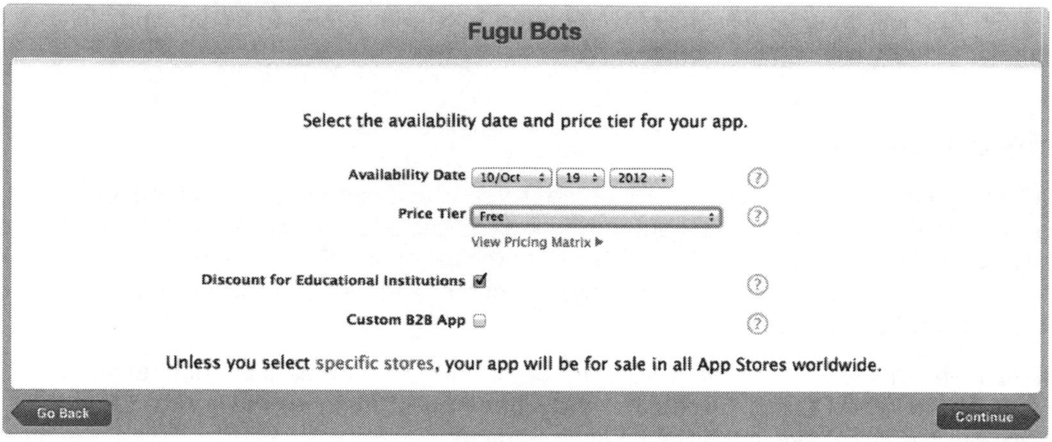

Figure 11-17. Setting the app availability and price on iTunes Connect

The availability is contingent on when Apple approves the app, so if you specify an availability date one week from the day the app is submitted and the approval takes two weeks, then it will be made available on the approval date. If you want the app released as soon as possible, just use the default date, which is the day you're entering this information.

The prices range from free to $.99 to $1.99 to $2.99 and so on. There's no need to worry too much about charging the right price, it can be changed anytime later.

The next page is the kitchen sink of this process. Most of the app information is added here, and, fortunately, this huge form is broken into sections.

Version, Category, and Copyright

The first section is the version number, copyright, and category information (Figure 11-18).

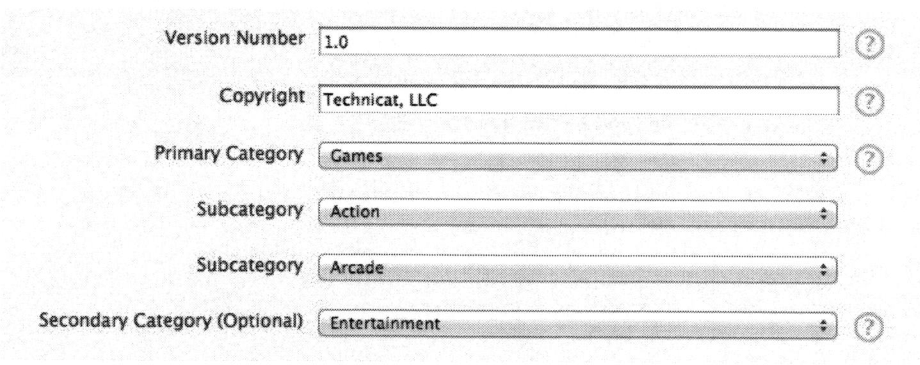

Figure 11-18. The app version, category, and copyright information on iTunes Connect

The version number must match the version number specified in the Unity Player Settings.

The copyright field should be filled in with the name of the copyright holder, normally you or your company. Don't add any extraneous Copyright text; that will be added automatically in the App Store.

Select the appropriate category and subcategories. You might as well also select a secondary category to increase the exposure of your app.

Rate the App

The Rating section is pretty straightforward (Figure 11-19). Fill it out, it's all mandatory.

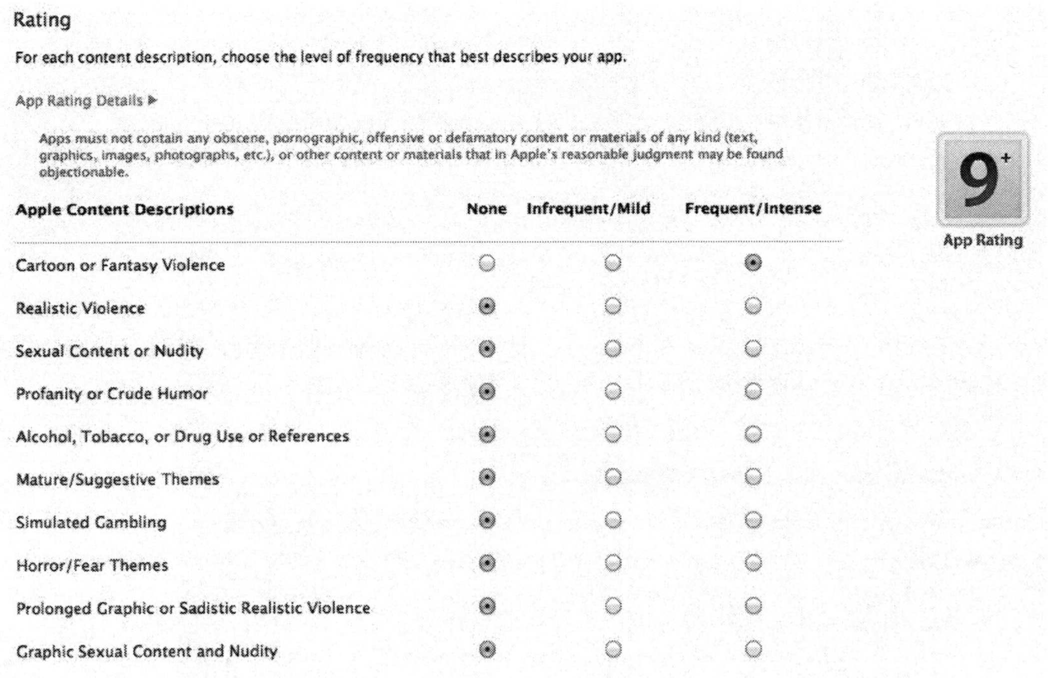

Figure 11-19. Setting the app content rating in iTunes Connect

If the ratings don't match the content, at least in Apple's eyes, the app may be rejected. For example, I tried submitting a version of Angry Bots and had the app rejected because the game has shooting, albeit against irate automata, and according to Apple that qualifies as Realistic Violence that should be marked as Frequent/Intense.

Metadata

The Metadata section is the most important for marketing (Figure 11-20).

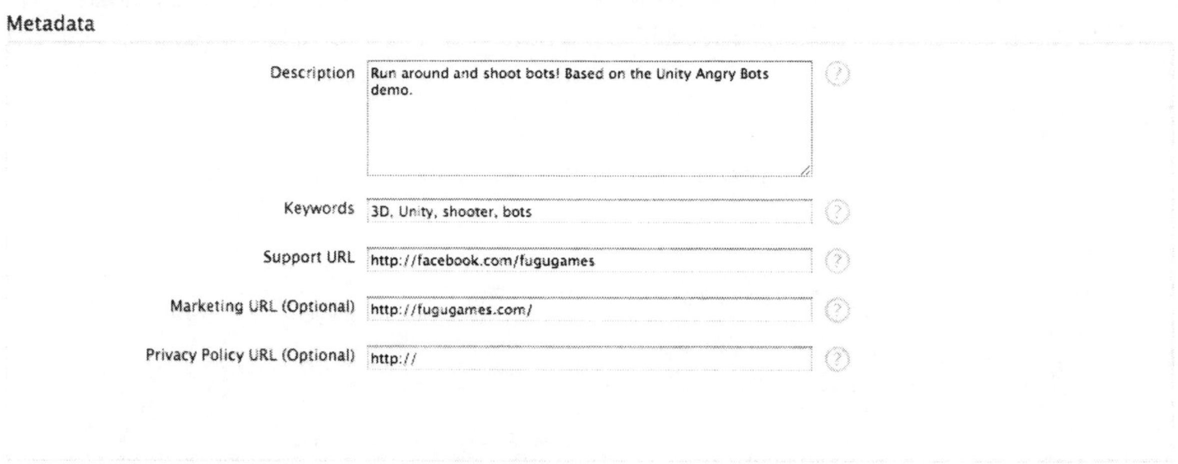

Metadata

Description	Run around and shoot bots! Based on the Unity Angry Bots demo.
Keywords	3D, Unity, shooter, bots
Support URL	http://facebook.com/fugugames
Marketing URL (Optional)	http://fugugames.com/
Privacy Policy URL (Optional)	http://

Figure 11-20. The product description for the app in iTunes Connect

This section includes the description of your app as it will appear on the App Store and keywords that help your app show up in searches on the App Store .

Upload the Icon and Screenshots

Finally, this is where you upload the icon and screenshots you prepared earlier (Figure 11-21). The icon must be 1024 × 1024 and resemble the app icons that are built into the app or the app may get rejected by Apple.

Figure 11-21. Uploading the app icon and screenshots in iTunes Connect

iTunes Connect will not allow us to proceed without uploading the icon and at least one screenshot, although we really need to upload a screenshot for each screen type (aspect ratio) that the app will run with. If a Unity iOS app is built for the iPhone and iPad, then we need to upload screenshots for all three categories, basically corresponding to the iPhone 4, iPhone 5, and iPad.

> **Caution**   iTunes Connect will time out pretty quickly. If it times out before you complete this page, the entire app description disappears, and you'll have to start over. That's why we prepared the icon and screenshots beforehand.

Prepare for Upload

After filling out the data in the previous section and then advancing to the next page, we're almost done. The app status is now Prepare to Upload (Figure 11-22).

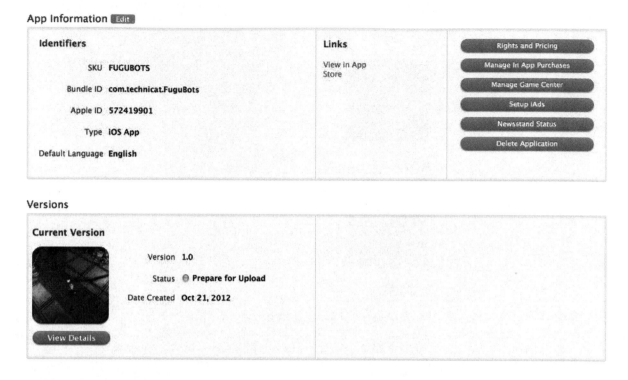

Figure 11-22. The app in Prepare for Upload status

Before you can submit your app you have to click the View Details button, which returns to the Version Information page (Figure 11-23).

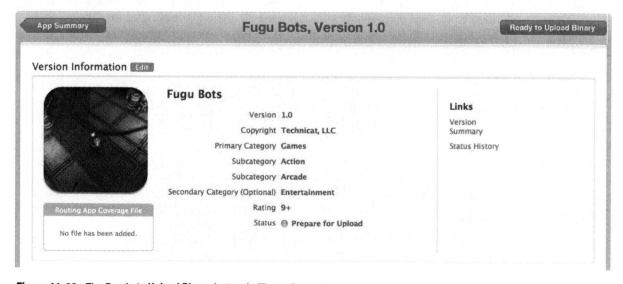

Figure 11-23. The Ready to Upload Binary button in iTunes Connect

That page now has a Ready to Upload Binary button in the upper right. Click that and iTunes Connect will ask you if the app uses cryptography, for consideration of export laws (Figure 11-24).

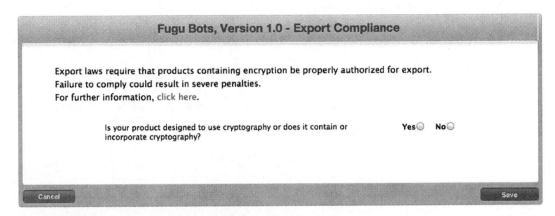

Figure 11-24. *Checking if the app has encryption in iTunes Connect*

Finally, iTunes Connect will present you with a message saying you can upload the app using a program called Application Loader. Ignore that—you can upload the app directly from Xcode (and the message is obsolete anyway). After that, you're back in the app page, now showing Waiting for Upload as the app's status (Figure 11-25).

Figure 11-25. *An app in Waiting for Upload status in iTunes Connect*

> **Caution**   The status colors for Prepare to Upload and Waiting for Upload are indistinguishable, so it's easy to forget to go through the Prepare for Upload steps.

Submit the App

Now you're ready to submit your app. Go back to Xcode and select your project and the build target. In Build Settings, scroll down and select the Distribution Provisioning Profile (Figure 11-26).

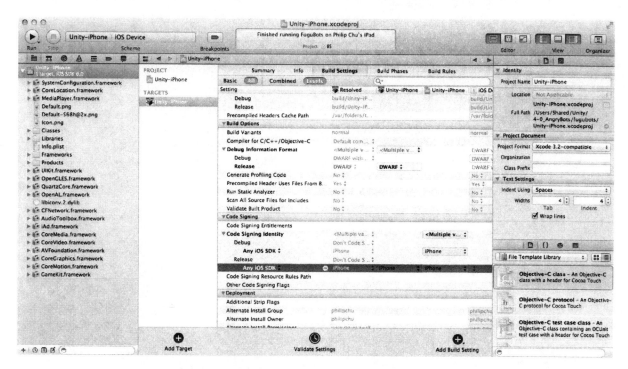

Figure 11-26.   Selecting a distribution provisioning profile for a Release build in Xcode

From the Project menu in the menu bar, select Clean, which will ensure that you rebuild everything with the Distribution Provisioning Profile (Figure 11-27).

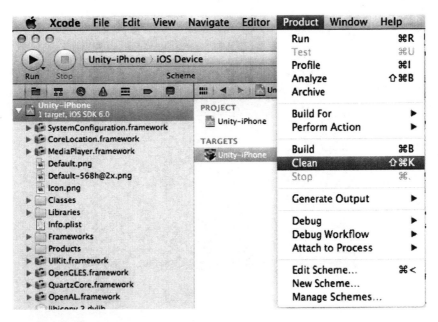

Figure 11-27. Clean the build before archiving in Xcode

Then select Archive, which will build a distribution version of the app (Figure 11-28).

Figure 11-28. Archiving a build for distribution in Xcode

When the build is complete, the Organizer window will appear showing the app, with buttons to Validate and Distribute (Figure 11-29).

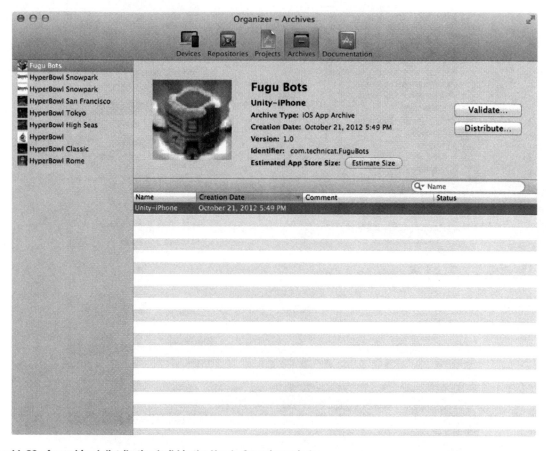

Figure 11-29. An archived distribution build in the Xcode Organizer window

Notice there is also an Estimate Size button. Your app will be processed by Apple before showing up on the App Store, which will increase the app size. Clicking this button will give you an idea what the final size of the app will be.

Clicking the Validate button will check if the app would be immediately rejected for various build or packaging problems (e.g., if the app was built using a development profile instead of a distribution profile).

> **Tip**   I don't find that using the Validate button saves me any time, since any errors reported by Validate are quickly reported by the app submission process anyway. Overall, it's more efficient to just go ahead and submit the app.

Clicking the Distribution button will initiate the app submission process, consisting of a series of pop ups (Figure 11-30).

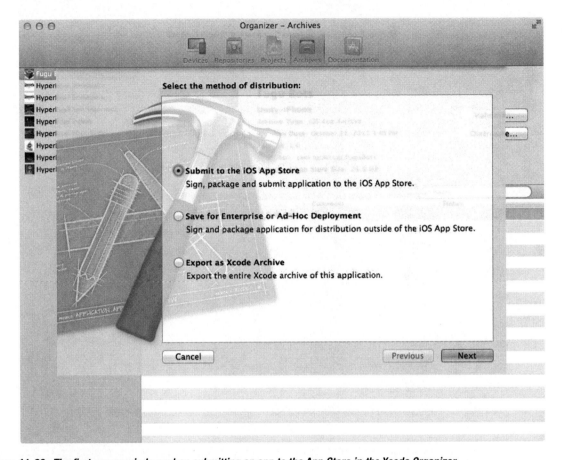

Figure 11-30. The first popup window when submitting an app to the App Store in the Xcode Organizer

The first pop up basically asks what you want to do with this app. The default selection, Submit to the iOS App Store, is what you want, so just click Next, which brings you to another pop up that asks which app you're submitting and what distribution provisioning profile you used for the app (Figure 11-31).

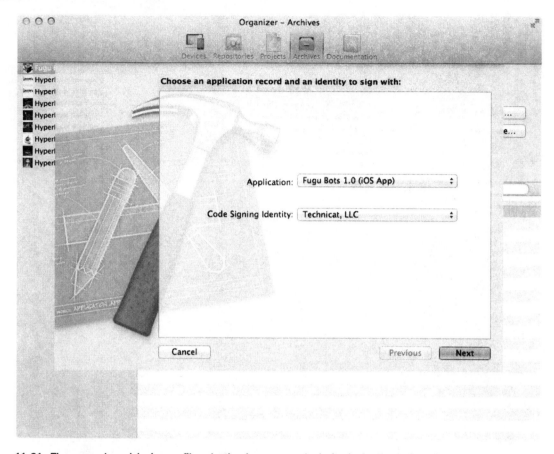

Figure 11-31. The app and provisioning profile selection for an app submission in the Xcode Organizer

The pull-down list of apps includes all your apps that are in Waiting for Upload status on iTunes Connect. Select the app that you're submitting (and if it's not in the list, you probably forgot to hit the Ready to Upload button for that app in iTunes Connect).

After selecting the matching app and provisioning profile and then clicking Next, the app will be uploaded to Apple for submission. If all goes well, the final screen will say your app has been submitted to the App Store (Figure 11-32).

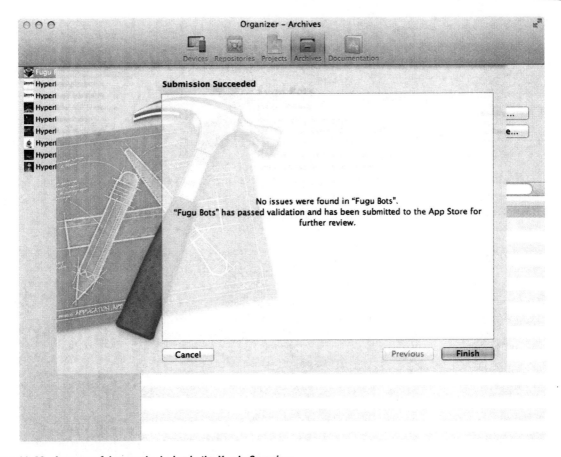

Figure 11-32. A successful app submission in the Xcode Organizer

Then it's a matter of waiting for Apple to approve or reject it.

> **Tip**   It's a good idea to log back into iTunes Connect after your submission and verify the app status
> is Waiting for Review. Even if the app binary is valid, the review may be held up because of a missing
> screenshot, for example.

You'll eventually receive an e-mail notifying you that the app is available on the App Store, that it's
been rejected, or that Apple needs more time to review it. This response usually arrives within a
couple of weeks after submission, but I've had apps accepted within twenty-four hours or rejected
after two months. When the review period is extended, Apple will typically send an e-mail stating
they need more time to review your app.

Be Prepared for Rejection

If the app is rejected, then the e-mail will tell you to return to your app in iTunes Connect and click the Resolution Center button to view and optionally respond to the rejection reasons, which may include technical issues, crash bugs, or violations of Apple's App Store Review Guidelines (which you can read on the Apple Developer Site after becoming an registered iOS Developer).

If you elect to revise your app, you will have to click Reject Binary and Ready for Upload again before uploading. The Resolution Center also allows you to file an appeal to the App Review Board if you feel the rejection is unreasonable.

If accepted, the app will appear shortly on the App Store if you selected the automatic release option in iTunes Connect. Otherwise, the app is placed in Pending Developer Release status until you log in to iTunes Connect, click View Details on the app, and click the Release this Version button.

Update the App

After an app has been approved, you can always return to the iTunes Connect page for the app and click View Details to edit the app description, and the modified text will show up on the App Store within a few hours. The iTunes Connect page will also display an Add New Version button. Clicking this will lead you through a condensed version of the original submission process to submit an update of the app. You can change nearly all the details except the bundle ID, but the only required change is an increment of the bundle version.

> **Tip**   When updating apps, remember to increment the bundle version both in iTunes Connect and in the Unity Player Settings.

Note the period-separated components of the bundle ID are treated as numbers, rather than strings, so updating version 247 to 2.049 is (surprisingly) okay because it's comparing the numbers 47 and 49 (Figure 11-33).

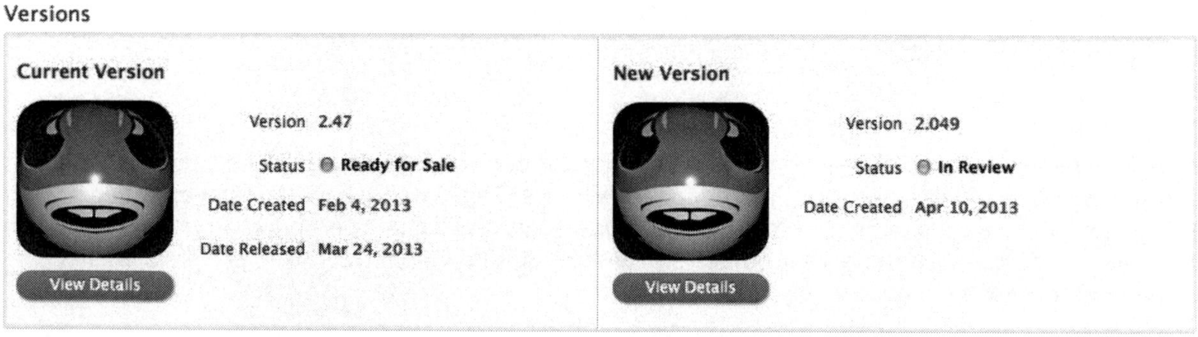

Versions

Figure 11-33. Successfully upgrading the app version number from 2.47 to 2.049 in iTunes Connect

But updating version 1.65 to 1.7 compares the numbers 65 and 7, which results in a submission error message (Figure 11-34).

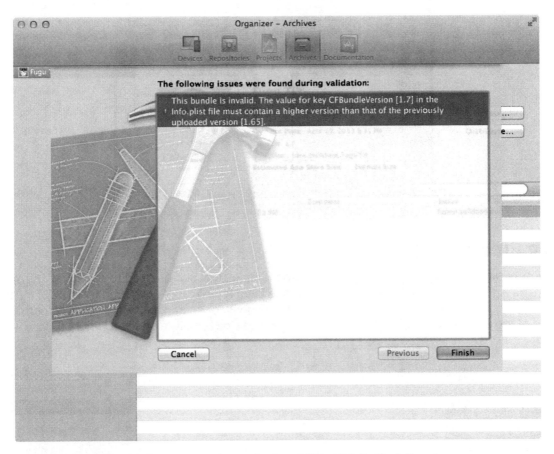

Figure 11-34. Unsuccessfully updating an app version number from 1.65 to 1.7 in the Xcode Organizer

Track Sales

After the first version of an app appears on the App Store, you can track its downloads and revenue (if it's a paid app) by logging on to iTunes Connect and clicking the Payments and Financial Reports link. The resulting page displays a time-based graph of sales, a breakdown of sales per country, and the option to generate reports (Figure 11-35).

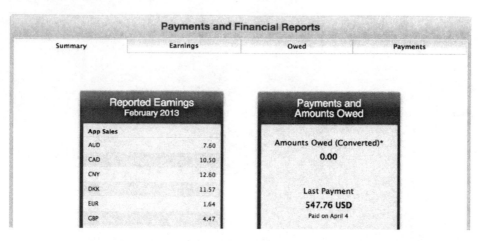

Figure 11-35. The Payment and Financial Reports page in iTunes Connect

Issue Promo Codes

For each version of an app, Apple provides 50 promo codes that can be used to download the app free on the App Store (the promo codes are available even for free apps, although there's not much point in using them in that case). To obtain the promo codes for an app, click View Details for that version of the app in iTunes Connect and then the Promo Codes button on the top right (Figure 11-36).

Figure 11-36. Clicking View Details on a live app in iTunes Connect

After agreeing to a contract, you'll be presented with a download button and field to specify the number of codes to download (Figure 11-37).

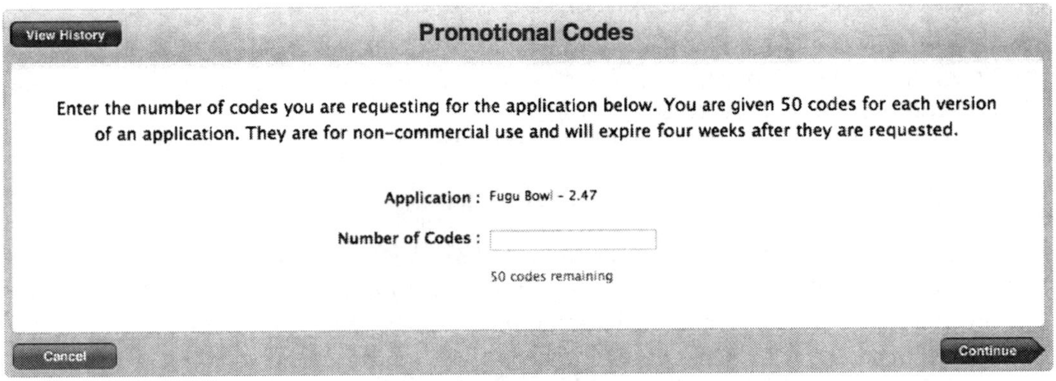

Figure 11-37. *The entry form for the number of promo codes to download*

After clicking Continue, you'll be presented with an App Store Volume Custom Code Agreement governing the use of the codes and then a download button for the codes. Clicking the button will download a text file with the number of codes you requested (Listing 11-1 shows some example promo codes) and it will e-mail you a copy of the agreement you just agreed to (if that sounds awkward, it's similar to Apple's phrase by the confirmation checkbox, "agree to the agreement").

Listing 11-1. *A Promo Code File with Five Promo Codes*

```
XY9LJRKMN7JM
TANFXAHR9EM9
XP6TMAFFHFLT
TXJ44ELTHETL
F9W3WEK7JL4Y
```

Once downloaded, the codes are valid for 28 days, even if the app is updated in the meantime.

Tip   Since the expiration date of the codes is based on their download dates, you can conserve the codes by only downloading them from iTunes Connect as needed, instead of all 50 at the same time.

The codes no longer allow users to write reviews for the app on the App Store, but the codes are ideal for sending out to sites that host their own reviews.

Explore Further

Testing Unity iOS apps in the Unity Editor and in the iOS Simulator is convenient, but there's no substitute for the real thing! The good news is that building for real hardware doesn't change much on the Unity side (really, just setting the SDK Version to Device SDK in the Player Settings). The bad news is that you have to go through the entire Apple developer registration, Provisioning Portal setup for your test devices and provisioning profiles, and iTunes Connect setup for all your apps. In a sense, this is the chapter where you became an iOS developer!

Now that we've got that out of the way, we can leave the Angry Bots project again and return to our bowling game and spend the remainder of this book adapting the game for iOS. However, we haven't seen the last of iTunes Connect. We will use iTunes Connect later when we incorporate Game Center (Chapter 14) and iAd (Chapter 15).

Unity Manual

Since the the simulator and device builds for Unity iOS involve nearly identical steps, the Unity Manual sections mentioned in the previous chapter also apply to this chapter. In addition, the "Getting Started in iOS Development" section of the Unity Manual has a page that briefly lists the steps required by Apple for submitting an app to the App Store, and the "Debugging" page in the "Advanced" section explains how to attach a MonoDevelop debugging session to a Unity iOS app running on a device.

Apple Developer Site

The road to all Apple developer information begins at the Apple Developer site (http://developer.apple.com/), so that should be your first stop. From there, you can find descriptions of the iOS Developer Program (and other Apple developer programs) and commence the registration process.

Even before the registration is complete, you can explore the iOS Dev Center, which includes the iOS Developer Library, which in turn contains the iTunes Connect Developer Guide (listed under Languages and Utilities).

> **Tip**   The documentation in the iOS Developer Library is also available in the Xcode Organizer. As you might gather from all the work that takes place in the Organizer (provisioning profiles, screenshots, app submissions), you'll be spending a lot of your Xcode time there!

Once your registration is approved, you can access the iTunes Connect site and the Provisioning Portal on the Apple Developer Site to complete the mobile provisioning and app submission steps covered in this chapter.

Chapter 12

Presentation: Screens and Icons

Now that our Angry Bots break is over, and the basics of building and running a Unity iOS project have been covered, it's time to resume our work on the bowling game and get it working on iOS!

From this point on, I will generally assume you're testing by building and running on a device, but in many cases you can test in the Editor with the Unity Remote or test in the iOS Simulator.

> **Tip** It's a good idea to always do some testing in the Unity Editor to catch errors that might not show up when testing on a device. And if you run into a weird problem on a device, go back to the Editor and see if you can debug it there.

This chapter focuses on making the game look right on an iOS device. This includes making sure the game shows up in the correct orientation and all the game elements show up at an appropriate resolution on the screen, which is a precursor to making the game playable (it's hard to start playing when you can't read or tap the Play button).

Furthermore, besides providing required attributes such as the app name and icon, we'll add some polish by including a splash screen and the familiar iOS activity indicator to indicate the game is loading.

Some of these presentation details might seem to be cosmetic and easy enough to implement that they could be deferred until the end of a project (and typically they are), but easy work could and should be done early. Tasks that can be accomplished quickly help you get into a development groove. And when you're working crunch-time hours trying to finish your game, the last thing you want to see is unfinished work you could have gotten out of the way early.

Besides, packaging is important. In fact, when I'm creating desktop software, I like to start with the installer, because that is the first customer experience. For iOS apps, the customer first sees the app icon and name and then the splash screen while launching the app. This will form the customer's first impression of whether the app is polished or amateurish. And you're the first customer of your app.

You'll feel better about your project and have a clearer idea of what you want your app to be if it's packaged like a finished product from the very beginning. And you never know when you'll need to demo it!

The corresponding Unity project is available online at `http://learnunity4.com/`, and, as usual, I recommend typing in the scripts rather than copying them from the online project. But there are some textures in the project files that will be used for the icon and splash screen, so, from the online project for Chapter 12, copy the additional files in the Textures folder to the Textures folder into the Textures folder of your bowling project (remember, you can drag the files into the Project View). You should have three Fugu Games splash textures of different resolutions, one splash screen displaying a book cover (of this book), and an icon texture (Figure 12-1).

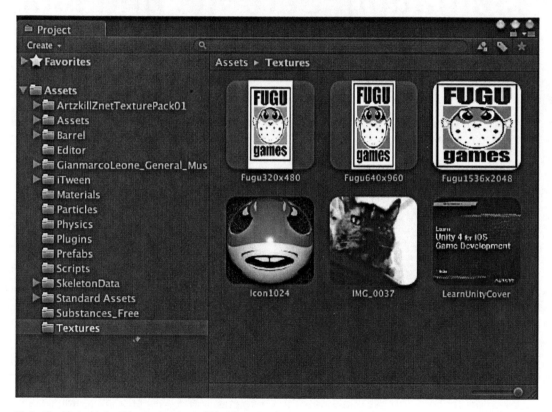

Figure 12-1. The Textures for this chapter copied from `http://learnunity4.com/`

Bowling for iOS

In the Unity Editor, bring up the Project Wizard (Open Project in the File menu), and select the bowling project as you last left it in Chapter 9, before we switched to Angry Bots. You should now be familiar with the process of switching build targets.

Bring up the Build Settings window (select Build Settings in the File menu), select iOS as the build target, and click the Switch Platform button.

If you have the Necromancer GUI installed from Chapter 9, some script errors will appear in the Console View after switching the build target to iOS, because a test script in that package wasn't written with #pragma strict and is missing some type declarations. This can be resolved quickly by just removing GUITestScript.js from the Project View or wrapping #if !UNITY_IPHONE around all its contents (bonus points for going in and fixing the code by appending :int to the function parameters). Removing the script will disable the Necromancer GUI test scene but otherwise the GUISkin is still usable in your pause menu. All of the changes introduced by this chapter will work with or without the Necromancer GUI (but the screenshots show the Necromancer GUI because it's prettier).

Once the asset reimport is complete, go to the Edit menu, and under Settings, select Player to bring up the Player Settings in the Inspector View. In the Cross-Platform Settings, fill in your Company Name and Product Name (the app name). Select the iOS tab to display the iOS Player Settings and fill in the bundle ID of the app (Figure 12-2).

Figure 12-2. The Player Settings for Fugu Bowl

Both the original and iOS versions of HyperBowl are portrait-mode games (and it turns out that portrait mode is best for the swipe-to-roll control that will be implemented in the next chapter), so let's restrict this game to portrait mode (and portrait upside down, because that kind of symmetry is required on the iPad).

Therefore, set the Orientation property in the Player Settings to Auto Rotation, with only the Portrait and Portrait Upside Down options selected (Figure 12-3).

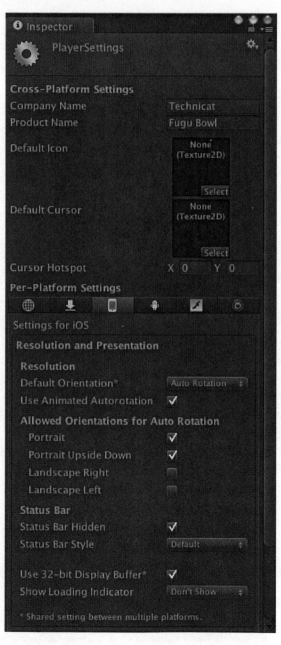

Figure 12-3. The Resolution and Presentation settings for Fugu Bowl

Scale the GUI

We now have enough set up to build and run, and the initial screen of our game looks fine, if we run it on a low-resolution iOS device (i.e., the iPhone 3GS), which has a 320 × 480 pixel screen. But on any of the newer devices, all of which have at least double the screen resolution, the pause menu looks really small, to the point where it's difficult to read or even tap an individual button. For example, Figure 12-4 shows the pause menu on the 640 × 960 screen of an iPhone 4.

Figure 12-4. The pause menu looking tiny on a high-resolution screen

To scale the GUI, you first need to figure out the scaling factor you want to use, which is the current screen width divided by the screen width you were originally targeting. The GUI looks alright on the iPhone 3GS, at 320 × 480 pixels, so let's say the base screen width we're targeting is 320. So if we're actually running on an iPhone 4, for example, at 640 × 960 pixels, we'll have to scale up the GUI by a factor of two.

The next step is to apply the scaling factor. This can be done in UnityGUI by setting the static variable GUI.matrix, which is a *transformation matrix.* In computer graphics, a transformation matrix encompasses and applies a translation (change of position), rotation, and scale.

In fact, the local position, rotation and scale of a Transform Component corresponds to a 4 × 4 transformation matrix for that GameObject. And the world position, rotation and scale are calculated by combining (multiplying) all the transformation matrices of a GameObject's parent GameObjects. In the good old days, you had to include this linear algebra code when programming in computer graphics. Now you can let the game engine hide this from you, but you're getting a little taste of it here.

Scale the Scoreboard

Let's start with the scoreboard, because that's a little bit simpler, by making the modifications shown in Listing 12-1 to the FuguBowlScoreboard script. The addition is a variable named baseScreenWidth that specify the base screen width, defaulting to the 320-pixel width of the iPhone 3GS. The variable is public, so you have the option of adjusting it in the Inspector View.

Then, at the beginning of the OnGUI function, so it takes effect before any GUI rendering takes place, two lines of code construct the scaling matrix and assign it to GUI.matrix.

Listing 12-1. Scaling Added to the FuguBowlScoreboard.js Script

```
var baseScreenWidth:float = 320.0;

function OnGUI() {
#if UNITY_IPHONE
        var guiScale:float = Screen.width/baseScreenWidth;
        GUI.matrix = Matrix4x4.TRS (Vector3.zero, Quaternion.identity, Vector3(guiScale,
                                                              guiScale, 1));

#endif
```

The new code is only intended for iOS (although it would work on any platform), so new lines of code are wrapped between #if UNITY_IPHONE and #endif. UNITY_IPHONE is a built-in preprocessor definition that is only defined when the build target is iOS (you can also use UNITY_IOS). The end result is that the additional code only turns into executing code for iOS and essentially disappears if you're building to any other target (we don't do that for baseScreenWidth because we don't want to lose its Inspector View setting if the build target is changed).

Of the two lines of real code, the first calculates how much you need to scale the GUI, based on Screen.width, the current screen width, and baseScreenWidth, the screen width the GUI is coded to render on. The result is assigned to a local variable guiScale.

You might have wondered why we declared baseScreenWidth as a float instead of an int. Well, this is why: Screen.width is an int, and if you divide an int by an int, then the compiler assumes you want the result as an int, which works out okay if, for example, you're dividing 640 (iPhone 4) by

320 and end up with 2. But if you're running on an iPad 2, then you would be dividing 768 by 320, and the result will round down to 2, which is wrong in this case. But as long as one number in the operation is a float, then the compiler will treat the whole thing as a floating point computation.

> **Caution** Watch out for operations where you're supplying ints as inputs and expecting float results. It's a common source of errors.

The result is passed to a call to Matrix4x4.TRS, which constructs a 4x4 matrix with a translation, rotation and scale. The translation is Vector3.zero (x, y, and z are 0), Quaternion.identity (the identity quaternion represents no rotation), and a Vector3 representing the scale. The scale factor based on the screen size is applied in the x and y directions, and the z-axis is left unscaled since that's the direction pointing into the screen.

Scale the Pause Menu

Scaling the pause menu is almost exactly the same process. Let's add the same baseScreenWidth public variable and the same code to set GUI.matrix in the beginning of the OnGUI function in the FuguPause script (Listing 12-2).

Listing 12-2. Scaling the Pause Menu in FuguPause.js

```
var baseScreenWidth:float = 320.0;

function OnGUI () {
        if (IsGamePaused()) {
                #if UNITY_IPHONE
                var guiScale:float = Screen.width/baseScreenWidth;
                GUI.matrix = Matrix4x4.TRS (Vector3.zero, Quaternion.identity,
                                                        Vector3(guiScale, guiScale, 1));

                #endif
                if (skin != null) {
                        GUI.skin = skin;
                } else {
                        GUI.color = hudColor;
                }
                switch (currentPage) {
                        case Page.Main: ShowPauseMenu(); break;
                        case Page.Options: ShowOptions(); break;
                        case Page.Credits: ShowCredits(); break;
                }
        }
}
```

However, one more alteration is required. The BeginPage function centers the GUI using Screen.width, so you need to use baseScreenWidth instead. Listing 12-3 shows this code change.

Listing 12-3. Modified BeginPage Function to Work with Scaled GUI

```
function BeginPage(width:int,height:int) {
#if !UNITY_IPHONE
        GUILayout.BeginArea(Rect((screenWidth-width)/2,menutop,width,height));
#else
        GUILayout.BeginArea(Rect((baseScreenWidth-width)/2,menutop,width,height));
#endif
}
```

Notice how we used #if !UNITY_IPHONE. The exclamation mark means *not*, so the first line of real code exists for any built target except iOS and the other line is just for iOS. We could have flipped the order of the two lines of code and started with #if UNITY_IPHONE.

While we're at it, we should remove the Quit button from the pause menu, as Apple rejects any app with a quit option. The Quit button in the ShowPauseMenu function of the FuguPause script is already excluded from Unity webplayer builds by checking the UNITY_WEBPLAYER preprocessor definition, so we can just add a check for UNITY_IPHONE (Listing 12-5).

Listing 12-4. Excluded Quit Button from the iOS Build of FuguPause.js

```
function ShowPauseMenu() {
        BeginPage(150,300);
        if (GUILayout.Button ("Play")) {
                UnPauseGame();
        }
        if (GUILayout.Button ("Options")) {
                currentPage = Page.Options;
        }
        if (GUILayout.Button ("Credits")) {
                currentPage = Page.Credits;
        }
#if !UNITY_IPHONE && !UNITY_WEBPLAYER
        if (GUILayout.Button ("Quit")) {
                Application.Quit();
        }
#endif
        EndPage();
}
```

The Quit button is only included in the build #if !UNITY_IPHONE && !UNITY_WEBPLAYER, which is true when the build target is not iOS *and* not a webplayer. When you build the game now, you should see the pause menu running on a device (or the iOS Simulator) scaled up with the screen resolution and missing the Quit button, like the iPhone 4 screenshot in Figure 12-5.

Figure 12-5. The scaled pause menu

Set the Icon

By default, the icon for your app will be the Unity logo. Figure 12-6 shows the icons for several demo apps published by Unity Technologies on the App Store. Aside from Angry Bots, they all have the default Unity icon, albeit an older one because they were built with Unity 3 (and at the time of this writing haven't been updated).

Figure 12-6. Apps with the default Unity icons

Figure 12-6 also shows the icon for our Fugu Bowl app if we were to build it right now. It looks a bit different because it's published with Unity 4 and also has the gloss that is automatically applied by Apple, since we didn't select Prerendered Icon in the iOS Player Settings.

To customize the icon, you can drag any texture into the Default Icon field of the Player Settings. Let's use the Icon1024 texture in the Textures folder, copied from the project for this chapter at http://learnunity4.com/. I often indicate the original texture size in the file name (a 1024x1024 texture in this case), which saves a lot of time in assigning icon and splash screen textures.

Since you're using the texture as an icon, you should adjust the import settings appropriately.

Select the Icon1024 texture in the Project View, and then in the Inspector view, set the Texture Type to GUI instead of Texture (Figure 12-7). This will prevent Unity from applying settings that are suitable for textures with 3D models but not for GUI display. For example, textures used with models should have dimensions that are powers of 2, such as 256 × 256 or 512 × 512, because that's what graphics hardware likes to operates with, and the textures are stretched around models, anyway. But, generally, GUI textures should stay at their original resolution, since they're usually sized according to their intended display (which is usually not at a power of 2 resolution).

You can switch the Texture Type to Advanced to compare the underlying settings of the Texture and GUI preset texture types, i.e., select Texture then switch to Advanced, then select GUI and switch to Advanced. And within Advanced, you can override any of the preset values for more control over the import settings.

Figure 12-7. The import settings for the icon texture

Tip   If you're going to use a texture for two different purposes, duplicate it so you can apply different import settings for each.

Below the Texture Type area is where texture maximum size and compression level is specified. Unity will generate a warning at build time if you have used a compressed texture as an icon, pointing out correctly that compressed textures may not look good as icons. So select the Default tab so these settings apply to all platforms unless overridden, set the Max Size as 1024 to avoid scaling the texture, and set Format to TrueColor for full color resolution and no compression. Click Apply to reimport the texture with the adjusted settings, and the Preview at the bottom will reflect the new format, size, and memory usage.

Now drag the icon texture into the Default Icon field of the Player Settings in the Cross Platform area. Examine the Icon foldout of the iOS Settings (Figure 12-8). As long as the Override for iPhone check box is not selected, automatically scaled versions of the Default Icon will appear for all the other icon sizes (Figure 12-8).

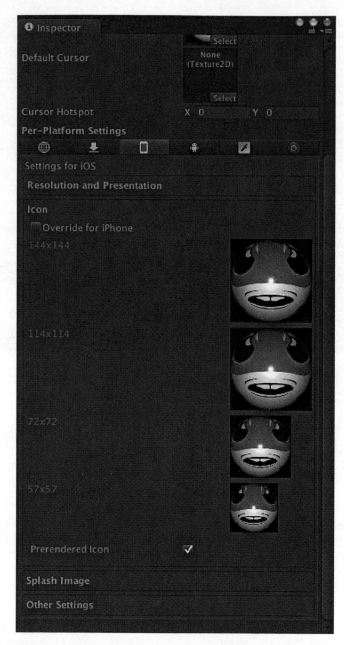

Figure 12-8. The Default Icon scaled to different icon sizes in the Player Settings

The various icon sizes correspond to the screen resolutions of the various iOS devices:

- 57 × 57: Any iPhone or iPod touch preceding the fourth generation (the iPhone 3GS or the third-generation iPod touch)
- 114 × 114: Fourth generation and later iPod touch and iPhone
- 72 × 72: The original iPad, iPad 2, and iPad Mini
- 144 × 144: The "new" iPad (or as I like to call it, the iPad 3)

Ideally, there would be an icon tailored for each size, in which case you would check mark the Override box, and then drag the various versions of your icon to each appropriate box. Any box that you leave unfilled with use the Default Icon. But Unity does a good job of scaling textures down (it is far preferable to scale down then up), so I often reuse the same 1024 × 1024 texture that I upload for the iTunes Connect app description.

> **Tip** If you don't use the same icon file for iTunes Connect and the Player Settings, make sure the various icons at least resemble each other. I've had an app rejected because its icon iTunes Connect did not resemble the app icon as displayed on a device.

I recommend you always select the Prerendered Icon option to avoid the gloss that otherwise would be automatically added by Apple.

Besides the optional shine, the portion of the build executed from Xcode also automatically rounds the corners of the icon and adds a drop shadow. So don't do that yourself! Just keep it square with sharp corners and no special borders.

Set the Splash Screen (Pro)

All iOS apps display a static "splash" screen on startup. Like the default app icon, the default splash screen in a Unity-built app shows the Unity logo (Figure 12-9).

Figure 12-9. The default Unity splash screen

If you're using Unity iOS Basic, you're stuck with the default splash screen. But if you're using Unity iOS Pro, you can supply your own splash screen in a manner similar to the way you customized the app icon.

The Splash Image foldout is located beneath the Icon foldout in the iOS Settings, and, as with the icon selection, it has slots for multiple resolutions appropriate for the various iOS screens and also for both portrait and landscape orientations (Figure 12-10):

- *Mobile splash screen*: 320 × 480 for any iPod touch or iPhone preceding the fourth generation (i.e., the iPhone 4)

- *iPhone 3.5"/Retina*: 640 × 960 for the Retina display of the iPhone 4, iPhone 4S, and fourth generation iPod touches

- *iPhone 4"/Retina*: 640 × 1136 for the iPhone 5 and fifth-generation iPod touch

- *iPad Portrait*: 768 × 1024 for the original iPad and the iPad 2

- *iPad Landscape*: 1004 × 768 for the original iPad and the iPad 2

- *High-Res. iPad Portrait*: For the Retina display of the new iPad (the iPad 3)

- *High-Res. iPad Landscape*: For the Retina display of the new iPad (the iPad 3)

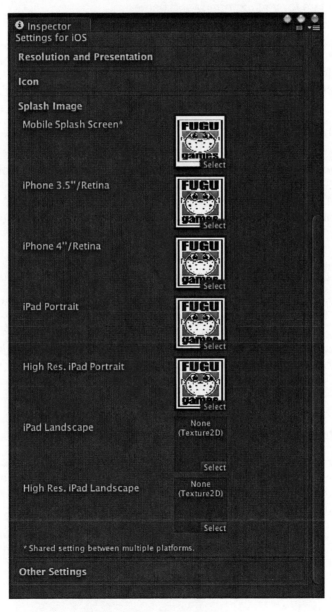

Figure 12-10. Splash screens for different screen resolutions and orientations

There is no single default splash screen that Unity will automatically resize for all the splash resolutions, so you have to populate the splash screen boxes for the resolutions and orientations that your game will use. Since only Portrait and Portrait Upside Down orientations (along with Auto Rotation) are selected in the Resolution and Presentation settings, only the portrait splash screens need to be assigned. Like icons, the splash screens can be any textures, and Unity will scale them as needed, but you'll get the best results with textures that are already the target size. You'll want to use something appropriate for your company and game.

> **Note** Apple recommends that the splash screen resemble an actual screen of your game, but it's typical to just present a company logo. Personally, I think it's confusing to have a screen that acts like an unresponsive game screen.

Drag each splash screen texture from the Textures folder into the matching Splash screen box in the Player Settings (Figure 12-10): Fugu320x480 into Mobile Splash Screen, Fugu640x960 into iPhone 3.5"/Retina, and Fugu1536x2048 into High Res. iPad Portrait. The iPhone 4"/Retina needs a texture, so drag the closest match, Fugu640x960 into it. And Fugu1536x2048 can be used for iPad Portrait.

A Second Splash Screen

Although you can't change the splash screen in Unity iOS Basic, you can make a splash screen that appears right after the built-in one. You just need to make a scene that displays the splash texture on the screen for a few seconds and then loads the first game scene. This can also be useful with Unity iOS Pro if you want to have more than one splash screen. For example, in HyperBowl I have some HyperBowl artwork displayed by the built-in splash screen and then my Fugu Games logo in the second splash screen.

Create the Splash Scene

Invoke the New Scene command from the File menu to create a new empty scene. Save it as Splash. Bring up the Build Settings window and click Add Current to add the new scene to your build. It will appear at the bottom of the list of scenes, so drag it up to the top. Its scene index should now display as 0, meaning it's the first scene loaded (Figure 12-11).

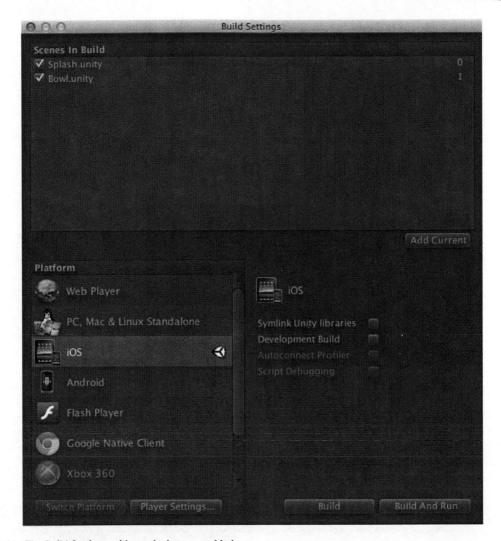

Figure 12-11. The Build Settings with a splash scene added

Create the Splash Screen

The easiest way to display a full-screen texture is with a GUITexture. In the splash scene, go to the Create Other submenu in the GameObject menu and choose GUI Texture (Figure 12-12).

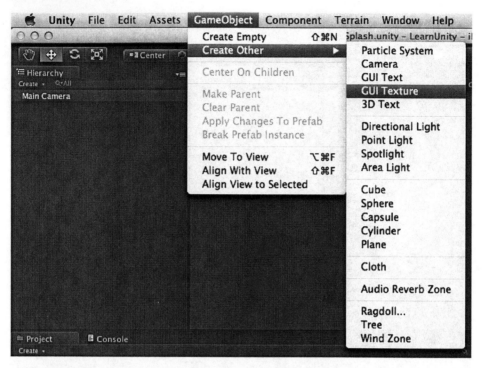

Figure 12-12. Creating a GUITexture

Rename the resulting GameObject to Screen and examine it in the Inspector View. The newly created GUITexture displays a Unity watermark centered in the screen (Figure 12-13). Unlike UnityGUI, GUITexture uses normalized screen coordinates: x and y range from 0 to 1, where 0,0 is the top left corner of the screen and 1,1 is the bottom right, so setting x and y to 0.5 each specifies that the texture is centered on the screen.

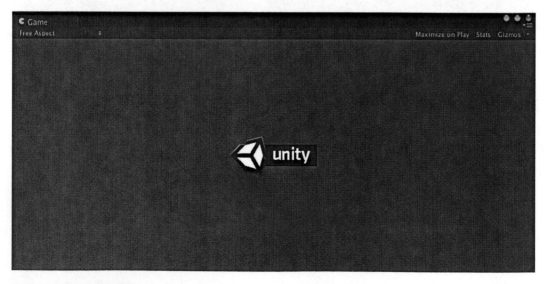

Figure 12-13. A default GUITexture

Let's replace the watermark texture with our splash texture. Drag the LearnUnityCover texture from the Textures folder in the Project View into the Texture field of the GUITexture component. To make the texture stretch across the entire screen, change the scale to 1,1,1 and set all the Pixel Inset values to 0 (Figure 12-14).

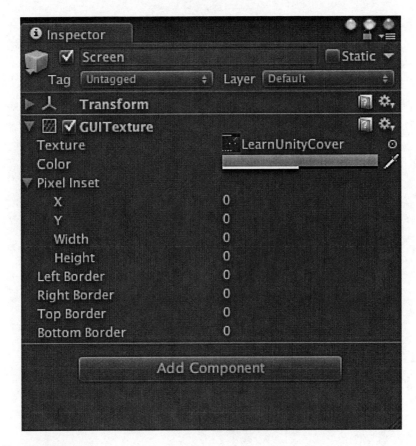

Figure 12-14. A full-screen GUITexture

Now if you run the game, you'll see the splash texture stretched to fill your screen. When running on a device or the iOS Simulator, it will appear after the built-in splash screen (Figure 12-15).

Figure 12-15. The full-size secondary splash screen

Load the Next Scene

As a splash screen, this scene should stay up for just a few seconds and then begin to load the game scene. Like any real game level, this scene could use a main logic script, so create a new JavaScript, name it FuguSplash, and add the contents of Listing 12-5.

Listing 12-5. Wait-and-Load code in FuguSplash.js

```
var waitTime:float=2; // in seconds
var level:String;     // scene name to load

function Start() {
        yield WaitForSeconds(waitTime);
        Application.LoadLevel(level);
}
```

There are two public variables that can be customized in the Inspector View: the time (in seconds) to wait before loading the next scene and the name of the scene to load. The Start function is really simple; it waits for the built-in coroutine WaitForSeconds to finish, passing in the specified wait time, and then it calls Application.LoadLevel to load the level you specified. In the process, the current scene will be unloaded so the splash screen will disappear.

Let's add the script to the splash scene. Create an empty GameObject, name it Splash, and attach the FuguSplash script to it. Then in the Inspector View, enter the name of the bowling scene in the Level field (Figure 12-16). Now if you run the game, either in the Editor or in an iOS build, the splash screen will appear for a couple of seconds and then the bowling scene will appear.

Figure 12-16. The FuguSplash script added to the splash scene

Just a few words about WaitForSeconds; it is convenient, but you could have implemented your own version. Listing 12-6 shows a hypothetical implementation.

Listing 12-6. An Implementation of WaitForSeconds

```
function WaitForSeconds(waitTime:float) {
        var startTime:float = Time.time;
        while (waitTime > Time.time-startTime) {
                yield;
        }
}
```

Note that the specified wait time is game time, not real-world time, so WaitForSeconds isn't useful, for example, while the game is paused and game time is stopped. But if you need to wait in real seconds, you can use the hypothetical implementation of WaitForSeconds and replace Time.time with Time.realtimeSinceStartup, which returns the time in real-world seconds since the game was started (Listing 12-7).

Listing 12-7. A Real-Time Version of WaitForSeconds

```
function WaitForSecondsRealtime(waitTime:float) {
        var startTime:float = Time.realtimeSinceStartup;
        while (waitTime > Time.realtimeSinceStartup-startTime) {
                yield;
        }
}
```

Display the Activity Indicator

When something is taking a while, it's nice to have some kind of loading indicator. For the initial scene load, there's a convenient way to display the iOS spinner that you often see in apps as an activity indicator. You can enable this by choosing one of the activity indicator styles for Show Loading Indicator at the bottom of the Resolution and Presentation foldout in the Player Settings (Figure 12-17). Given the splash screen is providing a mostly white background, Gray is the best style (the other styles are white).

Figure 12-17. *The Player Settings with Gray Show Loading Indicator selected*

Now when you run the game in an iOS build, you'll see the Gray activity indicator spinning on the built-in splash screen.

Script the Activity Indicator

It would be nice to use the activity indicator elsewhere, especially when loading other levels. Fortunately, Unity has a scripting interface for the activity indicator, in the form of static functions in the Handheld class. We just need a script that calls those functions to start and stop the activity indicator. Create a new JavaScript called FuguSpinner and add the contents of Listing 12-8 to the script.

Listing 12-8. Starting and Stopping an Activity Indicator in FuguSpinner.js

```
#pragma strict

#if UNITY_IPHONE
function Start() {
        DontDestroyOnLoad(this.gameObject);
        Handheld.SetActivityIndicatorStyle(iOSActivityIndicatorStyle.WhiteLarge);
        Handheld.StartActivityIndicator();
}

function OnLevelWasLoaded() {
        Handheld.StopActivityIndicator();
        Destroy(gameObject);
}
#endif
```

In the Start callback, the call to Handheld.SetActivityIndicatorStyle specifies the appearance of the activity indicator. The available options, represented by the iOSActivityIndicatorStyle enum, match the Loading Indicator options available in the Player Settings. We'll choose iOSActivityIndicatorStyle.WhiteLarge, since we know the secondary splash screen has a mostly black background.

The call to Handheld.StartActivityIndicator makes the activity indicator visible in the center of the screen. The Unity Scripting Reference documentation for Handheld.StartActivityIndicator says that the activity indicator will be activated after the current frame, so you need to yield at least a frame before calling Application.LoadLevel. Otherwise, the indicator won't appear until after the new level is loaded, which defeats the purpose of activating the indicator in the first place. We don't have to worry about that, here, because we know the FuguSplash script is yielding for some number of seconds before loading the next scene.

However, the activity indicator will keeps going even after the new scene is loaded by FuguSplash. To stop the activity indicator after the scene has finished loading, this script has to survive the scene load, which is why DontDestroyOnLoad is called at the beginning of the Start function, passing it the GameObject this script is attached to. This ensures the GameObject, and thus this script, survives when the next scene is loaded.

Because the GameObject survives the scene load, we can be assured the MonoBehaviour callback OnLevelWasLoaded is called after the new scene has finished loading. This is a perfect place to turn off the activity indicator with a call to Handheld.StopActivityIndicator. At this point, the script and the GameObject it's attached to aren't needed, anymore, so Destroy is called on the GameObject.

> **Tip** It's a good practice to destroy objects when you don't need them anymore. Besides freeing up space, you want to avoid the worst case where you loop back into the scene where the object was originally created, and then you end up with two versions of the same object!

Note that DontDestroyOnLoad and Destroy are both static functions in the Object class, so just as we called Instantiate in Chapter 7, instead of calling Object.Destroy, for example (or UnityEngine.Object.Destroy to avoid the name clash with System.Object class in .NET), here you're implicitly calling this.Destroy, which works because this is an Object.

Attach the FuguSpinner script to a new GameObject in the scene, called Spinner. Now when you Build and Run on a device, the activity indicator appears in the center of the splash image and disappears after the next scene has loaded (Figure 12-18).

Figure 12-18. Secondary splash screen with an activity indicator

Explore Further

Now our bowling game for iOS looks like a real app! It has an icon, a splash screen (or two), an activity indicator spinning away on the splash screen, it runs in portrait orientation, and the graphics scale to fit the screen including the UnityGUI scoreboard and pause menu. The menu is even automatically functional in iOS, with its buttons responding to taps on the screen. We can't quite say that about the actual gameplay, but we'll implement touchscreen game controls in the next chapter.

Reference Manual

Once again, we've spent some time in the Player Settings (a recurring theme now that we're making iOS builds), so the Reference Manual documentation on the Player Settings is worth a review.

We used just one new Component in this chapter, a GUITexture Component for our splash screen image. GUITexture and its parent class GUIElement have no relation to UnityGUI (in fact, GUITexture and its sibling GUIText were the closest things to user interface elements before UnityGUI arrived).

This chapter was devoted largely to icon and splash screen images, which should all be imported using the GUI preset import settings, which are documented fo Texture2D in the Asset Components section.

Scripting Reference

The one new UnityGUI feature introduced in this chapter was the "matrix" variable in the "GUI" class. At the time of this writing, the Scripting Reference page for that variable is nearly blank, but the "GUIUtility" class has some better-documented functions, including "ScaleAroundPivot", which can be used as an alternative to setting GUI.matrix (in fact, it is a helper function that sets GUI.matrix internally.

We only used the "Matrix4x4.TRS" constructor, but the Scripting Reference documentation on "Matrix4x4" is not bad, explaining how matrices are used in Unity and listing many class functions that will be useful if you ever have to start messing around with matrices.

The yield instruction "WaitForSeconds" was already introduced in Chapter 8 for the game over state, and it turns out to be convenient fordisplaying a splash screen a certain number of seconds. We took this opportunity to explore hypothetical implementations of WaitForSeconds and compare the static "Time" variables "Time.time" and "Time.realTimeSinceStartup". It's an important distinction when the pause menu is up and game time is suspended.

We called the static "Application" function "LoadLevel" to transition from the splash scene to the bowling scene, but we also could have called an asynchronous version of the function, "Application.LoadLevelAsync". As an asynchronous function, it doesn't suspend Unity while it's loading a new scene, so, really, you could have anything happen in the splash scene while waiting for the new scene to finish loading.

As demonstrated with our use of the activity indicator functions in the "Handheld" class, you can make Objects survive across scenes loads by calling "DontDestroyOnLoad" called on them and "Destroy" them when they're not needed anymore. These are both static functions in the "Object" class, which is always worth reading up on since it's the parent class of everything that can be in a scene.

To display and hide the activity indicator, we called the "StartActivityIndicator" and "StopActivityIndicator" functions in the "Handheld" class. See the documentation on the activity indicator functions about the necessity to yield before performing a scene load. "iOSActivityIndicatorStyle" enumeration for a list of the available activity indicator styles.

The Handheld class is worth a looking over, as it contains all the scriptable Unity mobile features (except those specific to iOS). For example, the Handheld class has a static "PlayFullScreenMovie" function that can play a movie from local storage or streamed from a web site, which is another possibility for a cool-looking splash scene. The Scripting Reference page for that function has details on the supported video formats and how to control the movie player (based, at the time of this writing, on the native iOS movie player, MPMoviePlayerController).

iOS Developer Library

As we explore Unity iOS features, more and more of the documentation in the iOS Developer Library is relevant. Remember, that documentation is available both on the Apple Developer site (http://developer.apple.com/) and from the Xcode Organizer window.

One document worth reading in its entirely, found in the "User Experience" topic of the iOS Developer Library, is Apple's iOS Human Interface Guidelines. The original guidelines dating back to the original Mac were the gold standard in user interface best practices. Since then, the guidelines have been split into Mac and iOS versions, but you should read the iOS version if only to avoid app rejections. Related to this chapter, the Custom Icon and Image Creation Guidelines lists requirements and recommendations for creating app icons and splash screens (known as "launch images" in their terminology).

Many Unity classes that are mobile-specific or iOS-specific will have an Objective-C counterpart. For example, the activity indicator controlled by Unity's Handheld class is accessed in Objective-C via the UIActivityIndicatorView class, also found in the User Experience topic in the Windows and Views section.

Asset Store

The Transitions Manager from DFT Games, available free on the Unity Asset Store, provides more sophisticated introductory screen behavior than what has been described in this chapter, including fading the screen in and out and using multiple screens. I use the Transitions Manager in all my apps.

Books

Josh Clark's *Tapworthy: Designing Great Apps* is the book that convinced me to eschew automatic icon gloss and always select Prerendered Icon in the Unity Player Settings. It's also a good treatment of app design in general.

There are plenty of textbooks on linear algebra (and even a hefty "matrix" article on http://wikipedia.org/), but any computer graphics book will have a primer on matrix math. For example, Real-Time Rendering (http://realtimerendering.com/) has an appendix on "Some Linear Algebra."

Handling Device Input

Although our bowling game is up and running on iOS, it's not quite in a playable state, because we don't have any working player controls. Which brings us to the issue of input handling, perhaps the most obvious difference between desktop and mobile games.

Instead of reading the mouse or keyboard, an iOS game has to use one of its device sensors, typically the touchscreen (tapping and swiping) or accelerometer (shaking and tilting). We'll opt for touchscreen input to control the bowling ball, but we'll do some shake detection with the accelerometer and play with the device camera a little bit, too.

The project for this chapter on `http://learnunity4.com/` has the script changes introduced in this chapter, and no other assets are added. This is true for the remainder of this book. It's all scripting from here on out!

The Touch Screen

UnityGUI already works with the touchscreen in iOS, so if you Build and Run our bowling game on a device right now, or test it with the Unity Remote in the Editor, you can operate the initial menu by tapping the buttons. When you tap the Play button on the pause menu, the bowling ball drops. So far, so good.

But what about the bowling ball control? `Input.GetAxis` does return values when swiping on the screen, but the results are unlikely to be exactly what you want (in older versions of Unity iOS, `Input.GetAxis` was not functional at all). In any case, we need to first define how the control will work in the iOS version of the bowling game.

Swipe the Ball

For Fugu Bowl, we'll adopt the touchscreen control that I use for HyperBowl. The player pushes the ball in a certain direction by swiping along the screen in that direction. Swiping up on the screen will push the ball forward, swiping down will push the ball back, swiping left will roll it left, and swiping right will roll it right.

The swipe control scheme is similar enough to the mouse controls that we can work within the framework of the existing `FuguBowlForce` script. Bring up that script and add some new public variables, `swipepowerx` and `swipepowery`, so we can adjust the swipe power, just like we did with the mouse control (Listing 13-1).

Listing 13-1. Adjustment Variables for Swipe Control in FuguBowlForce.js

```
var swipepowerx:float = 0.1;
var swipepowery:float = 0.08;
```

We added new variables instead of reusing `mousepowerx` and `mousepowery` so that we can switch between the standalone and iOS build targets without clobbering the power adjustment values for each platform. The properties for both will always show up in the Inspector View (Figure 13-1).

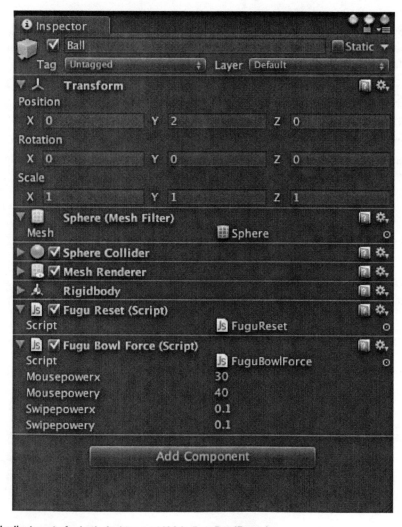

Figure 13-1. Control adjustments for both desktop and iOS in FuguBowlForce.js

The big change is our `CalcForce` function, which gets called by our `Update` callback once per frame. On iOS, instead of calling the static function `Input.GetAxis` to see how much the mouse has been moved, `CalcForce` calls the static function `Input.GetTouch` to check for swipes. The `UNITY_IPHONE` preprocessor definition makes sure the new code exists only on iOS and the old code on any other platform (Listing 13-2).

Listing 13-2. Detecting Swipes in FuguBowlForce.js

```
function CalcForce() {
        var deltatime:float = Time.deltaTime;
#if UNITY_IPHONE
        if (Input.touchCount > 0) {
                // Get movement of the finger since last frame
                var touch:Touch = Input.GetTouch(0);
                if (touch.phase == TouchPhase.Moved) {
                        var touchPositionDelta:Vector2 = touch.deltaPosition;
                        forcey = swipepowery*touchPositionDelta.y/deltatime;
                        forcex = swipepowerx*touchPositionDelta.x/deltatime;
                }
        }
#else
        forcey = mousepowery*Input.GetAxis("Mouse Y")/deltatime;
        forcex = mousepowerx*Input.GetAxis("Mouse X")/deltatime;
#endif
}

}
```

Like `Input.GetAxis`, `Input.GetTouch` returns information registered since the previous frame, so you can call it in `CalcForce`, which gets called from `Update`, thus once each frame.

`Input.GetTouch` returns a struct of type `Touch`, which describes the touch event, whether the finger was pressed, released, or moved, and if moved, by how many pixels.

We're now dealing with multitouch screens, so `Input.GetTouch` has one parameter, an integer indicating which of the latest `Input.Touch` events to return. The number of touch events is available in the static variable `Input.touchCount`, so we can process all touch events is a loop like this:

```
for (var i:int=0; i < Input.touchCount; ++i) {
        var touch:Touch = Input.GetTouch(i);
// do your stuff here
}
```

But to keep things simple here, we're only interested in one finger, so just check if there's one or more Touch events avallable, and if so, just check the first one:

```
if (Input.touchCount > 0) {
        var touch:Touch = Input.GetTouch(0);
```

Touch events can signify different finger actions: a press, release, or drag. This can be checked by inspecting the phase property of the Touch object, which is a TouchPhase enumeration. We're only interested in Touch events that signify a finger has dragged along the screen, so check if the touch phase is TouchPhase.Moved:

```
if (touch.phase == TouchPhase.Moved) {
```

If it is, then calculate the force used to push the bowling ball. It's similar to the mouse control, but instead of multiplying by Input.GetAxis, multiply by the deltaPosition property of the Touch event, which is the number of pixels the finger has dragged across:

```
var touchPositionDelta:Vector2 = touch.deltaPosition;
forcey = powery*touchPositionDelta.y/deltatime;
forcex = powerx*touchPositionDelta.x/deltatime;
```

Notice the deltaPosition property is a Vector2, which is just like a Vector3, but with only x and y properties, no z value.

Now if you click Play in the Editor and test with the Unity Remote, or if you perform a Build and Run on a device, the ball will roll in the direction you swipe.

The complete FuguBowlForce script with the touchscreen additions is available in the project for this chapter on http://learnuninty4.com/.

Tap the Ball

Although our bowling game doesn't care where on the screen the swiping takes place, many games require the ability to detect if a specific GameObject has been touched. On desktop and web platforms, mouse events over GameObjects with Collider Components can be detected with callbacks such as OnMouseDown, OnMouseUp, and OnMouseOver. For example, the OnMouseDown callback in a script is invoked at the beginning of a mouse click that takes place over the script's GameObject, or, rather, the GameObject's Collider Component.

> **Note** The OnMouse callbacks also work on GameObjects with GUIText and GUITexture Components. This was the closest thing to a built-in GUI system in Unity before UnityGUI was introduced.

To demonstrate how the OnMouse callbacks work, create a new JavaScript named FuguDebugOnMouse and attach it to the Ball GameObject (Figure 13-2).

Figure 13-2. Ball with the FuguDebugOnMouse script attached

Then add the contents of Listing 13-3 to the script.

Listing 13-3. Detecting a Mouse Click in FuguDebugMouse.js

```
#pragma strict

function OnMouseDown () {
        Debug.Log("GameObject "+ gameObject.name + " was touched");
}
```

Now the script contains an OnMouseDown callback that logs a message about the GameObject getting touched. When you run the game in the Editor and click the Ball, the debug message appears in the Console View (Figure 13-3).

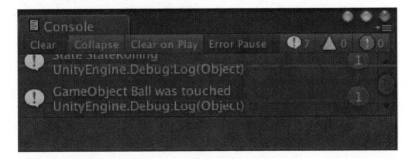

Figure 13-3. Debug message demonstrating the OnMouseDown callback

Unity iOS invokes the OnMouse callbacks in response to touch events, except in the cases where there's no obvious mapping. For example, what's the touch equivalent of OnMouseOver, which is called when the mouse hovers over a GameObject? But it makes sense to call OnMouseDown when a GameObject is tapped (and OnMouseUp when the finger stops touching the screen). And this is what happens, as you can see if you run the game again in the Editor with the Unity Remote or if you Build and Run on a device. In either case, tapping the Ball will produce the same debug message you saw when clicking it.

Although it's convenient that the OnMouse callbacks work for touches, at least to this extent, it's useful to know how to implement your own tap-object detection. It's a straightforward combination of checking for a tap and then performing a raycast from the screen position into the 3D world along the camera direction. *Raycasting* is the process of finding the first object that a ray intersects (as you may recall from high school math, a ray has a starting position and a direction, like an arrow).

To demonstrate, let's create a new JavaScript named FuguTap, attach it to the Main Camera (Figure 13-4), and add the contents of Listing 13-4 to the script.

Figure 13-4. Main Camera with the FuguOnTap script attached

Listing 13-4. A Script Mimicking OnMouseDown Events

```
#pragma strict

#if UNITY_IPHONE
function Update () {
                for (var i = 0; i < Input.touchCount; ++i) {
                        if (Input.GetTouch(i).phase == TouchPhase.Began) {
```

```
                    var ray:Ray = camera.ScreenPointToRay (Input.GetTouch(i).position);
                    var hit:RaycastHit;
                    if (Physics.Raycast (ray,hit,camera.far,camera.cullingMask)) {
           hit.collider.SendMessage("OnTap",SendMessageOptions.DontRequireReceiver);
                    }
                }
            }
}
#endif
```

The entire script consists of an Update callback, that loops through all the touch events registered in the past frame. But in this case, only the beginning of a tap is of interest, so only touches that are in the phase TouchPhase.Began are considered. The screen coordinates of each such touch is extracted and passed to the Camera function ScreenPointToRay to form a Ray that originates at the screen position and projects along the Camera direction into the 3D world.

The Ray is passed in as the first argument to the static function Physics.Raycast to see if the Ray intersects a Collider Component of any GameObject. Information about the first intersection, if any, is returned in the RayCastHit struct that is passed in as the second argument. The third argument is the raycast distance, and the fourth argument is the set of layers that will be tested for intersection. You restrict the possible raycast results by supplying the Camera far plane distance as the raycast distance and the Camera culling mask (set of visible layers) as the set of layers to test for intersection.

If the call to Physics.Raycast returns true, meaning there's been an intersection, then you retrieve the intersecting Collider Component and call SendMessage on it to invoke OnTap callbacks in attached scripts (calling SendMessage on a Component is equivalent to calling SendMessage on the Component's GameObject).

Notice that the call to SendMessage includes an optional second argument, SendMessageOptions. DontRequireReceiver. Without that argument, Unity will report an error if the message is sent to a GameObject that doesn't have any matching functions, or, in this case, any OnTap functions.

The entire Update callback is wrapped in a #ifdef UNITY_IPHONE, because it's only intended for iOS touchscreen input. Likewise, you can now use UNITY_IPHONE to rename the OnMouseDown callback to OnTap, so it will be called by the FuguOnTap script (Listing 13-5).

Listing 13-5. The FuguDebugOnMouse Script with an Alternate Callback Name for iOS

```
#pragma strict
if !UNITY_IPHONE
function OnMouseDown () {
#else
function OnTap () {
#endif
        Debug.Log("GameObject "+ gameObject.name + " was touched");
}
```

Now if you run the game again and tap the Ball, you'll still see the debug message, but it will result from the OnTap messages sent from FuguOnTap.

The Accelerometer

Every iOS device has an accelerometer that measures acceleration in three different directions. The three values can be examined in the static variable Input.accelerometer, which is a Vector3.

The x value corresponds to acceleration that runs left to right along the face of the device. The y value represents the acceleration running from top to bottom along the face of the device, and the z value is the acceleration from the front to the back of the device. Starting with Unity 4, the accelerometer values are adjusted for the device orientation, so if you're holding the device in landscape mode, the accelerometer x values still run from left to right.

Debug the Accelerometer

A time-honored way to figure out how code works is to print stuff out. Let's create a new JavaScript called FuguDebugAccel and attach it to a new GameObject named DebugAccel in the bowling scene. Add the Update function as shown in Listing 13-6 to the script.

Listing 13-6. Code to Print Out Accelerometer Values

```
function Update () {
        Debug.Log("accel x: "+Input.acceleration.x+" y: "+Input.acceleration.y+"
                                                    z: "+Input.acceleration.z);
}
```

The Update function takes the x, y, and z accelerometer values and concatenates them into a somewhat readable String. Debug.Log sends that String to the Console View if you're testing in the Unity Editor (with the Unity Remote) or to the Xcode debug area if you're running in the iOS Simulator or on a device.

Try tilting the device around and see how the values change. For example, the Debug.Log output shown in Figure 13-5 results from placing the device flat on a table. The x and y values are nearly 0 and the z value is close to –1. If the device is flipped upside down it would be close to 1.

Figure 13-5. Debug.Log output of accelerometer values

The acceleration values are in units of gravity. At rest, each accelerometer value ranges from –1 to 1, where 1 is full earth gravity (9.8 meters per second squared). Now try shaking the device. You should see the numbers spike up and down.

Detect Shakes

An issue with our pause menu on iOS is that we can't pause with the ESC key, since there's no ESC key on our devices (although Android devices typically have a Back button that behaves like an ESC key).

It's straightforward to add a pause button to the screen to FuguPause script by just adding a GUI.Button call inside the OnGUI function:

```
if (GUI.Button(Rect(0,0,100,50), "Pause") { PauseGame(); }
```

However, I don't like to have buttons on the screen during gameplay, especially on really small screens like the iPhone. So let's take advantage of the alternate input that iOS devices can provide and pause by shaking the device.

From our previous exercise in printout out accelerometer values, we saw that shaking the device causes at least one of the x, y, or z values of Input.acceleration to spike up or down. So we can check for a shake by checking if any of the values are much larger than 1 or much less than –1, for example. But we don't have to be very exact, so we can just take the square of the magnitude (length) of the vector:

```
if (Input.acceleration.sqrMagnitude>shakeThreshold)
```

Getting the sqrMagnitude of the Vector3 is faster than getting the magnitude, since the magnitude of a vector is the square root of $x^2 + y^2 + z^2$, and this way you avoid the square root operation, which is relatively expensive (remember learning to calculate square roots by hand in high school?).

So let's start by adding a public variable for the shake threshold to the FuguPause script:

```
var shakeThreshold:float = 5;
```

Now you can tweak that property in the Inspector View (Figure 13-6) and make it more or less sensitive to shakes.

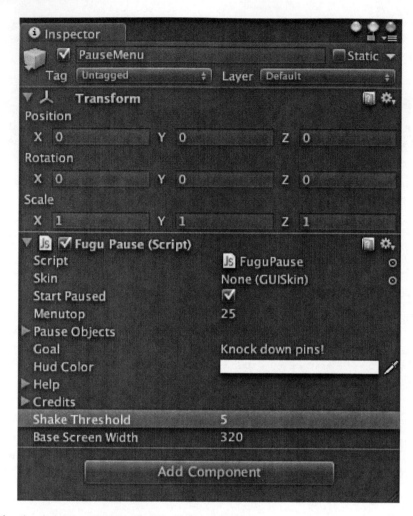

Figure 13-6. Adjusting the shake -to-pause threshold in the Inspector View

Next, add the check of Input.acceleration as a UNITY_IPHONE replacement for the check of the ESC key (Listing 13-7).

Listing 13-7. Adding Shake to Pause in the FuguPause.js

```
var shakeThreshold:float = 5;

function Update() {
#if UNITY_IPHONE
        if (Input.acceleration.sqrMagnitude>shakeThreshold)
#else
        if (Input.GetKeyDown(KeyCode.escape))
#endif
```

```
    {
                switch (currentPage) {
                case Page.None: PauseGame(); break;     // if the pause menu is not displayed, then pause
                case Page.Main: UnPauseGame(); break;   // if the main pause menu is displaying,
                                                                            then unpause
                default: currentPage = Page.Main;       // any subpage goes back to main page
                }
        }
}
```

That's all you need. Now when you test with the Unity Remote or on a device, shaking the device will pause the game! The augmented FuguPause script (just two lines of new code!) is in the project for this chapter on http://learnunity4.com/.

The Camera

Although Unity doesn't have much built-in support for iOS cameras, Unity does have cross-platform support for reading webcam video into a texture.

Reading the WebCam

Unity has a special kind of texture (like Texture2D, a subclass of Texture) called WebCamTexture that displays video from an attached hardware camera. It works on multiple platforms, including iOS. Let's give it a try. Create a JavaScript called FuguWebCam and add the Start function given in Listing 13-8. The Start function creates a WebCamTexture, assigns the texture to the Material of the GameObject you've attached the script to, and then calls Play to start updating the texture from the camera video.

Listing 13-8. Playing a WebCamTexture in FuguWebCam.js

```
function Start () {
var webcamTexture:WebCamTexture = WebCamTexture();
renderer.material.mainTexture = webcamTexture;
webcamTexture.Play();
}
```

Now attach the script to the Ball GameObject. If you click Play in the Editor you'll see video from the Mac camera appear on the ball. And if you Build and Run on a device, you'll see the same thing, only using the device camera. Figure 13-7 is a screenshot of the game on my iPod touch as I'm pointing the camera at my whiteboard.

Figure 13-7. A WebCamTexture rendered on the bowling ball

Explore Further

All in all, it didn't take much work (compared to the packaging effort in the previous chapter) to implement touchscreen input for the bowling game, although in practice you'll spend a lot of time testing and adjusting controls for a game to get it just right. In any case, with the shake-to-pause feature, the functional port of the bowling game is complete. In other words, the iOS version game is now playable!

And despite the fact there isn't a real use for the device camera in this game, we did activate it using Unity's WebCamTexture class to render a video texture on the bowling ball. Gimmicky, but game development is very much about learning! Especially in iOS, there's an opportunity to play around with a lot of different control schemes and input sensors.

Scripting Reference

Almost all the Unity features introduced in this chapter are members of the "Input" class. In fact, the Scripting Reference documentation on Input includes an overview of the iOS input features.

After reading the overview of the Input class, you should read the pages for each of the functions used in this chapter, in particular "Input.GetTouch" (and the associated "Touch" struct), which has code samples showing how to loop through all the Touch events in each frame, and "Input.acceleration", which has code samples showing how to check acceleration values in every frame.

One thing to keep in mind, the accelerometer can generate multiple values per frame. For most cases, it should be sufficient to just sample Input.accelerometer once per frame, but if finer-grained sampling is required, you can access the variables Input.accelerationEventCount and Input.accelerationEvents to obtain all acceleration events.

The Input class provides access to other iOS sensors. The static variables "Input.gyro", "Input.compass" and "Input.location" return data from the gyroscope, compass and location services, respectively. In addition to the pages documenting those variables, you should check out the pages on the classes of those variables: "Gyroscope", "Compass" and "LocationServices" classes. The documentation is sparse, but you can find code samples in the individual class functions. The static variable "Input.compensateSensors" controls whether the accelerometer, gyroscope and compass data are adjusted for the screen orientation.

Besides testing object selection, raycasting is used a lot in games and graphics, so you should familiarize yourself with the page on "Physics.Raycast", which has several code examples. For example, in HyperBowl, I use raycasting to keep the Main Camera from dipping below the ground and to set the initial positions of GameObjects to rest just on top of the ground. In both cases, I raycast down from the GameObject position toward the ground and check the resulting distance.

Finally, we covered the use of the WebCamTexture class. The page on "WebCamTexture" has a lot of stuff, but click the links to its Play, Stop, and Pause functions (the functions you'd most commonly use) to find code samples on each of those pages. Also check out the link to the "WebCamTexture" constructor. That page lists a variety of constructors that allow you to customize the texture size for different resolutions.

iOS Developer Library

It's a good idea to read the iOS Reference Library in addition to, or even before, reading the Unity Script Reference, so you'll know what iOS capabilities are available to be exposed through Unity and how Unity classes and functions map to their iOS counterparts.

You can view the iOS Reference Library, no login required, at http://developer.apple.com/library or from the Xcode Organizer, and from there select the Guides tab and browse the guides, in particular the following:

The "Event Handling Guide" provides an overview of touch events, which relate to Unity's Input.GetTouch and the Touch class, and motion events, which relate to Input.acceleration and the other Input accelerometer variables.

The guide "Camera Programming Topics for iOS" describes the UIImagePickerController class used by the Prime31 Etcetera plug-ins.

The "AV Foundation Programming Guide" describes the video capture functions most likely used for the WebCamTexture class in Unity.

Asset Store

The Unity Input class gives us access to basic touch information, but it doesn't provide access to the iOS Gesture Recognizers, which detect higher level "gestures," such as swiping and pinching. The Asset Store comes to the rescue again, offering third-party packages that provide high-level gesture detection. I use the Finger Gestures package, which has a nice callback system for detecting and handling various gestures.

For example, in HyperBowl I wanted the pause menu to come up when the player pinches the screen (two fingers on the screen coming together). With the Finger Gestures package, it just involves adding a callback for the gesture in the pause menu script:

```
function OnGesturePinchEnd(pos1:Vector2,pos2:Vector2) {
        PauseGame();
}
```

and then a line in the Start or Awake function that adds the callback to the FingerGestures callback list for that gesture:

```
FingerGestures.OnPinchEnd += OnGesturePinchEnd;
```

Unity doesn't provide script access to everything available in iOS, and that's where plugins come in. The Unity plugin system allows you to add new script functions that access "native" code. So, generally speaking, if you can code something in C, C++, or Objective-C, you can make a Unity plugin for it. For example, in the Unity Asset Store, you'll find there are plug-ins built around mobile ad SDKs and plugins for accessing iOS features.

Plugins are installed in the Assets/Plugins folder, which, as we mentioned before, is a good place to store scripts that have to be loaded before any other scripts. They also often require manual integration steps in Xcode, like adding entries to the Info.plist file or installing additional code libraries (preventing Build and Run from Unity—you have to Build, modify the Xcode project, then Run from Xcode). And then there's always the risk that multiple plugins installed in the same Unity project will have conflicts.

That's why I like to use the plug-ins provided by Prime31 Studios at http://prime31.com/unity. They provide a large variety of plugins that can coexist in the same Unity project, and all Xcode modifications are performed by a Unity postprocessor script, so Build and Run from Unity will still work and no messing around in Xcode is required.

For example, the Prime31 Etcetera plugin, available on the Asset Store, has a bunch of assorted features, including access to the iOS Photos gallery and the device camera, with one function call, like this:

```
EtceteraBinding.promptForPhoto(1.0);
```

The screenshot in Figure 13-8 shows the resulting prompt in my Fugu Maze app (where I use the photo chooser to allow players to customize the maze wall texture). If you want to try it out, download Fugu Maze Free from the App Store or one of the free HyperBowl lanes (I use the photo chooser to customize the bowling ball texture).

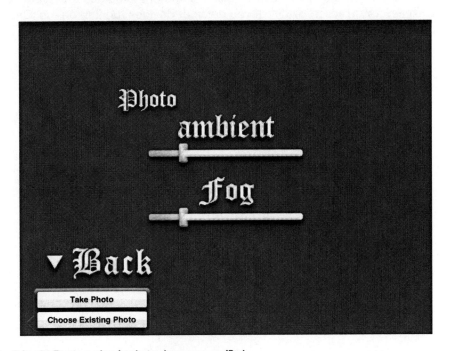

Figure 13-8. *The Prime31 Etcetera plug-in photo chooser on an iPad*

Another Prime31 plugin that makes available additional device input is the iCade plugin (only available on the Prime31 web site). The iCade is a retro-style arcade cabinet that provides joystick input to iOS devices through a Bluetooth connection. The iCade essentially pretends it's a Bluetooth keyboard, so any code using the iCade plugin is similar to the code for keyboard controls. If we added code for iCade controls to the CalcForce function of our bowling ball code, it would look something like the snippet in Listing 13-9 (this sample is actually taken from HyperBowl).

Listing 13-9. *iCade Additions to CalcForce Using the Prime31 iCade Plug-In*

```
var yinput:float = 0;
if (iCadeBinding.state.JoystickUp) yinput = 1;
if (iCadeBinding.state.JoystickDown) yinput = -1;
var xinput:float = 0;
if (iCadeBinding.state.JoystickLeft) xinput = 1;
if (iCadeBinding.state.JoystickRight) xinput = -1;
var deltatime:float = Time.deltaTime;
forcey += iCadePowery*yinput/deltatime;
forcex += iCadePowerx*xinput/deltatime;
```

Just as if we're checking if four different keys were pressed, we're checking if the joystick is moved in any of four directions. The joysticks aren't any more sensitive than that.

The product information for the iCade is on the Ion Audio site at `http://www.ionaudio.com/products/details/icade`, and the ThinkGeek blog lists some of the games that work with the iCade (`http://www.thinkgee.com/product/e762/`). If you get your devices running on the iCade, be sure to contact that blog to have your app listed!

Game Center: Leaderboards and Achievements

Now that we have a playable iOS game, it's time to add some bells and whistles. We'll start with one of the hot trends, social gaming, which, at the minimum, involves collecting high scores onto a global *leaderboard* and rewarding players with *achievements*.

Lucky for us, Unity provides a script interface to Apple's Game Center social gaming platform. As an iOS user, you've most likely played many games that submit scores and achievements to Game Center, and maybe you've used the Game Center app included with iOS to view game recommendations, to "friend" other players, or to issue challenges to those friends. We'll add Fugu Bowl to the ranks of those games by registering a Game Center leaderboard and a couple of achievements for the app and making the necessary script additions to submit those scores and achievements to Game Center.

As in previous chapters, if you're coming in late, you can download and open the Unity project for this chapter from `http://learnunity4.com/`, keeping in mind the projects on that web site don't include any packages from Standard Assets or the Asset Store. But for the purposes of this chapter, the project is ready to run and demonstrate its integration with Game Center.

So far, all of the iOS modifications to Fugu Bowl have been testable with the Unity Remote or iOS Simulator, and an Apple Developer membership hasn't been necessary. But the free ride is over, since integrating Game Center functionality into an app requires configuring Game Center for the app on iTunes Connect. If you still don't have an Apple Developer membership at this point, you can just read through this chapter and the next (which deals with iAds and also requires some set up on iTunes Connect), and then return here when you're ready.

Set Up Game Center on iTunes Connect

To set up Game Center for the bowling game in iTunes Connect, you first need to add the app to iTunes Connect, repeating the steps we rehearsed with the Angry Bots demo. Assuming you're a registered Apple Developer, go to `http://itunesconnect.apple.com/`, click Manage Apps, and add

Fugu Bowl (remember to prepare some screenshots in advance, again as we rehearsed with Angry Bots). For the App Store icon, use the same Icon1024.jpg file we set as the app icon in the Player Settings. You'll need to choose your own app identifier, of course. When you're finished, click View Details for the app you've just created to see the App Information page (Figure 14-1).

Figure 14-1. *The top portion of the App Information page in iTunes Connect*

Once Fugu Bowl is set up in iTunes Connect, bring up the Game Center management page for the app buy clicking the Manage Game Center button at the top right of the App Information page.

Add a Leaderboard

The Game Center management page has three functions: it allows you to move the app into a Game Center group, manage the leaderboards for this game, and manage achievements for this game (Figure 14-2 shows the top of the page and the first two options, achievements are below).

Fugu Bowl

Game Center

To share leaderboards and achievements of this app with other apps you have provided, move this app to a Game Center group.

[Move to Group]

Leaderboards

Leaderboards allow users to view the top scores of all Game Center players of your apps in this group. Leaderboards that are live for any app version cannot be removed.

[Add Leaderboard] [Delete Test Data] (?)

0 Leaderboards				Q Search
Reference Name	Leaderboard ID	Type	Default	Status
Click Add Leaderboard to get started.				

Figure 14-2. *The top portion of the Manage Game Center page in iTunes Connect*

Placing an app in a Game Center group allows the app to share leaderboards and achievements with other apps. As an example, HyperBowl has six bowling lanes, each with its own leaderboard. Each lane is also available as a free ad-supported app. Using Game Center groups, the same leaderboard is shared between the free lane and its equivalent in the full-paid app. So a player who attained a high score and some achievements in the free HyperBowl Classic lane will still see that score and those achievements after buying the full game, and from the developer's point of view, it nicely augments the number of players shown in the leaderboard. Because we're just dealing with one game for now, there's no need to worry about groups (you can always move the app to a group later).

Create a Single Leaderboard

Create a new leaderboard by clicking the Add Leaderboard button. That brings up a window that presents the options to create a Single Leaderboard or a Combined Leaderboard (Figure 14-3). The latter combines the results from several leaderboards. Using HyperBowl as an example again, the combined leaderboard for that game lists high scores from the leaderboards for each of the six lanes.

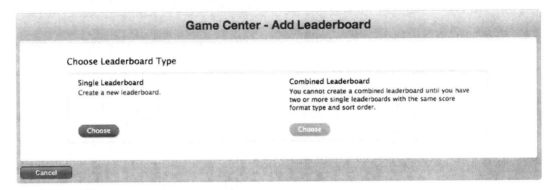

Figure 14-3. Selecting a leaderboard type in iTunes Connect

You can always add a Combined Leaderboard later when it's merited. In fact, Figure 14-3 shows the Combined Leaderboard option is dimmed until you actually have leaderboards that can be combined. So for now, just start by selecting Single Leaderboard, which will bring you to a page where you can fill out the leaderboard information (Figure 14-4).

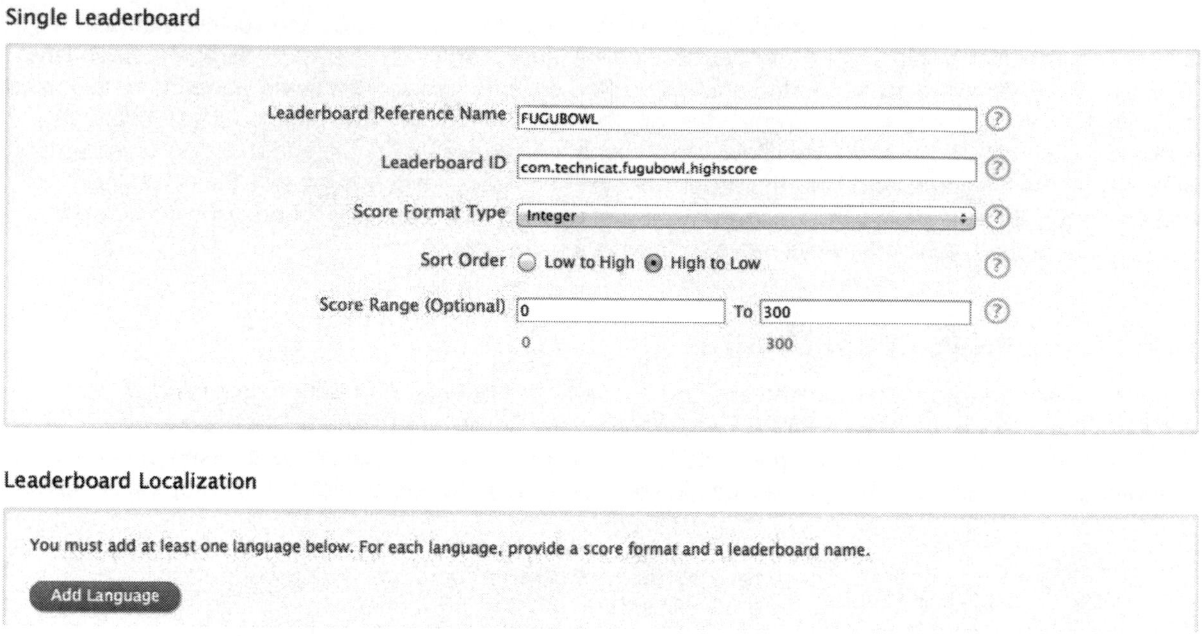

Single Leaderboard

Leaderboard Localization

You must add at least one language below. For each language, provide a score format and a leaderboard name.

Add Language

Figure 14-4. *Creating a leaderboard in iTunes Connect*

The Leaderboard Reference Name is the name displayed for the leaderboard within iTunes Connect. I like to use an entirely capitalized word for the reference name so I can tell immediately it's not used anywhere else, e.g., as an ID or display text in code.

The Leaderboard ID is the identifier that will be referenced in code. It's convenient to make that a variation of the app ID (but it doesn't have to match exactly), so when you see the Leaderboard ID, you can tell immediately which app the leaderboard belongs to. This also helps ensure that the ID is unique.

The next three fields provide information about the scores submitted to the leaderboard. Choose Integer for the Score Format Type (you'll never have a bowling score of 200.5, for example), and specify that the Sort Order is High to Low, meaning higher scores are better and the leaderboard should display the scores in descending order. Finally, indicate the range of possible scores as 0 to 300, so Game Center won't display any score outside that range (for a while, I had HyperBowl submitting scores of -1 if the player quit the game prematurely).

Add a Language

Located below the fields you just filled out is the Leaderboard Localization section. *Localization* is the process of adapting a program for different regions of the world (or *locales*) and largely involves specifying which text should be used for the user interface in various languages. You need to add at least one language to this listing, so click the Add Language button to bring up the corresponding form (Figure 14-5).

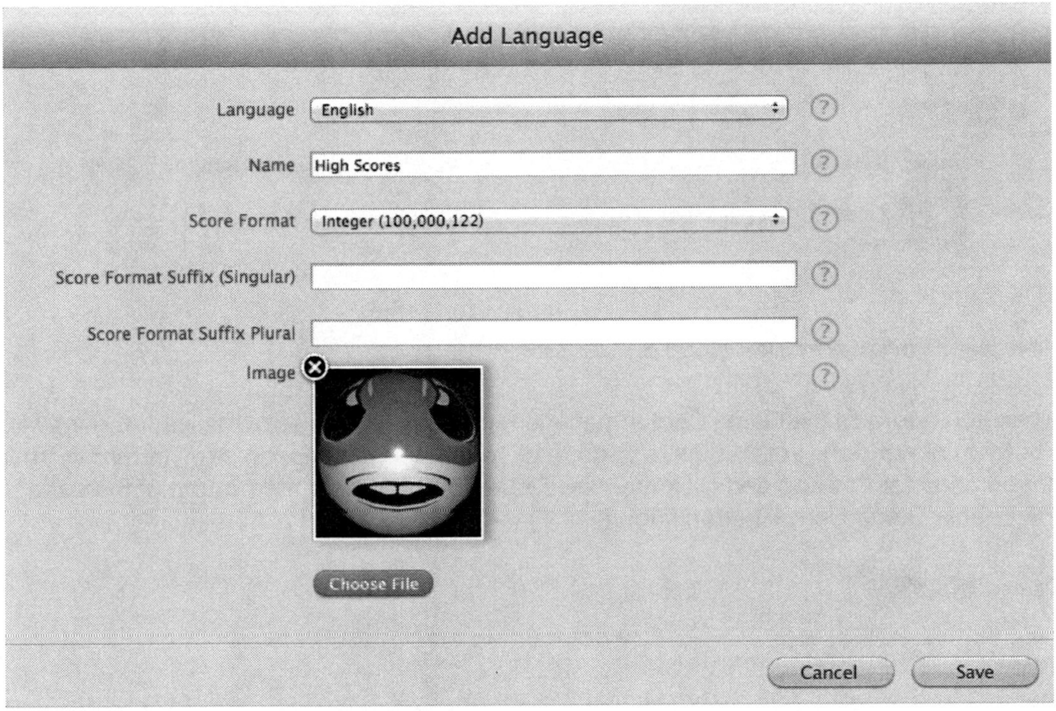

Figure 14-5. Adding localization for a leaderboard in iTunes Connect

Specify the Language for this localization as English and the Name of the leaderboard in this language as High Scores. This is the name that will appear when viewing this leaderboard in the Game Center app or in a standard Game Center leaderboard display.

The Score Format specifies how the scores are displayed. Bowling scores never exceed 300, so it doesn't matter whether commas or decimal points separate groups of digits.

A Score Format Suffix isn't necessary, either, but if you did supply one, you might use Point as the Singular suffix and Points as the Plural.

For the image, which is displayed with the leaderboard Name, you can choose the Icon1024.jpg file again from the project's Textures folder (like the app description icon, iTunes Connect wants a 1024 × 1024 image for Game Center icons). Ideally you would have a different icon custom designed for each leaderboard.

After the settings for this Language are saved, the Language will be listed in the Localization section of the page for this leaderboard (Figure 14-6).

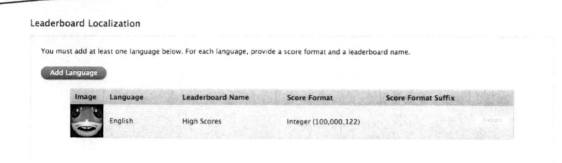

Figure 14-6. *Saved localization for a leaderboard on iTunes Connect*

Now when you return to the Game Center management page for this app, the leaderboard will be listed, but you're not done yet. You have to go back to the app description page (return to the App Information page for this app and click the View Details button). Near the bottom of the page, click the Enable Game Center button (Figure 14-7).

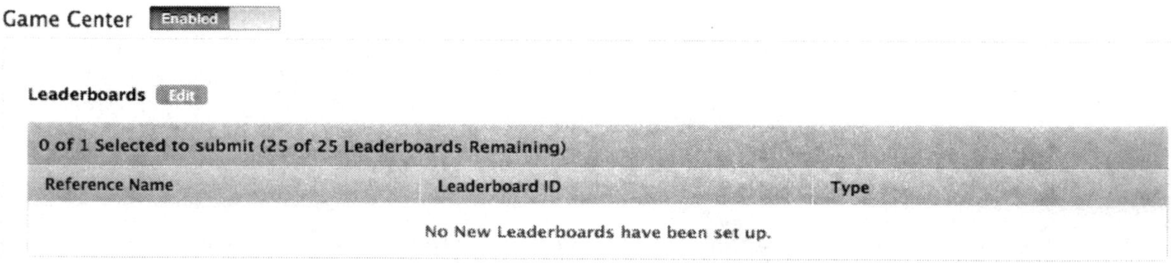

Game Center `Enabled`

Leaderboards `Edit`

0 of 1 Selected to submit (25 of 25 Leaderboards Remaining)		
Reference Name	**Leaderboard ID**	**Type**
No New Leaderboards have been set up.		

Figure 14-7. *Enabling Game Center in iTunes Connect*

Then click the Edit button, which will bring up a dialog box that allows you to select any new leaderboards that have been defined for this app (Figure 14-8).

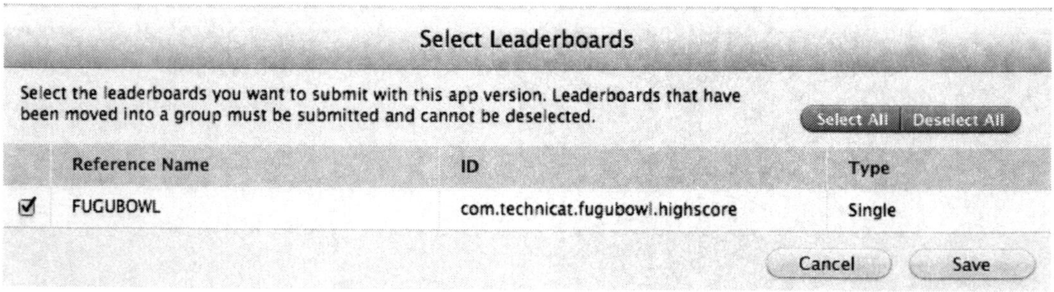

Select Leaderboards

Select the leaderboards you want to submit with this app version. Leaderboards that have been moved into a group must be submitted and cannot be deselected.   `Select All` `Deselect All`

	Reference Name	**ID**	**Type**
☑	FUGUBOWL	com.technicat.fugubowl.highscore	Single

`Cancel` `Save`

Figure 14-8. *Enabling leaderboards in iTunes Connect*

Usually, you will want to add all the leaderboards displayed, except for any that are intended for future releases.

Set Up Achievements

Now that you have a leaderboard, it's time for achievements. The possibilities for achievements are plentiful. In HyperBowl, achievements are awarded for rolling spares, strikes, consecutive strikes, bowling a perfect game (300 points), even an achievement for each lane if the player completes a full game. For Fugu Bowl, let's just define achievements for rolling a spare and rolling a strike, since the FuguBowl script already detects those situations.

The process of adding achievements is similar to that of adding a leaderboard. In iTunes Connect, go back to the Game Center page for this app (Figure 14-9).

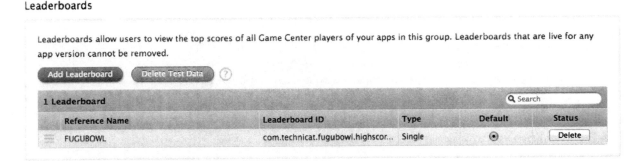

Figure 14-9. The Add Achievement section in iTunes Connect

Beneath the section where you clicked Add Leaderboard (where now there is a leaderboards list consisting of the leaderboard that was just created), you will see the Achievements section. Click the Add Achievement button to bring up the Add Achievements page (Figure 14-10).

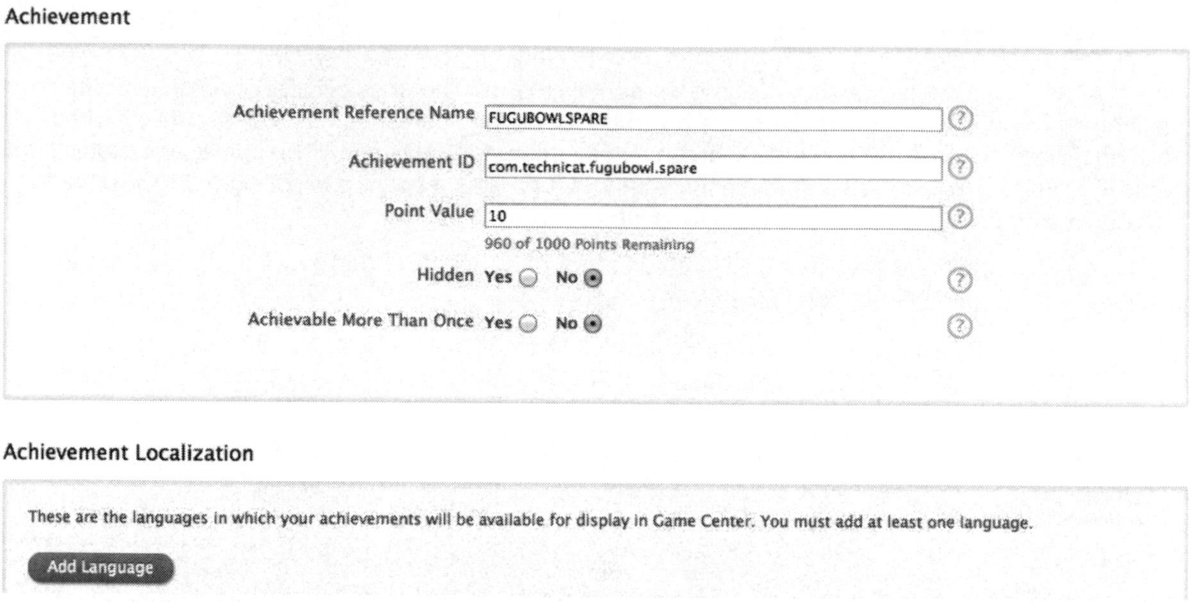

Achievement

Achievement Reference Name FUGUBOWLSPARE (?)

Achievement ID com.technicat.fugubowl.spare (?)

Point Value 10 (?)

960 of 1000 Points Remaining

Hidden Yes ○ No ⦿ (?)

Achievable More Than Once Yes ○ No ⦿ (?)

Achievement Localization

These are the languages in which your achievements will be available for display in Game Center. You must add at least one language.

Add Language

Figure 14-10. Adding achievement information in iTunes Connect

Just like a leaderboard, an achievement has a Reference Name that is used within iTunes Connect and an ID that will be referenced from scripts to refer to this achievement. Let's use FUGUBOWLSPARE for the reference name and append .spare to the app ID to form the Achievement ID (again, it doesn't have to be exact—this is just a convention).

Below the name and ID fields, specify a Point Value, which is the number of points that the Game Center awards to the player once this achievement has been completed. Let's choose 10 points for rolling a spare.

> **Tip**   The total number of points allotted to achievements in this game cannot exceed 1000, so it's a good idea to anticipate all the achievements you plan to add to a game and make sure you allocate points to them within that budget.

Below the Point Value field are two Yes or No options. *Hidden* specifies whether the achievement can be shown to the player before it has been earned. *Achievable more than Once* specifies whether the achievement can be earned multiple times (with points awarded each time). If you selected Yes for this option, then the player would receive ten points for each spare, rather than just ten points for just the first time a spare was rolled (Figure 14-11).

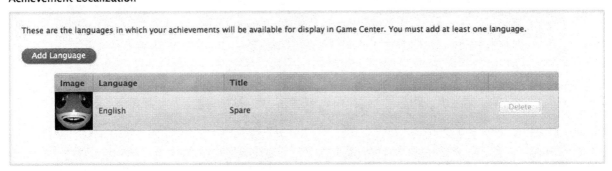

Figure 14-11. *Adding a localization for an achievement in iTunes Connect*

Just like the leaderboard, the achievement needs a Language added in the Localization section. Clicking the Add Language button brings up a window where you can specify the language (English), Title of the achievement (Spare), a Pre-earned Description, which will be displayed for the achievement before it's been earned, and an Earned Description, which is displayed for the achievement after it has been earned (Figure 14-12).

Achievement Localization

These are the languages in which your achievements will be available for display in Game Center. You must add at least one language.

Add Language

Image	Language	Title	
	English	Spare	Delete

Figure 14-12. *A saved localization for an achievement in iTunes Connect*

Again, for expedience let's choose the Icon1024.jpg image in our project Textures folder as the achievement icon, but in a polished game you may have a different icon for each achievement.

When you click Save, the new Language will be listed in the Achievement Localization section. Click Save on the Achievement page, and the achievement will now be listed on the Game Center management page.

Repeat the process to create an achievement for rolling a strike. The only difference for a strike is that you'll have a different reference name and ID, and you'll award 20 points instead of ten. And you should provide different earned and pre-earned descriptions, too. When that's done, visit the App Description page again, where Game Center was already enabled when you added a leaderboard, and click the Edit button above the Achievements section to add the available achievements.

At this point, you have a leaderboard and two achievements set up in Game Center. Now it's time to get back to scripting!

Integrating Game Center

Unity provides access to Game Center through static functions in the Social class, which provides a general interface to social gaming platforms. In principle, you could access other social gaming networks without even changing (much) code, but at this time, Social only supports Game Center.

Our game will be making calls to functions in the Social class to connect to Game Center and submit achievements and scores. We could place all of those calls directly in our game controller script, but we can minimize code bloat and maximize code reusability by with a new script.

From the Project View, create a new JavaScript, place it in the Scripts folder, and name it FuguGameCenter (Figure 14-13).

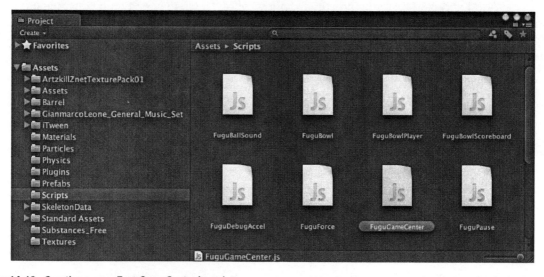

Figure 14-13. Creating a new FuguGameCenter.js script

Initialize Game Center

In the new FuguGameCenter script, let's place the Game Center initialization code in the Start callback (Listing 14-1), so the initialization will take place as soon as the script is enabled. The body of the Start callback is enclosed by an #ifdef UNITY_IPHONE so that any non-iOS build will treat the callback as empty.

Listing 14-1. Game Center Initialization in FuguGameCenter.js

```
import UnityEngine.SocialPlatforms.GameCenter;

var showAchievementBanners:boolean = true;

function Start() {
#if UNITY_IPHONE
        Social.localUser.Authenticate (function (success) {
        if (success && showAchievementBanners) {

        GameCenterPlatform.ShowDefaultAchievementCompletionBanner(showAchievementBanners);
                Debug.Log ("Authenticated "+Social.localUser.userName);
        }
                else {
                        Debug.Log ("Failed to authenticate "+Social.localUser.userName);
                }
        });
#endif
}
```

The function Social.authenticate performs the Game Center login of the player (prompting the player for login information if necessary) and takes a callback function as an argument. When Game Center reports a true or false result, indicating if the operation was a success, that value is passed to the callback function. Instead of defining the callback function as we've defined all our functions so far, separate with its own name, for convenience we pass the function definition directly as the argument, without a name. Functions passed in this manner are called *anonymous functions*. Our anonymous callback calls Debug.Log with a message based on the success value. This gives us an easy way to check if the login has failed when we're testing.

The callback also optionally activates achievement banners, which are briefly displayed notifications that an achievement has been awarded. This Game Center feature was introduced in iOS 5, so the feature is often referred to as iOS 5-style notification banners. I happen to like seeing them, but it's a matter of preference, so we have a public boolean variable showAchievementBanners that we can select or deselect in the Inspector View.

If the callback was passed true for the authentication success value and showAchievementBanners is true, then the callback calls the static function GameCenterPlatform. ShowDefaultAchievementCompletionBanner, which takes a true or false argument to turn the banners on or off, and also takes a success callback function as an argument.The achievement banner function is not considered a cross-platform feature, which is why the function is not exposed in the Social class and instead has to be accessed from the GameCenterPlatform class. That class is in the UnityEngine.SocialPlatforms.GameCenter namespace, so we import that namespace at the top of the script to avoid typing out the entire namespace name when referencing GameCenterPlatform.

Submit Achievements

Submitting an achievement is as simple as calling the static function Social.ReportProgress. But that function also takes a success callback function, and we should first check if the player is actually logged into Game Center. To avoid duplicating all that in every piece of code that submits an achievement, we'll add a wrapper function for Social.ReportProgress to the FuguGameCenter script (Listing 14-2).

Listing 14-2. Submitting an Achievement in FuguGameCenter.js

```
static function Achievement(name:String,progress:double) {
#if UNITY_IPHONE
        if (Social.localUser.authenticated) {
                Social.ReportProgress(name,progress, function(success) {
                        if (success) {
                                Debug.Log("Achievement "+name+" reported successfully");
                        } else {
                                Debug.Log("Failed to report achievement "+name);
                        }
                } );
        }
#endif
}
```

This wrapper function which we'll call Achievement, is a static function, so it can be called from any script as FuguGameCenter.Achievement. It takes an achievement ID and a progress number (in the range 0-100) and passes those along to Social.ReportProgress, along with a success callback that prints the result with Debug.Log.

> **Note** The achievement progress is passed in as a double, not an int or float, just because that is what Game Center expects. A double is a double-precision floating point number (float is a single-precision floating point number). Game engines, including Unity, typically stick with single floats.

But first, Achievement checks Social.localUser.authenticated to see if the player is logged into Game Center before calling Social.ReportProgress.

Submit Scores

The code for submitting a score to a Game Center leaderboard looks nearly identical to the code for submitting an achievement (Listing 14-3).

Listing 14-3. Submitting a Score in FuguGameCenter.js

```
static function Score(name:String,score:double) {
#if UNITY_IPHONE
        if (Social.localUser.authenticated) {
                Social.ReportScore (score, name, function(success) {
                        if (success) {
                                Debug.Log("Posted "+score+" on leaderboard "+name);
                        } else {
```

```
                            Debug.Log("Failed to post "+score+" on leaderboard "+name);
                    }
            } );
        }
#endif
}
```

The only difference between the static function FuguGameCenter.Score and the static function FuguGameCenter.Achievement is that one calls Social.ReportScore and one calls Social.ReportProgress. Off course, also, they have different Debug.Log messages and Social.ReportScore takes a leaderboard ID and score instead of an achievement ID and progress number.

The Complete Script

You now have a very trim Game Center wrapper script with just a Start callback, one public variable, and a couple of static functions for use from other scripts. The FuguGameCenter script in its entirety is available in the project for this chapter on http://learnunity4.com/.

Attach the Script

Because the Game Center initialization takes place in the Start callback of FuguGameCenter.js, the script has to be attached to a GameObject in the scene. Make sure you have the bowling scene open, create an empty GameObject, name it GameCenter, and drag the FuguGameCenter script onto it. The script has just one property that you can tweak in the Inspector View, the option to display iOS 5-style achievement banners (Figure 14-14).

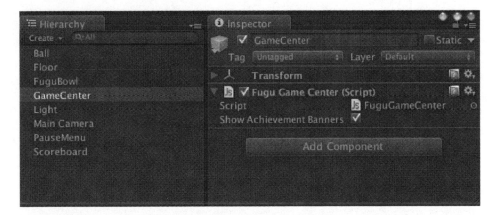

Figure 14-14. The FuguGameCenter script in the scene

You could have attached the FuguGameCenter script to a GameObject in the splash scene instead, as the static functions defined in that file can be called whether or not the script is attached in any scene. Placing the script in the splash scene would have the advantage of initializing Game Center earlier, but it is less confusing if the FuguGameCenter script is in the same scene as the scripts that will call it (in this case, the FuguBowl script).

Integrate the Game

Although the FuguGameCenter script takes care of Game Center initialization and provides static functions to report scores and achievements, you still need the FuguBowl script to call those static functions. Fortunately, this part is really easy.

Submit Achievements

So far we've set up two achievements, one for rolling a spare and the other a strike, so now the game needs to report spares and strikes when they happen (at least the first time). This is where organizing the game controller as a state machine really pays off. There's already a game state for a spare and a game state for a strike, so let's just add calls in them to the FuguGameCenter.Achievement function (Listing 14-4).

Listing 14-4. Submitting Achievements in FuguBowl.js

```
var spareAchievementID:String = "com.technicat.fugubowl.spare";
var strikeAchievementID:String = "com.technicat.fugubowl.strike";

function StateSpare() {
    FuguGameCenter.Achievement(spareAchievementID,100);
    state="StateNextBall";
}

function StateStrike() {
    FuguGameCenter.Achievement(strikeAchievementID,100);
    state = "StateNextBall";
}
```

Instead of hardcoding the achievement IDs that are passed to FuguGameCenter.Achievement (your achievement IDs will likely be different from mine), declare public variables for spare and strike so you can customize them in the Inspector View.

Submit the Score

Submitting the final game score is similar to submitting achievements. We were already printing the final score with Debug.Log in the game-over state, so that's an obvious place to submit the final score to Game Center (Listing 14-5).

Listing 14-5. Submitting a Game Score in FuguBowl.js

```
var leaderboardID:String = "com.technicat.fugubowl.highscore";

function StateGameOver() {
    Debug.Log("Final Score: "+player.GetScore(9));
    FuguGameCenter.Score(leaderboardID,player.GetScore(9));
    yield WaitForSeconds(gameOverTime);
    state="StateNewGame";
}
```

Again, the leaderboard ID is declared as a public variable, so it can be customized in the Inspector View (Figure 14-15).

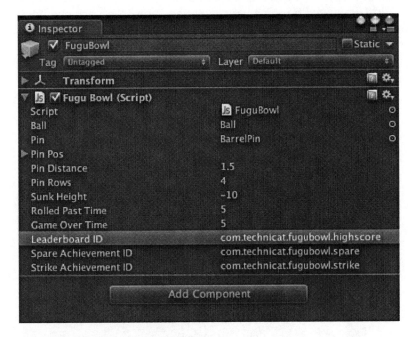

Figure 14-15. Custom Game Center IDs in the FuguBowl script

This was such a small change to our game controller code, just two additional lines (and it could easily have been one), so I won't bother listing the entire FuguBowl script again, but the modified script is of course available in the project for this chapter at http://learnunity4.com/.

Test the Game

Until the app is released on the App Store, the achievements and leaderboards are only available in the Game Center Sandbox, which is basically an alternate universe for Game Center, with its own user IDs and leaderboard and achievement data. When an app in development (a version that has not been approved yet for the App Store) attempts to connect to Game Center the player will be prompted to log in to or create a Sandbox account, and the outside world won't see any scores and achievements you earn in the test session, since they are only recorded in the Sandbox.

> **Tip**   If you seem to be stuck in the Sandbox version of Game Center or stuck in the non-Sandbox version, try bringing up the iOS Game Center app and then logging out (tap your Apple ID).

When you build and run Fugu Bowl on the iOS Simulator or on a device (but not in the Editor) and play a whole game, you should have a score on the leaderboard and up to two achievements, if you bowled a strike or a spare. At this point, Fugu Bowl should be visible in the Game Center app (Figure 14-16), and when you tap on it, you'll see the scores and achievements that have been submitted (Figure 14-17).

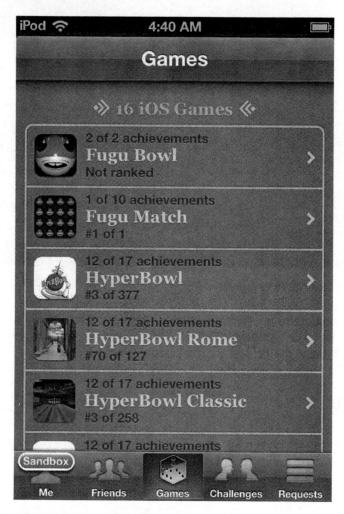

Figure 14-16. Fugu Bowl listed in the Sandbox version of Game Center

Figure 14-17. Test results in the Game Center Sandbox

Scores and achievements don't always show up in Game Center in a reliable or timely manner, particularly when testing in the Sandbox, so check the Xcode debug area to see if Game Center operations succeeded (remember, we added logging functions in all of the FuguGameCenter functions).

Show Game Center In-Game

Although the Game Center app's display of the achievements and leaderboard looks pretty nice, players of the bowling game might not bother checking the Game Center app, or they might not even know about it. Ideally, the player would be able to view the leaderboard and the achievements within the game, so let's add a couple buttons to the main pause menu in the FuguPause script for that purpose (Listing 14-7).

Listing 14-7. Buttons to Show Achievements and High Scores in FuguPause.js

```
function ShowPauseMenu() {
      BeginPage(150,300);
      if (GUILayout.Button ("Play")) {
            UnPauseGame();
      }
       if (GUILayout.Button ("Options")) {
            currentPage = Page.Options;
      }
       if (GUILayout.Button ("Credits")) {
            currentPage = Page.Credits;
      }
#if UNITY_IPHONE
      if (GUILayout.Button ("High Scores")) {
            Social.ShowLeaderboardUI();
      }
      if (GUILayout.Button ("Achievements")) {
            Social.ShowAchievementsUI();
      }
#endif
#if !UNITY_IPHONE && !UNITY_WEBPLAYER
      if (GUILayout.Button ("Quit")) {
            Application.Quit();
      }
#endif
      EndPage();
}
```

The code for those two buttons are wrapped with #if UNITY_IPHONE, so they will only appear on iOS builds. They're labeled High Scores and Achievements (Figure 14-18).

Figure 14-18. Pause menu with buttons for the leaderboard and achievements

The Social class provides functions to query Game Center for leaderboard and achievements information that can be used to construct custom displays. But it's easier to just call the functions Social.ShowLeaderboardUI and Social.ShowAchievementsUI to bring up the standard Game Center presentation of leaderboards and achievements, respectively. So the High Scores button calls Social.ShowLeaderboardUI and the Achievements button calls Social.ShowAchievementsUI.

When you run Fugu Bowl and connect successfully to Game Center and tap one of the new Game Center buttons, a standard Game Center interface appears. Figure 14-19 shows the results of tapping on the Achievements button.

Figure 14-19. In-game achievements displayed with Social.ShowAchievementsUI

The display is similar to the one in the Game Center app but simpler. For example, the in-game display doesn't need all the navigation buttons that switch its view to other portions of the Game Center app. Also, the iPad version of this display is much different because the iPad has a lot more screen space to work with.

You might think we should have added wrapper functions for these two calls in FuguGameCenter, but these functions are so simple there's no real need to. They don't take success callback functions as arguments, and it's not necessary to check `Social.localUser.authenticated` beforehand. In fact, it's better not to, as both `Social.ShowLeaderboardUI` and `Social.ShowAchievementsUI` will provide a user-friendly alert to the player if there is no current Game Center login.

As with the change to the game controller code, the enhanced pause menu only required a couple of additional lines and doesn't warrant a complete relisting of `FuguPause.js` here. The modified script is in the project files for this chapter at `http://learnunity4.com/`.

Explore Further

This has been one of the more efficient scripting chapters. With just a few lines of code, our game is now connecting to Game Center, submitting achievements and scores, and displaying the achievements and the leaderboard from the pause menu!

The bulk of the work was spent in the Game Center setup on iTunes Connect. Even there, designing the leaderboard and set of achievements for a bowling game is straightforward, since the rules and traditions are so well-defined. Chances are, if you design a new game, you'll have to put some thought into what leaderboards and achievements you want in your game, and you should probably think about that early in the design process.

Scripting Reference

This chapter used the "Social" class almost exclusively to access the Game Center features used in this chapter. The Scripting Reference page for that class explains its role in encapsulating access to Game Center and potentially other social gaming platforms (although for now, Game Center is the only one).

We made do with the minimum set of functions required to report scores and achievements and display the results: accessing "Social.localUser" to connect to Game Center, calling "Social.ReportProgress" and "Social.ReportScore" to submit achievements and scores, respectively, and calling "Social.ShowAchievementsUI" and "Social.ShowLeaderboardUI" to bring up the Game Center display for the player's achievements and game's leaderboards. The documentation for the Social class lists several other functions that allow finer-grained control, for example, to retrieve information from Game Center to populate a custom leaderboard display.

We bypassed Social and accessed the "GameCenterPlatform" class directly to invoke its "showDefaultAchievementsCompletionBanner" function, enabling iOS 5-style achievement banners. The page for the GameCenterPlatform class explains what namespace it's in and includes some notes on the Game Center Sandbox.

iOS Developer Library

The Game Center chapter of the iTunes Connect Developer Guide is the definitive source on setting up achievements and leaderboards. The Guide is available within the iOS Developer Library (available on http://developer.apple.com/library/ios or in the Xcode Organizer).

The inner workings of Game Center are explained in the Game Center Programming Guide in the iOS Developer Library, under the "Networking and Internet" topic. The portion of the Game Center that can be integrated into apps, as opposed to the server portion operated by Apple, is actually called Game Kit and also features support for networked multiplayer gaming.

Asset Store

Game Center isn't the only social gaming platform available for iOS. Many have come and gone (OpenFeint, Agon Online), but there are still some other options. Under its Services category, the Asset Store offers plug-ins for PlayHaven (http://playhaven.com/) and Swarm (http://swarmconnect.com/), both offering leaderboards, achievements, and other social gaming features. Another Game Center plugin, from Hippo Games, is listed under Scripting/Integration.

Before Unity had built-in Game Center support, Prime31 Studios provided a Game Center plugin, which is still available at http://prime31.com/ (but not on the Asset Store) and is an option for developers who need some features not provided by Unity. For example, the Prime31 plugin includes a function for issuing achievement challenges (a feature of iOS 6). Prime31 also offers a Game Kit plugin for multiplayer gaming support that is on the Asset Store.

iAd: Banner Ads and Interstitial Ads

Frankly, in these freemium days, it's not easy to get a lot of people to pay for an app. So an alternative is to incorporate ads. iAd is not the only mobile ad product available, but it is the official ad service for iOS, paying developers 70% of revenue, the same as the revenue share for paid app sales. And, conveniently, Unity has scripting support for iAd. In this chapter we'll incorporate the two ad types offered by iAd—banner ads and interstitial (full-screen) ads—into our bowling game.

The project project for this chapter on `http://learnunity4.com/` includes the iAd scripts developed in this chapter and is sufficient to demonstrate iAd functionality. However, even if you start with the that project to avoid adding the scripts by hand, you'll still need to enable iAd in iTunes Connect.

iTunes Connect

As with Game Center, you need to enable iAd for our app on iTunes Connect in addition to calling Unity's iAd functions from scripts. Besides the Manage Apps page, iTunes Connect has two other pages relevant to iAd: the Contract, Banking and Taxes page and the iAd Network page (Figure 15-1).

Sales and Trends
View and download your sales and trends information.

Contracts, Tax, and Banking
Manage your contracts, tax, and banking information.

Manage Your Applications
Add, view, and manage your App Store apps.

iAd Network
View ad performance and manage the ads that appear in your apps.

Figure 15-1. The iAd-related pages on iTunes Connect

Sign the Contract

The first page you need to visit is the Contracts, Banking and Taxes page, so you can agree to Apple's iAd contract, in the same way you had to agree to the paid sales contract to start charging for apps.

Once the iAd contract has been processed, as shown in Figure 15-2, you're ready to enable iAd for individual apps.

Contracts In Effect

Contract Region	Contract Type	Contract Number	Contact Info	Bank Info	Tax Info	Effective Date	Expiration Date	Download
All (See Contract)	iOS Paid Applications	MS9055375	Edit	Edit	View	Oct 27, 2012	Oct 04, 2013	📄
Worldwide	iOS Free Applications	MS8438372	N/A	N/A	N/A	Sep 12, 2012	Oct 04, 2013	N/A
World	iAd Network	MS6839814	Edit	Edit	View	Apr 01, 2012	Oct 04, 2013	📄

Figure 15-2. A completed iAd Network contract listed on iTunes Connect

Enable iAd

Just as you did with Game Center, enable iAd for Fugu Bowl by going to the Manage Apps page in iTunes Connect, selecting Fugu Bowl, and visiting its App Information page. On the top right, in the same section as the Game Center button, is the Manage iAd Network button (Figure 15-3).

App Information Edit

Figure 15-3. The top portion of the App Information page in iTunes Connect

Click the Manage iAd Network button to start the process of enabling iAd. It's much simpler than enabling the Game Center. No leaderboards or achievements to set up, just click the Enable iAd Network button (Figure 15-4).

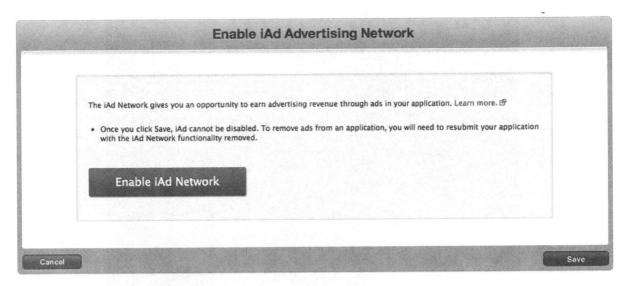

Figure 15-4. Enabling iAd on iTunes Connect

Like Game Center, iAd can only be enabled or disabled for an app after a New Version of the app has been added to iTunes Connect and before that version has been approved and released. The iAd change will affect that upcoming version, and there's no way to change the iAd status of an app already on the App Store.

> **Tip** I've had apps rejected for having screenshots that showed test ads, so you may want to take screenshots of your app before enabling iAd.

iAd is now enabled for our app on the server side, and you just need to add the code for iAd to the app itself.

Add a Banner Ad

Let's start by adding a banner ad to our bowling game. Unlike, interstitial ads, which only run on iPads, banner ads run on all devices. And frankly, banner ads are easier to incorporate in a game. You just need to allocate some space at the top or bottom of the screen.

> **Tip** Think about where to incorporate ads when designing the app, not as an afterthought.

Create the Script

Similar to how we created a script in the previous chapter to initialize the Game Center, let's write a script to instantiate and place a banner ad. Create a new JavaScript in the Project View, place it in the Scripts folder, and name it FuguAdBanner (Figure 15-5).

Figure 15-5. Creating the FuguAdBanner script

Then edit the script and add the contents of Listing 15-1 to it.

Listing 15-1. The Complete Listing of FuguAdBanner.js

```
#pragma strict

public var showOnTop:boolean = true; // banner on top or bottom of screen
public var dontDestroy:boolean = false; // keep this GameObject around for next scene

#if UNITY_IPHONE

// don't make this a local variable, or else it'll get garbage collected
private var banner:ADBannerView;

function Start () {
        if (dontDestroy) {
                GameObject.DontDestroyOnLoad(gameObject); // keep ad alive across scenes
        }
        Debug.Log("Creating iAd banner");
        banner = new ADBannerView();
        banner.autoSize = true;
        banner.autoPosition = showOnTop ? ADPosition.Top : ADPosition.Bottom;
        while (!banner.loaded && banner.error == null) {
                yield;
        }
```

```
        if (banner.error == null) {
                Debug.Log("iAd banner shown");
                banner.Show();
        } else {
                Debug.Log("iAd banner error: "+banner.error.description);
                banner = null;
        }
    }
}
#endif
```

The code in FuguAdBanner is similar to the Scripting Reference example for AdBannerView. The Start callback creates an AdBannerView instance and waits in a while loop for either the banner to load, indicated by the loaded variable of the AdBannerView, or for an error to happen, indicated by the error variable in AdBannerView. The while loop calls yield to avoid blocking the rest of the game from running.

If there is an error, the error message is logged with Debug.Log. If the banner has loaded successfully, the ad will immediately display by with a call to the Show function of AdBannerView. You can call Show and Hide on the ad at any time, but with banner ads, the easy thing to do is just leave it up.

The Variables

To provide some flexibility and reuse of the script, let's add a couple of public boolean variables, which will show up as check boxes in the Inspector View. The ShowOnTop variable to determines whether the banner is displayed at the top or the bottom of the screen (the only two options), by passing in the enum values AdPosition.Top or AdPosition.Bottom accordingly. The iAd banners are automatically sized correctly to stretch across the screen.

If the other variable, DontDestroy, is true, then we call the static function GameObject.DontDestroyOnLoad, passing in the GameObject the script is attached to. This keeps the GameObject alive if another level is loaded, so if you have multiple scenes, you don't have to add an AdBanner GameObject to each one.

> **Caution**   Calling GameObject.DontDestroyOnLoad in a scene that will be loaded again later can result in duplicate GameObjects.

For example, if you place your AdBanner GameObject in the splash scene instead of the bowling scene, setting dontDestroy to true will allow the banner ad to persist through the load of the bowling scene without getting destroyed.

Garbage Collection

Speaking of destroyed objects, notice that we declare the banner variable outside the Start function, although it looks like it could have been declared inside. Normally, it's better to declare variables within the narrowest scope possible, but in this case, you want the ADBannerView to exist as long as this GameObject exists. If you declare banner as a variable inside the Start function, then there is no reference to the ADBannerView object after the Start function returns, and the object can be destroyed at any time to free up the memory it's taking up, and the ads will disappear as soon as that happens.

This reclamation process is called *garbage collection* (GC), as objects that are lying around with no way for code to access them are effectively garbage. GC is not an issue for objects in the scene (basically anything whose class is a subclass of UnityEngine.Object), because as long as they are in the scene there is an implicit reference to them. Generally, those objects have to be explicitly cleaned up with a call to the static Destroy function of the UnityEngine.Object class.

Attach the Script

To add the FuguAdBanner script to the bowling scene, make sure that scene is open, create a new GameObject in the Hierarchy View, name it AdBanner, and drag the FuguAdBanner script onto it (Figure 15-6).

Figure 15-6. The FuguAdBanner script added to the scene

Because we have our scoreboard at the top of the screen, lthe banner ad is best left at the bottom, so leave Show On Top unchecked. And because the AdBanner GameObject is placed in the bowling scene, which doesn't load any other scene, it doesn't really matter whether you call DontDestroyOnLoad or not, but let's leave DontDestroy unchecked, too.

Test the Script

An iAd won't show up when running the game in the Editor, but you can test it by running the game in the iOS Simulator or on a device. Until the app is approved, it will show only test ads, as shown in Figure 15-7.

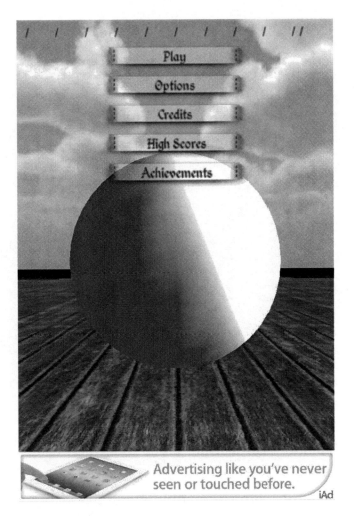

Figure 15-7. A test iAd banner

If an ad doesn't appear, check the Xcode debug area for the Debug.Log error messages emitted by the FuguAdBanner script. But if there are no error messages, don't worry. Sometimes ads take a while to show up, and sometimes the iAd server fails to provide an ad, in which case a *No inventory* message will appear in the debug area. Even after an app is approved, there is typically a delay until iAd is really activated. During that time, users will see test ads, but again, don't panic!

Add an Interstitial Ad

Now we're ready to try an interstitial ad. Since interstitial ads are full-screen ads, we have to treat them differently from banner ads. When an interstitial ad appears, it has to be dismissed before the game can proceed, much like dismissing a modal dialog. For that reason, interstitial ads are usually placed strategically at transition points in the game (interstitial means in between). No one would like a full-page ad popping up in the middle of a game! For this reason, let's place our interstitial ad in the splash scene, so it appears, if it appears, before the bowling scene is loaded.

Again, let's start by creating a new JavaScript, named FuguAdInterstitial (Figure 15-8). Add the contents of Listing 15-2.

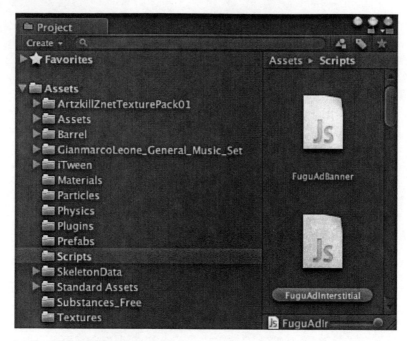

Figure 15-8. Creating the FuguAdInterstitial script

Listing 15-2. The Complete Listing for FuguAdInterstitial.js

```
#pragma strict

var waitTime:float = 2.0;

#if UNITY_IPHONE
private var ad:ADInterstitialAd = null;

function Start() {
        if (iPhone.generation == iPhoneGeneration.iPad1Gen ||
                iPhone.generation == iPhoneGeneration.iPad2Gen ||
                iPhone.generation == iPhoneGeneration.iPad3Gen ||
                iPhone.generation == iPhoneGeneration.iPad4Gen ||
                iPhone.generation == iPhoneGeneration.iPadMini1Gen ||
                iPhone.generation == iPhoneGeneration.iPadUnknown) {
                ad = new ADInterstitialAd();
                var startTime = Time.time;
                while (!ad.loaded && ad.error == null && Time.time-startTime<waitTime) {
                        yield;
                }
                if (ad.loaded && ad.error == null) {
                        Debug.Log("iAd page shown");
                        ad.Present();
                } else {
```

```
                    if (ad.error != null) {
                            Debug.Log("iAd page error: "+ad.error.description);
                    } else {
                            Debug.Log("iAd page timed out");
                    }
                    ad = null;
                }
            }
}
#endif
```

Because interstitial ads are only available on iPads, the first thing to do in our Start function is check if its running on an iPad. Unfortunately, there's no succinct way to test for that, but you can check the static variable of iPhone.generation and see if its value matches one of the iPad models, each with a value defined in the iPhoneGeneration enumeration.

The way you test iPhone.generation illustrates the iPad values of the iPhoneGeneration enumeration, but it does have the disadvantage of requiring an update when future versions of Unity add values to accommodate new iPad models. Another way to do it, either more robust or a kludgy, depending on your viewpoint, would be to convert the enum value to a string and check if it starts with "iPad," like this:if(iPhone.generation.ToString().StartsWith("iPad")).

After the iPad check, the code resembles the FuguAdBanner script. Instead of the ADBannerView class, we have Unity's ADInterstitialAd class. As FuguAdBanner did with ADBannerView, the code instantiates an ADInterstitialAd and, within a while-yield loop, waits for the ADInterstitialAd to load or fail with an error. But we don't want to wait for an indeterminate duration, especially if it's going to delay the start of the game, so we also set it to stop waiting after a certain amount of time, waitTime, has expired.

waitTime is in seconds and declared a public variable so it can be adjusted in the Inspector View. Before the loop begins, the current game time, available in the static variable Time.time (also in seconds), is saved in a local variable startTime. The loop, along with checking if the ad has loaded or resulted in an error, checks if Time.time minus startTime is still less than waitTime.

When the while loop terminates, the ad is displayed if it has loaded successfully, using the ADInterstitialAd Present function (essentially the same as the Show function used for ADBannerView). If it hasn't loaded successfully, an "iAd page has timed out" message is logged with Debug.Log.

Attach the Script

With our FuguAdInterstitial script in hand, we're ready to add it to a scene. As mentioned earlier, we're going to add it to our splash scene, so let's switch to that scene (double-click the splash scene file in the Project View). Then create an empty GameObject and name it AdPage (you could name it AdInterstitial, but why not name it something easier to type). Drag the FuguAdInterstitial script onto the AdPage GameObject (Figure 15-9).

Figure 15-9. Adding the FuguAdInterstitial script to the splash scene

Test the Script

Now we're ready to roll. As with banner ads, you won't see any ads when running in the Editor, but when testing on the iOS Simulator or on a device, you should see a full-page ad while the splash screen is up (Figure 15-10). As with banner ads again, there's no guarantee that the iAd servers will send the ad, but if it does, it will be a test ad until the app is released on the App Store.

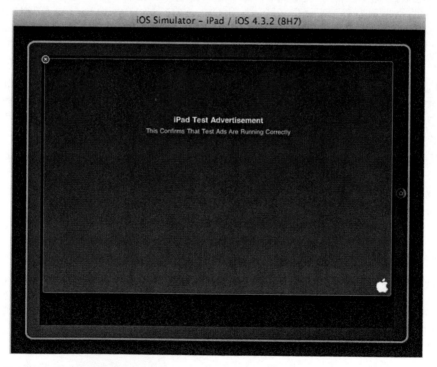

Figure 15-10. Test interstitial iAd on the iOS Simulator

Track Ad Revenues

Like app sales revenue, iAd revenue is reported on iTunes Connect, under the iAd Network page link, shown in Figure 15-1. The top of the iAd Network page displays a graph of iAd revenue for all your apps (Figure 15-11).

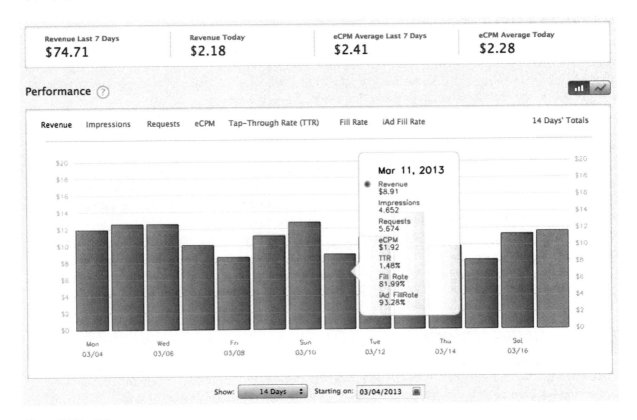

Figure 15-11. iAd revenue

Below the revenue graph is a list of your iAd-enabled apps, both those that have gone live and those that are still test ads (Figure 15-12).

	AppleID: 586137589	$0.00	$0.00	0	0	0.00%	0.00%	0.00%	⊘ Test Ads	View ▾
	Elektra Dance	$0.37	$4.36	200	84	42.00%	75.00%	4.76%	● Live Ads	View ▾
	Fugu Bowl	$9.43	$2.30	5,918	3,944	66.64%	84.44%	2.33%	● Live Ads	View ▾
	Fugu Match	$0.60	$3.91	189	152	80.42%	85.88%	1.97%	● Live Ads	View ▾

Figure 15-12. An app listing on the iAd revenue page

Clicking an app in the list brings up a similar page displaying revenue just for that app. That page also displays ad revenue broken down by country and provides options for editing the app description (what advertisers see) and specifying competing companies and apps that you don't want displayed in your ads.

Explore Further

This chapter has been the shortest by far, and that's a good thing. It means our game is functionally complete and adding ads is really simple. Even the setup on iTunes Connect wasn't bad! In practice, though, you may need to put some thought into where and when to place ads, especially interstitial ads, and the earlier in the design process that takes place, the better.

Scripting Reference

We managed to do a lot with just a little code in this chapter. Only two classes were required to make use of iAds: "ADBannerView" and "ADInterstitialAd," and in a typical app you would only use one of those classes (having both banner ads and interstitial ads is a bit much!). The pages for both of those classes have script examples.

The "iPhone" class contains anything that is specific to iOS (much of what used to be iOS-specific is now also applicable to Android and is now in the "Handheld" class). For example, we check the static variable "iPhone.generation" to find out if we're running on an iPad. It's worth checking the page on the "iPhoneGeneration" enum to see the set of iOS hardware recognized by Unity.

iOS Developer Library

The Unity `ADBannerView` and `ADInterstitialAd` classes correspond to same-named classes in Objective-C. The iAd Programming Guide in the iOS Developer Library describes those classes and provides a lot of details on how to effectively deploy banner and interstitial ads.

General information about iAd for both developers and advertisers is available on `http://developer.apple.com/iad`.

Asset Store

iAd isn't your only in-app advertising option. Once you start releasing apps, you will probably start receiving e-mails from numerous account managers at various mobile ad vendors. In fact, iAd originated as a product of Quattro Wireless before Apple acquired that company to gain its advertising product. Third-party ad vendors typically have their own iOS SDK and thus require a Unity plugin to access that SDK. Some of these SDKs are available on the Asset Store under the Services category, including PlayHaven and Inneractive.

Outside the Asset Store

As with their Game Center plugin, Prime31 Studios offered an iAd plugin before Unity introduced their iAd scripting support. Prime31 offers plugins for many other advertising services, including AdMob, AdWhirl, MobClix, and many more, available at `http://prime31.com/`.

Kiip (`http://kiip.com/`) provides an interesting twist on ads. A Kiip-enabled app features coupons that resemble banner ads but are presented like achievements. Their Unity plugin is available on GitHub at `http://github.com/kiip`.

Optimization

Consistent with Donald Knuth's much-ballyhooed quote that "premature optimization is the root of all evil," I've left the topic of optimization until nearly the end of this book. In this chapter we'll optimize our bowling app and go over the precursors to that process, establishing the target performance and measuring the current performance. The project for this chapter on `http://learnunity4.com/` contains the optimized scripts and optimization helper scripts developed in this chapter.

Choose Your Target

There's a saying, "Fast, good, or cheap. Pick two." That's generally the case with optimization. Among quality, space, and speed, you can often at best achieve two of the three, at the expense of the third.

Frame Rate

Before you start optimizing, you should establish your target frame rate. iOS devices refresh their screens 60 times per second, but by default, Unity iOS builds attempt to achieve 30 frames per second (fps). Targeting a frame rate at half the device refresh rate is less demanding on the device battery, and 30 fps is a lot easier to achieve than 60 fps. Our bowling game is simple, so you should be able to hit 60 fps if you're willing to make some compromises.

It might seem obvious to always target the highest possible frame rate, but if a game switches frequently between 30 fps and 60 fps, the discontinuity may be more distracting than just steadily running at 30 fps. Nevertheless, it makes sense to start with a target of 60 fps before profiling, so you can see your peak performance and then lower it later if you need to.

Create the Script

There's no way to set the target frame rate in the Unity Editor, but fortunately, you can adjust the target frame rate in a script by setting the static variable Application.targetFrameRate. So let's create a new JavaScript script, place it in the Scripts folder, and name it FuguFrameRate (Figure 16-1).

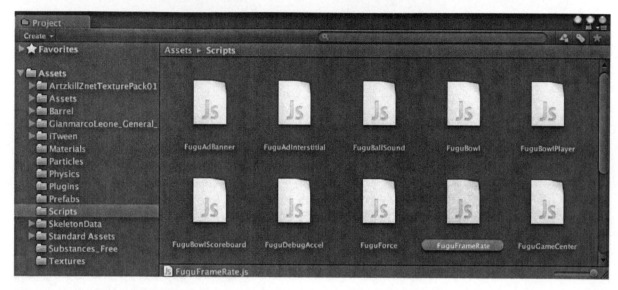

Figure 16-1. Adding a script in the Scripts folder

This will be a really short script, with one public variable and a Start callback containing just one line of code (Listing 16-1).

Listing 16-1. Complete Script for FuguFrameRate.js

```
#pragma strict

public var frameRate:int = 60;

function Start() {
        Application.targetFrameRate = frameRate;
}
```

The script sets the target frame rate by changing the value of the static variable Application.targetFrameRate to the value of frameRate, which is a public variable so it can be adjusted in the Inspector View. Since iOS devices all have a screen refresh rate of 60 fps, that's the best frame rate you can achieve, and thus a reasonable default value for frameRate.

Attach the Script

To utilize the FuguFrameRate script, it has to be added to a scene so that its Start callback is executed when the game starts. So let's create an empty GameObject in the bowling scene, name it FrameRate, and drag the FuguFrameRate script onto it (Figure 16-2).

Figure 16-2. Frame rate script included in the bowling scene

This script was added to our bowling scene, but you could just as well have added it to our splash scene instead, since `Application.targetFrameRate` only needs to be set once and it stays at that value even when a new scene is loaded. Our current splash scene doesn't really do anything, so running at Unity's default 30 fps is fine.

However, if the splash scene were to display a cool animation, you might want to set it at 60 fps, and in that case, you would also add the frame rate script to that scene. In fact, if the splash scene looked best at 60 fps and the bowling scene ran more smoothly at 30 fps (rather than jittering between 30 fps and 60 fps), you would add the frame rate script to both scenes, setting the target frame rate to 60 fps in the splash scene and 30 fps in the bowling scene.

Targeting Space

Besides frame rate, you should also set a goal for the app size. You have to compete for room on iOS devices with songs, photos, videos, and all the other apps that users install. A smaller footprint makes the decision easier for a user to keep your app.

A smaller app also downloads in less time and loads faster (both the app load and level loads). Especially important, the App Store limits downloads over cellular connections to apps under 50MB in size. You don't want to miss out on impulse buys, so 50MB is a good app size target. This constraint is much easier to meet than the App Store's original 20MB limit, but any app with significant content can still easily exceed that size (HyperBowl, with six lanes, is around 40MB).

Profile

Before you start optimizing, you need to know what to optimize. That's where profiling, obtaining performance information about the game, comes in. You have options ranging from statistics displayed in the Editor, to profiling the app itself, and even writing some of your own performance measurement code.

Game View Stats

In the Editor, you have immediate access to performance-related information about the scene using the Stats overlay in the Game View (Figure 16-3).

Figure 16-3. The Game View statistics overlay

When you click Play, you'll see these statistics update while the game is in progress. This information is convenient, but it's no substitute for profiling the actual app.

The Build Log

Minimizing your app size is not as important as it used to be, when exceeding 20MB meant that an app could only be downloaded onto a device over Wi-Fi, not 3G wireless. Now the limit is a more generous 50MB, but this is still easy to reach if you've got a big game, and smaller means faster downloads and more people can fit your app into devices with less free storage (I always fill up my iPads fairly quickly).

You can see a breakdown of assets that went into your app by checking the Editor log after a build, as shown in Listing 16-2.

Listing 16-2. Build information in the Editor Log

```
Textures      5.2 mb      16.9%
Meshes        17.4 kb     0.1%
Animations    0.0 kb      0.0%
Sounds        21.2 mb     69.1%
Shaders       0.0 kb      0.0%
Other Assets  19.1 kb     0.1%
Levels        10.7 kb     0.0%
Scripts       175.2 kb    0.6%
Included DLLs 4.1 mb      13.3%
File headers  16.6 kb     0.1%
Complete size 30.6 mb     100.0%
Used Assets, sorted by uncompressed size:
```

```
21.1 mb          69.0% Assets/Assets/Free/Assets/Sci-Fi_Ambiences/Sci-fi_AmbienceLoop1.wav
4.0 mb           13.1% Assets/Textures/LearnUnityCover.jpg
170.8 kb          0.5% Assets/Standard Assets/Skyboxes/Textures/Sunny3/Sunny3_up.tif
170.8 kb          0.5% Assets/Standard Assets/Skyboxes/Textures/Sunny3/Sunny3_right.tif
170.8 kb          0.5% Assets/Standard Assets/Skyboxes/Textures/Sunny3/Sunny3_left.tif
170.8 kb          0.5% Assets/Standard Assets/Skyboxes/Textures/Sunny3/Sunny3_front.tif
170.8 kb          0.5% Assets/Standard Assets/Skyboxes/Textures/Sunny3/Sunny3_back.tif
170.8 kb          0.5% Assets/Standard Assets/Light Flares/Sources/Textures/50mmflare.psd
170.8 kb          0.5% Assets/Barrel/Barrel_D.tga
31.2 kb           0.1% Assets/Assets/Free/Assets/8Bit/Coin_Pick_Up_03.wav
17.4 kb           0.1% Assets/Barrel/Barrel.fbx
17.3 kb           0.1% Assets/Substances_Free/Wood_Planks_01.sbsar
10.8 kb           0.0% Assets/Standard Assets/Skyboxes/Textures/Sunny3/Sunny3_down.tif
1.0 kb            0.0% Assets/Prefabs/BarrelPin.prefab
0.6 kb            0.0% Assets/Standard Assets/Light Flares/50mm Zoom.flare
0.3 kb            0.0% Assets/Standard Assets/Skyboxes/Sunny3 Skybox.mat
```

The log lists a breakdown of your app size by type of asset—textures, audio, meshes, scripts—and a list of the individual assets that went into it. Unfortunately, the size contributions are based on uncompressed sizes and not the final compressed asset sizes, but it still give you an idea of which assets are taking the most space.

The log also provides a way to find out which assets in your project are used or not used, via the handy search field in the Console app. For example, all the textures for Fugu Bowl are in the Textures folder, so to check which of those Textures are used and which ones can be remove from the project, select Editor Log in the Console View menu, which should launch the Console app with the Editor log selected (Figure 16-4).

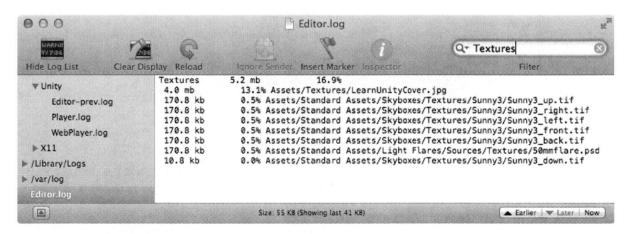

Figure 16-4. Filtering the build log using the Console app search field

In the search box type "Textures" to filter the display. Then you can compare the resulting list with the Textures folder in the Project View and see if there's anything in the Project View that didn't end up in the build.

Run the Built-In Profiler

After the Unity iOS build has generated its Xcode project, you have the option of activating the built-in profiler, which reports information similar to the Stats overlay in the Game View. To activate the built-in profiler, also referred to in the Unity documentation as the internal profiler, select the header file iPhone_Profiler.h in the Xcode project, listed inside the Classes folder, and change the value of ENABLE_INTERNAL_PROFILER from 0 to 1 (Figure 16-5).

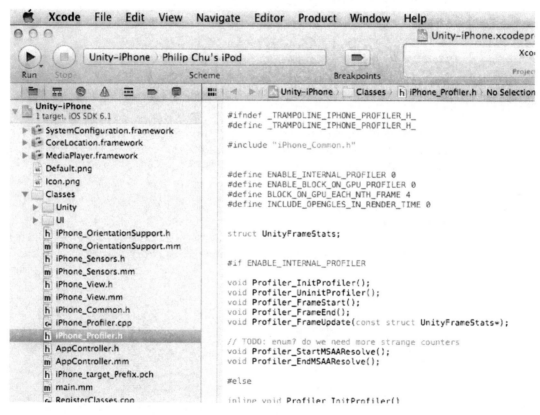

Figure 16-5. Built-in profiler switch in the Unity Xcode project

Now when you click Play, the app will recompile with the built-in profiler enabled, and the debug area of Xcode will display statistics, as shown in Listing 16-3, after every 30 frames while the game is running.

Listing 16-3. Built-In Profiler Output on a Fourth-Generation iPod Touch

```
iPhone Unity internal profiler stats:
cpu-player>    min: 39.8   max: 63.2   avg: 58.0
cpu-ogles-drv> min:  2.1   max:  3.7   avg:  2.4
cpu-present>   min:  0.7   max:  6.6   avg:  1.8
frametime>     min: 47.7   max: 72.2   avg: 64.5
draw-call #>   min:  40    max:  40    avg:  40    | batched:   0
tris #>        min: 5544   max: 5544   avg: 5544   | batched:   0
verts #>       min: 4358   max: 4358   avg: 4358   | batched:   0
player-detail> physx:  0.0 animation:  0.0 culling  0.0 skinning:  0.0 batching:  0.0 render: 58.0
```

```
fixed-update-count: 0 .. 0
mono-scripts> update: 0.2   fixedUpdate:  0.0 coroutines:  0.1
mono-memory>   used heap: 405504 allocated heap: 524288  max number of collections: 0 collection
total duration:  0.0
```

The first number to look at in the profile is the frametime, which is the total amount of time taken by a frame, in milliseconds. If you're running at 60 fps, you should see an average of around 16.7 ms for the frametime. If the frametime is above 34, then you're not even getting 30 fps. The line below the frametime is pretty important, too, as it tends to have a big impact on the frametime. Draw calls are distinct drawing operations. Generally, each rendered mesh incurs a draw call, and lighting and shadows on top of that can add more draw calls.

The player-detail breaks down the time listed in the cpu-player line at the top. The player-detail time is apportioned among physx (physics), animation, culling (determining objects that don't need to be rendered), skinning (updating the skin position on animated characters), batching (combining meshes that have the same materials so they are rendered with a single draw call), rendering, and the fixed update count.

The profile results in Listing 16-3, taken on a fourth-generation iPod touch, show a frametime not even close to 30 fps, much less 16 fps, and the player-detail is dominated by the render time. One thing that is known to have a big performance impact is dynamic shadows, so let's disable shadows in our Light (Figure 16-6).

Figure 16-6. Disabling shadows from the bowling scene Light

Then Build and Run again to start a new profile session (Listing 16-4).

Listing 16-4. Built-In Profiler Output After Removing Shadows

```
iPhone Unity internal profiler stats:
cpu-player>     min:  5.0   max:  7.6   avg:  5.7
cpu-ogles-drv> min:  3.1   max:  7.0   avg:  3.7
cpu-present>    min: 14.4   max: 42.9   avg: 28.1
cpu-waits-gpu> min: 14.4   max: 42.9   avg: 28.1
 msaa-resolve> min:  0.0   max:  0.0   avg:  0.0
frametime>      min: 28.5   max: 55.5   avg: 39.5
draw-call #>    min: 29     max: 29     avg: 29      | batched:    10
tris #>         min:  4584  max:  4584  avg:  4584   | batched:  3420
verts #>        min:  3712  max:  3712  avg:  3712   | batched:  2750
player-detail> physx:  0.0 animation:  0.0 culling  0.0 skinning:  0.0 batching:  1.9 render:
3.1 fixed-update-count: 0 .. 0
mono-scripts>  update:  0.2   fixedUpdate:  0.0 coroutines:  0.1
mono-memory>   used heap: 401408 allocated heap: 524288  max number of collections: 0 collection
total duration:  0.0
```

If you're not running Unity iOS Pro or you turned off shadows earlier for performance reasons, then you're already here. Anyway, the results are dramatic. Turning off shadows significantly reduces draw calls, and the frametime and render time are lower, although the frame rate is still below 30 fps.

Run the Editor Profiler (Pro)

The built-in profiler gives you a general idea of the bottlenecks in your game's performance—whether it's draw calls, physics computation, or script execution, for example. But it's still a bit of a guessing game figuring out exactly what's taking up the frametime. Unity Pro users have the luxury of using the Profiler included in the Unity Editor. The Profiler can record the performance of a game run in the Editor or profile remotely, capturing performance data from a test device. To profile our bowling game running on a test device, you need to check the Development Build option in the Build Settings, which will enable the Autoconnect Profiler option (Figure 16-7).

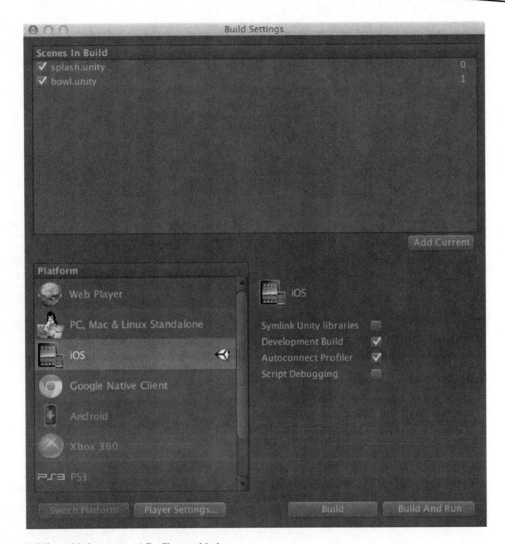

Figure 16-7. Building with Autoconnect Profiler enabled

Perform a Build and Run, and the Profiler window should appear automatically, running a profiling session of the game running on the device (Figure 16-8).

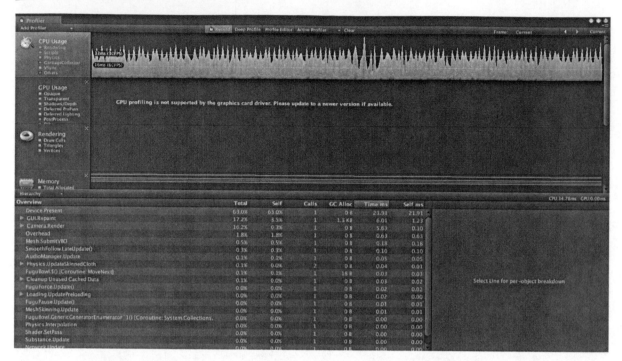

Figure 16-8. The Profiler window

The topmost bar displays the computer processing unit (CPU) usage. This particular profile indicates we're hovering around 30 fps. The area below shows a breakdown of the CPU usage by function calls (Figure 16-9).

Overview	Total	Self	Calls	GC Alloc	Time ms	Self ms
Device.Present	53.3%	53.3%	1	0 B	16.80	16.80
▽ Camera.Render	21.1%	1.0%	1	0 B	6.67	0.33
▽ Drawing	19.6%	0.6%	1	0 B	6.18	0.21
▶ Render.OpaqueGeometry	9.0%	0.1%	1	0 B	2.86	0.03
▶ Camera.RenderSkybox	8.7%	8.5%	1	0 B	2.77	2.70
Clear	0.5%	0.5%	1	0 B	0.16	0.16
Render.Prepare	0.2%	0.2%	1	0 B	0.08	0.08
▶ Render.TransparentGeometry	0.1%	0.0%	1	0 B	0.05	0.02
Camera.ImageEffects	0.0%	0.0%	1	0 B	0.02	0.02
▶ Culling	0.4%	0.3%	1	0 B	0.12	0.09
Camera.ImageEffects	0.0%	0.0%	1	0 B	0.02	0.02
Camera.GUILayer	0.0%	0.0%	1	0 B	0.01	0.01
RenderTexture.SetActive	0.0%	0.0%	1	0 B	0.00	0.00
▽ GUI.Repaint	18.8%	1.5%	1	1.3 KB	5.94	0.48
▶ FuguPause.OnGUI()	10.2%	4.1%	1	428 B	3.23	1.30
▶ FuguBowlScoreboard.OnGUI()	5.0%	2.6%	2	0.8 KB	1.57	0.84
GUIUtility.BeginGUI()	1.1%	1.1%	4	64 B	0.35	0.35
GUIUtility.EndGUI()	0.8%	0.8%	4	0 B	0.26	0.26

Figure 16-9. The Profiler breakdown of CPU usage

You can expand the items to reveal the nested function calls. Figure 16-9 indicates we're spending a lot of time in our UnityGUI functions, both the scoreboard and pause menu (this profile is taken with the pause menu up).

Manually Connect the Profiler

If for some reason the profiler doesn't start automatically, the Profiler can be brought up from the Window menu (Figure 16-10).

Figure 16-10. The Window menu item to display the Profiler

The Profiler is actually a view, which is why it's listed among the other views in the Window menu. But, like the Asset Store, the Profiler takes up so much screen space it is best left by itself in a floating window .

Once the Profiler window is up, it will automatically start recording the game in the Editor (even if the game is not actually running), so click the Record button to stop it. Then select your iOS test device in the Active Profiler window (Figure 16-11) and click the Record button again to start profiling.

Figure 16-11. Selecting an iOS device as the Active Profiler

Add a Frame Rate Display

Enabling the built-in profiler or attaching to the Editor Profiler over the network is inconvenient just to see the frame rate. That's where an on-screen frame rate display would come in handy. You could just toggle it on while you're lying on the sofa watching TV and play testing your game (at least that's what I do).

For an on-screen frame rate display, you could use a UnityGUI label like we did with the bowling scoreboard. However, there's another way to display 2D text on screen, using the GUIText Component. You can create a GameObject with a GUIText Component already attached using the GameObject menu on the menu bar, or the Create menu in the Hierarchy View (Figure 16-12).

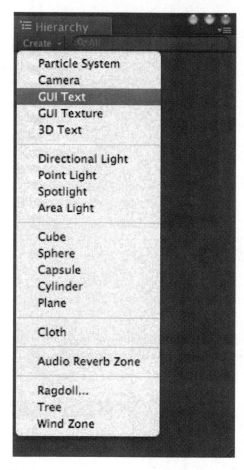

Figure 16-12. Creating a GUIText GameObject

Let's go ahead and create that GUIText GameObject and name it FPS (Figure 16-13).

Figure 16-13. The FPS GameObject with a GUIText Component

Like the GUITexture we used for our secondary splash screen, GUIText is positioned on the screen in normalized coordinates, where the bottom left corner is 0,0 and the top right is 1,1, specified in the Transform x and y values of the GameObject. Set the x and y positions of our frame rate display to -.1 each, placing it near the bottom left corner, and change the text value from GUIText to FPS.

Don't bother customizing the font because the frame rate display is only for development use and you won't activate it in the released app (although in HyperBowl, the frame rate display can be activated by users so they can report performance issues). The default size value of 0 indicates the font size specified in the font's import setting is used, but that's pretty small, so let's set it to a reasonably large size, 40. All this time, the GUIText is visible in the Game View, so you can see the effect of the size changes (Figure 16-14).

Figure 16-14. The Game View with a GUIText

Just as GUITexture is more convenient for displaying static textures than UnityGUI, requiring no scripting, GUIText is a more straightforward way to display static text on the screen than UnityGUI. But the frame rate display does need to change the text by setting the text variable in the GUIText instance. Let's implement our frame rate display script now. Create a new script, place it in the Scripts folder, and name it FuguFPS (Figure 16-15).

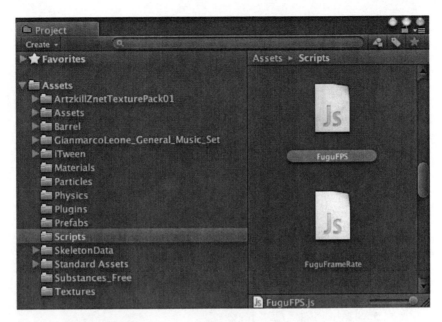

Figure 16-15. Creating a new FuguFPS.js script

Then add the Update function in Listing 16-5 to the script. The script's Update callback sets the text variable, of GUIText with the calculated frame rate. The calculation is simplistic, based on Time.delta time, the most recent frametime. Normally, frames per second would be calculated as 1/Time.deltaTime, but since Time.deltaTime is scaled by Time.timeScale, you can easily take that into account by using Time.timeScale/Time.deltaTime.

The text variable in GUIText is a String variable, so you need to convert the frame value to a String by calling the number's ToString function (every built-in type has a ToString function). And then append the "FPS" so you won't wonder what those two numbers are on the screen!

Listing 16-5. The Complete Frame Rate Display Script FuguFPS.js

```
#pragma strict

function Update()
{
        if (Time.deltaTime>0) {
                var fps:float = Time.timeScale/Time.deltaTime;
                guiText.text  = fps.ToString("f0")+"FPS";
        }
}
```

Now attach the script to the FPS GameObject. When you click Play in the Editor, you should see the frame rate display flicker among different numbers. And when you perform a Build and Run to a test device, you should see the frame rate display correspond to the numbers you got in the built-in and Pro profilers (Figure 16-16).

Figure 16-16. *A frame rate display running on a test device*

Just remember, you should deactivate the FPS GameObject before you release this app!

Optimize Settings

The proper way to optimize is to methodically go through the bottlenecks starting with the largest, profiling the improvements at each stage until you achieve your target. But for the purposes of getting through a number of optimization procedures in this chapter, we'll plow through a bunch of them in sequence.

Quality Settings

Let's start by tweaking the global settings that relate to our optimization effort. The settings that are most likely to affect performance are the Quality Settings, which control the visual quality of the game (Figure 16-17).

Figure 16-17. Optimizing the Quality Settings

We're going for speed, so set the current iOS quality to Fastest and then adjust the settings from there. Zero pixel lights is fine for the lighting set up. If you had a spotlight, then the lack of a pixel light would be obvious.

You don't want to force all textures to half resolution though. Relying on the Texture Import settings to limit the resolution on a case-by-case basis gives you more flexibility. So let's set the Texture Quality to Full Res.

Similarly, you'll want to change the setting for Anisotropic Textures from none to per-texture. Anisotropic Texture are textures that compensate for being viewed at an angle, which is appropriate for a texture used for a road in a racing game, for example. Like texture resolution, anisotropy can be adjusted for a Texture in its Import Settings.

Multisample Anti Aliasing (full-screen smoothing) is an expensive operation, as you would expect a full-screen per-pixel operation would be.

You don't have any particle systems in this game, so the Soft Particles setting doesn't matter, but it's another pixel-dominated operation (these types of features are often called fill-rate limited).

Shadows are disabled, so all the shadow parameters below it are irrelevant, but if shadows were enabled, the two key properties are the Shadow Resolution and Shadow Distance. Both properties affect the shadow's resolution; increasing the Shadow Resolution naturally allows for a more sharply defined shadow at the expense of more memory consumed for a larger shadow map, and much like the improved depth buffer precision of a shortened Camera frustum, a shorter Shadow Distance reduces the need for a large shadow map texture. Reducing the Shadow Resolution saves space while introducing more jaggy shadows, while reducing the Shadow Distance potentially reduces the number of objects involve in the shadows.

Physics Manager

Rigidbodies go to sleep when they're at rest to avoid unnecessary physics computation. "At rest" means the Rigidbody's motion has stopped moving and rotating. You can specify the threshold for the Sleep Velocity and Sleep Angular Velocity in the Physics Manager (Figure 16-18), available under the Settings portion of the Edit menu.

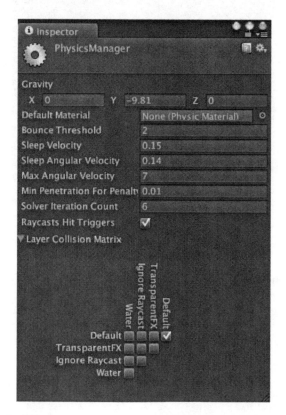

Figure 16-18. Optimizing the Physics Manager

At the bottom of the Physics Manager, you can also specify which layers of GameObjects can collide with one another. This doesn't make a difference with our bowling game, because all of our colliding objects are in the Default layer. But to demonstrate this point, let's modify the collision table to only allow GameObjects in the Default layer to collide with other GameObjects in the Default layer.

Time Manager

Because the physics updates take place at fixed intervals, you can reduce physics computation time by increasing the fixed timestep in the Time Manager (Figure 16-19). Ideally, the fixed timestep should be set as high as possible without degrading the physics simulation. For now, we'll increase the fixed timestep from 0.02 to 0.03.

Figure 16-19. Optimizing the Time Manager

The property immediately below Fixed Timestep is also related to physics updates: Maximum Allowed Timestep. This value caps how much time can be spent on physics updates in each frame. This prevents the runaway situation where the fixed updates take up a lot of time and increase the frametime, thus including more fixed updates in the next frame and so on. Lowering the Maximum Allowed Timestep minimizes the FixedUpdate impact on the frametime but risks degrading the physics simulation.

Audio Manager

There is also an optimization tradeoff in how the audio is played. In the Audio Manager (Figure 16-20), you can specify the audio latency, which is how much delay is allowed before the sound is played.

Figure 16-20. Optimizing the Audio Manager

For games where responsive sound is important (e.g., the collision sounds in our bowling game), selecting Best latency (i.e., lowest latency) is appropriate.

Player Settings

The Player Settings can have a great effect on optimization. In the Resolution and Presentation Settings, we opted for the highest native screen resolution, and we also have the maximum 32-bit per-pixel color resolution selected for the Display Buffer (Figure 16-21). If the box is unchecked, the display buffer uses 16 bits for each pixel, which can result in some color banding. Thus we're going for more visual fidelity at the expense of taking up more memory.

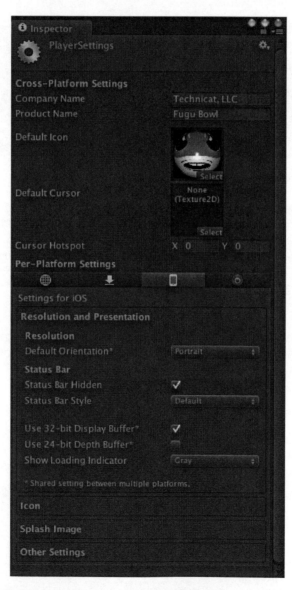

Figure 16-21. Optimizing the Resolution and Presentation in Player Settings

Let's leave the Depth Buffer at the default 16 bits per pixel, but if that precision is not enough to prevent z-fighting (the case where an object close behind another pokes through), you can raise it to 24 bits per pixel, again improving visual quality but using more memory.

The Other Settings section is filled with optimization options, and not just in the portion labelled Optimization (Figure 16-22).

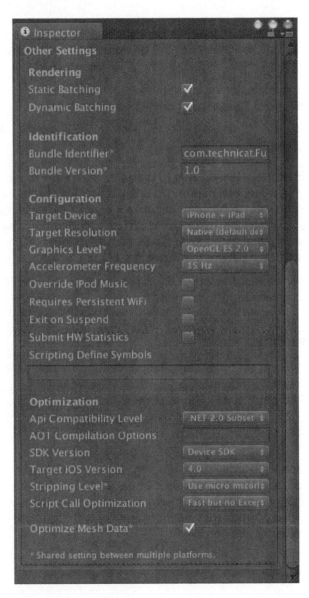

Figure 16-22. Optimizing Other Settings in Player Settings

Static Batching (Pro)

As I pointed out in the first profiling session, draw calls tend to have a big impact on performance. Static batching, only available to Unity iOS Pro users, reduces draw calls by combining meshes at build time that can be rendered together in the same draw call. For meshes to be combined, their GameObjects must be marked as static in the Inspector view and they must share the same material or set of materials.

Static batching is a very flexible system; it remembers the distinct identity of each GameObject, so a GameObject with a statically batched mesh can still be deactivated at will and is still subject to culling.

Our bowling game only has one static mesh, the Floor, so enabling static batching won't make any difference here. In general, static batching provides a good performance boost but at the expense of taking up more memory, because it essentially copies each batched mesh.

Dynamic Batching

The next option, dynamic batching, is available to both Pro and non-Pro users and takes place at runtime. Like static batching, it requires meshes to share materials before they can be combined, but dynamic batching can handle moving objects, because it checks every frame if it needs to rebatch objects. For example, the bowling pins in our game can be batched because they all obviously have the same material. They were instantiated from the same prefab, after all. However, the bowling ball cannot be batched with any of the pins or the bowling surface.

Batching does take some time, which is why it shows up in the built-in profiler, but, like static batching, it generally is a big win for performance.

Accelerometer Frequency

The Accelerometer Frequency is set to 60 samples per second by default. You can save some processing time by lowering that frequency to 15, which is sufficient for our shake detection code. If you don't use the accelerometer at all in an app, set it to 0.

Stripping Level (Pro)

Unity Pro users have the option to apply iOS Stripping. Three cumulative levels are available: String Assemblies, Strip Bytecode, and Use micro mscorlib. Let's choose the latter, which is the most aggressive optimization and includes the other two. The micro mscorlib is a custom, slimmed down version of the core Mono library, which may be incompatible with additional .NET libraries you might import, but that's not an issue for this game.

Script Call Optimization

The Script Call Optimization level determines how calls to native code are made. The default setting, Slow and Safe, incurs overhead, so let's set it to Fast with No Exceptions. As the label signifies, this setting is faster but will fail if the native code throws an exception (essentially, an error that is expected to be handled by calling code).

Optimize Mesh Data

The Optimize Mesh Data option removes at build time any unnecessary per-vertex mesh information. If a mesh is not using a bump-map shader, then the tangents can be removed, and if the mesh is using an unlit shader, then normals can be removed. This saves space and facilitates batching, since batching copies all of those Mesh data. Of course, if you're going to change the shader of a Mesh at runtime via script to a shader that requires more per-vertex information than the original shader, you shouldn't use this option.

Optimizing GameObjects

After adjusting the Quality Settings, Physics Manager, and Time Manager, we're ready to tweak individual GameObjects.

Camera

Cameras are a focal point (no pun intended) of optimization because they dictate what is rendered and how it is rendered. The Camera frustum automatically provides one source of optimization. Any GameObject that resides entirely outside the frustum is not visible to the Camera, so no attempt is made to render the GameObject. This optimization is called *frustum culling* and also benefits animation and particle systems. The system has no need to play an animation or simulate particles when there's no one to see it.

> **Tip**   The fastest way to render a GameObject is to not render it all.

Therefore, adjusting the Camera's frustum so it includes fewer objects in a scene is one source of optimization. You can narrow the frustum by lowering its field of view, and you can shorten the frustum by decreasing the far distance value, bringing the far plane closer to the Camera (Figure 16-23).

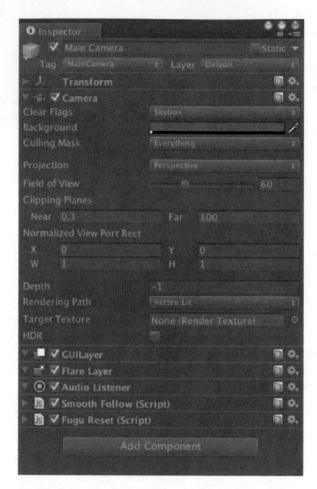

Figure 16-23. Optimizing the Main Camera

For example, the default value of 1000 for the far plane value in the Main Camera is overkill, considering the bowling Floor is much smaller. Setting the far value to 100 still leaves everything visible (Unity skyboxes are conveniently visible independent of the frustum).

Minimizing the far plane value has the additional benefit of storing a smaller range of values in the depth buffer when rendering. This avoids the problem of z-fighting, where an object that is barely behind another seems to poke through the one in front because of the limited numerical precision in the depth buffer.

Another way to cull GameObjects from rendering by a Camera is to specify that it renders only GameObjects in a certain set of layers, listed in its Culling mask. This is really a matter of correctness—you want to make sure the Camera is rendering only what it's supposed to be rendering, and not, say, HUD elements that are already rendered by a separate HUD camera. But it does affect performance. I once had a bug where the Main Camera was unintentionally rendering GUI elements, but far enough in the distance that I didn't notice it.

Each Camera also has an eventMask variable that is similar to its Culling mask (or, equivalently, its cullingMask variable), but instead of specifying what layers are rendered by the Camera, the eventMask determines what layers receive onMouse events from the Camera. Minimizing the layers present in eventMask can reduce the overhead of onMouse processing, but as it's not visible in the Inspector View, that variable has to be set from a script.

The last Camera optimization to make is to specify the Render Path. There are two render paths available on iOS: Vertex Lit and Forward Rendering (Deferred Rendering is not available for mobile platforms). Forward Rendering is more flexible and powerful than Vertex Lit. For example, the Vertex Lit path won't display bump-mapping. But in this chapter, we're aggressively going for a high frame rate, so let's set the render path to Vertex Lit.

Lights

We already disabled shadows on our Light (except for non-Pro users who didn't have shadows in the first place), which is a big performance improvement because it reduces draw calls. And lighting is already influenced by the Quality Settings, which specify no pixel lights and disabled shadows (Figure 16-24).

Figure 16-24. Optimizing the Light

But we can perform some additional adjustments on the Light similar to our Camera tweaks. Like the Camera, Lights have a specified range, which we can minimize to reduce the number of lit GameObjects. Lights also have a Culling Mask, which, as in the case of the Main Camera, can be set to the Default layer, but with judicious assignment of layers you can reduce unnecessarily lit GameObjects.

Pins

In pursuit of speed, we've chosen the simplest lighting and the simplest render path. You can also simplify the shaders you're using for each Mesh. The bowling pins comprise most of the objects in our scene, so let's modify the BarrelPin prefab first (Figure 16-25).

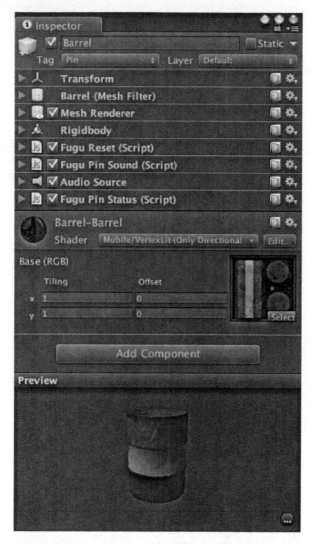

Figure 16-25. Optimizing the BarrelPin prefab

In the Project View, select the Barrel GameObject in the prefab and click the Shader selector in the Inspector View. There are many simpler shaders than Bumped Specular; anything with less than two materials is likely to be faster, and Vertex Lit will be more efficient than any of the pixel shaders. There is even a set of shaders specifically implemented for mobile devices, including Mobile/Vertex Lit. But there's one that is even better for our situation, a Mobile/Vertex Lit shader implemented specifically for use only with directional lights. So let's choose that one, Mobile/Vertex Lit (Only Directional Light).

Floor

The Floor GameObject has a few Component properties that can be tweaked for optimization (Figure 16-26). Starting with the MeshRenderer Component, we have the Cast Shadows and Receive Shadows options enabled. Although we have Shadows disabled in the Light and in the Quality Settings, you should pay attention to the per-object settings just in case you enable shadows in the future. If shadows were enabled, you would want shadows cast on the floor, so Receive Shadows should be enabled. But because we don't expect the Floor to cast a shadow (at least not on anything we can see), let's disable the Cast Shadows option. For performance, the fewer shadow casters, the better.

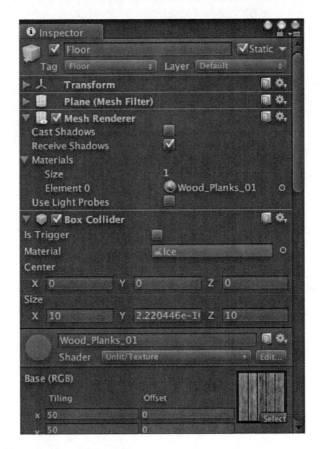

Figure 16-26. Optimizing the Floor

Turning to physics, there is another opportunity for optimization. Although we have primitive colliders for the bowling pins and bowling ball, our Floor has a MeshCollider Component. Because the Floor is a flat and square surface, you could use a BoxCollider instead. Replacing it is a simple process: when you add a BoxCollider Component to the Floor, either using the Add Component button in the Inspector View or the Component menu on the menu bar, Unity asks if you want to replace the existing MeshCollider (say yes), and the new BoxCollider Component will automatically be sized to fit the Floor mesh.

As with the bowling pins, you could also change the shader from the fairly complex Bumped Specular shader to Mobile/VertexLit (Only Directional Lights), as we did with our bowling pin prefab. But the floor is a special case because it's flat. The lighting across its surface is uniform. So you can use the Unlit Texture shader and avoid any lighting calculations at all.

Ball

The last GameObject we will optimize is the Ball. It's already using a SphereCollider Component, so the one thing we'll change is the shader. Like the bowling pins, the Ball is going to move, so let's use a lit shader, in particular the same Mobile/VertexLit (Only Directional Light) shader that we selected for the pins. However, the Ball is currently using the default diffuse Material that was automatically assigned when you created the Ball, and you can't change the shader on that Material. So you'll need to assign a different Material to the Ball.

You can create a new Material in the same way you created the other types of assets. In the Project View, bring up the Create menu and select Material (Figure 16-27).

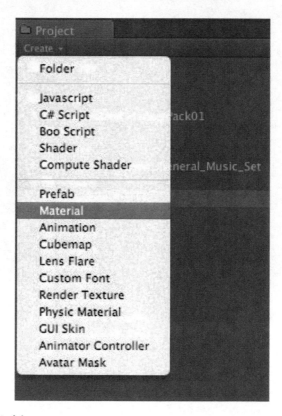

Figure 16-27. Creating a new Material

Place the new Material in the Materials folder and name it Ball. Select it (Figure 16-28), and in the Inspector View you can adjust its shader, selecting Mobile/VertexLit (Directional Light).

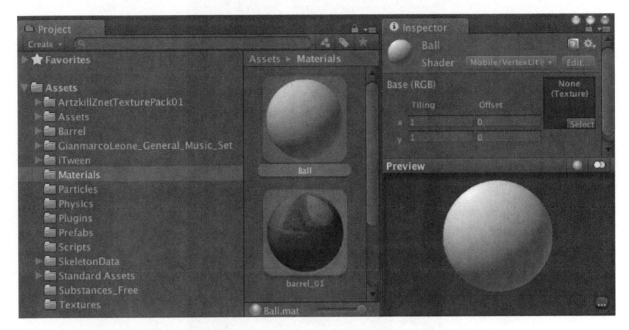

Figure 16-28. Setting the shader for a new Material

Then drag the Ball material onto the Ball GameObject, and you're all set (Figure 16-29).

Figure 16-29. Optimizing the Ball

Both of the Mobile/VertexLit shaders will display a white color if no texture is supplied. If you want the ball to have a color other than white, you would use the standard Vertex Lit shader, which allows you to specify a Main Color and Specular (shininess) Color.

Optimize Assets

It's easy to overlook the fact that a lot of optimization can take place when the asset is imported, and you have control over this in the Import Settings for each asset.

Textures

Our textures are already imported with reasonable default settings, but let's look at a couple of textures so we can understand those settings. In the Project View, let's look in the Textures folder and compare the cat texture we used for the example scene in Chapter 3 (Figure 16-30) and the texture we used for the secondary splash screen in Chapter 12 (Figure 16-31). The cat texture used the Import Settings corresponding to the Texture preset, while the splash texture used the Import Settings of the GUI preset. In both cases, switching from the preset to Advanced reveals the specific settings of the preset.

Figure 16-30. Import Settings for a texture

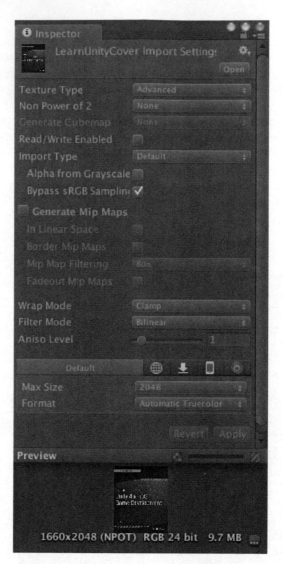

Figure 16-31. Import Settings for a GUITexture

There are two major differences between the Texture and GUI presets: Texture has Mip Mapping enabled, while GUI has the sRGB bypass option enabled. The *mip* in mipmapping stands for the phrase *multim in parvo*, meaning "many in little." Mipmaps are precomputed smaller versions of the texture that provide a smoother visual quality and transition as the texture comes nearer or farther away from the Camera.

The filter type determines how a pixel from the texture (or *texel*) is calculated for rendering purposes. For point filtering, the texel is chosen from the mip map closest to the desired size. Bilinear filtering averages the surrounding texels from the closest smaller mipmap, while trilinear filtering combines the bilinear filtering results from the closest larger mipmap and the closest smaller mipmap. Point sampling is the simplest and fastest filter, while trilinear filtering is the most expensive. Bilinear filtering is the middle ground and a reasonable default.

Mipmapping is usually appropriate, despite the increased memory usage. Besides improving the texture display, mipmapping allows the graphics processor to work with a smaller version of the texture, which can improve performance. For a texture used in a GUI (e.g., UnityGUI or GUITexture), you'll typically view the texture at just one size, and ideally at the texture's original size, so mipmapping is unnecessary. That's certainly true for the splash screen, especially when it isn't even loaded into a scene.

> **Tip**   For a texture with sharp details (e.g., one use as a street sign), it may be better to use point sampling or even disable mipmapping entirely to avoid blurring the texture.

The anisotropic (directionally dependent) filtering level compensates for the case where a texture is tilted with respect to the Camera, such as the road surface in a racing game. In those cases, filtering uniformly across a texture in both directions may not look right. For regular textures in a scene, the anisotropic level should be chosen on a case-by-case basis. For GUI textures, which are viewed face on from the Camera, no anisotropic filtering is required.

Normally, textures are imported taking into account gamma space, the nonlinear color space of screens. In general, this isn't necessary for GUI textures, so in those cases, the bypass sRGB option is selected. If it doesn't look quite right, try both options.

For mipmapping, textures need to be square and have dimensions that are a power of two (POT), because mip maps are generated at successively halved dimensions. For example, a 256×256 texture would have mip maps at 128×128, 64×64, and so on. Even a non-mipmapped texture benefits from POT dimensions, because that's what the graphics hardware ultimately uses. Most textures designed for games have POT dimensions, but if they don't, the Texture imports settings can automatically size the texture to the nearest POT.

For GUI textures, you usually don't want this. Our splash screen has None set for its POT scaling, and the resulting preview displays its original dimensions and NPOT (Non-Power of Two). If you try to use it as a regular texture in the scene, Unity will issue a warning in the Console View that you're using a NPOT texture in a non-GUI way and will incur a performance penalty.

The max texture size and compression level of the texture are listed in the preset settings and are specified independently of the presets. For regular textures, the default Max Size of 1024 is reasonable (2048×2048 is the maximum supported by all devices), but it should be chosen on a case-by-case basis. For example, if a large texture has just one color, you might as well make it a 2×2 texture. And if a texture is only used on a Mesh that is small or far away on screen, then there's no reason to make it a big texture. For the splash screen, we set the Max Size to 2048 so we don't scale the texture to be smaller than the iPad Retina screen.

> **Tip**   Setting the max scale to the maximum allowable and the compression level to TrueColor allows you to see the original format of the texture in the preview area of the Import settings.

For a regular texture, the default compression level, 4-bit PVRTC (PowerVR Texture Compression), is reasonable. A texture with less detail may work with the more aggressive 2-bit PVRTC. As with mipmapping, texture compression reduces the memory taken by texture mapping, and the graphics processor support for PVRTC provides an additional performance advantage. And as with mipmapping, particularly detailed textures may be degraded too much by compression, in which case leaving the texture at uncompressed 16-bit or uncompressed TrueColor (24-bit) may be better. For GUI textures, you might not want to compress the texture for that reason, or in the case of the splash screen that we assign in the player settings, you should leave it alone in its native format.

Audio

We adjusted the DSP Buffer Size in the Audio Manager for more responsive collision sounds, lowering the latency at some processing expense. As with textures, you can also adjust the Import Settings for AudioClips. Analogous with having two general categories of texture usage, for 3D and GUI, you also have 2D and 3D sounds, where 3D sounds are associated with GameObjects, or at least a position in the 3D world, while 2D sounds are used for ambient audio or music (like the song we added to our dance scene in Chapter 5).

Let's compare a couple of our bowling sounds: the pin collision sound (Figure 16-32) and the ball rolling sound (Figure 16-33). They're both sounds that emanate from a position in the world and even move with respect to the Main Camera (or rather, more precisely, they move with respect to the AudioListener Component attached to the Main Camera). Thus, they're both marked as 3D sounds in their Import Settings. 3D sounds should be mono, not stereo. Fortunately, the original audio files for both of these sounds are mono, so you don't have to select Force to mono.

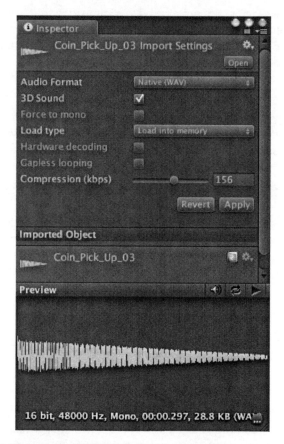

Figure 16-32. Optimizing Import Settings for the pin collision sound

Figure 16-33. Optimizing Import Settings for the ball rolling sound

The collision sound is fairly small, so let's leave it uncompressed to avoid the processing involved in uncompressing the sound and to maximize the quality of the playback. The rolling sound is a larger sound file, so let's compress it and leave it compressed in memory. Because this is the only compressed sound, and iOS has hardware support for decoding one compressed sound at any time, you're not incurring any software decoding overhead. However, if you also had ambient sound or music playing in the scene, chances are that would be a much larger sound file and you would want to compress that instead.

> **Tip**   Import uncompressed sounds to allow flexibility in deciding which sounds to compress in the Editor. There's no reason to import compressed audio unless you've found a compression tool that gives you better quality than Unity's compression.

With compression selected, the gapless looping option becomes available. That forces the compression to process the end of the audio clip so it can loop seamlessly, which is what you want, since you're playing this sound in a loop.

For compressed audio, there is one other load option besides Uncompress on load and Compressed in memory: Stream from disc. There is some additional overhead in streaming from disc, but that's a good option for a scene that plays multiple songs in succession, in which case it would be prohibitive to keep all of those songs in memory.

Meshes

Most of the Mesh Import Settings (Figure 16-34) that affect optimization have an impact principally on memory usage.

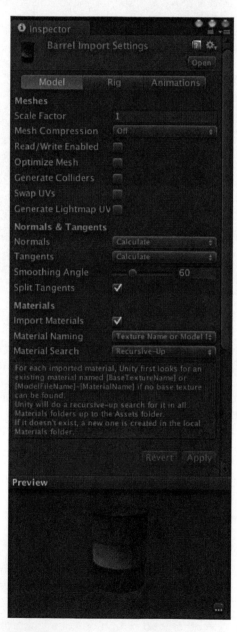

Figure 16-34. Optimizing Import Settings for a Mesh

The first is Mesh Compression, which reduces the amount of space and memory used for a mesh by reducing the numerical precision (i.e., number of bits used to represent the vertices, normals, texture coordinates, and tangents). This can also reduce the visual quality, so it's best to experiment and find the maximum compression level that doesn't degrade the appearance. The available levels are low, medium, high, and none. The default is none.

Listed below Mesh Compression is Read/Write Enabled. This is by default on, creating a copy of the Mesh that can be modified. But if you don't have any scripts that read or write Mesh variables, such as vertices and normals, and you usually don't need any, then you can leave this option off.

Optimize Mesh, not to be confused with the Mesh Optimization option in the Player Settings, offers some performance improvement by optimizing the arrangement of the Mesh's triangle list.

Leave Generate Colliders off if you're not going to use a Mesh Collider. In fact, it's not a bad idea to leave this option off as a rule, because you can always add a Mesh Collider manually if you need one, but it's often preferable to add one or more primitive Colliders instead.

If you know the shader for this Mesh will not require normals or tangents, you can set the Normals and Tangents options, respectively, to none. But if you have Mesh Optimization selected in the Player Settings, unused vertex data will be removed at build time anyway.

Optimize Scripts

The usual tips for optimizing code apply to scripting in Unity. For example, we've already made a point of calling the magnitudeSquared function of Vector3 instead of magnitude to avoid its internal square root operation. But I'll describe some of the less obvious ways to improve script performance or use scripts to improve performance in the following sections.

Cache GetComponent

In general, it's a good idea to assign a value to a variable if you're going to calculate that value more than once, whether it's a math expression, the result of a function call, or even accessing the value of an instance or static variable, which might in fact be internally performing a function call.

This is the case with the component shortcut variables we've been accessing in our scripts like transform, audio, and rigidbody, each of which results in a call to GetComponent that searches among all the Components attached to the GameObject for a Component with the matching type.

So any time you're going to reference a Component shortcut variable more than once in a script, whether it's listed more than once in the script or referenced repeatedly in callback like Update, or especially if the shortcut is referenced in a loop with many iterations, you should assign the Component to a variable early on. Listing 16-6 shows how to apply this optimization to our FuguReset script.

Listing 16-6. Caching Component Shortcuts in FuguReset.js

```
#pragma strict

private var startPos:Vector3;
private var startRot:Vector3;
```

```
// for performance
private var trans:Transform = null;
private var body:Rigidbody = null;

function Awake() {
        // cache the Transform reference
        trans = transform;
        body = rigidbody;
        // save the initial position and rotation of this GameObject
        startPos = trans.localPosition;
        startRot = trans.localEulerAngles;
}

function ResetPosition() {
        // set back to initial position
        trans.localPosition = startPos;
        trans.localEulerAngles = startRot;
        // make sure we stop all physics movement
        if (body != null) {
                body.velocity = Vector3.zero;
                body.angularVelocity = Vector3.zero;
        }
}
```

The original version of FuguReset.js referenced two Component shortcut variables: transform and rigidbody. So we add two private variables, named trans and body, to reference those Components and initialize trans and body in the Awake callback.

This cleanup is applicable to many of our scripts, because we commonly reference transform, rigidbody, and audio. I won't list all of the revised code, but the updated scripts are available in the project files for this chapter on http://learnunity4.com/.

UnityGUI

The detailed profile results indicate that UnityGUI takes up a significant portion of our frametime. One source of slowdown in UnityGUI is the overhead of using GUILayout to automatically place GUI elements. We don't use GUILayout in the scoreboard, so you can add an Awake callback which sets useGUILayout to false in the FuguBowlScoreboard script (Listing 16-7).

Listing 16-7. Setting useGUILayout to False in FuguBowlScoreboard.js

```
function Awake() {
        useGUILayout = false;
}
```

The pause menu still uses GUILayout, but because the menu is only up when the game is paused and won't affect gameplay, its performance is less of a concern.

Runtime Static Batching (Pro)

Dynamic batching can combine similar meshes that weren't candidates for static batching at build time because they're moving or happened to be created during the game. But dynamic batching has to constantly update the batching, which is why the batching time is listed in the profile results. This rebatching seems like a waste if the batched objects are moving together or if they are not moving but were instantiated at runtime. Also, since batching takes memory, there is an upper limit on the amount of dynamic batching that will occur (the Unity documentation currently says 30,000 vertices, but that is subject to change).

Fortunately, there is a class called StaticBatchingUtility (in Unity Pro and Unity iOS Pro) that allows you to perform static batching at runtime by calling a Combine function. Listing 16-8 shows a really simple script that just calls StaticBatchingUtility.Combine on the script's GameObject.

Listing 16-8. Script for Statically Batching an Object Hierarchy

```
#pragma strict

function Start() {
        StaticBatchingUtility.Combine(gameObject);
}
```

Although simple, the script is fully functional. For example, in the rotating cube scene, if we dragged this script onto the main rotating Cube that has two child cubes (and disabled the individual rotation scripts of the child cubes), all three cubes would be statically batched together when the scene starts playing. The batched GameObjects don't have to be in a hierarchy together. StaticBatchingUtility.Combine is an overloaded function, and with another version it takes two arguments: an array of GameObjects to batch together and a GameObject designated as the parent.

Share Materials

For batching to take place, whether statically, dynamically, or through a call to StaticBatchingUtility.Combine, the Meshes to be batched must share the same Material or set of Materials. But for dynamic batching in particular, you need to be careful that you don't break that sharing if you modify the Material.

For example, the script in Listing 16-9 animates the texture of a Material by constantly changing its texture offsets. This provides a scrolling texture effect; in HyperBowl, this script is used to animate textures for scrolling neon signs, drifting clouds in the sky, and flowing water. However, when the script modifies the Material by calling its SetTextureOffset function, a new Material is created if the original Material happens to be shared.

Listing 16-9. Script That Animates the Texture Coordinate Offsets of a Material

```
#pragma strict

var speed:Vector2;
var materialIndex:int=0;

private var offset:Vector2;
private var material:Material;
```

```
function Start() {
        offset=new Vector2(0,0);
        material = renderer.materials[materialIndex];
}

function Update () {
        var dtime:float = Time.deltaTime;
        offset.x=(offset.x+speed.x*dtime)%1.0f;
        offset.y=(offset.y+speed.y*dtime)%1.0f;
        material.SetTextureOffset("_MainTex",offset);
}
```

This makes sense, of course. If you create two GameObjects with the same Material and decide you want to alter the appearance of one by modifying its Material, you don't necessarily want to make the same change to the other GameObject.

However, if you're going to apply the same animation to all the GameObjects that are sharing the Material, then there's no reason to stop sharing the Material. So you can modify the script to access the sharedMaterials variable of the MeshRenderer instead of the materials variable. Accessing sharedMaterials (or sharedMaterial if you assume only one Material on the GameObject) means you really do want to change the shared Material and avoids creating a new one, thus preserving eligibility for batching. To handle both shared and nonshared Material cases, let's add a public variable that allows you to specify whether the animation breaks Material sharing, and let's use that value to determine whether to modify renderer.materials or renderer.sharedMaterials (Listing 16-10).

Listing 16-10. Texture Animation Script with Option to Share Material

```
#pragma strict

var speed:Vector2;
var materialIndex:int=0;

var shared:boolean = true;

private var offset:Vector2;
private var material:Material;

function Start() {
        offset=new Vector2(0,0);
        if (shared) {
                material = renderer.sharedMaterials[materialIndex];
        } else {
                material = renderer.materials[materialIndex];
        }
}

function Update () {
        var dtime:float = Time.deltaTime;
        offset.x=(offset.x+speed.x*dtime)%1.0f;
        offset.y=(offset.y+speed.y*dtime)%1.0f;
        material.SetTextureOffset("_MainTex",offset);
}
```

An additional, although less significant, optimization is available when using this script to animate a shared Material. It would be redundant for every GameObject with the same Material to run the same texture animation script; just one instance of the script is sufficient to drive the animation for everyone.

Minimize Garbage Collection

I alluded to automatic memory management when we developed our iAd banner script in the previous chapter, noting that you have to keep a reference to the ad object to keep it from getting garbage collected, and you should remove the reference to allow the garbage collector to reclaim the space used by the object. In the worst case, if you're constantly creating objects and never allowing them to be garbage collected (let's say you've added the objects to an Array and never remove them, so they're always referenced), you'll eventually run out of memory.

Garbage collections can introduce noticeable pauses into a game. The most effective way to minimize those pauses is to minimize the necessity for garbage collection, and that can be accomplished by minimizing the number of objects that are eventually reclaimed by the collector. One technique is to keep objects in a *pool* so they can be reused, instead of letting them get garbage collected.

You can also explicitly invoke the collector by calling System.GC.Collect. For example, you can add that call to the Awake callback in our bowling game controller to make sure a garbage collection takes place before the game starts, which will immediately clean up any unused objects left over from the previous scene (Listing 16-11).

Listing 16-11. Adding a Call to the Garbage Collector in FuguBowl.js

```
function Awake() {
        player = new FuguBowlPlayer();
        CreatePins();
        System.GC.Collect();
}
```

Optimize Offline

All of the changes we've made so far are quick optimizations that you can immediately try out with a test run and profile to see their effect. Unity also integrates some commercial scene preprocessing tools that can greatly improve performance: Beast and Umbra. These won't be used in this chapter because they can take quite a while to set up and run, and frankly, they won't do much for our simple scene. But I'll describe them briefly in the following sections.

Beast

It's difficult to add high-quality, real-time lighting without a heavy performance penalty. Each additional pixel light generates more draw calls, shadows are expensive, and the resulting visual quality is not as good as on the desktop much less a computer-generated scene that has been rendered offline. Beast solves both problems by generating lightmaps, which is precalculated lighting that is "baked" into textures. Of course, nothing is free—besides the set up and baking time, the lightmapped scene ends up with additional large textures that take up more memory, increase the app size, and lengthen the scene loading time.

To generate lightmaps for the current scene, you would first have to mark all the nonmoving GameObjects, including Lights, as static, because you can only precalculate lighting for fixed lights and surfaces. A lightmap is layered as a second texture over the mesh, so most likely, you would have to reimport your static meshes with the Generate Lightmap UVs option selected to create that second set of texture coordinates. Then you would bring up the Lightmapping window from the Window menu on the Editor menu bar (Figure 16-35).

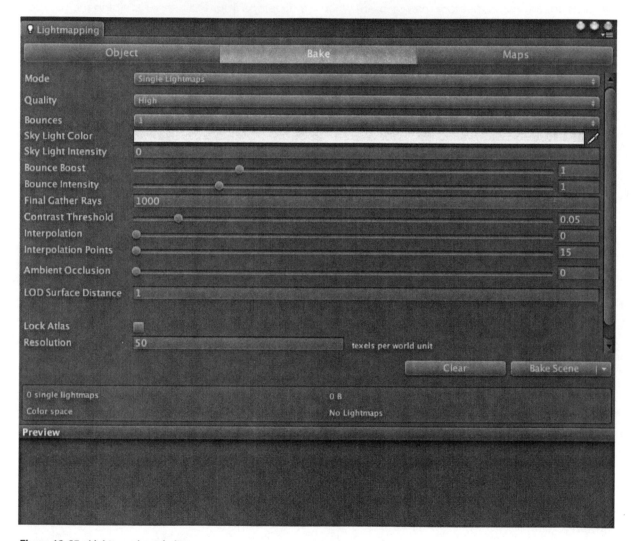

Figure 16-35. Lightmapping window

In that window, you can adjust the lightmapping properties for each object in the Object pane, then switch to the Bake pane to set the lightmapping properties and initiate the lightmapping.

Note that dual lightmaps are unavailable on Unity iOS, because that feature requires deferred lighting, so single lightmaps is the only option and dynamic and static lighting won't mix as well, especially with shadows.

Umbra (Pro)

I mentioned how each Camera performs frustum culling, ignoring any GameObject that lies outside the Camera's view volume. Those not familiar with real-time computer graphics might assume that an obscured object (i.e., blocked from view by another) is also culled, but that's not the case. All objects within the frustum are rendered, and the depth buffer is used to determine on a pixel-by-pixel basis which object is in front of another. Determining whether an object is positioned outside the frustum is a relatively straightforward calculation, but determining which objects are occluded requires some preprocessing. That's where Unity's integrating of Umbra as an occlusion culling tool comes in.

Adding occlusion culling to the scene is similar to the process of lightmapping the scene. You would mark nonmoving objects as static and then bring up the Occlusion Culling window from the Window menu on the Unity Editor menu bar (Figure 16-36).

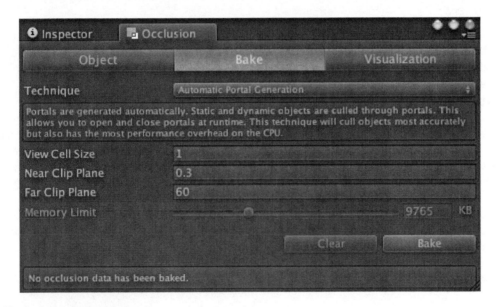

Figure 16-36. Occlusion Culling window

From there, you can adjust per-object occlusion culling settings in the Object tab, and then in the Bake tab specify the occlusion culling settings and then bake the occlusion culling data.

Final Profile

Now that you've completed an optimization pass through our project, it's time to profile the game again (Listing 16-12), although if you want to be methodical, you should run a profile after each change to see its effect.

Listing 16-12. Built-In Profile Results After Optimizations

```
iPhone Unity internal profiler stats:
cpu-player>    min:  5.0   max:  9.7   avg:  6.1
cpu-ogles-drv> min:  3.4   max:  7.4   avg:  4.2
cpu-present>   min:  0.9   max: 10.5   avg:  4.2
```

```
cpu-waits-gpu> min:  0.9    max: 10.5    avg:  4.2
 msaa-resolve> min:  0.0    max:  0.0    avg:  0.0
frametime>     min: 13.5    max: 22.1    avg: 16.6
draw-call #>   min:  30     max:  30     avg:  30     | batched:    10
tris #>        min: 4592    max: 4592    avg: 4592    | batched:  3420
verts #>       min: 3728    max: 3728    avg: 3728    | batched:  2750
player-detail> physx:  0.0 animation:  0.0 culling  0.0 skinning:  0.0 batching:  2.2 render:  3.4
fixed-update-count: 0 .. 0
mono-scripts>  update:  0.1    fixedUpdate:  0.0 coroutines:  0.0
mono-memory>   used heap: 389120 allocated heap: 524288  max number of collections: 0 collection
total duration:  0.0
```

The profile lists an average frametime of 16.6 ms, which is just about 60 fps. Target achieved! This profile was run on a fourth-generation iPod touch (equivalent to an iPhone 4), so depending on your device, your mileage may vary.

The player-detail line indicates the frametime is dominated by batching and rendering, so graphics is the remaining bottleneck and any more time spent on script optimization would not be time well spent. And if you decided that 30 fps isn't so bad, then you're in a good situation to add more content and features.

Explore Further

I began this chapter by citing the perils of optimizing too early, at the risk of complicating things before you even got something working. But you should keep your performance target in mind from the very beginning of development. Start simple (the Unity documentation recommends rendering no more than 40,000 vertices on the iPhone 3GS), get something working, optimize enough to meet your performance target, continue adding content and functionality, and stop and optimize every time the game's performance falls below your target. And remember to profile and optimize the bottlenecks. It will do you no good to optimize something that's taking 10% of your frametime and leave alone something else that's taking 50%.

Unity Manual

In the Unity Manual, the section "Getting Started with iOS Development" has several pages on "Optimizing Performance in iOS," covering the "Player Settings" we adjusted to optimize builds, description of the built-in profiler, and optimizing the build size.

The "Advanced" section documents the Profiler available with Unity Pro and also the offline optimization features mentioned: lightmapping and occlusion culling. The "Advanced" section includes many other pages related to optimization: "Optimizing Graphics Performance," "Reducing File Size," "Automatic Memory Management" (garbage collection), and "Shadows" (in particular, "Shadow Performance"). The pages on "Asset Bundles" and "Loading Resources" explain how assets can be downloaded and brought into a scene on demand, which is a technique that can be used to manage the installed app size.

Reference Manual

The Reference Manual describes all the Components and Asset types we optimized. Among those Components, we tweaked the "Camera" frustum and visibility mask, also adjusted the culling mask and distance for the Light in addition to disabling its shadow, minimized the number of shadow casters and receivers per "MeshFilter", simplified the shaders for each "MeshRenderer", and replaced a "MeshCollider" with a "BoxCollider". We looked over the Import Settings for the various Asset types referenced by the Components: "Texture2D", "AudioClip", and "Mesh". The Reference Manual also documents the Settings Managers we customized, including the "QualitySettings", "PhysicsManager", "TimeManager", and "AudioManager". We also used the "GUIText" Component, sibling of the "GUITexture" we use for a splash screen, for our frame rate display.

Scripting Reference

The "Scripting Overview" section of the Scripting Reference has a "Performance Optimization" page with some tips on how to write faster scripts. The one new function we learned in this chapter is the static function "Combine" in the "StaticBatchingUtility" class (Combine is the only function in that class), which we called to batch a hierarchy of GameObjects at runtime. The one new variable we learned in this chapter is the "useGUILayout" variable in the "MonoBehaviour" class, which when set to true provides a performance increase by telling the UnityGUI system that the current "OnGUI" callback will not be performing any automatic layout using the "GUILayout" functions.

The Settings Managers all have corresponding classes so that their settings can be queried and set with scripts. Even though all of the Settings Managers except Render Settings are active for the entire game and not per scene, script access allows us to adjust settings for each scene. For example, we might define a Quality Level for each scene and add a script to each scene that loads the appropriate Quality Level. The classes corresponding to the Settings Managers discussed in this chapter include QualitySettings, AudioSettings, PhysicsManager, and Timemanager.

We also used the "Time" class, evaluating its "timeScale" and "deltaTime" variables and setting the "text" variable of a "GUIText" for our rudimentary frame rate display.

Asset Store

The Asset Store lists a few profiling systems (search for "profiler") and some object pooling systems (search for "pool"), such as PoolManager, Smart Pool and Pooling Manager. That last one, from DFT Games, is free.

On the Web

The Unity wiki at http://wiki.unity3d.com/ has some performance tips under its "Tips, Tricks and Tools" section and several performance-related scripts. In particular, the "FramesPerSecond" page lists several frame-rate display scripts more sophisticated than the one we created in this chapter (for example, they calculate the frame rate from a series of frames for a steadier display).

The Umbra occlusion culling system is developed by Umbra Software at http://umbrasoftware.com/. The Beast lightmapping system is an Autodesk product with a product page at http://gameware.autodesk.com/beast.

Books

I've mentioned Real-Time *Rendering* (http://realtimerendering.com) a couple of times, already, but it's really really relevant to the graphics optimizations in this chapter. Just the treatment on mipmapping is a good read.

Where to Go from Here?

You've now completed this introduction to Unity and Unity iOS development, from downloading and installing Unity, to developing a simple bowling game in the Unity Editor, to getting it to run on iOS, and finally optimizing it to run with decent performance. Although not every Unity feature or game development topic was covered (this book would start to resemble a multivolume encyclopedia set!), I'll wrap up with a chapter's worth of Explore Further.

More Scripting

We just scratched the surface with Unity scripting, not only in the variety of scripting languages offered and the extensive set of Unity classes, but also what can be scripted.

Editor Scripts

If you feel there's something missing in the Unity Editor, there's a good chance you can add the feature by writing Editor scripts. These are scripts also written in JavaScript, C#, or Boo, but they're located in the Editor folder in the Project View. Editor scripts have access to the Editor GUI, project settings, and project assets via a set of Editor classes, documented in the Scripting Reference under "Editor Classes."

As an example, let's create a menu on the Unity Editor menu bar with commands for activating and deactivating an entire hierarchy of GameObjects. In other words, the commands call SetActive on every GameObject in the hierarchy and is equivalent to clicking the checkbox of each GameObject in the Inspector View.

Before Unity 4, each GameObject just had one active state represented by the active checkbox in the Inspector View and the GameObject variable active. But starting with Unity 4, that checkbox in the Inspector View represents the local active state of the GameObject, settable in a script by calling SetActive and read from the GameObject variable activeSelf. The global or "really" active state that depends on all its parents also being locally active. Thus, ensuring all GameObjects in a hierarchy are locally active allows you to deactivate the entire group by toggling the active state of the root GameObject. Clicking all those checkboxes by hand can be laborious and error-prone, so a single command to perform that operation would be a boon, especially for developers upgrading projects to Unity 4.

The process of creating an Editor script is the same as creating a script intended for use in a scene, except the Editor script has to be located in the Editor folder. So let's create a new JavaScript in the Project View, name it FuguEditor, and place it in the Editor folder (Figure 17-1).

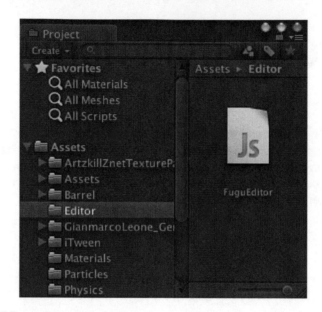

Figure 17-1. Creating a new Editor script

Now add the code in Listing 17-1 to the script.

Listing 17-1. The Complete listing for FuguEditor.js

```
#pragma strict

@MenuItem ("FuguGames/ActivateRecursively")
static function ActivateRecursively() {
        if (Selection.activeGameObject !=null) {
                SetActiveRecursively(Selection.activeGameObject,true);
        }
}

@MenuItem ("FuguGames/DeactivateRecursively")
static function DeactivateRecursively() {
        if (Selection.activeGameObject !=null) {
                SetActiveRecursively(Selection.activeGameObject,false);
        }
}

static function SetActiveRecursively(obj:GameObject,val:boolean) {
        obj.SetActive(val);
```

```
        for (var i:int=0; i<obj.transform.GetChildCount(); ++i) {
                SetActiveRecursively(obj.transform.GetChild(i).gameObject,val);
        }
}

@MenuItem ("FuguGames/ActivateRecursively", true)
@MenuItem ("FuguGames/DeactivateRecursively", true)
static function ValidateGameObject() {
        return (Selection.activeGameObject !=null);
}
```

The line `@MenuItem ("FuguGames/ActivateRecursively")` adds an `ActivateRecursively` item
to the FuguGames menu on the Editor menu bar, creating the menu if it hadn't already been
created. The function following the `@MenuItem` line is invoked when that menu item is selected.
`ActivateRecursively` checks if a GameObject has been selected in the Editor, and, if so, then
it passes that GameObject to the function `SetActiveRecursively` along with the value true.
`SetActiveRecursively` in turn calls `SetActive` with the passed value true call for each GameObject
in the hierarchy.

After that, a similar block of code adds a `DeactivateRecursively` item to the menu, differing only in
name and in passing false instead of true to `SetActiveRecursively`.

Although you can check if an object is selected before calling `SetActiveRecursively`, it's better user
interface design to deactivate a menu item if it's not going to have any effect. You can add this by
listing the `MenuItem` attributes again, but this time with an additional `true` argument, which indicates
the next function is a static function that returns true only if the menu item should be active. Both
`ActivateRecursively` and `DeactivateRecursively` use `ValidateGameObject`, which just checks if a
GameObject is selected in the Editor, to decide if the menu item should be available or grayed out.

Once this script has been compiled, the new menu should appear as shown in Figure 17-2 (there
may be a delay).

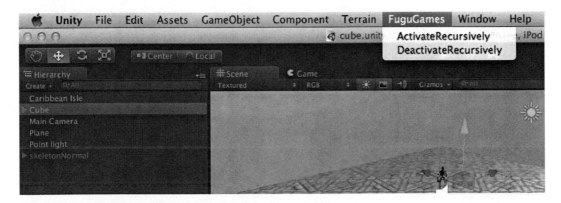

Figure 17-2. A menu added to the menu bar using an Editor script

This example has minimal user interface, just some menu items, but Editor scripts can create new windows and user interfaces using UnityGUI functions (and the Editor is actually implemented in UnityGUI, which is why occasional Editor errors show up as UnityGUI errors in the Console View). Editor scripts can also be used for batch processing, postprocessing assets after import, or preprocessing scenes before a build. I have simple Editor scripts that remove build files, show GameObject statistics, and even call the OS X say command so I can talk to myself.

C#

I've focused on using Unity's JavaScript as the scripting language in this book because, well, I had to pick one. But seriously, JavaScript does have more example code in the Unity documentation (although the gap is closing) and will likely look more familiar to JavaScript and Flash developers. JavaScript is also more succinct than C#, at least for small scripts. Just compare the empty JavaScript (Listing 17-2) and C# script (Listing 17-3) generated by the Create menu in the Project View.

Listing 17-2. A Newly Created JavaScript Script

```
#pragma strict

function Start () {

}

function Update () {

}
```

Listing 17-3. A Newly Created C# Script

```
using UnityEngine;
using System.Collections;

public class NewBehaviourScript : MonoBehaviour {

        // Use this for initialization
        void Start () {

        }

        // Update is called once per frame
        void Update () {

        }
}
```

In the C# script, the class declaration is explicit and you have to ensure that the class name matches the script name. At the top of the C# script, two namespaces that are commonly used in Unity scripts, UnityEngine and System.Collections, are explicitly imported—in JavaScript, they are implicitly imported.

A lot of JavaScript code will run in C# with little modification, but there are some syntactic differences: variables declarations begin with <type> <name> instead of var <name>:<type>. Functions are defined the same way, starting with the return type and name instead of starting with function. There's no reason to add #pragma strict to a C# file because C# is already strictly typed.

For small scripts, JavaScript is more convenient, but for large-scale Unity development, C# is arguably the more practical choice, given that it's a better-documented language with industrial-strength testing as the most popular Mono or .NET language. Furthermore, many Unity extension packages are written in C# (the Prime31 plugins, EZGUI, and NGUI among them), and mixing JavaScript and C# in Unity is inconvenient; if you have JavaScript code referencing C# scripts, those scripts must be placed in the Plugins or Standard Assets folders so they load earlier.

Another reason to use C# is the addition of namespace support for C# in Unity 4. This feature allows you to dispense with prefixing class names to avoid conflicts. For example, Listing 17-4 shows a C# version of our FuguFrameRate script, where the class is defined within a namespace declaration.

Listing 17-4. A C# Version of the FuguFrameRate Script

```
using UnityEngine;
using System.Collections;

namespace Fugu {

sealed public class FrameRate : MonoBehaviour {

        public int frameRate = 60;

        void Awake () {
                Application.targetFrameRate = frameRate;
        }

}

} // end namespace
```

Because the class is inside the namespace Fugu, you can safely call the class just FrameRate and name the script FrameRate to match. If you had to refer to this class from another script, you would have to use the fully qualified name Fugu.FrameRate unless you added a using Fugu; statement at the top of the script.

C# allows you to optionally prepend the class definition with sealed, which specifies that this class is not intended to be subclassed. A compiler error will result if you try to define a subclass of FrameRate. Java programmers will recognize this is the same as the Java final declaration.

In C#, coroutines must explicitly return type IEnumerator (which is in the System.Collections namespace and why it's convenient to always import that namespace). Although Unity automatically adds a Start callback that returns void in newly created C# scripts, that Start callback can be turned into a coroutine by changing the return type from void to IEnumerator. But it seems kind of weird to change the return type of a callback, so I prefer to move the coroutine out of the Start callback and invoke the coroutine with StartCoroutine, as I did in the C# version of the FuguAdBanner script (Listing 17-5).

StartCoroutine can be called from any callback, so this technique has the advantage of providing a uniform way to invoke coroutines and makes it unnecessary to use callbacks directly as coroutines (and also makes it unnecessary to remember which callbacks can be used as coroutines). This is not a bad practice to apply in JavaScript, too.

Listing 17-5. A C# Version of the FuguAdBanner Script

```csharp
using UnityEngine;
using System.Collections;

namespace Fugu {

public class AdBanner : MonoBehaviour {

        public bool showOnTop = true;
        public bool dontDestroy = true;

        private ADBannerView banner = null;

        void Start() {
                StartCoroutine (StartBanner());
        }

        private IEnumerator StartBanner () {
                if (dontDestroy) {
                        GameObject.DontDestroyOnLoad(gameObject);
                }
                banner = new ADBannerView();
                banner.autoSize = true;
                banner.autoPosition = showOnTop ? ADPosition.Top : ADPosition.Bottom;
                while (!banner.loaded && banner.error == null) {
                        yield return null;
                }
                if (banner.error == null) {
                        banner.Show();
                } else {
                        banner = null;
                }
        }
}
} // end namespace
```

You also can't just call yield within a coroutine as you did in JavaScript. In C#, you have to call yield return null to equivalently yield for a frame.

Another difference is the syntax of anonymous functions. In our FuguGameCenter script, I passed unnamed success or failure functions in the form of function(success:boolean) {...}, but in C#, anonymous functions are known as *lambda functions* (dating back to terminology from the Lisp language, which used (lambda (success) ...)) and is specified in the form (bool success) => {...} Listing 17-6 shows a C# version of the FuguGameCenter script.

Listing 17-6. C# Version of FuguGameCenter

```csharp
using UnityEngine;
using System.Collections;

using UnityEngine.SocialPlatforms.GameCenter;

namespace Fugu {

sealed public class GameCenter : MonoBehaviour {

        public bool showAchievementBanners = true;
        // Use this for initialization
        void Start () {
#if UNITY_IPHONE
        Social.localUser.Authenticate ( (bool success) => {
        if (success && showAchievementBanners) {
                GameCenterPlatform.ShowDefaultAchievementCompletionBanner(showAchievementBanners);
                        Debug.Log ("Authenticated "+Social.localUser.userName);
        }
                else {
                        Debug.Log ("Failed to authenticate "+Social.localUser.userName);
                }
        }
    );
#endif
        }

        static public void Achievement(string name,double score) {
#if UNITY_IPHONE
        if (Social.localUser.authenticated) {
                Social.ReportProgress(name,score, (bool success) => {
                        if (success) {
                                Debug.Log("Achievement "+name+" reported successfully");
                        } else {
                                Debug.Log("Failed to report achievement "+name);
                        }
                } );
        }
#endif
}

        static public void Score(string name,long score) {
#if UNITY_IPHONE
        if (Social.localUser.authenticated) {
                Social.ReportScore (score, name, (bool success) => {
                        if (success) {
                                Debug.Log("Posted "+score+" on leaderboard "+name);
```

```
                } else {
                        Debug.Log("Failed to post "+score+" on leaderboard "+name);
                }
        } );
    }
#endif
}


}
}
```

Finally, what you might miss about JavaScript the most is the ability to easily modify the Vector3 values in a Transform Component. Listing 17-7 shows a simple line of JavaScript that modifies just the x component of a Transform Component's position.

Listing 17-7. Modifying a Vector3 of a Transform in JavaScript

```
function Start () {
        transform.position.x=0;
}
```

That line of code will generate a compiler error in C# (Figure 17-3), because Vector3 is a struct, not a class, and thus a value type, not a reference type. The fact that it works in JavaScript is a convenience (albeit a misleading one, because it does make Vector3 look like a class, not a struct).

Figure 17-3. Error message when modifying a Transform's Vector3 in C#

Because Vector3 is a struct, you don't have to worry about the garbage collector having to clean up a bunch of unused Vector3 instances, since, well, there are no instances. But it does mean in C# you have to create a new Vector3 if you want to modify the Transform Component's position, as shown in Listing 17-8.

Listing 17-8. A Valid Way to Modify a Transform in C#

```
void Start () {
        transform.position = new Vector3(0,transform.position.y,transform.position.z);
}
```

Notice how in C# you have to specify new before the Vector3 constructor, whereas in JavaScript that is optional. That is a minor convenience of JavaScript (these types of conveniences are generally known as *syntactic sugar*), but C# has the advantage of allowing you to define your own structs, in a manner similar to how classes are defined. In JavaScript, you can use structs, but there's no way to define new ones. Andrew Stellman and Jennifer Greene's *Head First C#* (O'Reilly) is a good introduction to C#, but experienced programmers can get a quick start in C# with the *C# in* a *Nutshell* series (also published by O'Reilly). Java programmers in particular will find C# familiar (despite the name, C# has no relation to C or C++, unless you count distant ancestors).

Script Execution Order

Before leaving the topic of scripting, there's one more issue worth mentioning: specifying the order of execution among scripts. If you look in the SmoothFollow script used to control the Main Camera in the bowling game, you'll see the Camera position is updated not in an Update callback, but in a LateUpdate callback. LateUpdate is called in every frame just like Update, but all LateUpdate calls in a frame take place after all Update calls have completed. SmoothFollow calculates the Camera position in LateUpdate so it takes into account any position change that's taken place in its target's Update callback.

Having both Update and LateUpdate callbacks is a common technique in game engines, but it can only go so far. What if you want a GameObject to update after another GameObject's LateUpdate? Sorry, there's no LateLateUpdate callback! But Unity does have a more general solution, the Script Execution Order Settings, which can be brought up from the Project Settings submenu of the Edit menu (Figure 17-4).

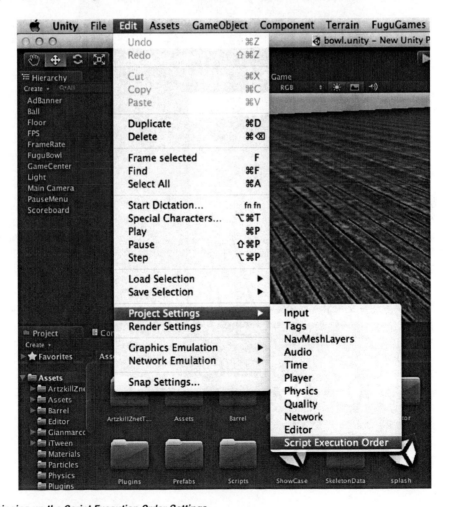

Figure 17-4. Bringing up the Script Execution Order Settings

The Script Execution Order Settings can also be brought up by clicking the Execution Order button displayed in the Inspector View when a script is selected. Either way, the Script Execution Order Settings show up in the Inspector View as a MonoManager (Figure 17-5) and has a list initially containing just one item, Default Time.

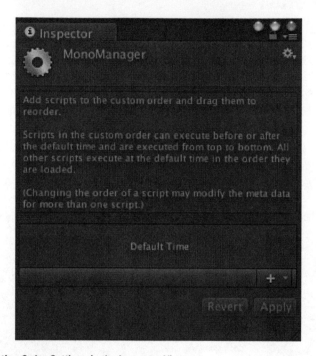

Figure 17-5. The Script Execution Order Settings in the Inspector View

Since SmoothFollow uses LateUpdate, you don't have to make any changes, but let's say you want to make sure the SmoothFollow script runs its Update callback after all other scripts. You would click the plus sign (+) button at the lower right of the Script Execution Order Settings and select the SmoothFollow script from the resulting menu. By default, the SmoothFollow script would appear in the Script Execution Order Settings below the Default Time, meaning SmoothFollow will run after all other scripts.

And then you might decide that the game controller script, FuguBowl, should run after every other script (since it's constantly checking the bowling position, for example) except for SmoothFollow. So again, you would click the + button to add the FuguBowl script and then drag FuguBowl, using the handle on the left, above SmoothFollow but below Default Time, resulting in a list as shown in Figure 17-6. Anything dragged above Default Time would execute before all the other scripts.

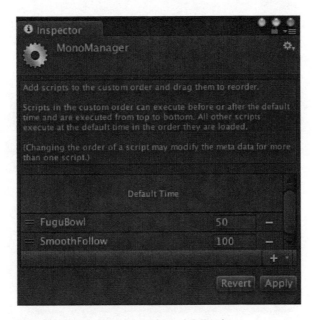

Figure 17-6. Specifing the execution order of FuguBowl.js and SmoothFollow.js

Clicking the minus (-) button on the right of a script will remove the script from the Script Execution Order Settings.

Plugins

Much mention has been made of third-party plugins, some available on the Asset Store, and many from Prime31 Studios. But if you happen to be conversant in C, C++, or Objective-C, you can write your own plugins, either to access more device functionality or to make use of libraries written in C, C+, or Objective-C. Besides including the native library, plugins require additional Unity wrapper scripts. The process is documented on the "Plugins" page in the "Advanced" section of the Unity Manual.

Tracking Apps

Although iTunes Connect provides download and sales figures (and the graph is a lot easier to read than the .csv report, which once was the only option), there are several third-party products that track app sales and other data like app rankings and reviews.

App Annie (http://appannie.com/) and AppFigures (http://appfigures.com/) are two of the more popular web-based products that both automatically perform daily downloads of app data from iTunes Connect (after you provide them your iTunes Connect log-in information during account set up). They both have nice graph presentations of the sales data and send daily email summaries of the app statistics. App Annie is currently free (technically in beta) while AppFigures charges a fee.

Figure 17-7 shows an App Annie graph of downloads over a month for Fugu Bowl. The number of downloads that are updates are overlaid over the downloads that are sales. There are spikes in the update line corresponding to releases of updates for FuguBowl.

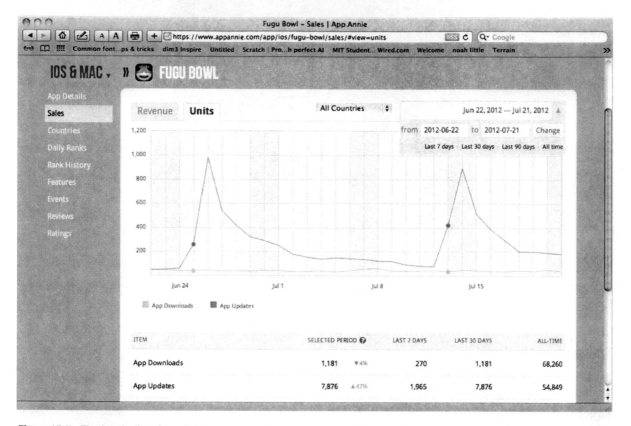

Figure 17-7. The App Annie sales graph

AppViz (http://appviz.com/) is an OS X application that performs the same function but downloads the data onto your Mac and features a variety of graphs, including sales by geography (Figure 17-8). AppViz is not free but it doesn't cost much and I think it's well worth it.

Figure 17-8. The AppViz geographic view

There's no reason to restrict yourself to just one of these products. I use AppViz to ensure I have all of my app sales data available locally and I like its variety of graphics and the App Store review downloads. I use AppAnnie for its automated e-mail reports of daily sales figures, rankings display (downloading of all that ranking data in AppViz takes a long time), and App Annie has support for some Android app stores. Also, it's free!

> **Tip** From AppViz, you can export all the data you've downloaded and then import that data into another product like App Annie. Since Apple only makes a year's worth of app sales data available on iTunes Connect, this is a way to ensure you can always import the entire sales history of an app into a sales tracking product.

Promo Codes

I have described how to download promo codes after an app is approved on the App Store, but I didn't explain what to do with them. There are plenty of options. Nearly every app review site accepts promo codes with review requests. Touch Arcade (http://toucharcade.com/) is one of those sites, but it also has a very active forum where developers issue promo codes. And AppGiveaway (http://appgiveaway.com/) runs promotions where they hand out promo codes over a set period of time. This is a lot more convenient than handing them out yourself, although you should do that, too. Keeping an inventory of promo codes is also a good reason to crank out app updates, since you get a fresh batch of 50 codes with each update.

More Monetization

Given the yearly Apple developer fee and Unity license costs (if you decide to go with the Pro licenses), chances are you want to at least make that money back. Besides iAd and third-party mobile ad services, there are other monetization strategies.

In-App Purchasing

Apple offers one other revenue channel for iOS besides app sales and iAd: an in-app purchasing (IAP) system called Storekit. Unity iOS doesn't have a script interface for IAP, but Prime31 Studios includes a Storekit plugin among its offerings. The Unity Manual has some tips for how you might download and activate additional content purchased with IAP, and the iTunes Connect documentation explains how to set up in-app purchases.

Asset Store

I use dozens of free and paid Asset Store packages in my apps, and you will surely find the Asset Store useful for your own projects. But the Asset Store is also another place to self-publish products and generate revenue (Unity takes a 30% cut, same as Apple does on the App Store). And you can release packages free on the Asset Store for recognition or as a contribution to the community (I've certainly taken advantage of that generosity for the examples in this book).

Conveniently, Asset Store submissions are made from within the Unity Editor, using the Asset Store Tools downloaded from, aptly, the Asset Store. You can submit any collection of assets from a project—audio, textures, models, scripts, plugins, or even the entire project itself.

> **Tip**   Use preprocessor directives to ensure there are no compiler errors when switching build targets, and add a custom UNITY_PRO preprocessor directive if you have Unity Pro features, so that Unity Basic users won't have problems.

Much of the work in an Asset Store submission, as with an App Store submission, involves creating screenshots, icons, app descriptions, and store artwork. The instructions for becoming a seller on the Asset Store are available at http://unity3d.com/asset-store.

Developing for Android

Unity Android requires an additional license, with the same Indie and Pro structure as for Unity iOS. The good news is that almost everything developed for Unity iOS in this book will work fine with Unity Android. Unsurprisingly, anything in the iPhone class is not available on Android either (e.g., the variable iPhone.generation, which we used to check the device type), but everything in the Input class that works for iOS also works the same on Android, including the touchscreen and accelerometer functions.

Game Center and iAd are Apple technologies, so those features aren't available on Android, but in the future, the Social, ADBanner, and ADInterstialAd classes might support equivalent offerings on Android. Prime31 Studio and other vendors offer Unity Android plugins to provide more access to device features and mobile services, such as the AdMob mobile ad service.

The build and submission process is different for Android, too. Instead of Xcode, Android requires installation of the Android SDK. You can still invoke a Build and Run from the Unity Editor, but instead of building an Xcode project for the app, Unity Android directly builds the executable app (an APK file). And unlike iOS development, Android development can be targeted to a number of app stores. Google Play in particular has no approval process, so it's a good avenue to self-publish quickly and a useful fallback channel for apps rejected by Apple.

Contract Work

While working on that next hit app, independent developers often keep the bills paid by taking contract work. Prospective clients can be found in the Paid Work topic of the Unity forum and on http://unity3dwork.com/ and even general contractor web sites like http://odesk.com/. Some marketplaces specialize in mobile app development, such as http://apptank.com/ and http://theymakeapps.com/.

And if you're looking for full-time game development work, whether it involves Unity or not, experience developing games with Unity, not to mention a portfolio of self-published games, can only help.

Final Words

Now I've come to the end, and hopefully you're ready and excited to start making your own Unity iOS apps. If there's one lesson that I hope you can take from this book, it's that you can start with something simple and keep building on it until it turns into something interesting. Don't be one of those people who want to start with a massively-multiplayer online (MMO) game as a first project!

Remember to keep learning and participate in the Unity community, both contributing and asking for help on the Unity forum and on the Unity Answers site, and don't forget to check the Unity wiki. It's fine to promote your work to the community (there is a Showcase topic in the Unity forum) and ask others to spread the word, but remember to return the favor!

As an unintended result of working on my own projects with Unity iOS, I've met a population of developers with whom I can commiserate and celebrate and trade valuable tips. I won't try to list them all, but you can find them on my twitter follow list at @fugugames. Twitter, by the way, is another great way to interact with other Unity developers, on a more personal level. I've communicated with many customers over twitter, also, and have had some success with setting up Facebook product pages for my games (in particular, HyperBowl). Although app customers can be legendarily snarky, I've found most of them are supportive and sympathetic of us independent developers and are enthused to be part of the process if we let them. In fact, I've benefited from a lot of free QA and some localization (translation) help, not to mention a lot feedback. So, set up those twitter feeds and Facebook fan pages and start talking!

Above all, have fun. Any other reward is a bonus!

Index

P, Q

R

S

◼T

◼U, V, W, X, Y, Z

CPSIA information can be obtained at www.ICGtesting.com
Printed in the USA
LVOW111324210613

339708LV00003B/23/P